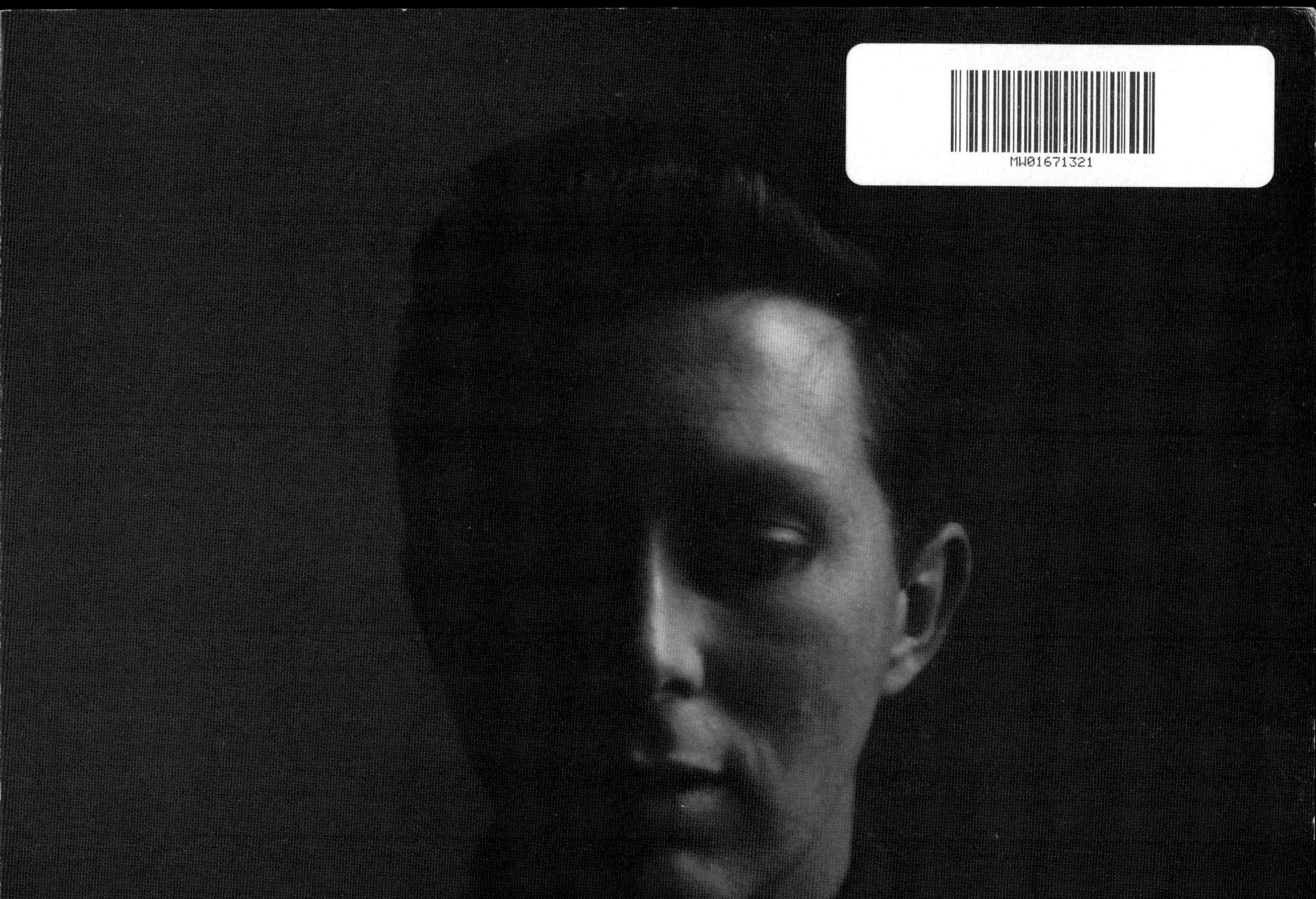

# George Tooker

Robert Cozzolino
Marshall N. Price
M. Melissa Wolfe

Contributing authors
Anna C. Chave
Thomas H. Garver
Jonathan Weinberg

Columbus Museum of Art

National Academy Museum
& School of Fine Arts

Pennsylvania Academy
of the Fine Arts

MERRELL
LONDON • NEW YORK

First published 2008 by Merrell Publishers Limited

Merrell Publishers Limited
Head office
81 Southwark Street
London SE1 0HX

New York office
740 Broadway, Suite 1202
New York, NY 10003

merrellpublishers.com

*in association with*

Columbus Museum of Art, Ohio
480 East Broad Street
Columbus, OH 43215

columbusmuseum.org

Published on the occasion of the exhibition *GEORGE TOOKER: A RETROSPECTIVE*
National Academy Museum, New York
October 2, 2008–January 4, 2009
Pennsylvania Academy of the Fine Arts, Philadelphia
January 30–April 5, 2009
Columbus Museum of Art, Ohio
May 1–September 6, 2009

*George Tooker: A Retrospective* is generously supported by the Henry Luce Foundation and the National Endowment for the Arts.
The New York presentation of *George Tooker: A Retrospective* is generously supported by the New York State Council on the Arts and the New York City Department of Cultural Affairs.
The Philadelphia presentation of *George Tooker: A Retrospective* is generously supported by the Richard C. von Hess Foundation.
The Columbus presentation of *George Tooker: A Retrospective* is generously supported by the Columbus Foundation, the Greater Columbus Arts Council, National City, Nationwide, and the Ohio Arts Council.
Support for the catalogue is generously provided by Furthermore: a program of the J.M. Kaplan Fund.



A catalog record for this book is available from the Library of Congress.

British Library Cataloguing-in-Publication Data
Cozzolino, Robert, 1970–
George Tooker
1. Tooker, George – Exhibitions
I. Title II. Price, Marshall N. III. Wolfe, M. Melissa
IV. Columbus Museum of Art
759.1'3

ISBN-13: 978-1-8589-4456-2 (hardcover edition)
ISBN-10: 1-8589-4456-2 (hardcover edition)
ISBN-13: 978-1-8589-4455-5 (softcover edition)
ISBN-10: 1-8589-4455-4 (softcover edition)

Printed and bound in Italy

Produced by Merrell Publishers Limited
Designed by Adam Hooper
Copy-edited by Matthew Taylor
Proof-read by Elizabeth Tatham
Indexed by Vicki Robinson

Front jacket:
George Tooker
*Subway* (1950) (detail)
Whitney Museum of American Art, New York
Purchase, with funds from the Juliana Force Purchase Award
Photography by Sheldon C. Collins
(see page 121)

Back jacket:
George Tooker
*Self-Portrait* (1947)
Curtis Galleries, Minneapolis, Minnesota
(see page 114)

Page 1:
*George Tooker* by C. Howard, *circa* 1947

# Contents

# Directors' foreword

The directors of the National Academy Museum (NAM), the Pennsylvania Academy of the Fine Arts (PAFA), and the Columbus Museum of Art (CMA) are thrilled to be partners in presenting this, the first retrospective of George Tooker's work in more than three decades. Such collaboration, especially among smaller institutions, is the way of the future. Our three institutions have equally shared the work and costs of this project, much to the credit and benefit of all. George Tooker himself, along with curators Marshall N. Price (NAM), Robert Cozzolino (PAFA), and M. Melissa Wolfe (CMA), selected the works for the exhibition. The curators, along with guest writers Thomas H. Garver, Anna C. Chave, and Jonathan Weinberg, wrote essays for this catalogue. Their essays, which entailed new research and provide new insights, contribute to our knowledge of the significance of this American artist's career.

The National Academy is a tripartite institution, conceived in 1825 by artists to promote American art. Its members, including more than three hundred and fifty artists, come from throughout the United States. The Academy's mission is to promote American art through exhibitions and education. This exhibition is the second in a series recognizing venerable artists who should be publicly acclaimed for their lifetime achievements. The Academy's exhibition committee, comprising artist–members, curators, and the director, conceived this series in 2000, beginning in 2002 with an exhibition of the work of Hyman Bloom.

Founded in 1805, the Pennsylvania Academy of the Fine Arts is the oldest public museum and art school in the United States and remains dedicated to American fine arts education. Starting with its founder, Charles Willson Peale, and continued by subsequent generations of artists ranging from Thomas Eakins and William Merritt Chase to the current faculty, the Pennsylvania Academy has long been a leading proponent of the highest-caliber American figurative art. The Pennsylvania Academy also has a deep commitment to Modernism, dating back to such early Modernist alumni and faculty members as Arthur B. Carles, Hugh Breckenridge, and Henry McCarter. While Tooker's realism fits soundly within the figurative tradition of the Academy, the compelling mystery of his work, and his exploration of what was once termed the "primitivism" of early Italian painting and the egg tempera technique, engage key Modernist concerns. It is this duality that makes Tooker an exciting modern master to add to our collection through the recent acquisition of the major painting *Dark Angel* (1996) and to participate in the collaboration on which this important exhibition and publication are based.

The Columbus Museum of Art had been developing an exhibition on Paul Cadmus, Jared French, and George Tooker when we discovered that the National Academy Museum was organizing a Tooker exhibition. This coincidence suggested a wonderful opportunity to join together to support an exhibition focused entirely on Tooker and presented during the artist's lifetime. The Museum has had a long commitment to the examination and promotion of American art, based in large part on its respected holdings in American Modernism and early twentieth-century figurative painting. In 2005, the Museum acquired more than four hundred works from the Philip J. and Suzanne Schiller Collection of American Social Commentary Art (1930–70), which includes Tooker's painting *Lunch* (1964). This acquisition has extended the Museum's focus to embrace those American artists who have engaged in social issues through visual expression. Tooker's own passion for issues of social equality, and his particular blend of figuration and abstraction, make this exhibition a perfect fit for our Museum. We also wish to take this opportunity to acknowledge and sincerely thank the Henry Luce Foundation and the National Endowment for the Arts. Their very generous financial support helped to make *George Tooker: A Retrospective* the wonderful reality that it is.

*George Tooker: A Retrospective*, as an exhibition and as a catalogue, provides a much-deserved and comprehensive examination of the scope of Tooker's art and of his important place in the history of the United States. We invite you to share in our appreciation of this iconic American artist.

Bruce Weber
Acting Co-Director and Senior Curator of Nineteenth-Century Art
National Academy Museum
New York

David R. Brigham
Edna S. Tuttleman Director of the Pennsylvania Academy Museum
Philadelphia

Nannette V. Maciejunes
Executive Director
Columbus Museum of Art, Ohio

# Introduction and acknowledgments

It has been more than thirty years since we have had a chance to examine a representative overview of George Tooker's work. Much has changed in the intervening three decades in the field of American art and in our cultural climate. Among the many reasons to look again at the hauntingly beautiful work of this quiet, independent artist is the capacity his paintings have to reflect both the public and the private aspects of humanity. By focusing on individuals and the lives they lead in society, whether evident in their choices of intimacy or their struggle against dehumanizing political systems, Tooker has given the world multiple stories about what it is to live in the second half of the twentieth century and now in the twenty-first. Although he has avoided specific traditional narratives, his work carries the moral, spiritual, and sensual power of the fourteenth- and fifteenth-century Italian and Flemish painting he loves. This is evident in such works as *Children and Spastics* (1946; plate 1) and *Bird Watchers* (1948; plate 9).

Looking again at Tooker entails re-examining the multiple ways that artists have made "modern" art. Scholars no longer consider the question of Modernism as one of abstraction *versus* representation. Such artists as Tooker integrated lessons learned from Cubism, Abstract Expressionism, and Minimalism as readily as they did those of Piero della Francesca (*circa* 1420–1492). In the 1940s and 1950s, Tooker was closely associated with Paul Cadmus (1904–1999), the photographer George Platt Lynes (1907–1955), the painter Jared French (1905–1988), and the curator/writer/dance director Lincoln Kirstein (1907–1996), and with their circles. Many of these figures were central to and supported an American transformation of Surrealism through a sharp and personal narrative focus that drew heavily on fourteenth- to fifteenth-century painting. While not an actual movement, this stylistic tendency was labeled "Magic Realism" by critics and curators in the 1940s and often compared to contemporary European paintings by Otto Dix (1891–1969) or George Grosz (1893–1959), who synthesized similar influences into something new for a world wounded by World War I, the Great Depression, and World War II. In this context, Tooker became a major figure in the postwar American art world, acclaimed by critics and peers alike for his social acuity and virtuoso technique. A critic reviewing Tooker's first solo show, at the Edwin Hewitt Gallery, New York (*Art Digest*, March 1, 1951), noted that his modern "allegories … are evocative of the haunting fear and suspense and the sure prescience of disaster … Tooker's visual world and allegorical comments are true; his recording is impeccable."

Tooker and others who continued to work with the figure and narrative painting have often been overshadowed by the attention that critics gave to Abstract Expressionism. The dominant critical narrative of the postwar American art world has associated abstraction with innovation and considered so-called representational art as retrograde. In this version of history, such artists as Tooker were either ignored or treated lightly as a kind of aberrant proof that people still made illusionistic paintings. In general, critics and art historians have emphasized realism and abstraction as polar opposites, pitting them against each other politically as irreconcilable styles.

*George Tooker: A Retrospective* builds upon recent scholarship in order to re-examine the abstract/representational dichotomy by exploring the multiple meanings of postwar realist painting. As the essays in this book show, postwar American artists reacted to similar cultural experiences and aesthetic choices in extraordinarily diverse ways. Realism, often erroneously considered retrograde in this period by such critics as Clement Greenberg, was an important site for modernity and new aesthetic approaches. Modernism was clearly a much broader stylistic and intellectual position that necessarily included such artists as Tooker, who drew upon abstraction and new approaches to form while constructing narrative and figurative paintings. The present exhibition and catalogue allow audiences to see the unexpected ways in which Tooker overlaps with what has been considered avant garde in American art and to appreciate the depth of his resonant and prescient imagery.

We would first like to thank George Tooker, who has been a gracious and enthusiastic collaborator in this project. Without his support and input, we would not have been able to make this exhibition the special event that it has become. Although he lives a quiet life in the heart of Vermont, he welcomed us and our colleagues into his home and endured numerous interviews, letters, and phone calls about myriad details of his life. He also accommodated Melissa Wolfe and her Columbus Museum of Art colleague Jeff Sims with unfailing patience during two non-stop days of questions and filming in Vermont to compile footage for a documentary to accompany the exhibition. We are grateful for George's good humor and dedication to the project. Similarly, his sister Mary Tooker hosted us at her home and shared anecdotes about her brother that added to our understanding of his range of work and family life. We are thankful for her cooperation.

Longtime friends and associates of the artist also granted interviews. We thank Father Robert Campbell of LaSalette Shrine, Enfield, New Hampshire; James David Draper, Distinguished Curator of European Sculpture, the Metropolitan Museum of Art, New York; Arnold Skolnik; and Perez Zagorin for their perspective on Tooker's work and the art world. Mr. Skolnik was instrumental in helping us to locate private collectors and guarantee important loans. He also generously shared rare publications from his collection, and photographic archives from what was previously the only monograph on Tooker. At the DC Moore Gallery, New York, Bridget Moore, Edward De Luca, Heidi Lange, and Kate Pollack provided advice, feedback, and research assistance at every stage of the project. They were tireless in their efforts to track down works in private collections and to obtain hard-to-find photographs. They joined us in viewing this project as a labor of love.

No exhibition can claim success without the collaboration of passionate collectors dedicated to fostering new scholarship by sharing their collections with researchers and the public. In this regard, the Tooker retrospective has been exemplary; George's collectors believe strongly in his vision and were eager to demonstrate the power and beauty of his art. We wish to thank all who responded to our request for loans and in many cases allowed us to visit their collections: Mr. and Mrs. James C. Biddle, Mr. and Mrs. Mark L. Brock, Barney A. Ebsworth, Linda Lichtenberg Kaplan, Myron and Anita Kunin, Barbara B. Millhouse, Andrew Nelson, James and

Barbara Palmer, Nicholas Miles Pentecost, Pilar and Vincente Pita, the Reis Private Collection, James Francis Trezza, Susan and Peter Tuteur, and several anonymous collectors.

The new and diverse perspectives on Tooker presented in this catalogue are the result of hard work by all three curators and our colleagues Anna C. Chave, Professor of Art History at the Graduate Center, CUNY, and Jonathan Weinberg, independent scholar, who immersed themselves in the project and produced analyses that exceeded our high expectations. Thomas H. Garver agreed to contribute a personal note at a late stage in the game and did so flawlessly, based on his unparalleled experience with Tooker's work.

Numerous archivists and librarians facilitated our research throughout the development of the exhibition and publication. We wish to thank especially the fantastic staff at the Archives of American Art, Smithsonian Institution, Washington, D.C., for their accommodation of our appointments and requests: John W. Smith, Director; Marisa Bourgoin, Richard Manoogian Chief of Reference Services; and Wendy Hurlock Baker and Elizabeth Botten, Archives Technicians in Reference. Thanks also to their colleague at the New York office, Joy R. Weiner. We also thank: Bob Dunkelberger, Bloomsburg University Archivist; Bret Sharlow, the Criterion Collection and Janus Films; Kevin Madill, Assistant Librarian, and MacKenzie Bennett, Assistant Archivist, The Museum of Modern Art, New York; and William B. Keller, Fine Arts Librarian, Anne and Jerome Fisher Fine Arts Library, University of Pennsylvania.

Colleagues and friends who provided invaluable moral and logistical support include: Brian T. Allen, The Mary Stripp and R. Crosby Kemper Director, and James M. Sousa, Associate Registrar for Collections and Archives, Addison Gallery of American Art, Phillips Academy; Mark Cole, Associate Curator of American Painting and Sculpture, The Cleveland Museum of Art; Jenny Sponberg, Curtis Galleries, Inc.; Kathleen P. O'Malley, Associate Registrar, Hood Museum of Art, Dartmouth College; Nancy Wallach, Director of Curatorial Affairs/Grants Officer, Katonah Museum of Art; Lisa Mintz Messinger, Associate Curator, and Cynthia Iavarone and Jessica Murphy, Department of Nineteenth-Century, Modern, and Contemporary Art, the Metropolitan Museum of Art; Isabelle Dervaux, Curator of Modern and Contemporary Drawing, Morgan Library; Max Weintraub, Curator of The Reis Collection of Modern and Contemporary Art; Michael Rosenfeld, Michael Rosenfeld Gallery; Nancy Walker, Father Paul, and the congregation of the church of St. Francis of Assisi, Windsor, Vermont; Barbara C.A. Santini; Katherine Hauser, Associate Professor, Department of Art and Art History, Skidmore College; Susan Rivers, *Vermont Catholic Tribune*; Barbara Haskell, Curator, and Diana Lada, Documentation Manager, Registration Department, Whitney Museum of American Art.

The exhibition would not have been possible in New York without the support of the Isaacson–Draper Foundation, the Bonnie Cashin Fund, the Cape Branch Foundation, the Bernard and Muriel Lauren Foundation, Kathleen and John Schobel IV, John Schobel V and Daniel D. Schmeder, and public funds from the New York City Department of Cultural Affairs and the New York State Council on the Arts. At the National Academy, former Director Annette Blaugrund enthusiastically supported this exhibition from its earliest stage. She and Bruce Weber, Acting Co-Director and Senior Curator of Nineteenth-Century Art, provided helpful insight and criticism on Marshall Price's essay. The Academy's President, Susan Shatter, and the Exhibition Committee proffered encouragement throughout, while every member of the National Academy's small staff assisted with this exhibition. Our sincere appreciation goes to: Charles Biada, Director of Operations; Paula Bartel, Senior Development Officer; Nancy Brody, Director of Special Events; Nancy Cafferty, Director of Finance and Human Resources; Jonah Ellis, Building Manager; Monica Griesbach, Associate Conservator; Jessica Gumora, Assistant to the Director; Lucie Kinsolving, Chief Conservator; Nancy Malloy, Director of Artist Membership; Anna Martin, Registrar; Paula Pineda, Associate Registrar; Thomas Sembros, Assistant to the Director of Finance; Jean Telljohann, Director of Development; Kristine Widmer, Curator of Education; and Christine Williams, Director of Communications. Additional thanks go to Janezee Bond, Curatorial Intern during the summer of 2007.

Our friends at the Pennsylvania Academy were dedicated and passionate about this project from the beginning. Judith Thomas and Barbara Katus deserve special recognition as they took on the gathering and review of images for this book. Judith's persistence and Barbara's flawless eye guaranteed that this publication would contain a rich, high-quality collection of images that do the art work and the artist justice. Thanks also to Jamie Biddle, Trustee and Chairman of the Academy's museum committee, for his constant support in all things Tooker. Also instrumental in making the exhibition a success were: David R. Brigham, Edna S. Tuttleman Director of the Academy Museum; Brian Murray, Chief Preparator, and Mark Knobelsdorf, his assistant; Judy Ringold, Director of Public Education; Monica Zimmerman, Program Coordinator; Brian Duffy, Academy Librarian; Marsha Braverman, Senior Vice President of Marketing and Communications; Gigi Lamm, Public Relations and Advertising Manager; Anthony Ciambella; Aella Diamantopoulos, Chief Conservator; Jimmie Greeno, Director of Security; Louisa Hanshew, Senior Vice President of Development; Lynn Marsden-Atlass, Senior Curator; and Gale Rawson, Registrar. Curatorial Intern Elizabeth McGoey provided research assistance at the beginning of the project—thank you, Liz. Finally, thank you to Thomas Cook and the Richard C. van Hess Foundation for their generous support of the exhibition and its programs in Philadelphia.

The exhibition in Columbus received generous support from the Columbus Foundation, the Greater Columbus Arts Council, National City, Nationwide, the Ohio Arts Council, and the Mrs. Richard M. Ross Publications Fund of the Columbus Museum of Art. The Columbus Museum of Art has a staff that readily takes on the enthusiasms of its curators, and the expertise of Catherine Evans, Chief Curator, and the rest of the curatorial staff; Maureen Carroll, Grant Writer; Christopher S. Duckworth, Director of Publications; Cindy Myers Foley, Director of Education, and her staff; Melinda Knapp, Chief Registrar; Jennifer Seeds Martin, Associate Registrar; Greg Jones, Exhibition Designer; Norma Sexton, Director of Development, and her staff; and Jeff Sims, Adult Programs and Film Specialist, has been especially helpful. Special thanks are due as well to Rachel Trinkley and Sarah Johnson, Curatorial Assistants, and especially to Nannette V. Maciejunes, Executive Director, whose interest in and respect for Tooker's work have supported this endeavor from initiation to completion.

Finally, we all have extra-special personal thanks to pass along: Marshall N. Price would like to thank his colleagues Robert Cozzolino and M. Melissa Wolfe. They have provided steadfast support, constant encouragement, and insightful feedback on every aspect of this project. Thanks to National Academician Simon Dinnerstein for his reflections on Tooker, Ulrike Müller for discussing philosophical issues relating to Marshall's essay, and to James David Draper for his unwavering support. Robert Cozzolino would like to thank fellow "leaf-peeper" Marshall for making this collaboration a wonderful and rewarding experience, and Melissa Wolfe for her dual sense of realism and the amusing, which has made our work seem purposeful and fun. He would like to thank Catherine Cooney for her valuable feedback on his essay and especially his curatorial assistant Thomas Cooney Cozzolino, who devoured everything on George Tooker within arm's reach and whose influence is surely felt in the project's final shape. Melissa Wolfe would also like to thank her two collaborators Marshall and Robert for their willingness to add yet another voice to this deeply worthwhile project. Their generous collaboration and intellectual curiosity have shaped this project from beginning to end.

Marshall N. Price
Associate Curator of Modern and Contemporary Art
National Academy Museum and School of Fine Arts
New York

Robert Cozzolino
Curator of Modern Art
Pennsylvania Academy of the Fine Arts
Philadelphia

M. Melissa Wolfe
Associate Curator of American Art
Columbus Museum of Art, Ohio

# On the art of George Tooker

Thomas H. Garver

**"Painting is a very isolated occupation."**
George Tooker, undated letter

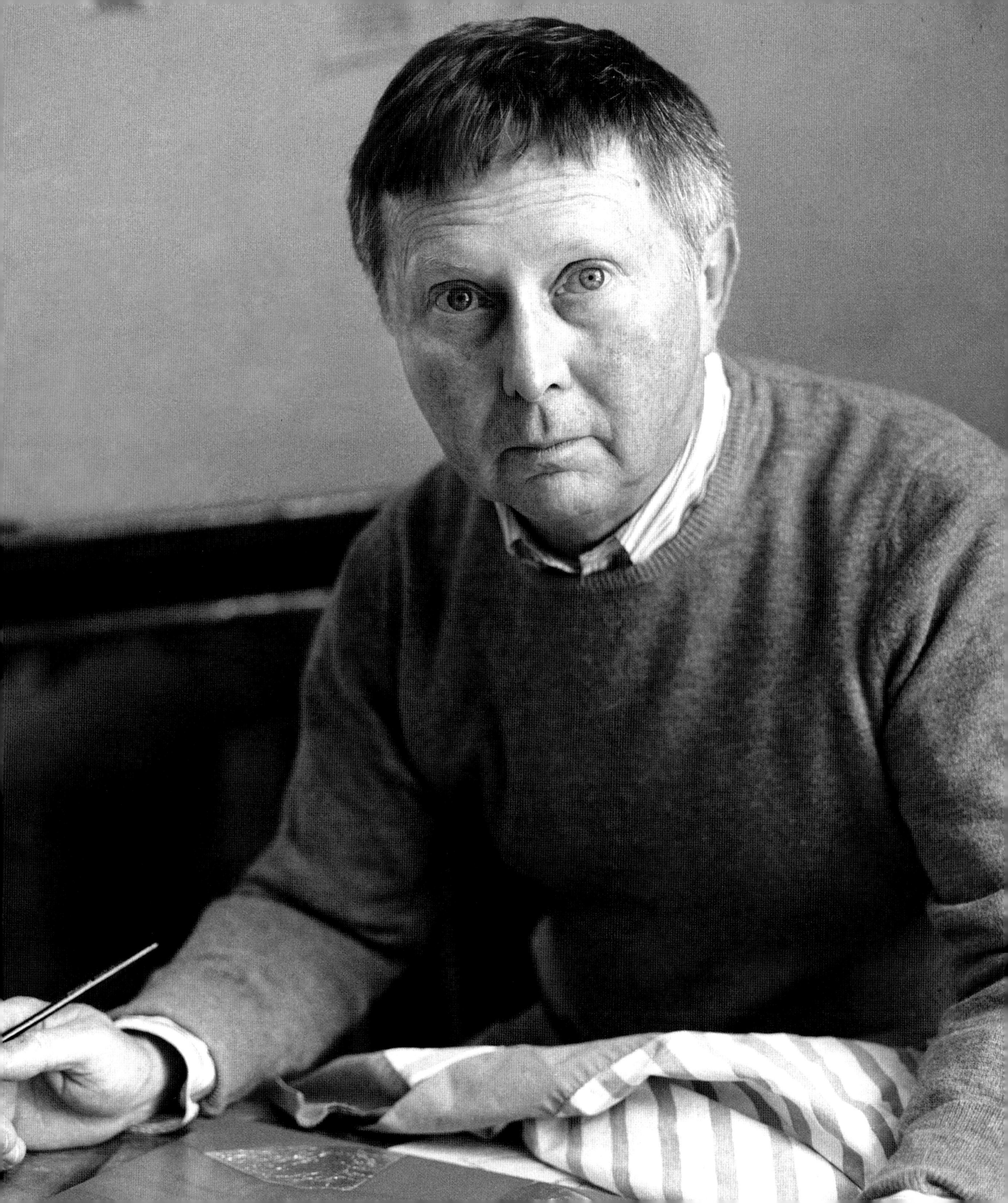

Previous page:
George Tooker working on *Stations of the Cross*, panel 4 (1983)
Photograph by Gregory Conniff

fig. 1
George Tooker in his studio with the sketch for *Sibyl* (2005), October 2006
Photograph by Thomas H. Garver



George Tooker is a gentle and articulate man. He chooses his words carefully under all circumstances, but he politely rebuffs questions about the forces that energize his paintings. "I don't want to explain in words what I'm about," he has said. "I can't explain it. I don't think about it myself and I don't want to." Any dialogue about his work that transpires is, therefore, not between the artist and another person but internal and silent, so it is not surprising to find that it is silence that marks the time when he is working in his studio. This is a room of modest size, hardly larger than a commodious bedroom, sparely furnished, in which he has painted for nearly fifty years.

In the mid-1950s, Tooker and his life partner, the late William Christopher (1923–1973), were living in a Brooklyn Heights brownstone they had revived from an all-but-derelict rooming house. (Tooker's painting *Government Bureau* (1956; plate 27) was created to document their struggle with Brooklyn's Borough Hall to obtain the

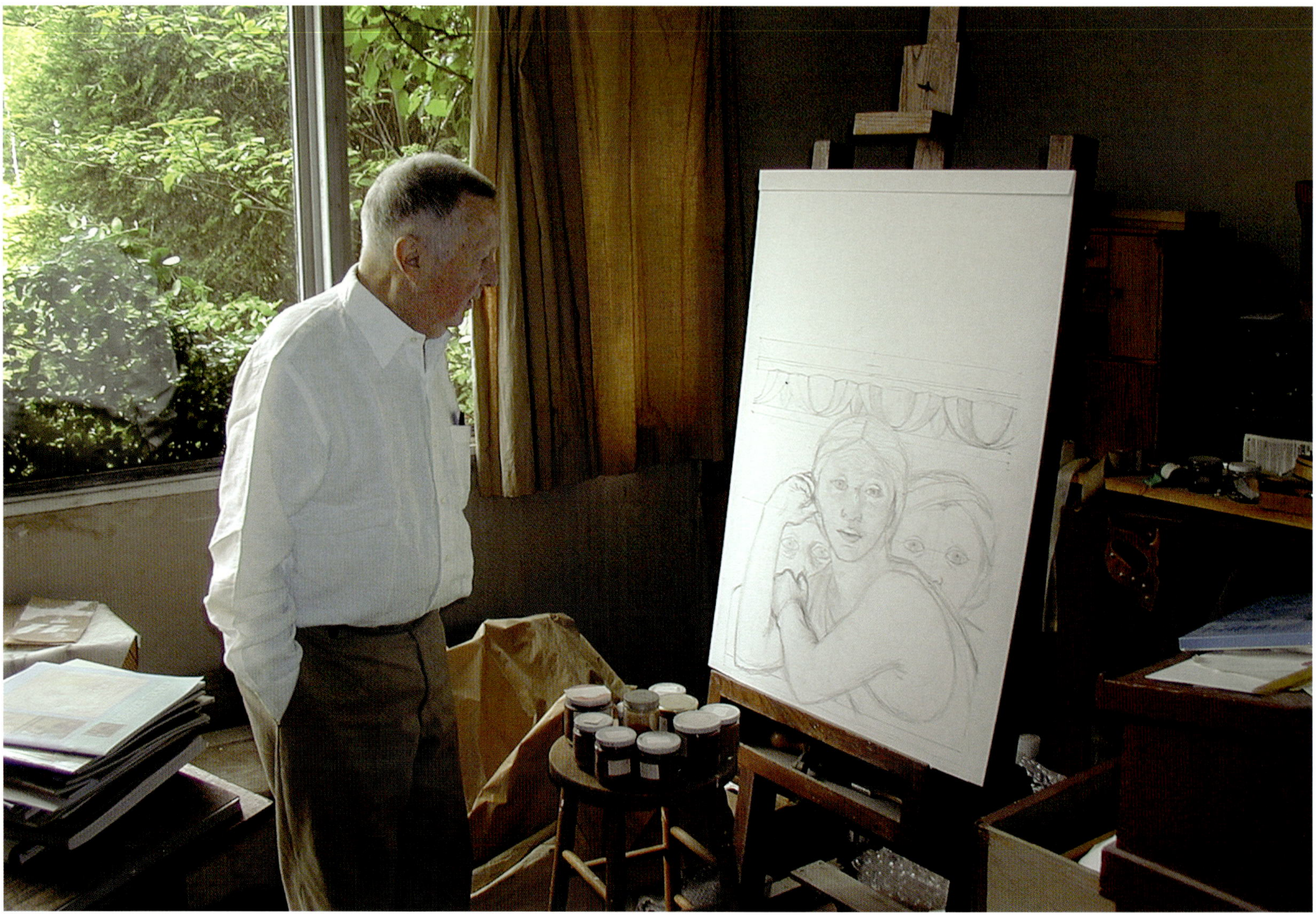

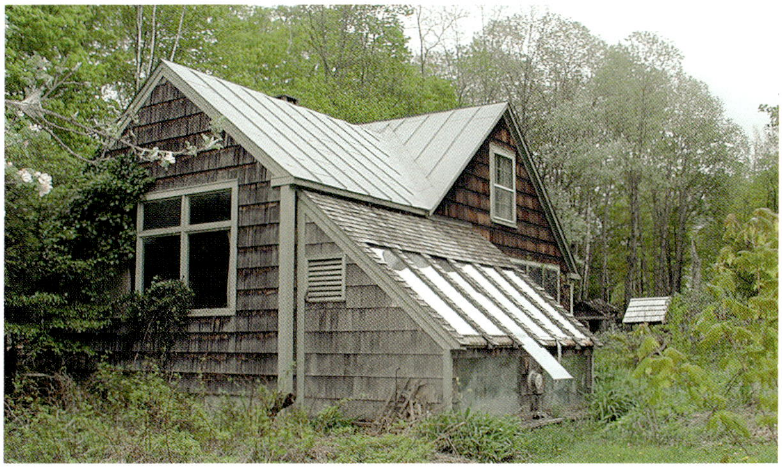

fig. 2
George Tooker's and William Christopher's home and studios at Hartland, Vermont (2006)
Photograph by Thomas H. Garver

fig. 3
Portrait of George Tooker (2006)
Photograph by Thomas H. Garver



permits necessary to renovate the building.) Around them, the creative life of New York was exploding. As other artists arrived in the city seeking recognition and reward, these two young painters went the other way, to rural Hartland, Vermont. While both were sustained by the cultural life of a great city, the very nature of their painting required a place where they could concentrate on their work without distraction. They bought a piece of rocky, worn-out farmland a few miles outside town and in the late 1950s started building a house on the cellar hole of a long-vanished structure, framing the central portion themselves with massive timbers from an eighteenth-century barn. In 1960, when the first part of the building was completed, they settled permanently in Hartland. The house is a simple dwelling of no particular style, filled with furniture and objects: some old, some made by its occupants, but all united by the beauty of their materials and orderly forms. The studio was one of several subsequent additions to the house, and, aside from a number of winters spent in Spain, Tooker has painted here ever since.

For George Tooker, painting is the supreme task of life, and for more than sixty years he has painted as though the frenetic art activity of New York City never existed. The center of this life is the studio, and the act of painting is a carefully established ritual, dictated both by Tooker's own steady and contemplative temperament and by the demands of the medium in which he works. Within this ritual, the selection of the subject for the painting is the first task, and this demands considerable reflection, for the pictorial decision, once made, will lead on to months of work to complete a painting. The image selected may be a reprise of an earlier theme, as the artist, like a composer, works to draw ever more variations from ideas developed over decades. For Tooker, these themes most often range from a muted eroticism or the destruction of the human soul by an indifferent society or its government, to an intense oracular spirituality. Once selected and sketched out, the image is transferred to a gessoed panel of modest proportions, never larger than something that can be easily held in both hands. The medium demands focused and intense concentration. Tempera—simply egg yolk, thinned with water and mixed with powdered pigment—must be applied steadily, as it dries almost instantly, and therefore any subsequent changes to the forms are possible only by over-painting.

Seated at a tilt-top table he built to hold the painting in progress, Tooker begins. The basic colors for that day's work are selected, mixed with the egg medium, and put into the little pots of a porcelain watercolor palette. Tooker takes a sable brush, lifts colors from the pots, mixes them, wipes excess liquid from the brush, then, stroke, stroke, stroke, as he applies paint to the panel, then rinses the brush,

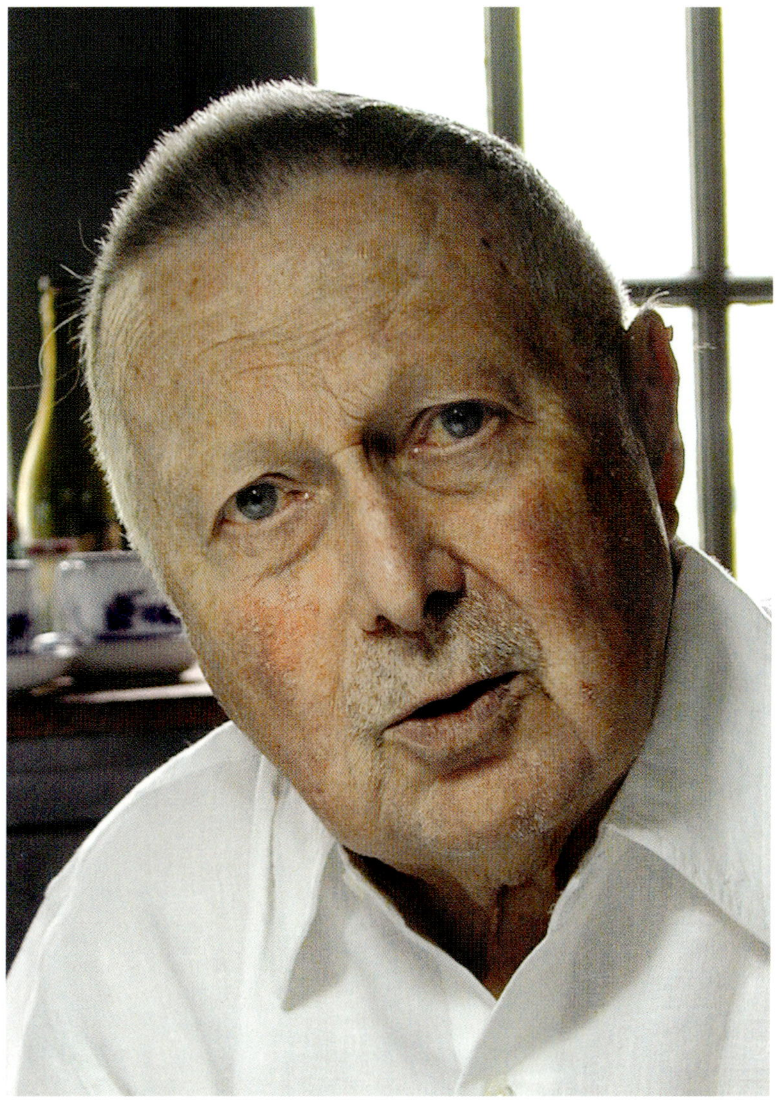

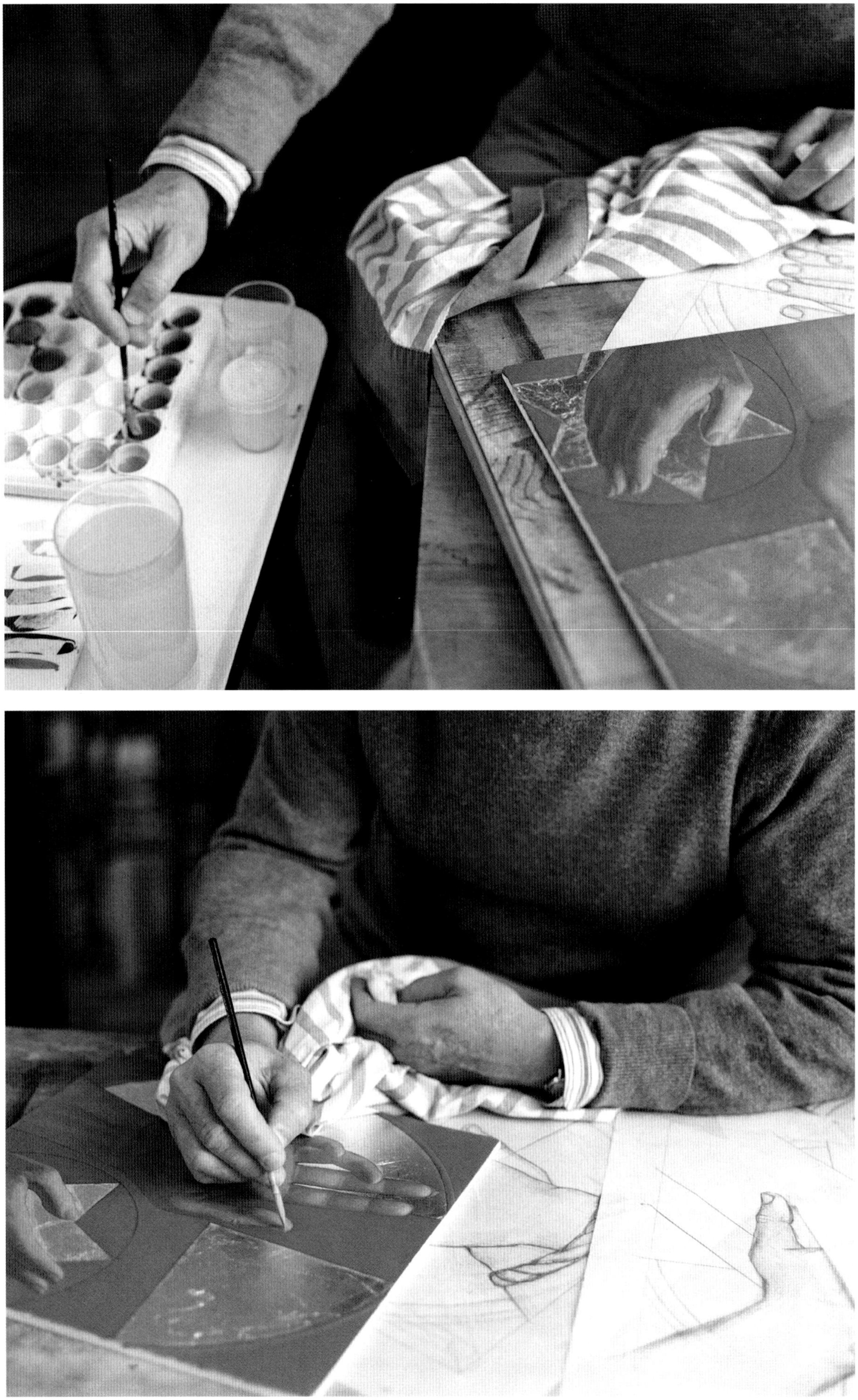

fig. 4
George Tooker working on *Stations of the Cross*, panel 4 (1983)
Photographs by Gregory Conniff

picks up more paint, adjusts the color, wipes the brush, and again, stroke, stroke, stroke. Again and again, day after day, month after month, thousands, perhaps tens of thousands of strokes, are laid down on the panel. These endlessly repeated gestures combine to build the surfaces and forms, while Tooker's use of layers of thinly applied color permits light to penetrate the surface to be reflected from the gesso ground, glowing through the layers of pigment.

Watching George Tooker paint is excruciating. Stroke, stroke, stroke, it goes on and on, yet to an observer almost nothing seems to be happening. Only the artist knows the glorious silent mantra that creates a work of art. Tooker does not think of himself as "creative" but rather regards his role in this process as that of a "passive vessel, a receptor or translator," whose function is to render an idea in visible form. The energy that sustains him over many months of work on a single picture comes from a sense of self-renewing wonder as the idea blossoms through the artist's own will. This is what Tooker calls "the discovery" within each painting. It is the nourishment he needs as the sketch traced on to the panel changes into an image that, in Lincoln Kirstein's prescient phrase, reaches for a "universal legibility rather than a limited correspondence."

The genesis of Tooker's art lies in two modalities. First is the germination of an idea, which may come from a visual event or a spiritual or intellectual construct. Secondly, the pictorial form is always embedded in Tooker's deep knowledge and grasp of art history and his love of the art of the past. For Tooker, "Art comes from other art"—a phrase he credits to Thomas Aquinas—for no matter what the subject, the new painting will be refracted by that "other art." His use of historical painting and sculpture is an act of respect, not one of visual appropriation. What Tooker creates is a new work of art, not a simulacrum of past endeavor.

While Tooker's paintings create a strong realistic presence, the absence of particular elements one might consider central to the documentation of life intensifies the focus and silence in his work. By Tooker's own admission, he is more involved in the creation of abstractions than in rendering reality. His paintings, however, always retain an essential representational structure. Within his work, the time of clocks disappears, even when time may be the essence of the picture. Additionally, other commonalities of life—age, gender, and race, all emblems of discrimination and judgment that we employ unthinkingly and repeatedly—are melded together. Even the line between life and death, the greatest divide of all, becomes swirled into a third state, where graves have opened and silent watchers watch.

As these are "cabinet pictures," paintings of an intimate size, to see them well one must stand within the circle of their creation and thus step into the space inhabited by Tooker as he painted them. We may study the myriad strokes on their surfaces, perhaps unaware of the thousands that lie beneath before we realize that what we are seeing would not have the same density of color and richness of modeling if the artist had not constructed them with such complete devotion. Tooker has reduced redundant information to reach the essence of experiences that are all too often clouded by the noise and clutter of daily life. These paintings may be small in size, but they are majestic in scale. Their generosity of spirit speaks directly to that "universal legibility," and they command absolute attention. Truth has come through that small sable brush. Perhaps that is why George Tooker's paintings continue to possess the power to silence a crowded room.

# George Tooker: a biography

M. Melissa Wolfe

"I am after painting reality impressed on the mind so hard that it returns as a dream, but I am not after painting dreams as such, or fantasy."

George Tooker quoted in Seldon Rodman, *Conversations with Artists*, 1957

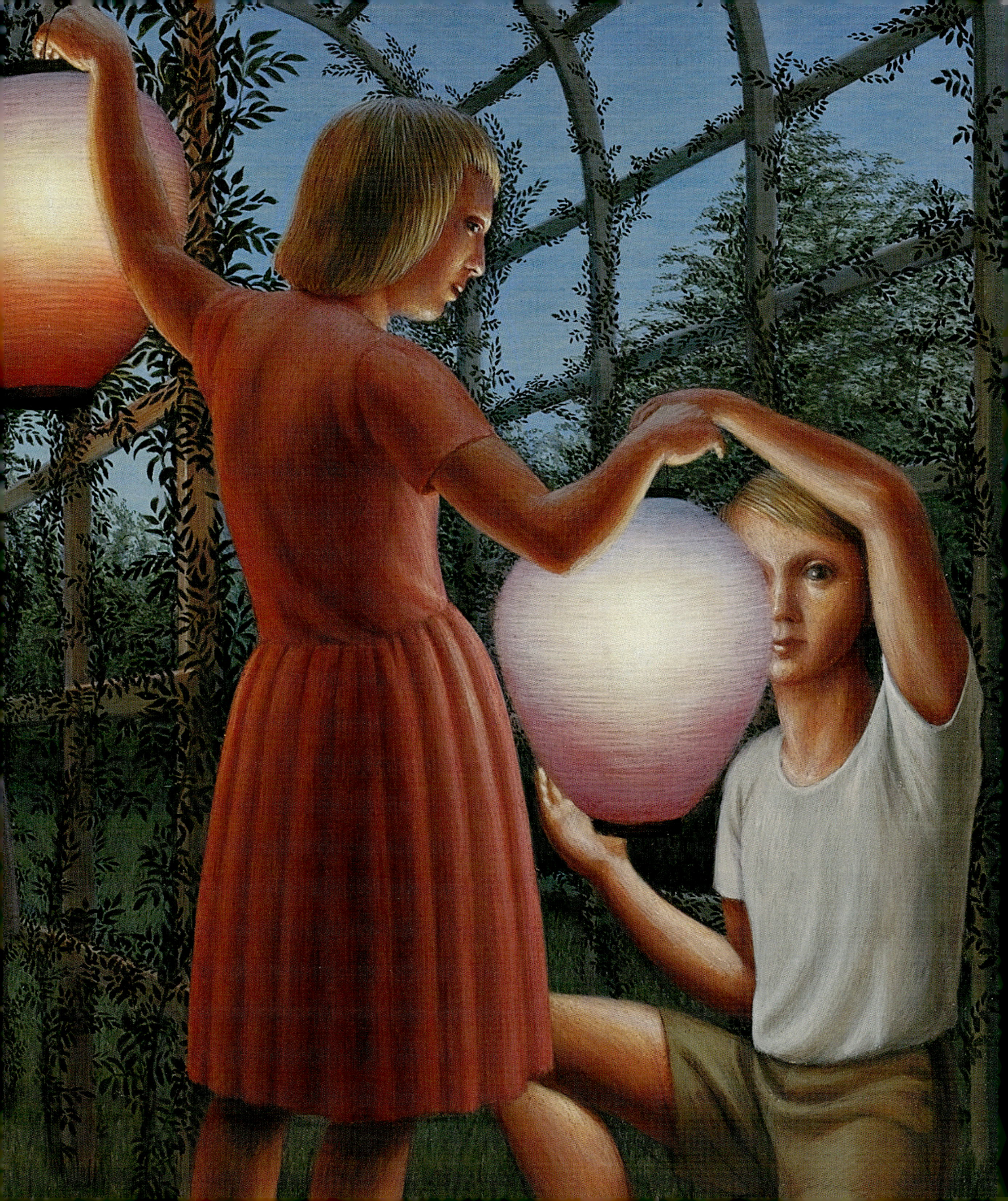

Previous page
George Tooker
***Garden Party*** (1952) (detail)
Private Collection, courtesy Debra Force Fine Art, New York
(see page 126)

Below
fig. 1
George Tooker (far right) at Pocono Summer Camp (early 1930s)
Courtesy of the George Tooker Papers, 1932–1973, Archives of American Art, Smithsonian Institution, Washington, D.C.

Right
fig. 2
Malcolm Fraser (1868–1949)
*Portrait of George Tooker* (*circa* 1924)
Oil on canvas
34⅜ × 18⅞ inches (87.2 × 47.8 cm)
Private Collection



George Clair Tooker, Jr., was born on August 5, 1920, in Brooklyn, New York. When he was five years old, his family moved to Long Island, the home of his paternal relatives, where his father was a municipal bond broker for several banks. Tooker recalls fondly his childhood in the (then) rather isolated countryside of Bellport (fig. 1). When he was seven, his parents enrolled him in art classes taught by a long-time family friend and neighbor, Malcolm Fraser (1868–1949), a European-trained artist who had painted several portraits for the family, including one of his young student (fig. 2). Though Tooker jovially admits that, as a seven-year-old, this experience was limited in its influence, he found Fraser fascinating, and it was from the older artist that he became aware at a very young age that one could be an artist—just the same as being a stockbroker or a teacher. George attended a local high school in Patchogue, but when his parents were told by the principal that his education there would not garner acceptance into college, they sent him to Phillips Academy in Andover, Massachusetts, where he graduated in 1938.

Throughout high school, Tooker had been visiting galleries and museums in New York City, and he was certain by this time that he wanted to be an artist. His parents were supportive of his interest in art; they had given their son a number of art books for his enjoyment, and his mother was a "Sunday painter." However, they

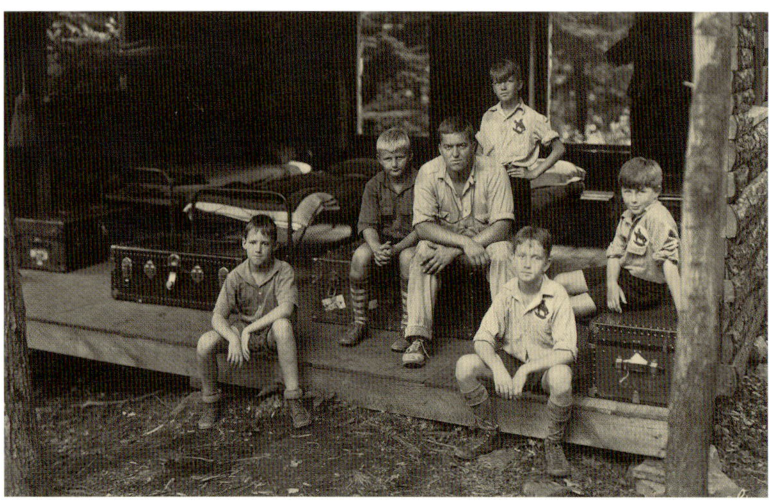

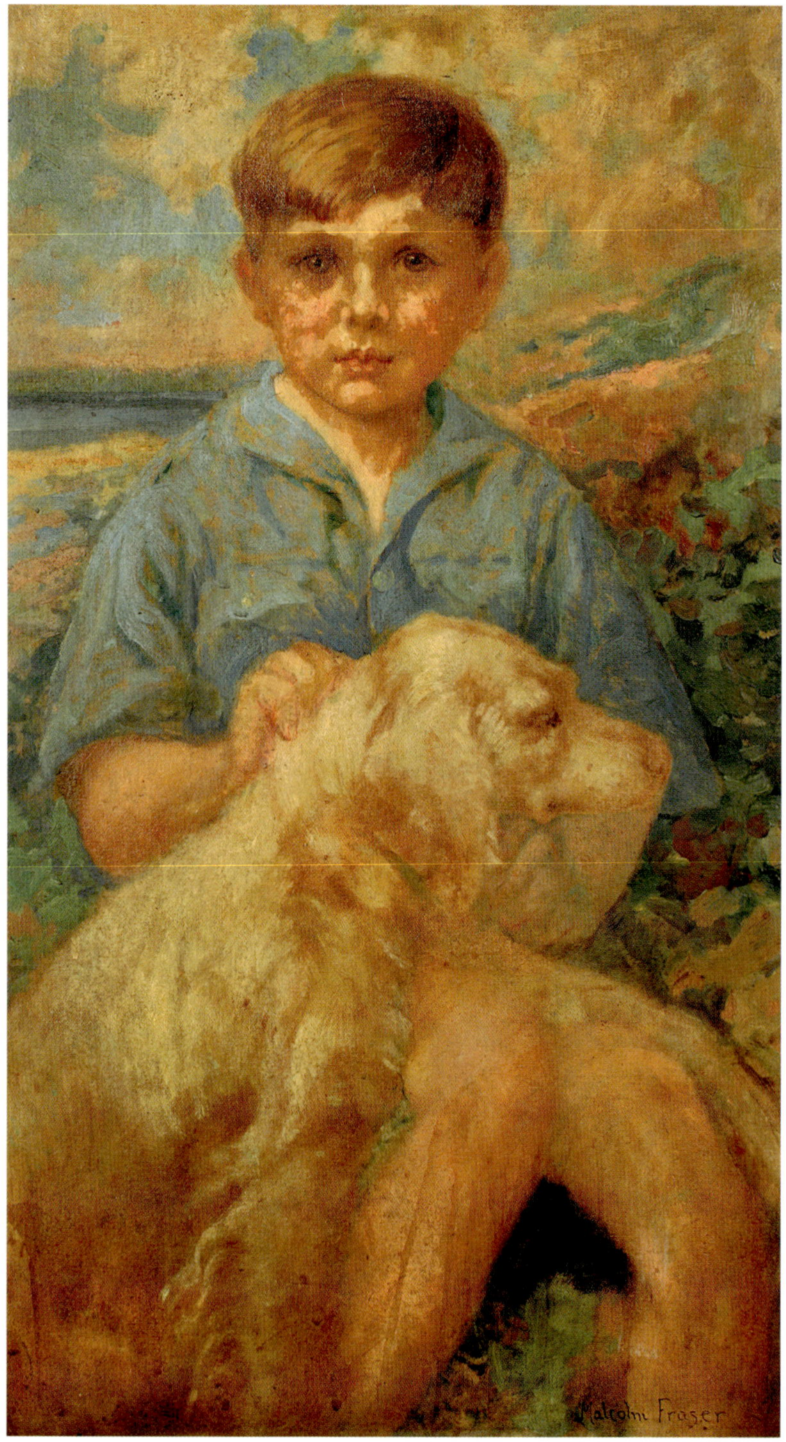


insisted that he first receive a formal university education. Not wanting to disappoint his parents, Tooker acquiesced, explaining, "I sort of gave in to them because I knew they loved me."[1] In a tacit rebellion against the business types at Phillips Academy, whom he disliked and who were going to Yale, Tooker applied to Harvard. Tooker was not interested in the art curriculum at the university; he wanted to study with a professional artist, not "someone who would have been teaching at Harvard."[2] Instead, he deepened his lifelong interest in literature, especially poetry, by majoring in English. He quietly continued to nurture his interest in painting, visiting galleries and exhibitions in Boston, taking a

fig. 3
George Tooker
*Old Inlet, Long Island* (1942)
Oil on board
15¾ × 19½ inches (40 × 49.5 cm)
Private Collection



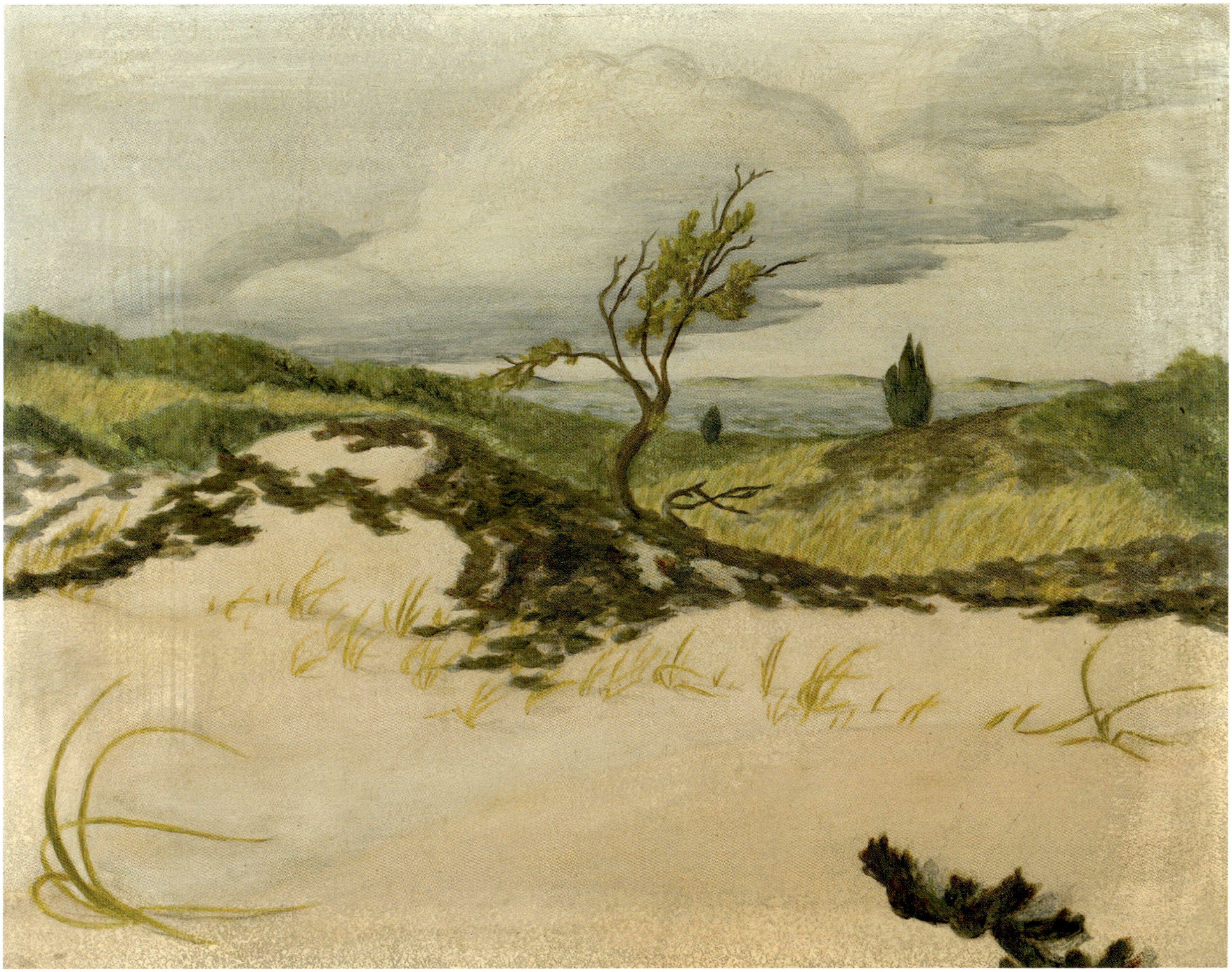

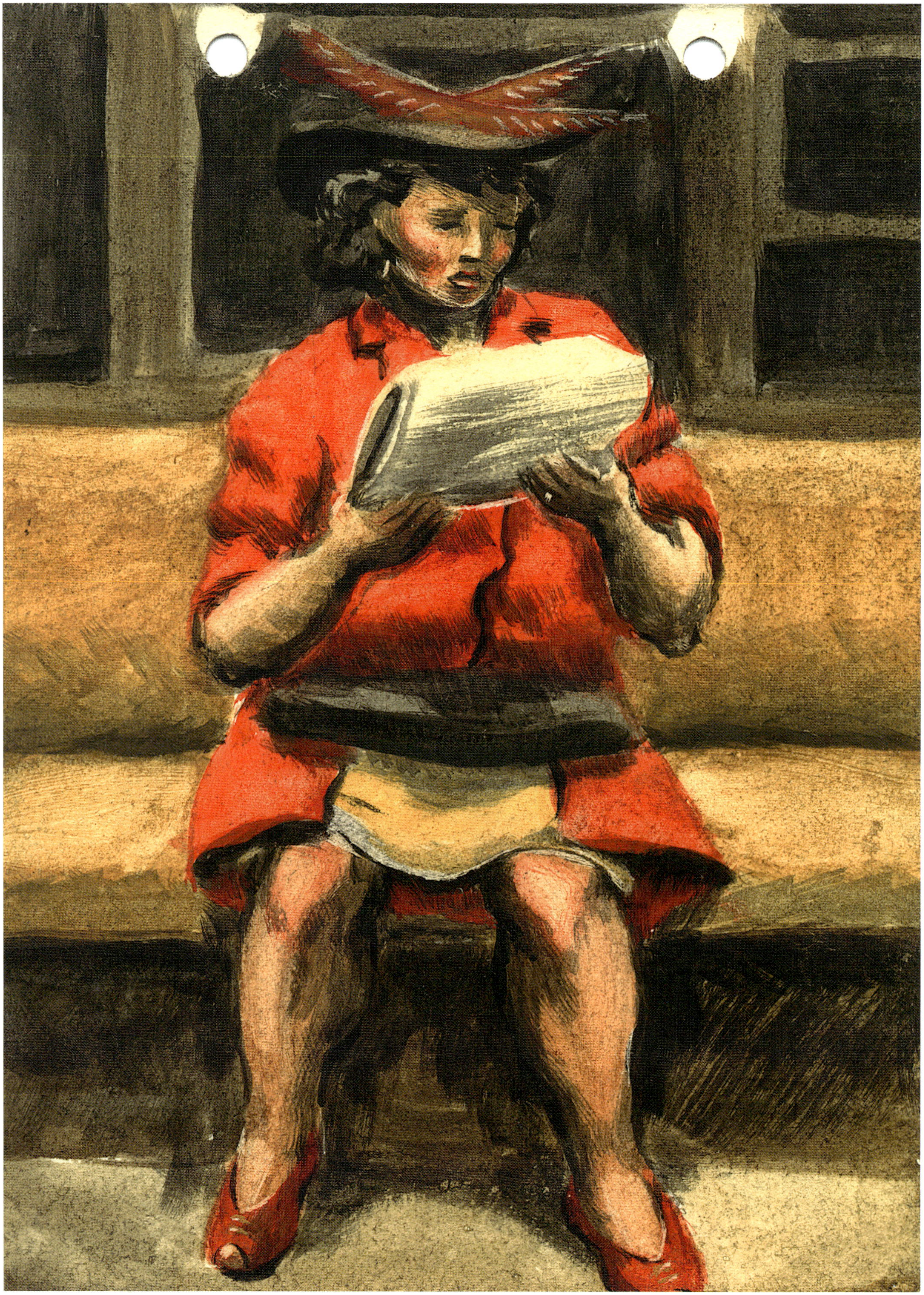

fig. 4
George Tooker
"Figure Sketch" (*circa* 1944)
Tempera on paper
7 × 5⅝ inches (17.8 × 14.3 cm)
Courtesy of the George Tooker Papers, 1932–1973, Archives of American Art, Smithsonian Institution, Washington, D.C.

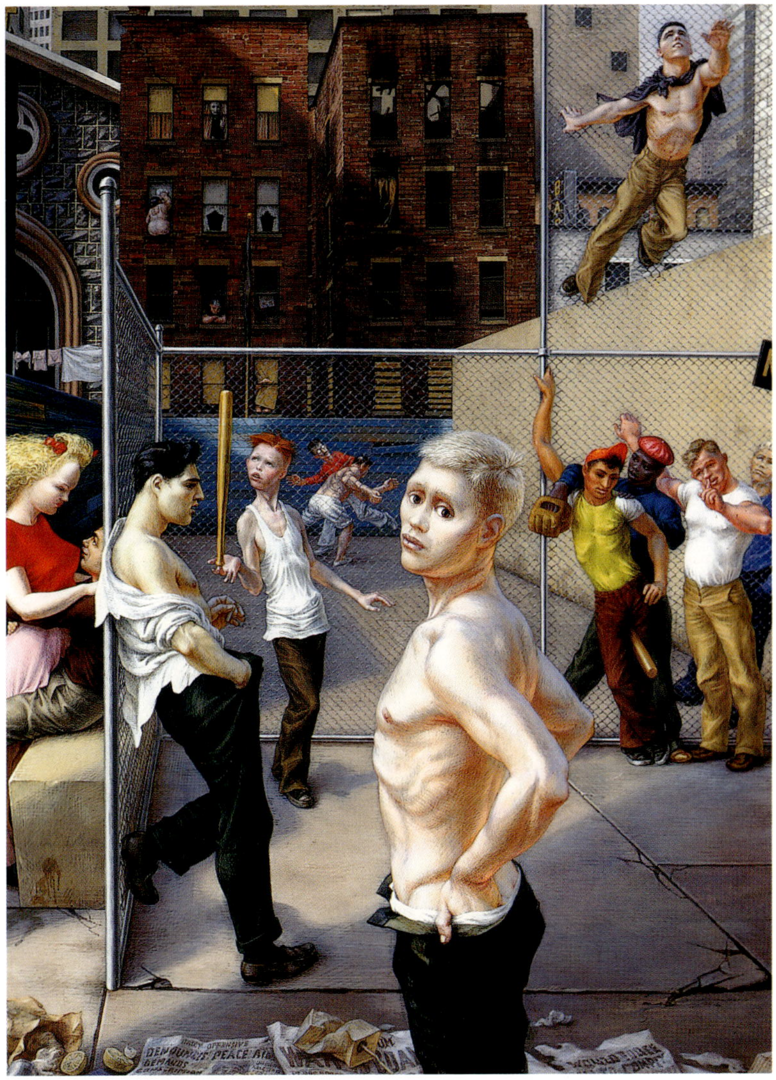

fig. 5
Paul Cadmus (1904–1999)
*Playground* (1948)
Egg-yolk tempera on hardwood panel
23½ × 17½ inches (59.7 × 44.4 cm)
Georgia Museum of Art, University of Georgia; University Purchase GMOA 1970.2619



course by Chandler R. Post at the Fogg Art Museum in Florentine Renaissance painting and sculpture, and sketching watercolor landscapes with his friend Francis Faust (fig. 3).

Tooker graduated from Harvard in 1942, and, with the entry of the United States into World War II, he felt it his duty to enlist in the Marine Corps Officer Candidate School. However, he has explained that he "didn't want to enter the military, but I hadn't wanted to go to college, either—I was doing these things because they were expected of me."[3] It was upon the realization only a few months later, during a bayonet drill, that he was being trained to stab another person "in the guts," that the pressure of acquiescence manifested itself in ulcerative colitis, and he was given a discharge. His family had moved back to Brooklyn, and, upon his return home, since he had complied with his parents' wishes, they "kept their word," and in the spring of 1943 Tooker enrolled at the Art Students League with their support.[4]

Tooker spent two years taking classes with Reginald Marsh (1898–1954), whose work he had admired in an exhibition in 1937. Marsh introduced him to tempera and encouraged him to make small, closely observed figure sketches as he moved about the city. Tooker's early work in the medium reveals his attempt to emulate the transparent, fluid brushwork of his mentor (fig. 4). Tooker became Marsh's class monitor, and the two artists established a lifelong friendship. Tooker studied with Kenneth Hayes Miller (1876–1952) for four months, and, though Tooker found Miller's personality difficult, his emphasis on compositional design was a lasting influence. Tooker also studied with Harry Sternberg (1904–2001), who helped him both focus his content and realize the viability of protest in his paintings.[5]

In 1944, Tooker met Paul Cadmus (1904–1999) through the Saturday drawing classes held at the League. Cadmus had established his reputation in the previous decade with works that excelled both in their draftsmanship and in their pointed satirical wit. He introduced Tooker to the artist's guidebook *The Practice of Tempera Painting*, published in 1936 by Daniel V. Thompson.[6] Cadmus worked in tempera, using a traditional, highly controlled application of paint that suited Tooker much better than the quick, fluid style of Marsh. As Tooker has explained, "It was only when Cadmus stepped in and encouraged me to slow down that I actually came into my own."[7] Cadmus and Tooker became lovers, and through Cadmus Tooker became acquainted with the artist Jared French (1905–1988) and his wife, Margaret Hoening (1889–1973), as well as with the dynamic gay community, which included Lincoln Kirstein (1907–1996), George Platt Lynes (1907–1955), and other prominent figures in the city's artistic world.

Tooker ended his study at the League in the summer of 1945. With financial support from his family, he began living and painting on his own in Greenwich Village in a cold-water flat on Bleecker Street, close to the studio that French and Cadmus shared. Not only did the three work in close proximity in the city, but the summers were spent on working vacations together as well.

It is remarkable in many ways how competent Tooker's painting was at this early stage in his career. Only one year after leaving the League, his work was included in the exhibition *Fourteen Americans* at The Museum of Modern Art, New York, and in the remaining years of the decade he was included in the annual exhibitions at the Carnegie Institute and the Whitney Museum of American Art. Tooker's output does, however, show evidence of focused

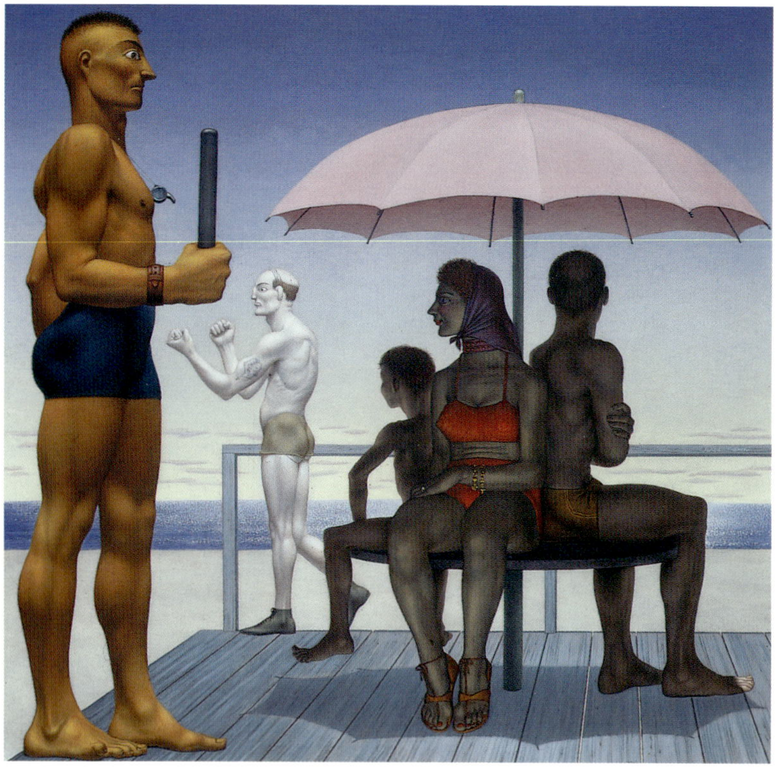

fig. 6
Jared French (1905–1988)
*State Park* (1946)
Egg tempera on composition board
23¼ × 23¼ inches (59.7 × 59.7 cm)
Whitney Museum of American Art, New York; Gift of Mr. and Mrs. R.H. Donnelley Erdman, 65.78

fig. 7
PaJaMa (Paul Cadmus, Jared and Margaret French)
*Margaret and Jared French and Umbrella, Nantucket* (*circa* 1946)
Courtesy of the George Tooker Papers, 1932–1973, Archives of American Art, Smithsonian Institution, Washington, D.C.

explorations, as he worked to find a language and a voice true to himself. As he has said of this time, "It gradually dawned on me that I had something to say, a certain point of view."[8]

Tooker cites Cadmus and French as two of the most important influences on his own style. His work from this period owes a clear debt to Cadmus's use of satire and to his overt exploration of homosexual themes. In *Children and Spastics* (1946; plate 1), the satirical voice is emphasized in the attenuated, overly affected postures of the three men and the Bosch-esque malevolence of the children. Such characters find parallels in Cadmus's painting of the same time. In *Playground* (1948; fig. 5), the threatening nature of the gang in the far right intensifies the vulnerability of the blond boy's eroticism in the foreground. Tooker's work is given explicit homosexual content by the exaggerated contrapposto (a "swish") and lightened hair, which were well-known stereotypical features of gay men at the time. The three figures present an obvious quotation of the Three Graces in *The Education of Marie de Medici* (1622–25), by Peter Paul Rubens (1577–1640), in essence turning exemplars of femininity into "exemplars" of effeminacy.[9] Homosexual content became much less explicit in Tooker's work as he moved away from the close association with Cadmus and French during this period, and as he further honed his own visual language. His later works address issues of homosexuality couched in a broader context of sexuality and difference, and filtered through multiple layers of meaning within each composition.

Tooker's emulations of Cadmus's satirical style and complicated groupings were mediated by his admiration for French's ability to create monumental figures whose emotional weight is both immediately felt and yet remains cryptic in intent. The figures in *Island* (fig. 8), painted in 1946, share the simplified, sculptural form seen in French's *State Park* (fig. 6) of the same year. The narrative has been distilled to a single gesture that unifies the three figures into a cohesive unit but remains enigmatic nonetheless. For more than a decade, Cadmus and the Frenches used Margaret's Leica camera to photograph themselves, and such other frequent visitors as Tooker, on the beach in self-consciously artistic arrangements (fig. 7). These photographs, collaboratively titled "PaJaMa," using the first two letters of each of their forenames, were not made as studies for paintings but were created as an aestheticizing practice. They are perhaps the most tangible manifestation of the artistic idealism that was cultivated by the entire group. *Island*, created during the summer of 1946 on Nantucket Island, shares with the photographs the endless scrubby beaches, the serene sky, and the aesthetic self-consciousness that permeated the group's activities.

In March 1949, Tooker, Cadmus, and the Frenches boarded the *Queen Elizabeth* to spend the spring and summer in Europe. The group started in Paris, where they spent nearly every day at the Louvre. They then moved on to Italy, where Tooker recalls they spent their time "just looking at museums, pictures. I loved Italy. I adored it" (fig. 10).[10] They spent a month in Florence absorbing the masters in the Uffizi, then another month traveling around Italy,[11] before ending with a few

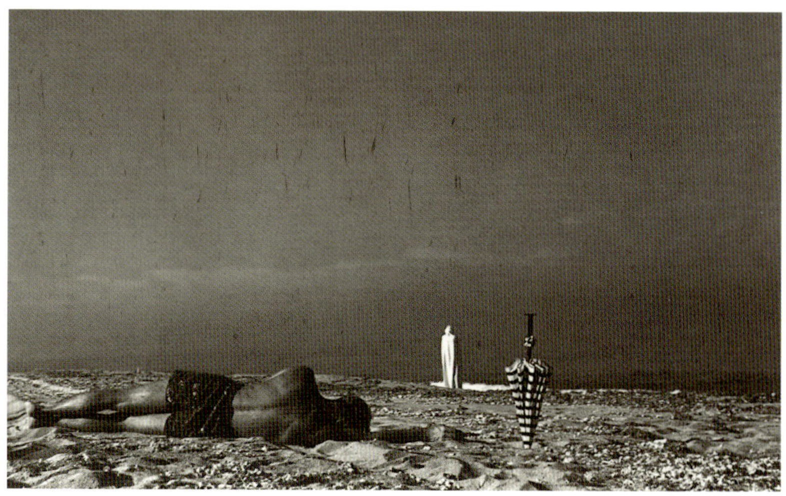

fig. 8
George Tooker
*Island* (1946)
Egg tempera on gesso panel
15¼ × 18½ inches (38.5 × 47 cm)
Location unknown

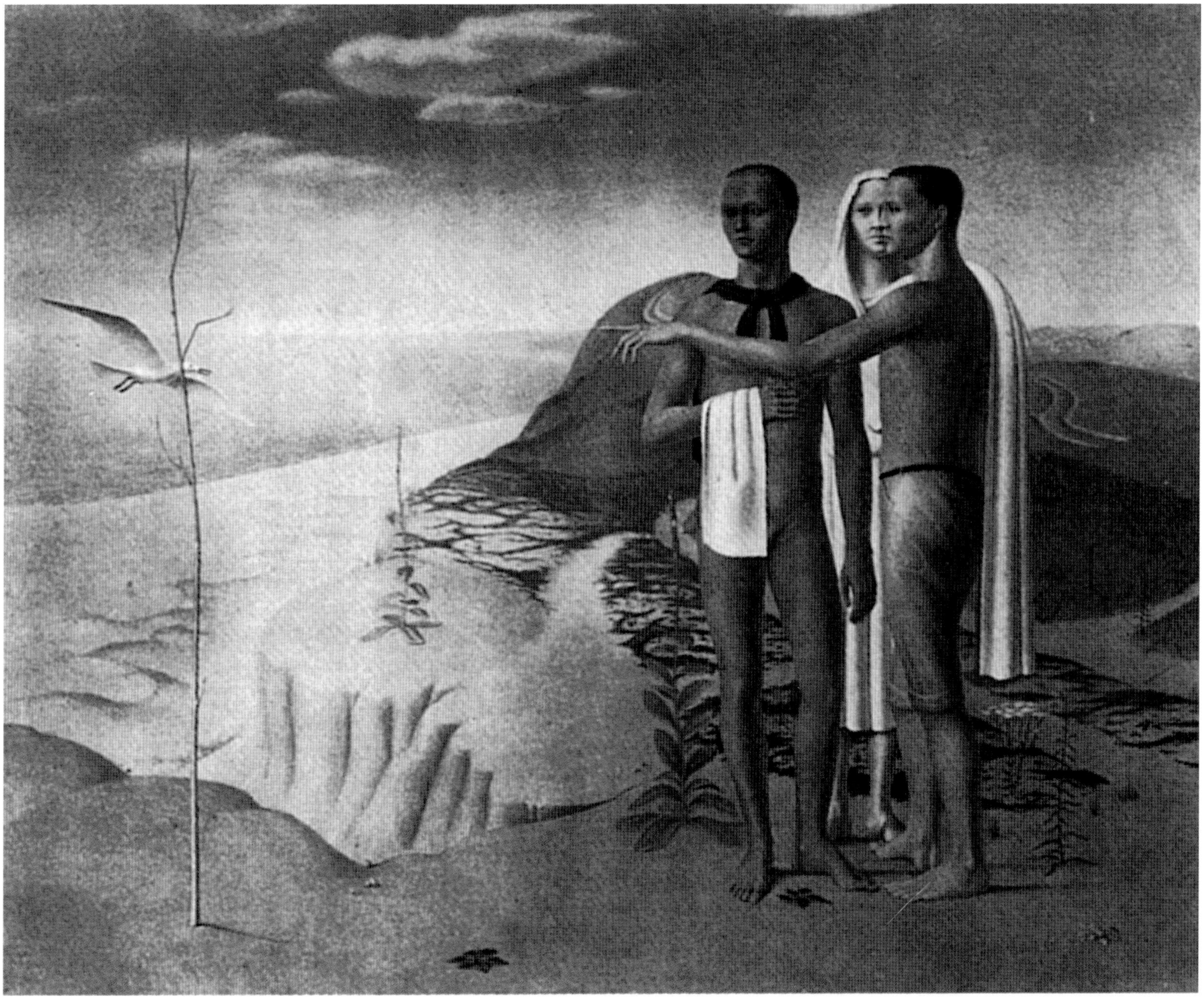

fig. 9
George Tooker
*Market* (1949)
Egg tempera on gesso panel
22 × 22 inches (55.9 × 55.9 cm)
John P. Axelrod, Boston, Massachusetts



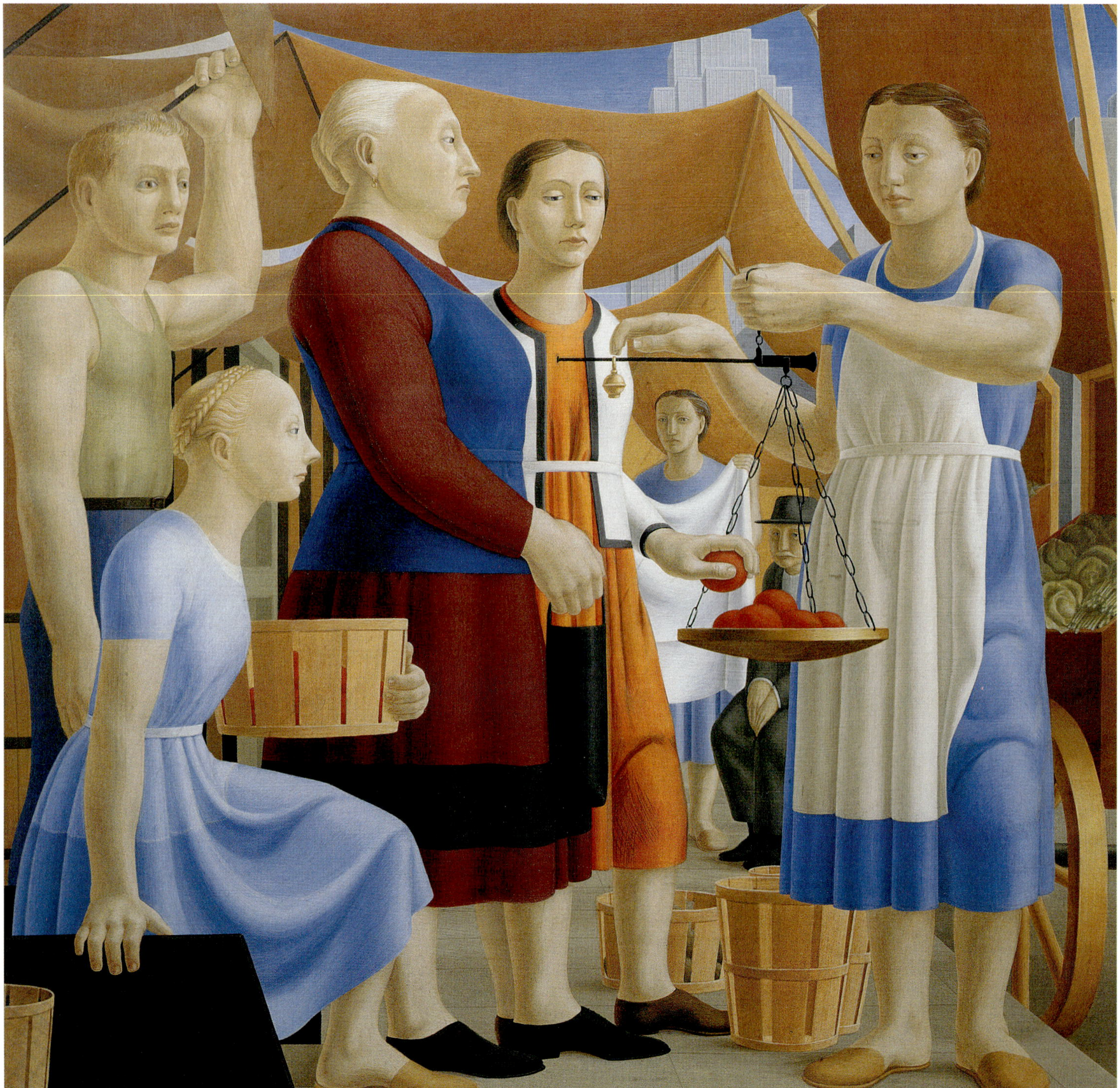

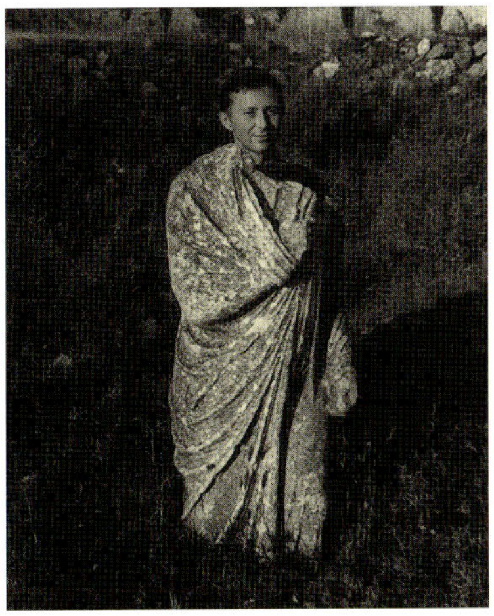

fig. 10
PaJaMa (Paul Cadmus, Jared and Margaret French)
*George Tooker on the Via Appia* (1949)
Courtesy of the George Tooker Papers, 1932–1973, Archives of American Art, Smithsonian Institution, Washington, D.C.



weeks in England. Tooker's experience in Europe only strengthened the training that had begun with Miller and Marsh, who, along with Cadmus, adopted Renaissance techniques and styles in their paintings. Throughout the trip, Tooker and Cadmus collected reproductions of the works they saw, for use as source material for later paintings.[12] Renaissance masters have remained a deep and consistent source of inspiration for Tooker. In fact, reproductions of relief sculptures on the Tempio Malatestiano, Rimini, are tacked to the storage doors of Tooker's studio still today.

Cadmus, Tooker, and the Frenches shared a great sense of harmony artistically; however, personally there had been long-standing tensions within the group. Cadmus and Jared French had a continuing intimate relationship that had begun in the late 1920s. The discord this caused the group was exacerbated by Jared's well-documented difficult personality. The friction seems to have accumulated to a point beyond Tooker's patience, and he returned to the USA from Europe earlier than the rest of the group. Though Tooker and Cadmus remained close friends to the end of Cadmus's life in 1999, this point marked the end of their sexual relationship. As Tooker later explained, "I was looking for a relationship, and my relationship with Paul always included Jared and Margaret French."[13]

Though works painted before his European sojourn, such as *Bird Watchers* (1948; plate 9), show Tooker's interest in the reduced, columnar forms found in early Renaissance painting, *Market* (1949; fig. 9), painted immediately after his return, exudes the enthusiasm of a convert. Massive sculptural figures dominate the space of the composition, and clean, rigid profiles serve as an obvious homage to Piero della Francesca. Tooker soon digested the lessons of the early Renaissance, and his own voice began to shape the dynamic dialogue with the Quattrocento masters that he continues today. Even in *Market,* a work predominantly couched in Renaissance language, Tooker has placed his action in a familiar, American vernacular—an immigrant Italian open market near his Bleecker Street home.

In late 1949, after his return from Europe, Tooker began a relationship with William Christopher that would last until the latter's death in 1973. Christopher was also an artist, and they had met several times before through a mutual circle of friends (fig. 11).[14] The couple moved to a loft on West 18th Street, New York, where they lived and worked for the next several years. In 1950, Tooker completed *Subway* (plate 15), the painting for which he is perhaps best known. Juliana Force, first director of the Whitney Museum of American Art, acquired it for the museum, placing the artist into a major museum collection before he had turned thirty.[15]

Though Tooker has continued to address new themes and compositions throughout his career, by this point he had settled on his basic working method and technique.[16] The majority of his paintings begin through an intuitive, reductive process.

> When I start working on pictures, I start, and frequently I don't know what the picture is going to be about. I use a lot of tracing paper. If I have a drawing, particularly if there's something I like about it, I start picking off elements. If I play around with the drawing itself, I might lose what's interesting. In order to find out what's interesting about it, I trace off different parts of the drawing and try to pinpoint what's interesting, what I can remove, what does not seem to be rewarding, and I start adding to it. My pictures start on a fairly unconscious level.[17]

fig. 11
*Donald Windham, George Tooker, Bill Christopher, Nag's Head, North Carolina (circa 1951)*
Courtesy of the George Tooker Papers, 1932–1973, Archives of American Art, Smithsonian Institution, Washington, D.C.

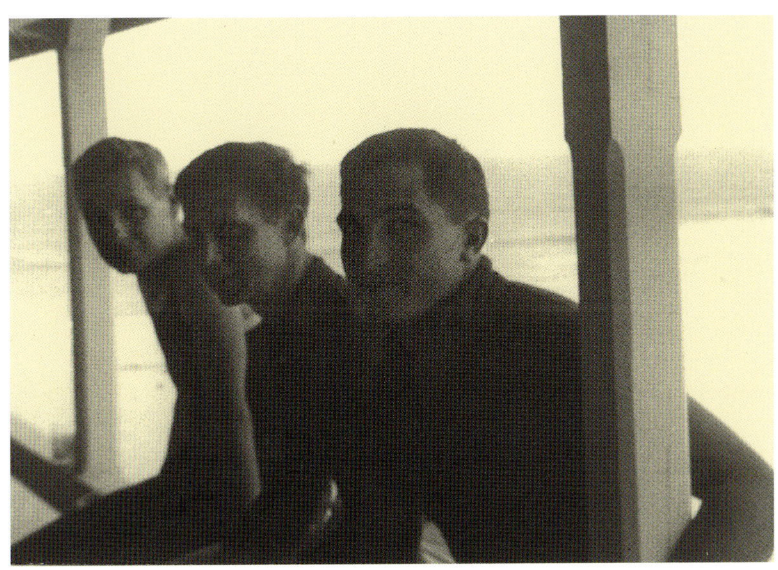

fig. 12
George Tooker
Compositional sketch (stairs) for *Subway* (n.d.)
Graphite on paper
1¼ × 1⅝ inches (3 × 4 cm)
Courtesy of the George Tooker Papers, 1932–1973, Archives of American Art, Smithsonian Institution, Washington, D.C.

fig. 13
George Tooker
Color design for *Subway* (n.d.)
Tempera and pencil on composition board
13⅞ × 10 inches (35.2 × 25.4 cm)
Courtesy of the George Tooker Papers, 1932–1973, Archives of American Art, Smithsonian Institution, Washington, D.C.



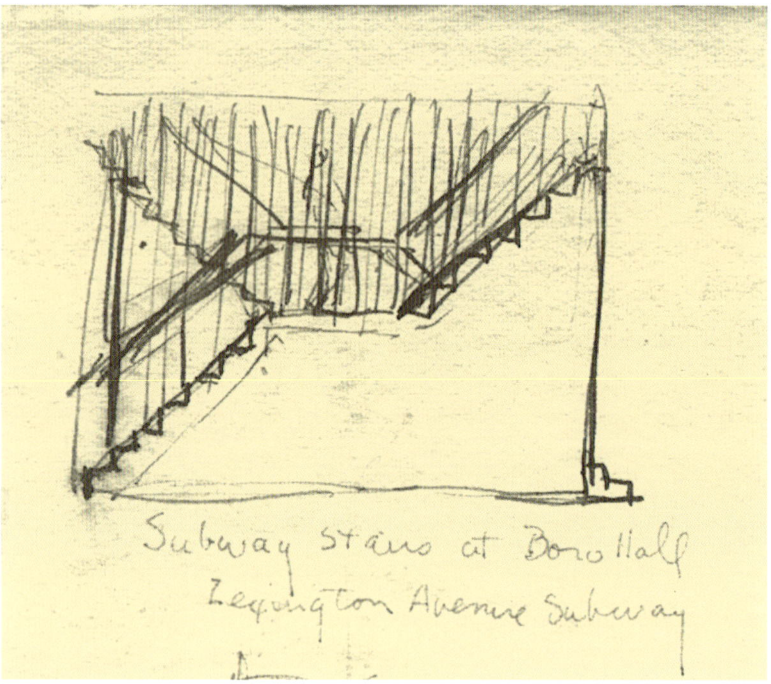


For more complex works, Tooker articulates a greater degree of planning in preparatory works. *Subway* has a number of quickly made sketches in which the artist worked out rudimentary compositional components or ideas (fig. 12), an annotated color sketch to set the basic palette (fig. 13), and full-sized perspectival studies (plate 14). The basic sculptural forms of nearly all Tooker's paintings are worked out in full-scale drawings (plate 26), however.[18] He then transfers the drawing to Masonite or illustration board. Tooker builds up his forms, painting from back to front, with small, repetitive—nearly obsessive, even—hatchmarks of color that, from a viewing distance, dissolve to emphasize sculptural form rather than surface texture. The process is "plodding," in Tooker's words, and often a single work takes more than three months to complete: "It's slow, and since I'm slow in knowing just what I want to do, it suits me well" (fig. 14).[19]

*Subway* marks the beginning of a sustained discourse that Tooker has maintained throughout his career, which addresses social injustices and oppression experienced by individuals as constituents of the modern American state. These paintings—such as *Subway, Government Bureau* (1956; plate 27), *Waiting Room* (1957; plate 31), *Landscape with Figures* (1965–66; plate 42), *Ward* (1970–71; plate 45), and *Waiting Room II* (1982; plate 55)—Tooker calls "protest paintings."[20] He has expressed on numerous occasions that it is the potential to motivate change that is important to him. When Grace George Alexander tried to clarify Tooker's subject in *Subway,* she asked, "In other words, when people look at [the painting] you are hoping that they ... will say, I see people who are strangers, and then perhaps they ask, why are they strangers?" To which Tooker replied, "And maybe, maybe they'll try to do something about making things better."[21] Other Social Realist painters of the time created works in order to compel change, but, whereas they generally protest at specific economic, class, or political conditions, Tooker's works protest at the spiritual state that results from existing under such conditions.[22]

Tooker moves the narrative from public, social exchanges to this inner, psychological (or spiritual, to use Tooker's term) state through his reductive processes. Narrative is distilled down to its essential components, beginning, as he characterizes it, with "picking off" elements of his sketches that seem extraneous, shedding the anecdotal. Action is concentrated down to the most essential gesture required to convey meaning. Such simplification creates clarity, and an immediacy, in the emotional state in which the central woman in *Subway* holds her hand to her stomach, the way the woman unsympathetically grips the boy's arm in *Men and Women Fighting* (1958), the way the boy peeks curiously over his fingers in *Pot of Aloes* (1974; plate 50), the way the woman clutches her mouth in anguish in *Standing Figures* (1973; plate 49), or the way the man caresses his lover's hair in *Lovers II* (1960).[23] Tooker embeds his protest in a setting that is equally distilled, employing it to play an integrated part in the evocation of protest. Such structures as the bureaucratic agency in *Government Bureau*, the medical facility in *Ward*, or the mass transit halls in *Subway,* divide, hide, and disorient the figures, and they re-create this experience for the paintings' viewers. Tooker identifies these power structures of the modern American state as the source of alienation of individuals from a healthy experience of community; they are the physical sites that subversively enable and perpetuate the disruption of community.[24]

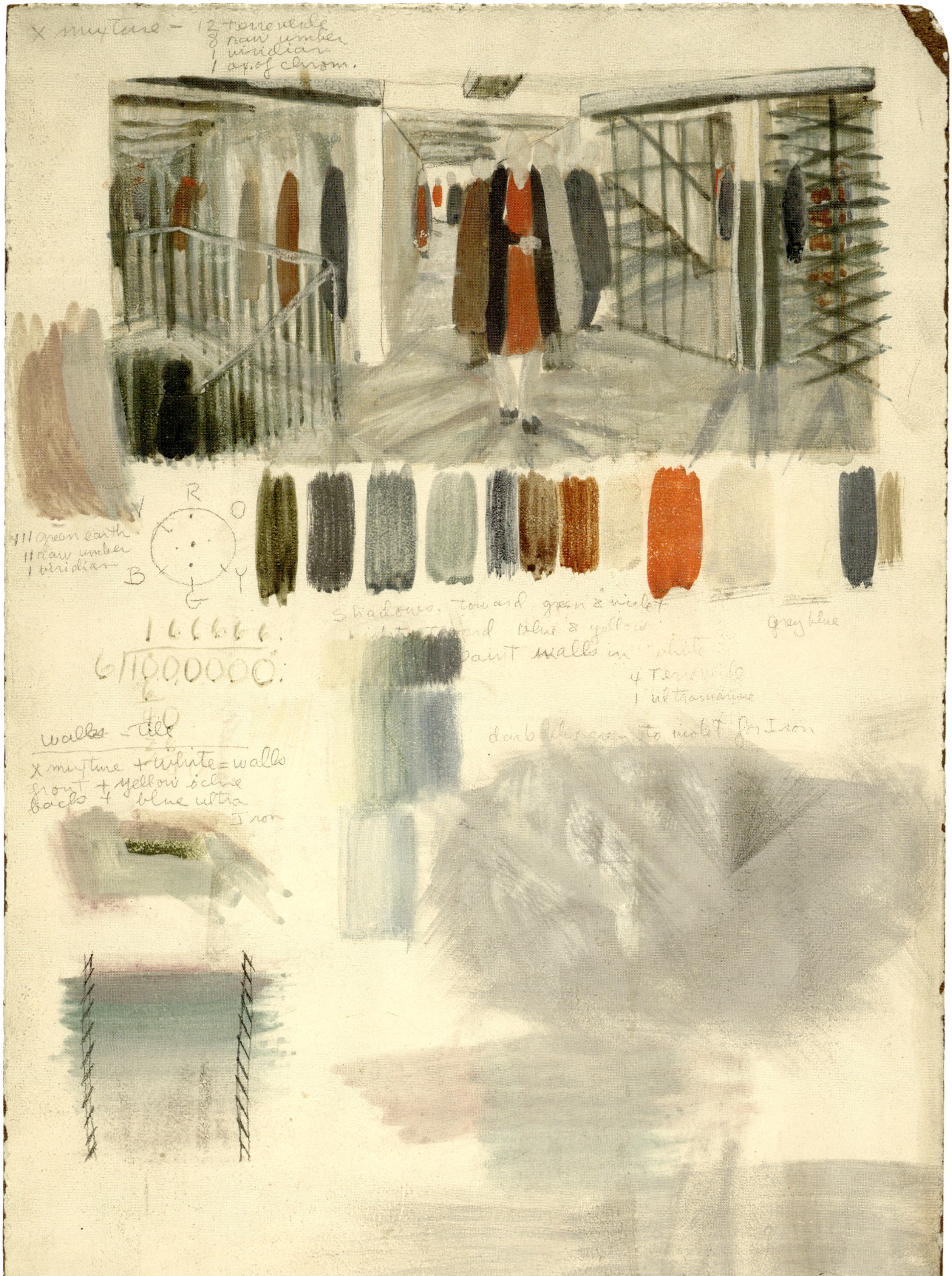

X mixture – 12 terre verde
8 raw umber
1 viridian
11 green earth
11 raw umber
1 viridian
R
O
Y
G
B
V
Shadows toward green & violet
paint walls in white
4 Terre verde
1 ultramarine
Grey blue
X mixture + white = walls
front + yellow ochre
backs + blue ultra
Iron


29

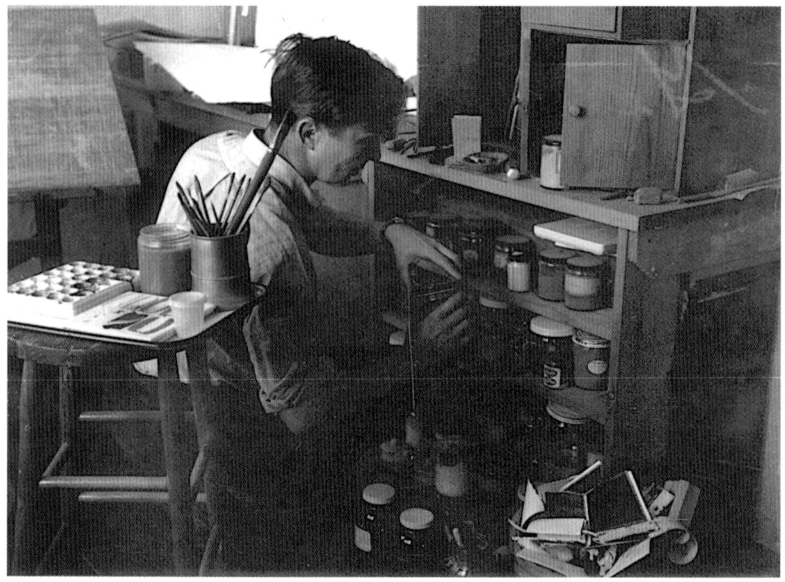

fig. 14
Tooker in his Hartland studio with palette and jars of pigment (*circa* 1940)
Courtesy of the George Tooker Papers, 1932–1973, Archives of American Art, Smithsonian Institution, Washington, D.C.

*Subway* and the other protest paintings of the 1950s—*Government Bureau* and *Waiting Room*—established Tooker's reputation. He exhibited actively throughout the decade, and in 1950 gained inclusion in exhibitions at the Metropolitan Museum of Art and again at the Whitney, followed by two major solo exhibitions, in 1951 and 1955, at the Edwin Hewitt Gallery, New York. In 1952, there was a fire behind Tooker's and Christopher's apartment on 18th Street, which forced them to move. Tooker's father had passed away suddenly in 1951, and his mother's health had deteriorated rapidly afterward. In 1953, the artists found a dilapidated brownstone at 77 State Street in Brooklyn Heights, around the corner from Tooker's mother's house. Not able to afford the mortgage, they renovated the structure themselves and rented out the top two floors. Though the couple did not enjoy being landlords, Tooker was able to visit his bedridden mother daily. Later in the decade, Tooker and Christopher purchased land near Hartland, Vermont, and constructed a home on an extant foundation, using timbers removed from an old barn. They spent the summers there, slowly improving the home and its surroundings (fig. 15). When Tooker's mother died in 1959, he felt free to move permanently to Vermont, and the couple readily did so the following year.[25] Christopher began teaching in the fine arts department at nearby Dartmouth College, Hanover, New Hampshire, and Tooker continued to show regularly in New York City.

Throughout his career, Tooker has sustained a focused meditation on the physical, emotional, and spiritual dynamics at the heart of his central artistic concerns: "people and their relations to each other and the outside world."[26] He has returned again and again, through the mode of seriality, to readdress specific compositions and ideas in groups of paintings given such titles as *Window*, *Sleepers*, *Lovers*, *Voice*, and *Embrace*. Many works in these series incorporate refined aspects from other, earlier works and experiences. Though his process of reduction often results in emphasizing the universal over the anecdotal, in fact, Tooker's works frequently begin from his observations of specific people or incidents he encounters in his daily life, revealing the close ties his work has with other figurative artists, such as Marsh, Miller, Edward Hopper (1882–1967), and others. Tooker has explained, for instance, that his house in Brooklyn Heights was "a very good place for paintings because there was a Puerto Rican rooming house opposite us, and I could just look out the window for subject matter … nearly all of the window paintings are based on what I saw through the windows."[27]

In 1950, Tooker's work was characterized by Lincoln Kirstein as "Magic Realism," which quickly became the predominant term used to describe it.[28] However, the label has been singularly disliked by Tooker (and many of the other artists whose work it is used to describe), because of its misleading suggestion that he shares an interest in the fantasy and dream worlds of Surrealism. Tooker's use of repetitive, reductive figures, odd perspectival space, and unsettling ambiguity does suggest an association with Surrealism. And even Tooker himself uses the term "dream" in his oft-repeated artistic statement "I am after painting reality impressed on the mind so hard that it returns as a dream."[29] For Tooker, however, the dream state and its manifestation are operative in very specific ways. Tooker seems naturally sensitive to the ineluctable mystery that certain life experiences evoke. His memory of childhood Fourth of July celebrations, in which he and his cousins would be allowed to hang lighted Japanese lanterns in the garden, is cherished for its "magical"

fig. 15
Tooker in Hartland (1958)
Courtesy of the William Christopher Papers, 1946–1972, Archives of American Art, Smithsonian Institution, Washington, D.C.



quality. Tooker's recollection of visiting the Pantheon for the first time with Cadmus also shares this sensitivity to the mystery of experience:

> We had just arrived in Rome. And it was about dusk. And Paul took me for a walk … the door was unlocked, it was open. We just walked in, and it was amazing. So little changed from Roman times … I took Chris there the same way, and I took Mary there the same way. Each time we'd arrived in Rome … close to dusk. And it was empty, there was nobody there, nobody in it. It was like walking into Rome. Ancient Rome. It was fascinating. … It was as if nothing had changed.[30]

Such moments stay with Tooker. They reappear in his works sometimes quite literally, as in *Garden Party* (1952; plate 20), and other times more elusively, as deep psychological vestiges of an experience that linger even after their association with the anecdotal experience is lost.

This dream-like ambiguity, in which images seem pregnant with meaning and yet evasive of precise (and comforting) interpretation, is the result of loading a multiplicity of meanings on to visual elements distilled to their most essential form. For instance, the death of Tooker's father, the "PaJaMa" photographs in Tooker's collection, and Matthew Arnold's poem "Dover Beach" (1867) all find resonances in *Sleepers I* (1951). Tooker embraces such multiplicity, allowing it to converge in the temporal and meditative space of the act of painting:

> I like not being too narrowed down as to only one reading. I like it when these things come together. … I think I'm happier if it's not too well defined because I think that limits it … [it] cuts down on the overtones and undertones … and I think that's important … it's better if it's not quite conscious … because I think there should be different interpretations, because we're all complex. Especially if you work on a picture for a while, different things come in, different days different things happen.[31]

While the expression of such diverse sources is not unique to the artist, their manifestation in his work is crowded into the barest of gesture, action, or object, conflating (but certainly not reducing) meaning beyond the easily identifiable.

The use of similar motifs common to Surrealism, however, does not necessarily imply similar intentions. Tooker's formal interests have remained committed to the tradition of figurative painting initiated by the early Renaissance masters he so admires.[32] This commitment put him at odds with the near monopoly on claims to "serious art" that abstraction, led by Abstract Expressionism, held in the decades following World War II. The review of the 1948 Worcester Biennial, in which Tooker, Cadmus, and French were included, is representative of the prejudice against realism at that time:

> I cannot pretend to find interesting (though it is still much practiced and one must presume useful as a perverse reminder of the Renaissance view of man) the hard realism and unimaginative explicitness—no matter what the fantastic content—shared by work from the hands of Castellon, Cuthbert, Evergood, Hensel, Tooker, Cadmus and Jared French … the more so as it occurs in a time when most art of living substance is determined to sweep away the dead tissue of mere realism … one misses the more

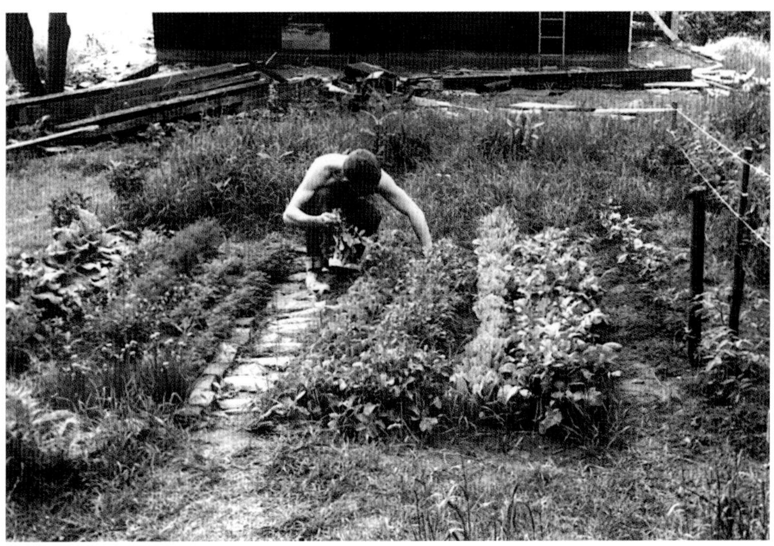

fig. 16
Bill Christopher (far right) and Martin Luther King, Jr., Boston University (September 14, 1964)
Courtesy of the George Tooker Papers, 1932–1973, Archives of American Art, Smithsonian Institution, Washington, D.C.



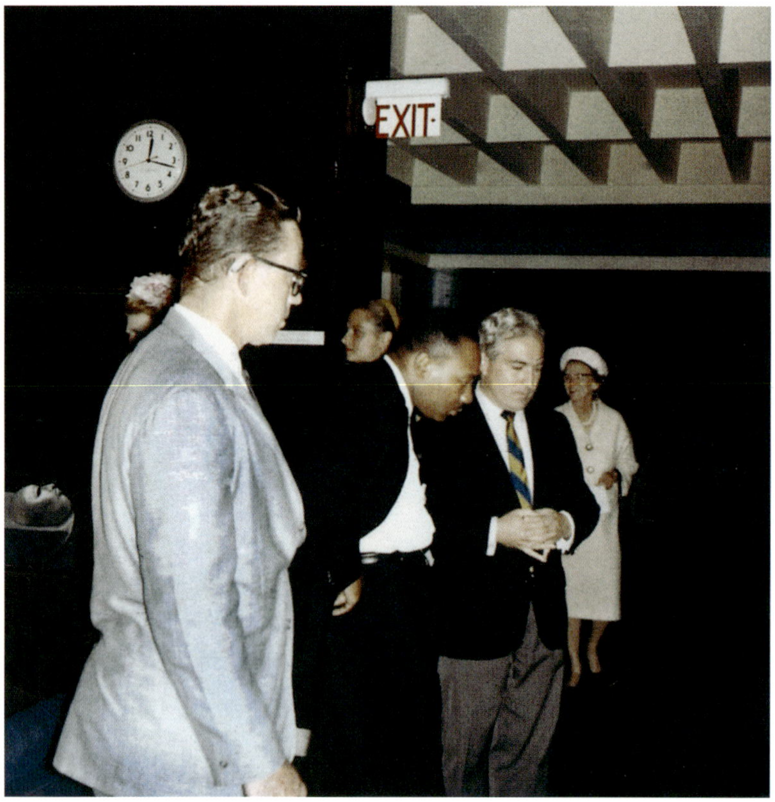


advanced abstract artists, who for all their rawness and hesitations, have proved their seriousness.[33]

The emphasis on the surreal aspects of Tooker's work can be seen as a strategy, more on the part of realism's apologists and gallery owners than on the part of the artist, to claim a continued viability and "seriousness" for the practice of realism. Surrealism's (and Tooker's) exploration of an inner world offered a basis of shared interests with non-objective painters.[34]

Tooker continued to participate in an art community engaged in figurative concerns (Reginald Marsh, Isabel Bishop (1902–1988), Edward Hopper, Jacob Lawrence (1917–2000), Honoré Sharrer (b. 1920)), most of whom were loosely associated with the Art Students League. If the interest of much of the art world marginalized, or even excluded, such work as Tooker's (though it would be accurate to say he has never been without an audience), the artist himself remained engaged with mainstream artistic developments and yet equally sure of his own artistic direction. He visited the city's galleries every Saturday, looking at "a lot of Abstract Expressionist work because I felt like that was what was being done and I wanted to see whether or not I could learn something from it."[35] He even admits trying it, but he wasn't happy painting in that manner, and felt that it was "painting without a purpose."[36]

Tooker's dedication to art's participatory role in social change only deepened his engagement with figurative painting. As Susan Baker has noted, "retaining the figure allowed Tooker to consider issues which abstraction could not address in a blatant manner: the problem of race, prejudice based on sex or sexual orientation, and other forms of social persecution. … An effective treatment of these particular social ills required a 'face,' not just the artist's gesture or mark."[37] Tooker's profound empathy with issues of equality has its genesis in his own sense of identity as a person of mixed race; in a recent census he identified himself as Anglo-Hispanic.[38] While Tooker's father descended from a Dutch family that had settled on Long Island in 1640, his mother was Cuban American. Her family maintained close ties with its Cuban relatives, and, though Tooker himself never knew them well, she (and her own mother, whom Tooker did know well) instilled in her son a deep sense of family identity.

The artist's engagement in the issue of racial inequality, and in the broader issue of oppression of difference, became especially pronounced in his work as his and William Christopher's personal involvement with the civil rights movement grew. Christopher, whose father died when he was young, had been raised in Georgia by blacks who worked for his family, and he identified strongly with them.[39] Christopher had done several paintings, including portraits, in honor of Dr. Martin Luther King, Jr., and the couple traveled to Boston to meet the leader (fig. 16).[40] They also traveled to Selma, Alabama, in March 1965 to participate in the memorial service that King led for the slain activist James Reeb. As Tooker says, "Dr. Martin Luther King, Jr., called for people to come to Selma, and we went. To march in

Selma."[41] Spoken in Tooker's characteristic plaintive manner, the statement does not reveal the deep commitment and courage their act took at a time when murders and violence were very real presences.

Tooker's *Supper* (1963; plate 37) is "an allusion to the supper at Emmaus and was painted because I was very moved by Dr. King."[42] The work situates Tooker's mode of protest against racial inequality. Two white men sit at either side of a black man who "breaks bread"—the traditional signifier that the participants have committed themselves to one another in a shared sense of identity, the formation of community. The image of racial equality is an assertion that the communion of individuals holds the potential, when multiplied, to sustain mass communities that, by their healthy nature, would overcome prejudice. The work shares its idealism with the compelling vision voiced by King later at Reeb's service, in which "we will be able to speed up the day when all of God's children ... black men and white men, Jews and Gentiles, Protestants and Catholics, will be able to join hands in unity and brotherhood to bring about the bright day of the brotherhood of man."[43]

The *Window* series further explores the dynamics of difference by siting the potential for racial harmony, and the benefits of that harmony, within an intimate, physical world revealed through a window. Tooker has said that he created the series "partly as an example of how people can relate to each other."[44] Most of the works include figures of minorities, or of ambiguous racial identity, and several, such as *Guitar* (1957; plate 29) and *Window VII* (1963; plate 38), are explicitly about interracial relationships. These Tooker quite specifically "meant ... as a challenge. ... I believed in racial intermarriage. And I wanted to ... paint about that."[45] The paintings work to convey Tooker's social challenge through their sensual and intimate eroticism, as a suffused light flows over bodies interlocked in various positions of relaxation. Tooker creates desire for these individuals, and, in basing desire within the physical relationships of marginalized and "othered" characters, including homosexuals, the works act to dissolve prejudices held by the viewer. These are acts that normalize communities of difference and offer the antidote to Tooker's protest paintings. He himself joins this community. To paint the figure as deliberately and meditatively as does Tooker, is, in a sense, to touch, caress, and care for it. Tooker's process—meticulous, intimate, time-laden—is a carrier itself of communication, a meditative merging with the community he visualizes.

During the 1960s, Tooker continued to exhibit frequently, both at the annual exhibition at the Whitney and in solo exhibitions, in 1960 and 1962 at the Robert Isaacson Gallery, New York, and then in 1964 and 1967 at Durlacher Brothers, New York. In 1965, he began teaching life drawing, painting, and composition at the Art Students League, taking the train into the city to stay for the week and then returning to Vermont. Tooker also had his first solo museum exhibition at Dartmouth College in 1967. However, in 1968, Christopher quit teaching at Dartmouth. He had had a heart attack when he was twenty-one years old, and at that time he was told he would not live long. The Vermont winters had become harder and harder on him, so the couple began to spend the winters in the port city of Malaga, Spain. By the early 1970s, they had decided to move there permanently. Sadly, in late 1973, William Christopher passed away. The couple's closeness is quietly characterized by Tooker, well known for his reticence to discuss his work, in saying, "You know, I never talk about painting, but we talked about painting."[46]

Tooker stayed in Spain through most of 1974, managing Christopher's estate and mitigating his grief through the process of painting. For Tooker, who had explored the theme of spiritual and physical communication throughout his career, the physical and psychological finality of death was profound. *Woman at the Wall* (1974; fig. 17), done just after Christopher's death, is a starkly honest depiction of a woman disheveled, exhausted, by the physical and emotional pain of grief. At the same time as Christopher's death and the trying process of closing his estate, Tooker was assisting Thomas Garver in the organization of his first nationally traveling museum exhibition, and he admits to being drained of energy and fighting depression.[47] Though Tooker was extremely helpful in interviews for the catalogue and assisted in the selection of the twenty-nine works that were included, he did not go to San Francisco for the opening at the California Palace of the Legion of Honor in 1974;

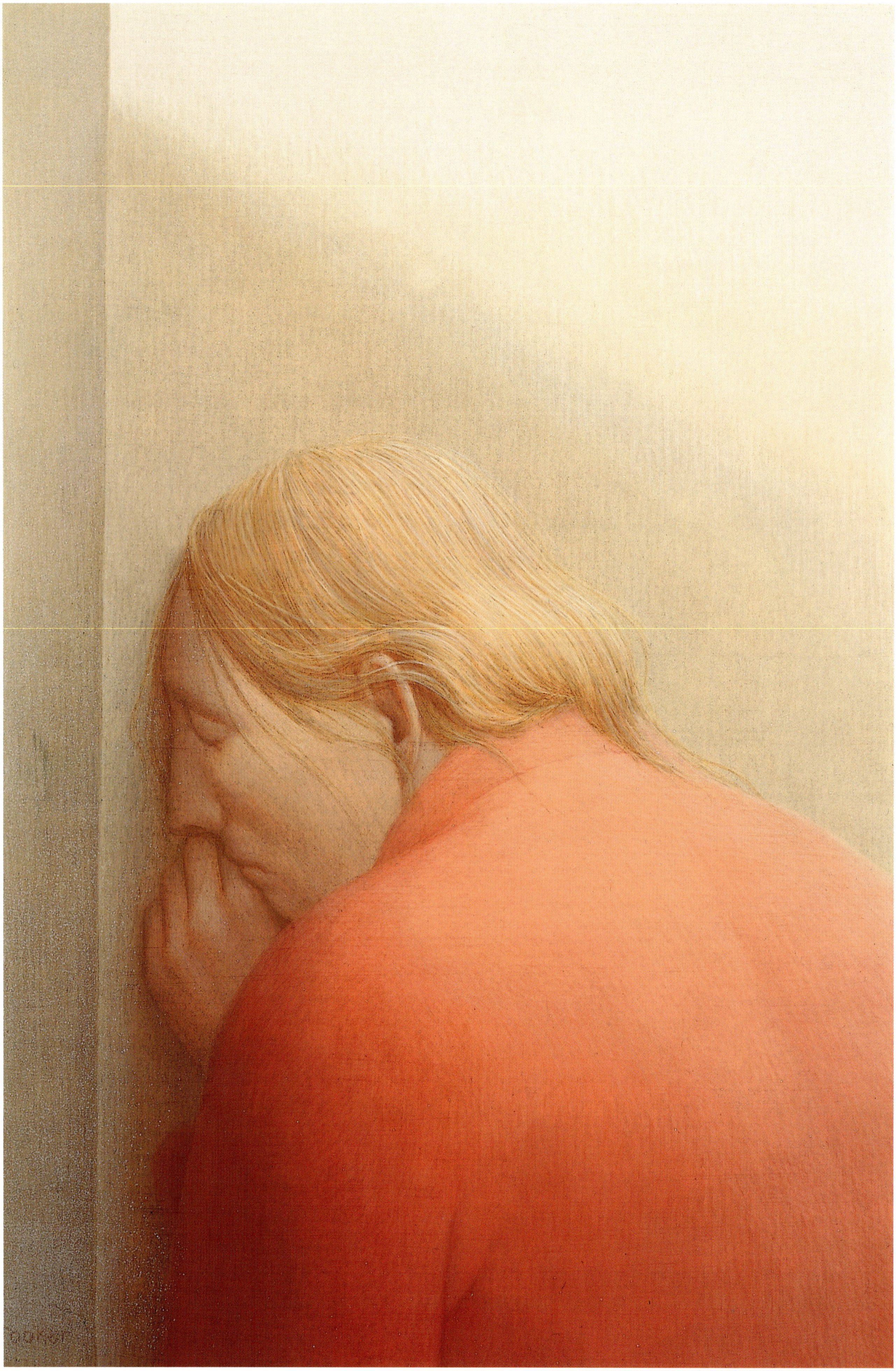

fig. 17
George Tooker
*Woman at the Wall* (1974)
Egg tempera on panel
18¼ × 12⅛ inches (46.2 × 30.8 cm)
New Britain Museum of American Art,
Gift of Olga H. Knoepke, 1992.40



he later explained, "It was just after Chris died and I didn't feel like going."[48]

After his return to Vermont, Tooker began going regularly to the meetings of the Episcopal Church, the denomination in which he had been raised, at St. Francis of Assisi Catholic Church in Windsor, Vermont. Tooker became friends with the Catholic Father, Forrest Rouelle, who confirmed the artist in the Catholic faith in 1976. Rouelle was a leader in social involvement in the Church, and the two shared many social and religious beliefs.[49] Though often voiced in a more explicitly religious context, Tooker's work after his confirmation continues the interests and beliefs that have consistently marked his œuvre. In *The Seven Sacraments*, the multi-panel altarpiece he created in 1980 for his parish church, the artist focused on the actions that sustain a community of individuals—the protective care of a mother for her child, an embrace between two people of different race, three generations partaking in a wedding, or the tender care of the sick. The depiction of the Embrace of Peace within the Reconciliation scene is an image of *agape*, or brotherly rather than carnal love, and its consequent breakdown of prejudice and oppression. In a later series of works done for the church, the *Stations of the Cross*, the artist took great care to avoid intruding upon the viewer's feeling of inclusion. Tooker used only hands for the figure of Christ because "I didn't want to interfere with the image that's already in somebody's head … but, I felt that hands could be expressive. And not interfere with anybody's image of Christ. Because I've been … put off by images of Christ. And I didn't want to do that."[50]

After 1981, Tooker no longer wintered in Spain. Looking for a second residence in the USA, in 1983 he purchased a home that had been owned by family friends near his hometown of Bellport, Long Island. However, Tooker found that the change experienced by the locale since he was young, and the passing of the people he associated with the area, were difficult for him; he explained, "when I was out there, I just remembered the past. … And that's why I didn't stay. I sold the house because I was living in the past when I was down there. And I thought, in Vermont I live in the present."[51] This sentiment seems to mark Tooker's work of the past few decades. He has continued to explore the themes that have compelled him throughout his career, continuing to focus the compositions, such as *Father and Child* (2000; plate 64), on the exchange between individuals. Though he did not have a gallery exhibition in New York City from 1967 until his show at the Marisa del Re Gallery in 1985, the renewed interest by artists in the 1980s in the expressive potential of figurative painting made Tooker's work a fertile source. In 2007, Tooker enjoyed another solo exhibition at the DC Moore Gallery. The art-history world has also come back to consider the artist again, as part of a renewed interest in those twentieth-century artists who, like Tooker, have remained committed to the power of the figurative tradition to engage both a humanist compassion and a shared wonder in the enigmatic qualities—the mysteries—of human experience.

## Notes

1 Interview with Jonathan Weinberg, Hartland, Vermont, June 7, 2007, 20.

2 Interview with the author, Hartland, Vermont, July 28, 2007, 16.

3 Justin Spring, "An Interview with George Tooker," *American Art*, 16:1 (spring 2002), 64.

4 Tooker sees the medical condition as being "a protest … from doing things I didn't want to do." Thomas H. Garver, interview with George Tooker, September 11, 1973, Archives of American Art, Smithsonian Institution, Washington, D.C.

5 "I had developed a rather meaningless mannerism at the time, he [Harry Sternberg] sort of straightened my head about that. … Like saying, now what is that picture about. He got me to look at a picture on the basis of what do you mean by this. You don't have to verbalize it, but clear it in your head." Interview with Garver, September 11, 1973, and interview with the author, 12.

6 Thompson was a preeminent scholar of Renaissance painting technique, and the text was essentially a translation of Cennino d'Andrea Cennini's fifteenth-century treatise *Il libro dell-arte*. Tooker, like Cadmus, Jared French, and Andrew Wyeth, worked specifically with egg-yolk tempera, which utilizes only the yolk rather than the yolk and albumen, as in the more common medium of egg tempera.

7 Spring, "An Interview with George Tooker," 65.

8 Interview with Garver, September 11, 1973.

9 Katherine Hauser, "George Tooker, Surveillance, and Cold War Sexual Politics," *GLQ*, 11:3 (June 2005), 391–425. Events that inspired Jared French's painting *State Park* (1946; fig. 6) further suggest homosexuality as the source of tension in Tooker's painting.

During the artists' summer at Saltaire in 1945, several residents along a favorite beach disapproved of the gay crowd, and they hired security guards who harassed them (including Tooker's group). *State Park*, which depicts a family at the beach protected by menacing guard-like figures, "embodies a critique of social mores that restrict acceptance of an individual's liberty, which through extrapolation encompasses the freedom of sexual orientation." Mark Cole, "Jared French (1905–1988)," PhD diss., University of Delaware, 1999, 137.

10 Interview with Garver, September 11, 1973.

11 Tooker recounts they went to "Arezzo, Siena, Assisi, and then to Rome, then Naples and Paestum, and Rimini—the Tempio Malatesta carvings by Agostino di Duccio—and Urbino. Of course we went to Padua, to the Arena Chapel for the Giottos, and to Venice, and Mantua, to see Palazzo del Te, and to Orvieto to see the murals by Luca Signorelli." Spring, "An Interview with George Tooker," 67. They also visited Pompeii. Gregory M. Hollister-Knepp, "The Sacred and the Profane: Christian and Mythological Imagery within the Œuvre of George Tooker," MA diss., Bloomsburg University, Pennsylvania, 1997, 62.

12 This practice comes from training at the Art Students League, where photographs were used for instructional purposes in the absence of original works. Cole, "Jared French," 48.

13 Quoted in Hauser, "George Tooker, Surveillance, and Cold War Sexual Politics," 410. Cadmus similarly characterized the reasons for the end of their intimate relationship. "George wanted me all to himself, but that was not possible. I was not going to give up Jerry in any case." Quoted in David Leddick, *Intimate Companions: A Triography of George Platt Lynes, Paul Cadmus, Lincoln Kirstein, and Their Circle* (New York: St. Martin's Press, 2000), 236.

14 Spring, "An Interview with George Tooker," 71. "We met many times; we had mutual friends. ... I thought of us as life partners from very early on."

15 Force's decision to acquire the painting also marked the first time Tooker's work had been purchased by someone other than an acquaintance.

16 Tooker's working methods are documented in Heidi D. Shafranek, "The World of George Tooker: Surreal or Real, " MA diss., University of Delaware, 1982, 160; Susan Jane Baker, "George Tooker and the Modern Tradition," PhD diss., University of Kansas, 1994, 56–57; interview with Grace George Alexander and George Kay on "Artists in New York," WNYC Radio transcript, New York City, 1967. George Tooker Papers, Archives of American Art, Smithsonian Institution, Washington, D.C.; and interview with Garver, September 11, 1973.

17 Quoted in Shafranek, "The World of George Tooker," 160.

18 He explains that "I look for the major shapes in the drawing so that I don't have to make any major changes. But I don't work it out too carefully … I want to discover as I'm doing the painting." Spring, "An Interview with George Tooker," 70–71.

19 Quoted in Thomas H. Garver, *George Tooker*, (New York: Clarkson N. Potter, 1985), 8.

20 Certainly issues of protest were an important aspect of Tooker's life very early on. He recalls that his mother had "social concerns," and while he was at Harvard he belonged to the Young Communists League for a short time and was even beaten up for handing out pamphlets. Though he admired David Alfaro Siqueiros and José Clemente Orozco already at this early date, his social convictions continued to be separate from his artistic production until his time at the Art Students League and later working closely with Cadmus. Hollister-Knepp, "The Sacred and the Profane," 67, and interview with Garver, September 11, 1973.

21 Interview with Grace George Alexander and George Kay, WNYC Radio transcript.

22 As Susan Jane Baker has noted, "Tooker removed the narrative specificity provided by Marsh, the Soyers, et alii. The figures in Tooker's paintings are not waiting for a job or a train, but are just waiting. Their 'homelessness' is of the spirit." Baker, "George Tooker and the Modern Tradition," 66–67.

23 As Tooker has said, "The significant gesture is something that fascinates me." Hollister-Knepp, "The Sacred and the Profane," 68. Tooker attributes his sensitive observation to Marsh. He also asserts that he specifically watches people's gestures and that he tries "to think of ones that are meaningful in relation to subject … I did specifically think of the way the woman is holding her stomach [in *Subway*]." Interview with the author, 20.

24 Such structures perpetuate the disempowerment of the individual through the act of alienation. As Tooker has said about *Subway,* the subject was "isolation … people being cut off from their fellow men in the city even though they're in crowds. And, it's my way of protesting it. Something I think is wrong." Interview with Grace George Alexander and George Kay, WNYC Radio transcript.

25 Interview with the author, 2–3. Given Tooker's interest in the urban environment, it would seem that this would be a difficult move; however, he has said that "it wasn't a difficult transition at all. We'd been wanting for some time to do it." Spring, "An Interview with George Tooker," 74.

26 George Tooker, Artist Questionnaire, January 30, 1951, Whitney Museum of American Art, New York.

27 Spring, "An Interview with George Tooker," 73. The *Window* series also evolved from more formal concerns. Tooker found the compositional conceit of overlapping figures

cropped at the torso and pushed to the surface of space a ready format to explore his conception of painting "in terms of carving, of bas-relief, a solid form supported from behind ... to compress space, to push it to the front as much as possible." Shafranek, "The World of George Tooker," 31.

[28] Lincoln Kirstein, *Symbolic Realism in American Painting,* 1940–1950, exhib. cat. (London: Institute of Contemporary Arts, 1950).

[29] Quoted in Garver, *George Tooker*, 10.

[30] Interview with the author, 13.

[31] Hollister-Knepp, "The Sacred and the Profane," 68–69. Or, as Tooker has succinctly put it, "I think it's very important for a painting to have a mystery." David Tunkl, "An Interview with George Tooker," in Merry A. Foresta and David Tunkl, *George Tooker*, exhib. cat. (Los Angeles: David Tunkl Gallery, 1980), n.p.

[32] When asked if he feels that his works relate to Surrealism, Tooker responded, "I don't," and, when asked why, he explained that "I like some Surrealist painting. But I don't think I ever tried to paint Surrealistically. I tried to be realistic." Interview with the author, 7.

[33] Sam Hunter, "Worcester Biennial," *New York Times* (November 28, 1948), George Tooker Papers, Archives of American Art. Tooker's work, with its precision of form and process, was often feminized in the hyper-masculine context of the aggressive, gestural Abstract Expressionism. A review of his 1955 gallery show described the works' style as "softly spread color [that] occasionally makes for sweet and pretty effects." *New York Times* (Undated clipping), George Tooker Papers, Archives of American Art. Such a description is also likely a covert response to the homoerotic undertones of many of them.

[34] In reviewing Tooker's 1955 show, Stuart Preston, in the *New York Times Magazine* (May 8, 1955), uses such language, writing that the work was "An art of powerfully imagined double meanings, it searches out links between the conscious and the unconscious." George Tooker Papers, Archives of American Art.

[35] Victoria Robinson, "Interview with George Tooker," in Elizabeth Langhorne-Reeve, *George Tooker: Paintings and Working Drawings* 1947–1988 (Richmond: Modlin Fine Arts Center, University of Richmond, 1989), 5. Tooker admired the skill with which the Abstract Expressionists constructed their compositions, though he has said that while he was in Provincetown in 1947 and 1948, "we didn't have anything to do with the [Hans] Hofmann school at all!" Spring, "An Interview with George Tooker," 67.

[36] Interview with Weinberg, 11. Tooker has shown a consistent, if not deeply influential, engagement with movements in the art world. Interview with the author, 9–10. *Farewell* (1966) owes a clear debt to the interests of the Op artists, whose landmark exhibition *The Responsive Eye*, at the Museum of Modern Art, had been held the year before. Similarly, *Supermarket* (1973; plate 48) evokes the interest in commercialism and mass marketing of the Pop artists.

[37] Baker, "George Tooker and the Modern Tradition," 15.

[38] Spring, "An Interview with George Tooker," 62. In an earlier interview, Tooker surmised that his deep feelings about the civil rights movement must be from "my own racial background ... I feel I am quite a mixture and identify with these." Robinson, "Interview with George Tooker," n.p.

[39] Interview with the author, 5.

[40] Notation on photograph (fig. 16), dated September 14, 1964. George Tooker Papers, Archives of American Art.

[41] Interview with author, 4–5. Following the service, nearly 3000 supporters marched, three abreast, from Brown Chapel to the Dallas County Courthouse, escorted by police cars and an angry crowd. Christopher recounted his and Tooker's experiences in Selma in a daily journal now held in the William Christopher Papers, Archives of American Art. Tooker's passion for civil rights continued, and he has at times directed payment for reproducing his works to the National Association for the Advancement of Colored People (NAACP: he was a member of the Dartmouth chapter) or, more specifically, to its legal defense fund.

[42] Quoted in Garver, *George Tooker*, 115.

[43] Martin Luther King, Jr., "A Witness to the Truth" (Eulogy for the Revd James J. Reeb, March 15, 1965), *Unitarian Universalists World*, XV: 2 (May/June 2001), 20–23.

[44] Interview with the author, 7.

[45] *Ibid.*, 4.

[46] Spring, "An Interview with George Tooker," 72.

[47] Garver, *George Tooker*, 112.

[48] Interview with Weinberg, 20.

[49] Father Rouelle had established a low-income advocacy group that grew to include a crafts cooperative, transportation service, and home-health nursing program, and he also initiated a senior center, dental clinic, and day-care center. Tooker has explained, "It was really Father Rouelle who was very important to me. But I read Dorothy Day and the *Catholic Worker*. And her ideas are ones I agree with. And I certainly don't think my conversion to Catholicism could ever have taken place before Vatican II." Spring, "An Interview with George Tooker," 78.

[50] Interview with the author, 21.

[51] *Ibid.*, 19.

# Tooker and company: identity and community in the early work

Jonathan Weinberg

"Paul and I differ in that my work is only implicitly homosexual, not outwardly so."

George Tooker interview with Justin Spring, *American Art*, 2002

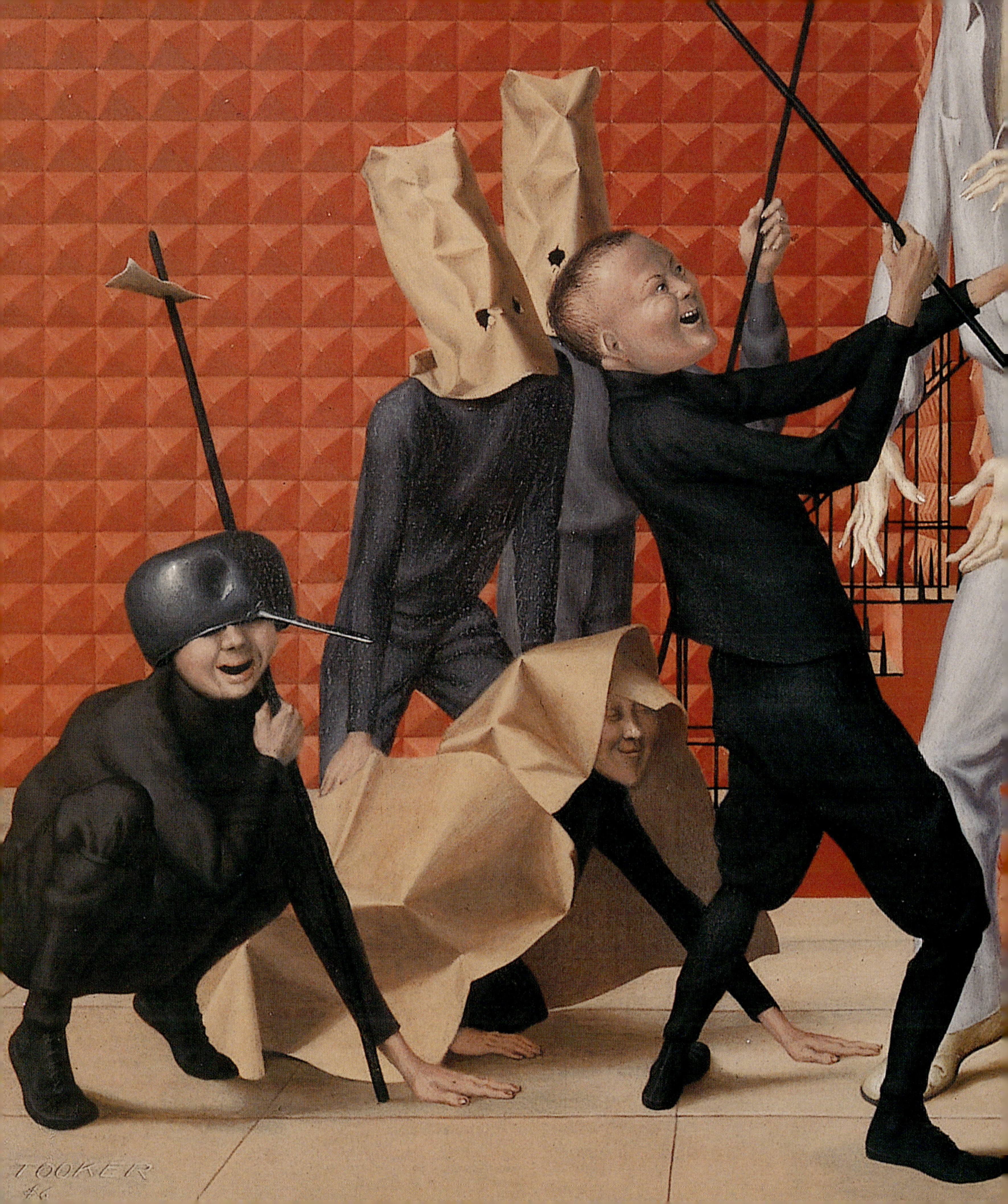
TOOKER

Previous page
George Tooker
***Children and Spastics*** (1946) (detail)
Collection Museum of Contemporary Art, Chicago
Gift of Mary and Earle Ludgin Collection
Photography © Museum of Contemporary Art, Chicago
(see page 107)

Below
fig. 1
George Tooker
*Self-Portrait* (1947)
Egg tempera on gesso panel
18¾ inches (47.6 cm) diameter
Curtis Galleries, Minneapolis, Minnesota

Opposite
fig. 2
George Platt Lynes (1907–1955)
*Paul Cadmus, George Tooker, and Jared French, 5 St. Luke's Place studio (circa 1949)*
Courtesy of the George Tooker Papers, 1932–1973, Archives of American Art, Smithsonian Institution, Washington, D.C.
© Estate of George Platt Lynes



Among George Tooker's papers in the Archives of American Art is a series of photographs by George Platt Lynes taken between 1945 and 1948 of Tooker and his artist friends. In one of these images (fig. 2), Paul Cadmus is in the midst of painting *What I Believe*, an allegorical picture that, like Lynes's photograph itself, conjures up an ideal artistic community. Behind him, in the next room, is Tooker at his easel, and in the far distance is Jared French. Lynes's picture seems to reveal three kindred spirits working in a communal space. The only problem with this Utopian vision is that, according to Tooker, the photograph was a fabrication; Tooker never made art in this Greenwich Village studio shared by Cadmus and French.[1] Yet the fictive nature of the picture does not so much negate its message of artistic community as make it more complex. Any concept of community has to encompass the principals' miscommunications and conflicts as well as their common purposes and sensibilities. Above all, Tooker's disavowal of the picture makes us wonder about the precarious position in which he found himself that day, consciously posed by Lynes between two older and more experienced artists as if he were a bridge or barrier between them.

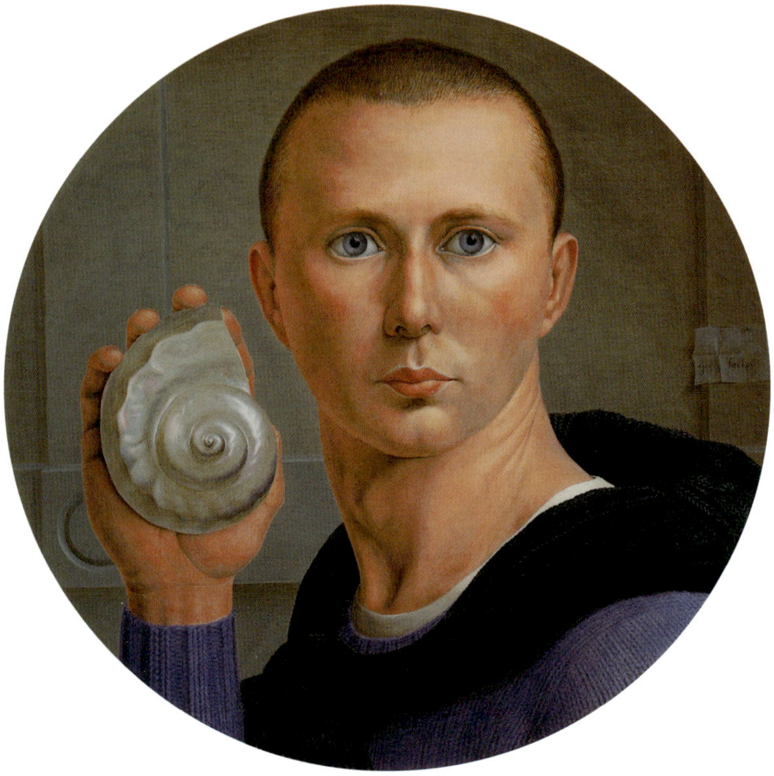

For the young Tooker to sit for Lynes, the celebrated *Vogue* and *Harper's Bazaar* photographer who had taken pictures of some of the most famous visual and performing artists of his day—the list includes Frederick Ashton, Alexandra Danilova, Jean Cocteau, Katherine Hepburn, Gloria Swanson, Gertrude Stein, Igor Stravinsky, and Yves Tanguy—must have been both exhilarating and intimidating. But you would never know it from Tooker's calm demeanor in most of Lynes's pictures. This is particularly true of the portrait of Tooker that years later was chosen to accompany Thomas H. Garver's authorized monograph of the artist (fig. 3). Sitting slightly forward in his chair with drawing board and brush, Tooker seems alert and active. To his right is an enormous oval mirror in which we can make out a bit of his left arm, the board, and his legs. The conceit is that the photographer might have just interrupted the artist in the process of self-scrutiny. It was at precisely this time that Tooker completed a small, round self-portrait (fig. 1), in which the oval shapes of Tooker's head and eyes are purposely exaggerated to rhyme with the circular forms of the shell in his hand and of the canvas itself. More than a tool to help reproduce the artist's likeness, the mirror is a symbol for the task of the realist painter who *mirrors* nature, even as it is a surrogate for Lynes's camera.

Mirrors both reflect and distort reality, depending on their angle of refraction. In other photographs from the same session (fig. 4), the mirror produces an entirely different reflection and effect. Instead of a fragment of Tooker's body, we see Cadmus and the somewhat taller and mustached French. Their relaxed stance and evident amusement at the proceedings undermine the formality of Tooker's pose. The strangest of the pictures (fig. 5) shows Tooker awkwardly looking away from the camera with his neck uncomfortably extended and his drawing board precariously resting on his lap. In the mirror, Cadmus turns his head in profile, perhaps to echo Tooker's pose. Cadmus's proximity to his friend's ear, and French's responding broad smile, suggest a whispered joke.

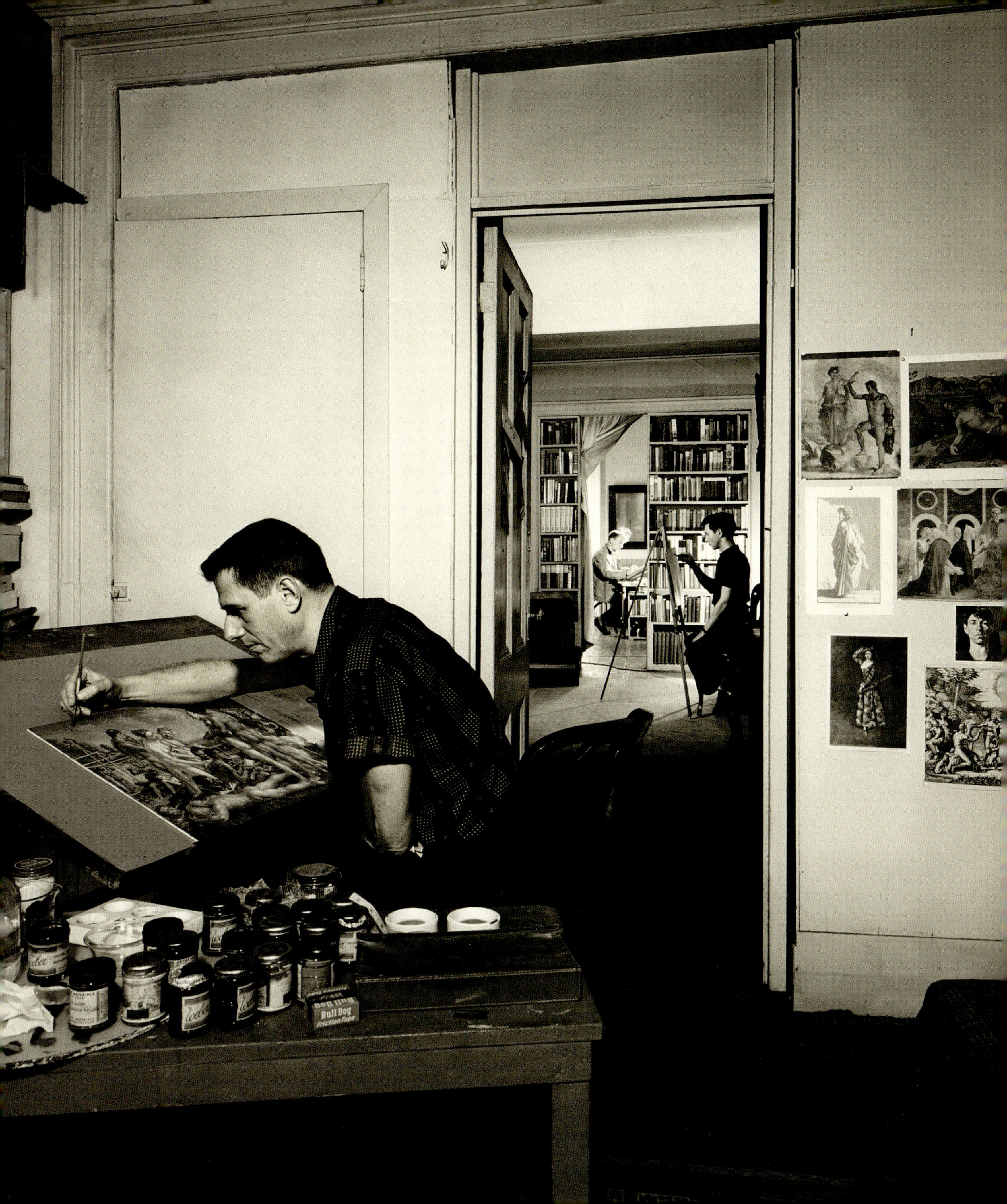
Bull Dog
Friction Tape

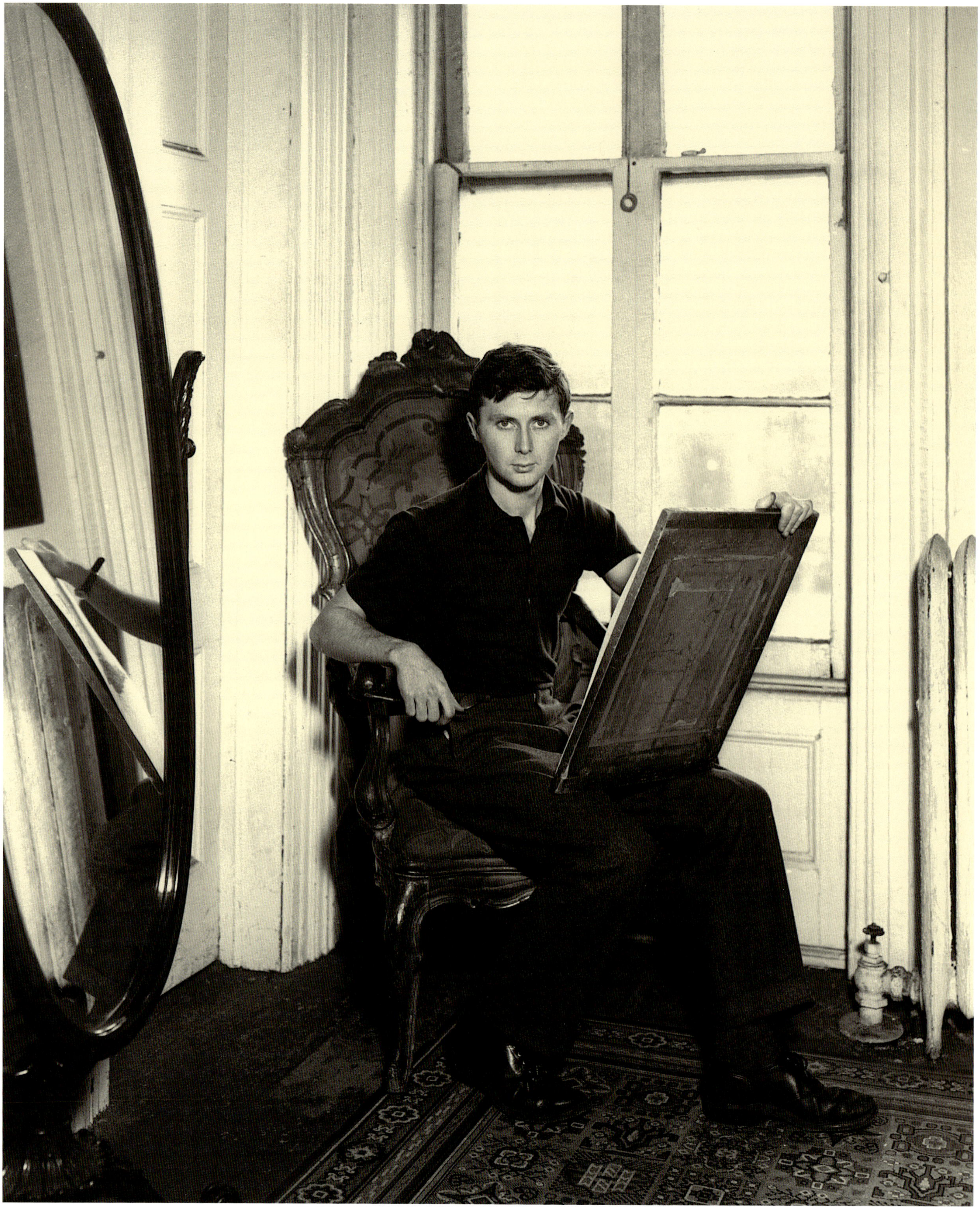

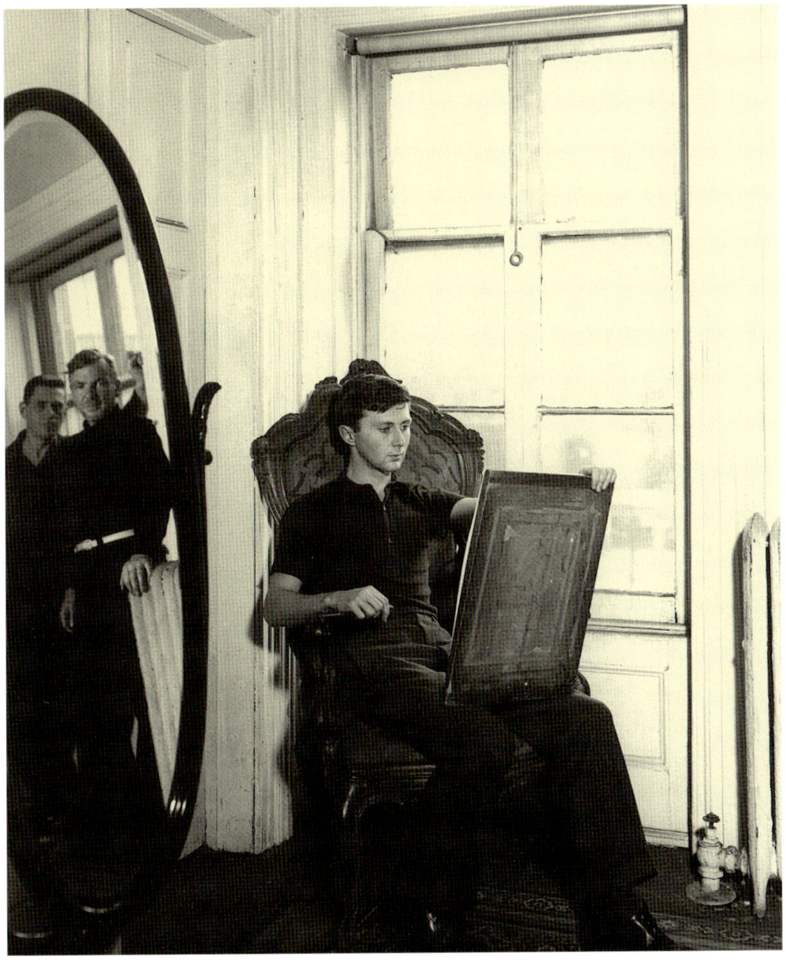

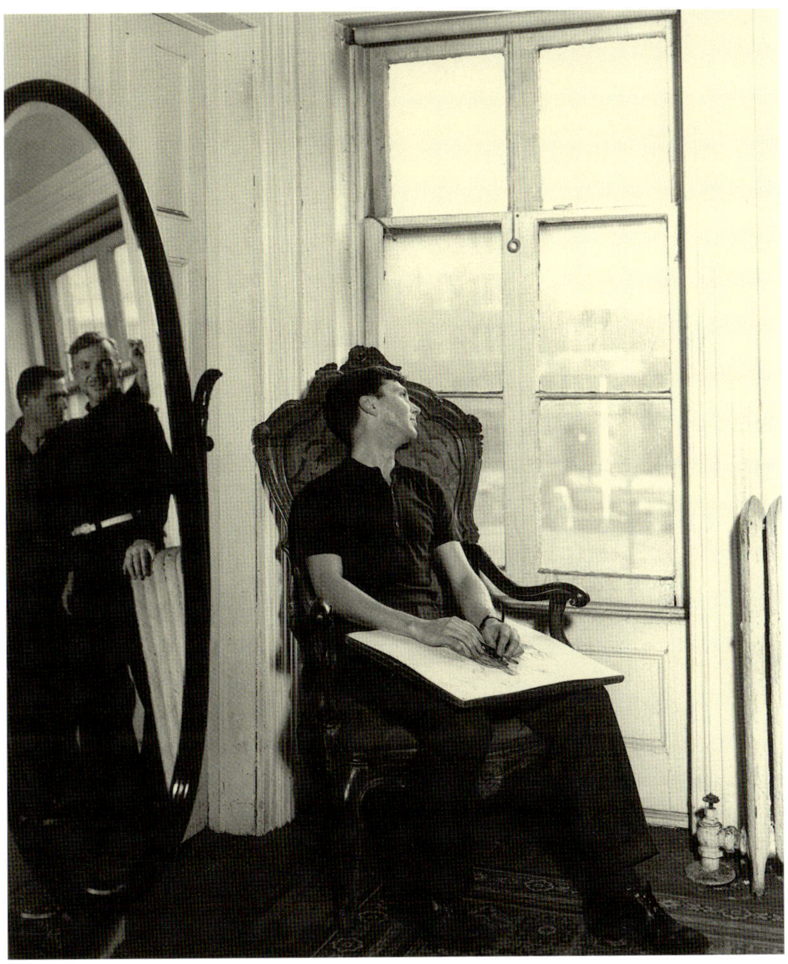

fig. 3
George Platt Lynes (1907–1955)
*George Tooker* (*circa* 1948)
Courtesy of the George Tooker Papers, 1932–1973, Archives of American Art, Smithsonian Institution, Washington, D.C.
© Estate of George Platt Lynes

fig. 4
George Platt Lynes (1997–1955)
*George Tooker with Paul Cadmus and Jared French in the Mirror* (*circa* 1948)
Courtesy of the George Tooker Papers, 1932–1973, Archives of American Art, Smithsonian Institution, Washington, D.C.
© Estate of George Platt Lynes

fig. 5
George Platt Lynes (1907–1955)
*George Tooker with Paul Cadmus and Jared French in the Mirror* (*circa* 1948)
Courtesy of the George Tooker Papers, 1932–1973, Archives of American Art, Smithsonian Institution, Washington, D.C.
© Estate of George Platt Lynes



What is strange about all the photographs in the series is Tooker's lack of acknowledgment of the presence of Cadmus and French. Ostensibly it is Tooker who is at the center of the photographs and Cadmus and French who are on its margins, but the intimacy of the two figures in the mirror creates precisely the opposite effect: Tooker seems vulnerable to their derision. In this way, Lynes uses the mirror device to forge a link between these three artists and simultaneously to hint at tensions between them. In fact, Tooker was Cadmus's lover at the time, but Cadmus had been lovers with French, and despite French's recent marriage to the painter Margaret Hoening, Cadmus and French continued to be intimate (supposedly Cadmus once boasted "I had Jerry in the daytime and George at night").[2] Apparently neither Tooker nor French was as enthusiastic about the arrangement as Cadmus later claimed to be. Tooker remembered that French refused to shake his hand when they met for dinner in public.[3] Yet, as Tooker himself admitted to me, French's influence was as crucial as Cadmus's in forging his own personal style.[4] Whatever their personal feelings for one another, the three artists were bound by a shared aesthetic sensibility. Together they helped form a close-knit artistic community that sustained and nourished their life and work.

It was Paul Cadmus who recruited Tooker into their little group:

> In 1944 I was seeing a great deal of a new friend, glamorous Bridget Chisholm ... Bridget and I were ardent sketch-class visitors pursuing the proper study of womankind and mankind on Saturdays at the Art Students League. Reginald Marsh's class was open to us and the monitor turned out to be twenty four year old George Tooker, immediately renamed by Bridget MISTERTOOKER, whom we took to at once, forming a trio which would repair to her place at the Plaza after class for sociability, tea, or drinks and assessment and discussion of our drawings. Her white rat RATRICK was part of the ménage.[5]

Cadmus was sixteen years older than Tooker and at the time of their meeting had already had considerable success in the art world. Through Cadmus, Tooker became part of an extraordinary aesthetic

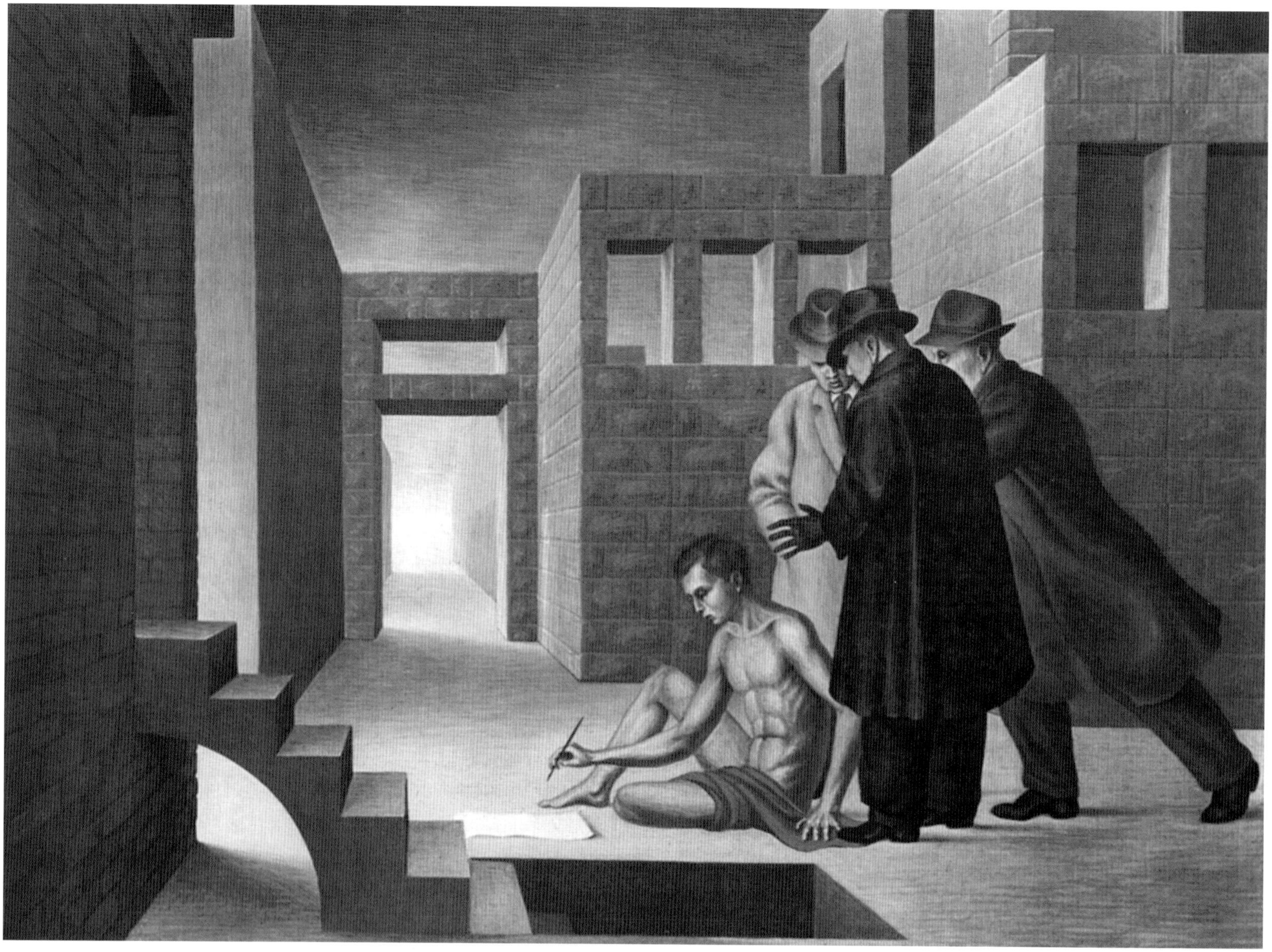

circle that included Lynes, W.H. Auden, Christopher Isherwood, Glenway Westcott, Monroe Wheeler, Bernard Perlin, and Pavel Tchelitchew. Above all, Cadmus introduced Tooker to his brother-in-law, the curator and ballet impresario Lincoln Kirstein, who became Tooker's great champion and patron. Although Tooker is shy by temperament, as Cadmus's companion he attended openings, ballet premieres and parties with a dazzling array of writers, dancers, composers, and visual artists. Postwar America was becoming increasingly conservative and conformist in terms of politics and sexual identity, but the bohemian circle in which Tooker found himself flouted traditional standards of behavior, particularly when it came to same-sex relationships. With Cadmus, Tooker summered with Jared and Margaret French in Fire Island and Provincetown, where they were visited by a constant flow of handsome young men who were not embarrassed to frolic nude on the beach. At a time when the young Tooker was struggling to accept his own sexual attraction to men, the relative openness with which Cadmus and his glamorous artist friends acknowledged and even celebrated their homosexuality must have been affirming.

Of course, Cadmus did more than expand Tooker's social life. Together with French, Cadmus instructed Tooker in the Old Master technique of egg tempera and, as Cadmus put it, Tooker has remained "faithful to egg-tempera ever since."[6] Tooker first put that method to good use in 1945 in *Audience* (fig. 6), a tiny painting that contains a half-naked self-portrait. Sitting on the floor of a stone court, the young Tooker draws on a sheet of paper. He is oddly oblivious to three nefarious-looking men who seem poised to attack him from behind. Garver writes that *Audience* "depicts clothed and unclothed figures in juxtaposition, where nudity may symbolize visionary truth opposed by the agents of obstruction, doubt and conventionality."[7] It is unclear what motivates the threatening men, who look like figures from a *film noir*. Is it lust or avarice? Do they want to possess the picture the artist makes, or his body? There is a poignancy to the slightness of Tooker's figure and the way a piece of cloth is awkwardly draped around his leg

fig. 6
George Tooker
*Audience* (1945)
Egg tempera on gesso panel
9 × 12 inches (22.9 × 30.5 cm)
Location unknown

fig. 7
George Platt Lynes (1907–1955)
*George Tooker* (1945)
Courtesy of the George Tooker Papers, 1932–1973, Archives of American Art, Smithsonian Institution, Washington, D.C.


fig. 8
PaJaMa (Paul Cadmus, Jared and Margaret French)
*George Tooker, Palisades Park, New Jersey* (1947)
Courtesy of the William Christopher Papers, 1946–1972, Archives of American Art, Smithsonian Institution, Washington, D.C.

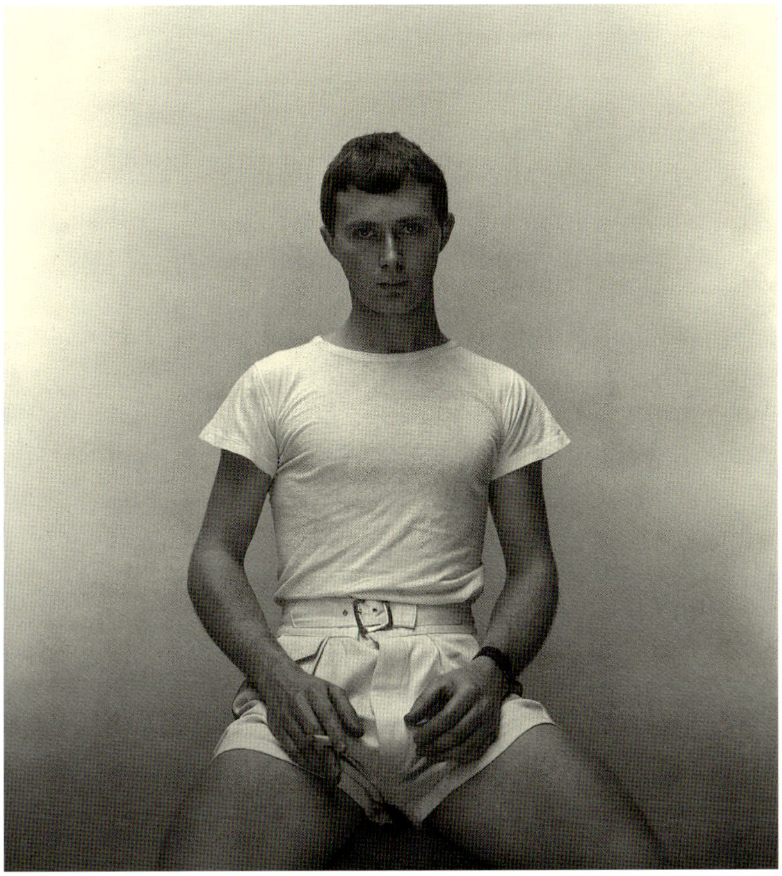

so as modestly to hide his genitals. The subject of the picture is mysterious, but it expresses a young man's vulnerability as an object of desire both in terms of his talent and his good looks.

Unlike many of the other handsome men that Lynes photographed at this time, Tooker was circumspect about showing too much of his body. In another series of portraits (fig. 7), Lynes posed Tooker against a simple white background to emphasize his lithe body and sweet, boyish features. Looking amused and sexy, in a tight-fitting T-shirt and skimpy shorts, Tooker was willing to play along but not to disrobe completely. Perhaps he was leery of being just another pretty boy in Lynes's expanding catalogue of nudes. Getting naked for an artist is not just a matter of modesty. It shifts the genre of a picture so that it ceases to be read as a portrait and becomes instead a nude. At a time when photographs of the naked male body were considered pornographic, getting naked for the camera was potentially dangerous. In essence, by keeping his clothes on, Tooker retained his selfhood. He was somewhat more daring when he spent time in Fire Island and Provincetown and posed for "PaJaMa," the nickname for the photographic collaboration of Paul Cadmus, and Jared and Margaret French. Yet even in these pictures, Tooker is mostly semi-clothed or facing away from the camera. The exception that proves the rule shows him naked front-on, but his hand partially covers his face, both to create a certain degree of anonymity and to insist that even in nakedness it is Tooker who controls what the camera sees (fig. 8).

Although Tooker told me, "I like painting the body. It's important to me. It's interesting. It is why I paint," he said he was not interested in painting genitalia: "I like painting the torso … I am not interested in painting the extremities."[8] His fascination with the upper regions of the body is explored most fully in his *Window* series. In these voyeuristic paintings, the languid eroticism of scantily clothed men and women is both heightened and contained by the window frame, which allows us to see only so much skin. Characteristically, Tooker's figures, whether semi-naked or clothed, are boxed in. This boxing-in, which is the central metaphor for alienation and oppression in Tooker's so-called "protest paintings," such as *Subway* (1950;

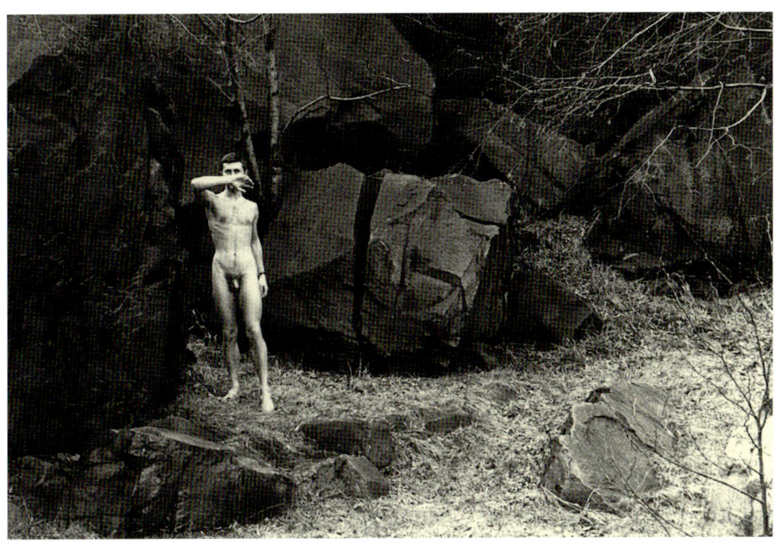

plate 15) and *Waiting Room* (1959; plate 31), is also reflective of Tooker's preference for restraint and modesty. Little wonder that Tooker brought this same quality of containment to his own presentation for the camera.

*Dance* (1946; plate 3), the painting that immediately follows *Audience*, can also be read as an image about the vulnerability of the body. As Garver points out, the painting is a modern retelling of the Dance of Death theme, complete with ghoulish skeletons snatching their victims from the night revelers that congregate in the city streets. Like the lurid warnings about venereal disease that were undoubtedly given to Tooker when he was a Marine recruit, the picture reinforces the idea that death is ready to strike down even the relatively young, particularly if they are promiscuous and drunk. In theme and form, *Dance* emulates *The Fleet's In!* (1934; fig. 9), the painting that made Cadmus's career a dozen years earlier. Cadmus's painting of drunken sailors cavorting with male and female civilians along the waterfront was removed from an exhibition of government-subsidized paintings because it supposedly showed the Navy in a bad light. The painting was a *succès de scandale*, appearing in major newspapers all across the country. Although it was left largely unsaid at the time, the military was undoubtedly upset by the depiction in the background of a man propositioning a sailor.[9] *The Fleet's In!* and *Dance* share a similar cast of seedy characters, as well as a tri-part composition and a frieze-like arrangement of figures across a long horizontal. But the moods of the two paintings are very different. The sailors and civilians of *The Fleet's In!* may be an ugly and immoral lot, but at least they are having fun as they degrade themselves. In contrast, the people of *Dance* are catatonic: they derive no joy from the various evening pleasures that will lead to their inevitable death.

Missing from Tooker's picture is Cadmus's representation of a homosexual pick-up as one of the vices of the city streets. Tooker does include in the left background a lone man who, if not gay, seems detached from the kind of heterosexual coupling that ends so badly at the painting's center. His Tookerish features suggest that he is a surrogate for the artist. He witnesses but does not participate in the dance between men and women. Garver insists that *A Game of Chess* (plate 5), completed the following year, with its overbearing matriarch and almost equally unappealing younger woman, is explicitly about Tooker's fear of marriage and being forced "to settle down, establish a family, and be socially correct and productive."[10] If Tooker's homosexuality is expressed in *Dance* and *A Game of Chess*, it is not as erotic longing for men but as a terror of conventional heterosexual relationships. Yet the contemporaneous *Children and Spastics* (1946; plate 1) suggests that Tooker was no more sanguine about homosexuality, at least in its most stereotypical form.

The "spastics" in question are three thin and exaggeratedly effeminate men cornered by a group of demonic children with aged features reminiscent of the images of hell in the paintings of Hieronymus Bosch (*circa* 1450–1516). Using broom and hoe as spears, they taunt the three youths, who with limp wrists and twisted faces passively submit to their abuse. Interestingly, in one of the sketches for the painting (fig. 10), the children and the spastics are nude, presumably so that Tooker can figure out the anatomical structure of their poses. But this nudity also expresses the possibility that underlying the children's hostility is some form of erotic allure and torment. The art historian Katherine Hauser, taking her cue from the way the makeshift weapons form crosses and the Renaissance tradition of children mocking religious figures, writes that the painting solicits "sympathy for the 'trinity' of men by linking them, through its many references to Christian iconography, with the ultimate martyr, Jesus Christ, and his Passion."[11] Yet, given the way Tooker made these men so grotesque, it is hard to believe that he meant them to be sympathetic. In fact, by labeling them "spastics" he joins in their derision. What did the artist have in mind in creating such a potentially homophobic image? When I asked Tooker directly, he claimed no longer to remember. In general, he has been loath to fix the meaning of his pictures by providing interviewers with explanations. My guess is that he intended the three figures to stand not for all homosexuals, but rather for a kind of outlandish behavior that was anathema to his own sense of decorum.

In this regard, it is interesting to compare *Children and Spastics* with a painting that Cadmus was working on at exactly the same time,

fig. 9
Paul Cadmus (1904–1999)
*The Fleet's In!* (1934)
Tempera on canvas
30 × 60 inches (76.2 × 152.4 cm)
Navy Art Collection, Washington, D.C.



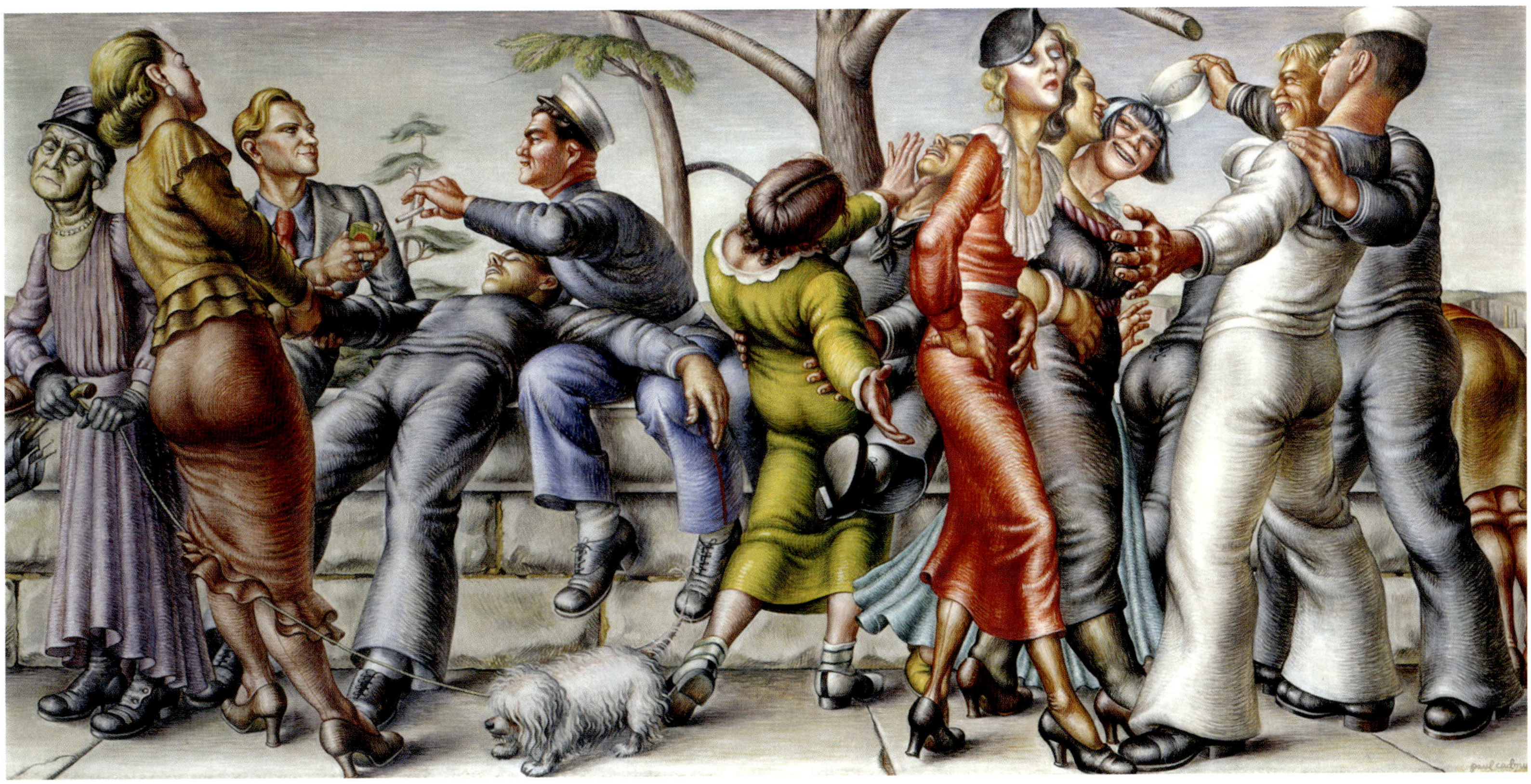

*Fantasia on a Theme by Dr. S.* (fig. 11). Both paintings involve a comparison of bodies. Hauser relates the poses of the trio of men in Tooker's painting to representations of the mythical Judgment of Paris, and its competition among three ideals of feminine beauty. Cadmus's painting also sets up a contrast of three body types, in this case to satirize the peculiar theories of the psychologist William Herbert Sheldon, the "Dr. S." of the painting's title. The three figures on the porch—obese, muscular, and thin—are exaggerations of Sheldon's "endomorph," "mesomorph," and "ectomorph." Sheldon's then recently published book *The Varieties of Temperament* (1942), which appears in the painting on the lap of the ectomorph, argued that these genetically derived body types were crucial in determining character.[12] In Cadmus's picture, Dr. Sheldon's pseudo-scientific studying of the human physique takes the form of the scrutiny of a pumped-up, half-naked sailor by two obviously gay men. The intensity of their lascivious gaze is mocked by the small phallic ornaments on the porch piers, which are aimed like missiles at the sailor's buttocks and chest. Another lewd joke is the hot dog in the fat man's hand.

The sign on top of the house in Cadmus's painting provides an alternative title to *Fantasy on a Theme by Dr. S*: reversed, it reads "JUST A MERE CAMP." In essence, both Tooker and Cadmus were ridiculing "camping," a behavior often associated with overtly gay men. As the historian George Chauncey succinctly puts it, camp uses "irony, incongruity, theatricality, and humor to highlight the artifice of social conventions, sometimes exaggerating convention to the point of burlesquing it, sometimes inverting it to achieve the same end."[13] When queers in private call each other by female names or behave with exaggerated lewdness toward a hyper-masculine man, they are in essence turning the language of homophobia on its head through

48

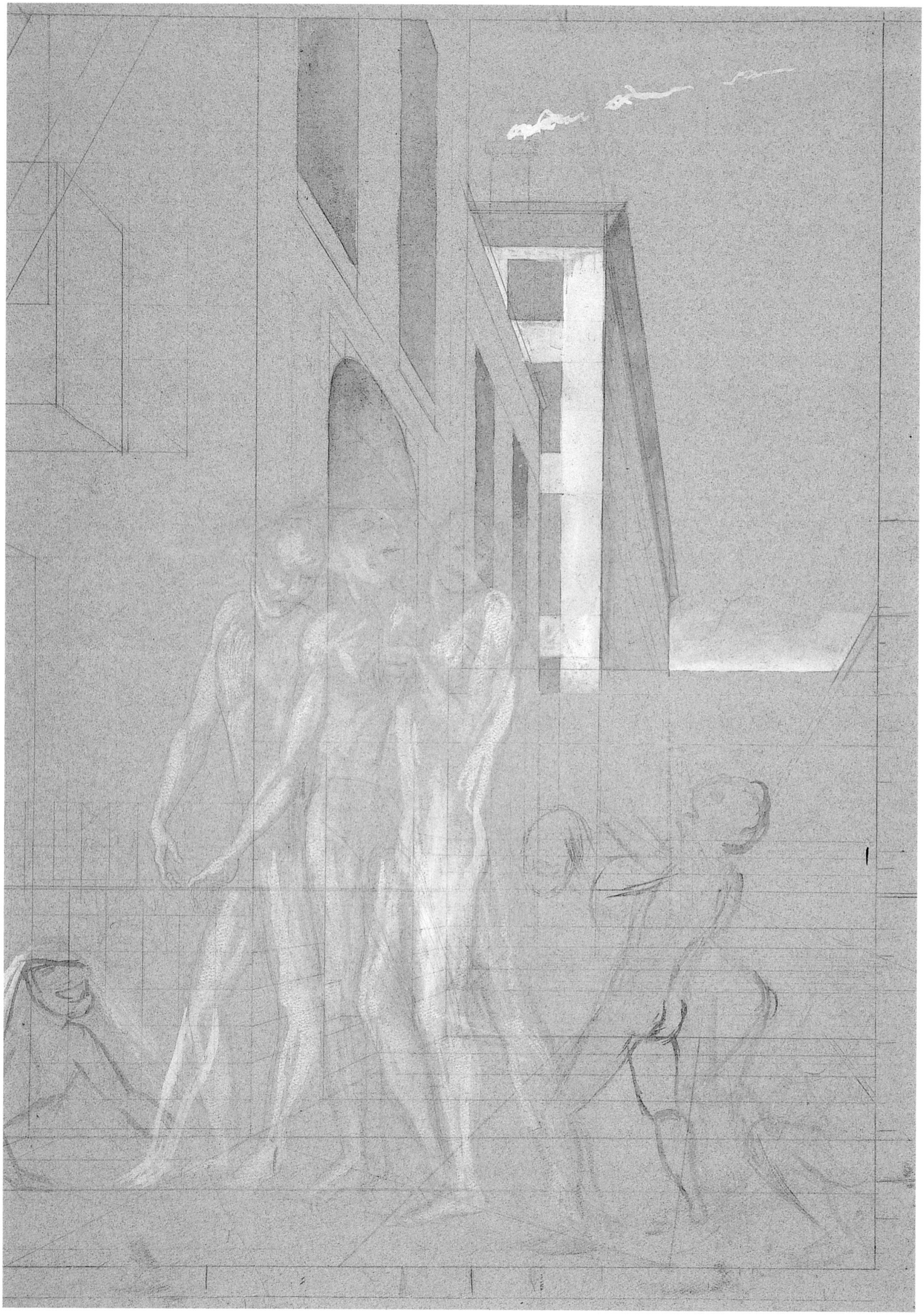

fig. 10
George Tooker
Study for *Children and Spastics* (*circa* 1946)
Drawing
26 × 20 5/16 inches (66.1 × 51.6 cm)
Addison Gallery of American Art; Gift of the artist (PA 1936) in memory of his parents, George Clair and Angela Montejo Roura Tooker, Addison Gallery of American Art, Phillips Academy, Andover, Massachusetts

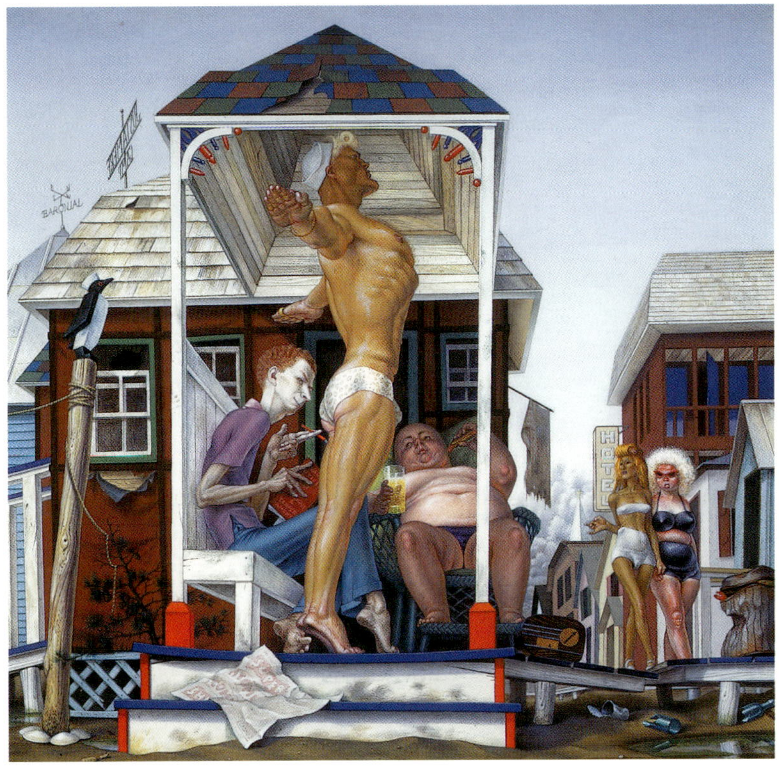

fig. 11
Paul Cadmus (1904–1999)
*Fantasia on a Theme by Dr. S.* (1946)
Egg tempera on pressed wood panel
13 1/2 × 13 inches (34.3 × 33 cm)
Whitney Museum of American Art, New York; Purchase 47.1
Photograph by Robert E. Mates



parody and humor. Tooker's "spastics," rather than fight with their accusers, *camp*: that is, they respond with a mock horror that is an exaggeration of the stereotype that gay men are weak. Camp is not a single way of acting, or a permanent aesthetic; it changes over time, under different circumstances and in different contexts. Although camp is often associated with effeminacy, even the most masculine man may indulge in it, given the right mood and social situation. For example, Kirstein, who supposedly was uncomfortable with "'fairies' and their campy ways," was, according to biographer Martin Duberman, "quite capable, with intimates, of camping himself."[14] In an era when the direct discussion of homosexuality was repressed, camp was one of the chief strategies by which queers "could make sense of, respond to, and undermine the social categories of gender and sexuality that served to marginalize them."[15]

In retrospect, the way certain men have used camp as a strategy of resistance by purposely playing up their difference was often courageous and ingenious. However, in rendering such camping heroic, we must not forget the ambivalent response such behavior elicited among members of the queer community. Even Susan Sontag, whose essay "Notes on 'Camp'" (1964) remains the most famous discussion of the term, admitted to being both "drawn to Camp, and almost as strongly offended by it."[16] Not all aspects of camping were liberating. To camp could be potentially subversive, but it might also be to act in ways that were predictable and circumscribed, cliquish and effete.

Such, at least, was the fear of Robert Duncan, the queer poet, whose extraordinary essay "The Homosexual in Society" was published in *Politics* in the very year that Tooker and Cadmus met and started working on similar themes. An early and courageous call for "homosexual rights," it was also an attack on "the *camp*, a tone and vocabulary that is loaded with contempt for the human."[17] Duncan's scorn was particularly directed at the private parties of the gay New York art world, which he likened to a cult dedicated to the idea of homosexual superiority: "They offered a family, outrageous as it was, a community in which one was not condemned for one's homosexuality, but it was necessary there for one to desert one's humanity for which one would be suspect, 'out of key.'" Duncan claimed that "the group language did not allow for any feeling at all other than this self-ridicule, this gaiety ... a wave surging forward, breaking into laughter and then receding, leaving a wake of disillusionment, a disbelief that extended to oneself, to life itself."[18] Significantly, Duncan alludes to his own past participation in these affairs, and so his criticism is as much directed against himself as it is against the queer elite that is his target. Likewise, Tooker and Cadmus, in caricaturing certain homosexuals, are ridiculing themselves. Indeed, Tooker's spastics are derived from the artist's own features, and the thin man with drawing pen in hand of *Fantasia on a Theme by Dr. S.* is surely a surrogate for Cadmus and his obsession with the male form. As Sontag declares, to understand camp, "to draw its contours and recount its history, requires a deep sympathy modified by revulsion."[19]

Duncan ends his essay by insisting on disowning "*all* the special groups (nations, religions, sexes, races) that would claim allegiance" in favor of "devotion to human freedom, toward the liberation of human love, human conflicts, human aspirations."[20] Duncan's solution is not to abandon the cause of gay rights or exclude queer subject matter from art; rather, it is to see the homosexual cause as part of a larger struggle for civil rights. He specifically relates it to the plight of the Jews and of African Americans, with the difference that few homosexuals in the 1940s had the courage to stand up for their own rights. Tooker has told me he knew nothing of Duncan's work, and it is possible that neither did Cadmus; however, these two painters shared many of Duncan's worries about ghettoizing gay experience as well as his hopes for an art devoted to the cause of human dignity.[21]

fig. 12
Paul Cadmus (1904–1999)
*What I Believe* (1947–48)
Tempera on panel
16¼ × 27 inches (41.1 × 68.6 cm)
Collection of the McNay Art Museum, San Antonio, Texas, Gift of Robert L.B. Tobin

fig. 13
Jared French (1905–1988)
*Figures on a Beach* (1940)
Egg tempera on gesso on linen mounted on panel
21½ × 33⅜ inches (54.6 × 84.7 cm)
Private Collection
Photo courtesy DC Moore Gallery, New York



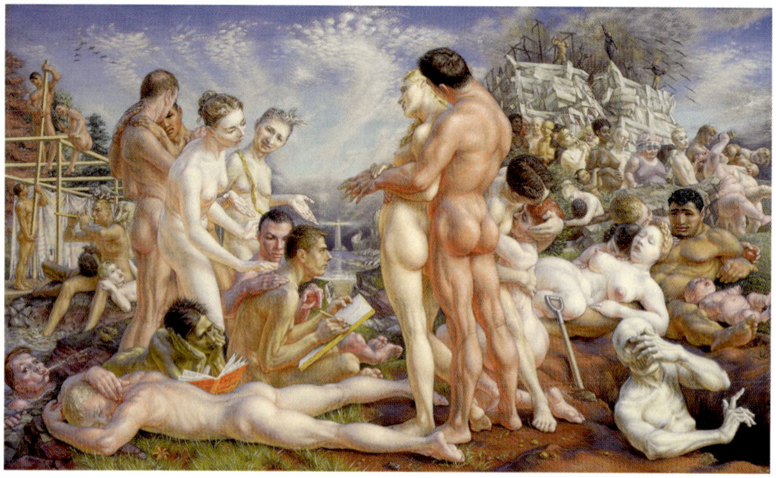

Cadmus's art contradicts some of Duncan's conclusions, however. It demonstrates how representing the specifics of a particular queer community may also be expressive of a wide-ranging humanism. Indeed, Cadmus's *What I Believe* (1947–48; fig. 12), with its portrait of friends on one side and images of fascism and avarice on the other, is an allegory in which the very queer elite that Duncan castigates is idealized as a counterfoil to the agents of intolerance and inhumanity.

Perhaps even more than Cadmus, Tooker has identified with the humanist goals outlined in Duncan's essay, particularly as they relate to the rights of human beings to express themselves unfettered by the state or by group pressure. As he matured, he avoided the type of caricaturing of social types that was Cadmus's forte. His figures became more generalized and abstract, and therefore perhaps more easily invested with the kind of broad moral values and conflicts that Duncan felt should be at the basis of any humanist art. Some fifty years after they first met, Cadmus described this quality of Tooker's later work: "his œuvre has become more universal, his characters fewer, their garments of no particular style or period, their features timeless, their emotions deep and restrained and their settings everywherenowhere."[22]

Ironically, Tooker's tendency toward abstraction and a generalization of facial features was greatly influenced by the art of his chief rival for Cadmus's affection, Jared French. The power that French's art had over Tooker at this time is best measured by *Coney Island* (1947–48; plate 11), a painting that Tooker claimed "was a kind of homage to Reginald Marsh, and to Paul [Cadmus], too, because they both painted Coney Island," but which is actually closer to French's work.[23] Tooker is less interested in carnality than are Marsh or Cadmus; nor does he share their interest in the working classes. Already we can sense Tooker's propensity to give all his figures similar features, a tendency he shares with French, whose *Figures on a Beach* (1940; fig. 13) was equally an inspiration for Tooker's *Coney Island*. Both paintings include the central motif of a sleeping figure paired with an awake companion. Where Marsh and Cadmus looked to Rubens as the basis for their tangle of human bodies, Tooker and French employ the classical structure and sense of calm of Nicolas Poussin (1594–1665). Even in extreme movement, Tooker's running and diving figures appear serene against the kind of bright, clear sky and sand that are also so essential to French's beach painting. Tooker's *Fountain* (1950; fig. 14) is even more dependent on French's example. Its circle of half-naked young men seemingly cloned from one another is closely linked to French's *Crew* (1941–42; fig. 15), in which identical *kouros* figures make up the rowers of a sculling-boat.

In the end, it was not so much a matter of Tooker choosing between the styles of Cadmus and French as of taking what was useful from both to find his own voice. Above all, Tooker shared their dream of reviving the craft of such Quattrocento masters as Piero della

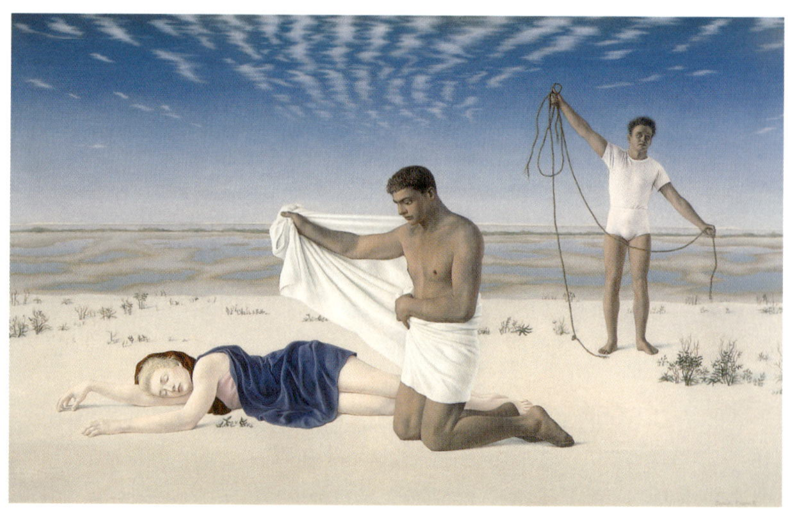

fig. 14
George Tooker
*Fountain* (1950)
Egg tempera on gesso panel
24 × 24 inches (60.9 × 60.9 cm)
Location unknown



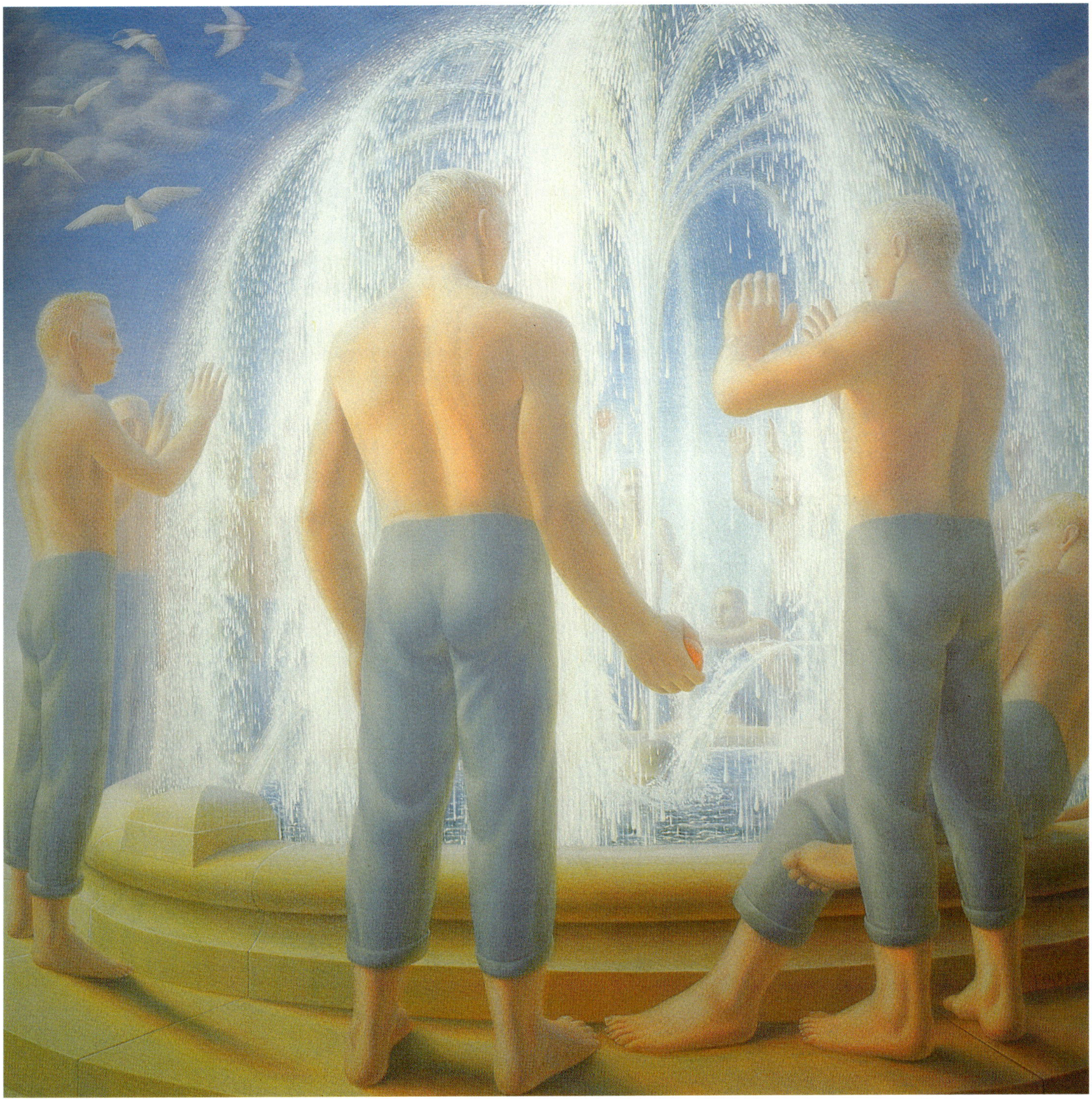

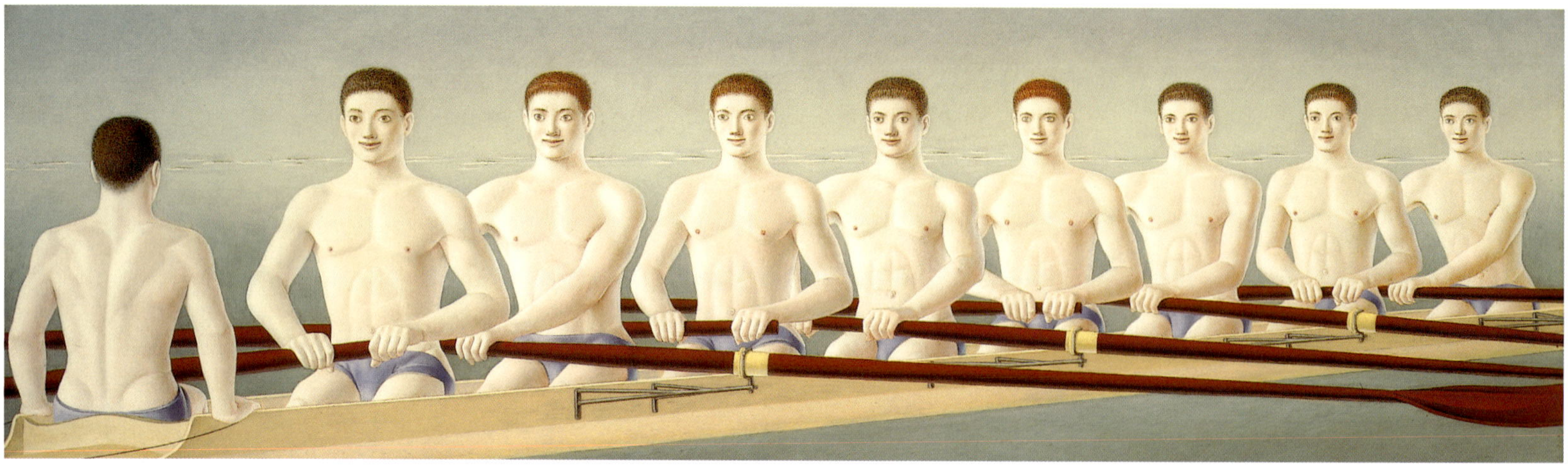

fig. 15
Jared French (1905–1988)
*Crew* (1941–42)
Egg tempera on gesso panel
9½ × 30½ inches (24.1 × 77.5 cm)
Private Collection
Photo courtesy DC Moore Gallery, New York

Francesca (*circa* 1412–92) and Paolo Uccello (1397–1475), which he studied first hand on his trip to Europe with Cadmus in 1949. At a time when Abstract Expressionism was on the rise, and so many American artists were jettisoning figuration, Cadmus and French encouraged Tooker's realist depiction of the human body using a method of painting in vogue some 500 years earlier. But, as Cadmus admitted, the process of influence was never one-sided: "I've been influenced by George Tooker since I've known him … but he has mysterious qualities that I can't emulate."[24]

Perhaps Cadmus's most generous act toward the younger artist was to introduce him to Lincoln Kirstein. As ballet impresario, producer, curator, and critic, Kirstein was one of the most powerful figures in the art world of the 1940s. He was instrumental in the foundation of New York's Museum of Modern Art, and probably was responsible for the last-minute inclusion of Tooker's work in the Museum's *Fourteen Americans* exhibition (1946), where *Children and Spastics* went on view to positive reviews. Kirstein bought several of Tooker's most important early paintings, which he came to hang alongside key paintings by French and Cadmus in his home. Perhaps recognizing the link between them, Kirstein purchased Tooker's *Coney Island* and French's *Figures on a Beach*. He also owned Cadmus's idealized portrait of Tooker, *The Inventor* (fig. 16), which shows Tooker holding a mobile of shells that he had made for Kirstein and his wife, Cadmus's sister Fidelma. Repeatedly Tooker paintings owned by Kirstein appeared in the annuals of the Whitney Museum of American Art and in several exhibitions that Kirstein personally curated.

Kirstein's patronage came at a price. In 1948, he published in *Harper's Magazine* "The State of Modern Painting," an essay that attacks abstract art as being mostly "decorative" and unfinished "improvisations." So much of modern art was "an amusement manipulated by interior decorators and high-pressure salesmen." Henceforth, to be taken under Kirstein's wing was to be considered part of his crusade against what he called "the canonization of abstract painting."[25] Tooker had always disliked the terms "Magic Realist," "Symbolic Realism," and "Metaphysical Painting," which Kirstein used to describe the art of Tooker and his friends. But I think he was even more ambivalent about being seen as anti-Modernist and anti-abstract just because he chose to work in a realist mode favored by Kirstein. Tooker was so alarmed by what he called Kirstein's tendencies to "pigeonhole artists" that he found a way diplomatically to head off his offer to write the catalogue for his 1973 retrospective.[26]

If Kirstein's advocacy brought unwanted baggage, it did provide a rallying cry for a mode of realism that was increasingly undervalued by mainstream Modernist critics and curators. Kirstein's dislike of improvisation and his emphasis on craft were undoubtedly colored by

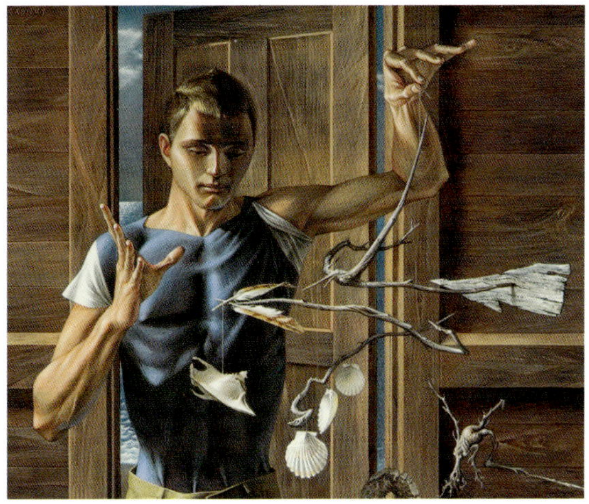

fig. 16
Paul Cadmus (1904–1999)
*The Inventor* (1946)
Egg tempera on pressed wood panel
7⅝ × 9⁹⁄₁₆ inches (19.4 × 23 cm)
Collection of James and Barbara Palmer

his passion for the ballet and his close collaboration with the choreographer George Balanchine. Kirstein wanted modern painting to be more like classical dance, a collaborative medium in which technique, order, and tradition are valued over individual invention and self-expression: "The essence of ballet is order. It is a classic or rational form … Its organization rests on an inherited academy, its presentation on equanimity and a body of long-tested practices … the academic dance speaks in miniature for the orderly, the productive, but also the vigorously active."[27] Little wonder Kirstein was such an advocate of Tooker's painting, with its display of technical virtuosity and its carefully choreographed placement of figures in space. Yet he was less sanguine about Tooker's painful subject matter. His praise of *Subway* was full of misgivings: "The disgust of your … picture is balanced by its pity or rather beauty. I hope your next picture will relax us from the anxious horror of half your vision. Simply because, since it's almost unbearable I see no reason one should attempt to bear it."[28]

What was most essential to Kirstein about the classical ballet was its deployment of beautiful bodies in space; even Balanchine's most abstract innovations always remained figurative. Indeed, Kirstein's obsession with the dance began with his teenage crush on Vaslav Nijinsky. Desire for the male body continued to motivate many of Kirstein's aesthetic enthusiasms for the rest of his life. His own art collection was filled with homoerotic imagery, just as so many of the artists he patronized were attractive men. I mention this, not to trivialize Kirstein's extraordinary career of nurturing artists, but rather to emphasize how important homoeroticism was to his aesthetic. As Kirstein himself insisted, the carnal is often a source for the highest achievement in art. He wrote Cadmus a letter about his painting *Lust* (1945): "I don't think anything as impermanent as flesh is corrupt … Lust isn't so bad, it lasts no time at all and is not destructive … maybe the nicest thing about all of us is our poor half-stiff peters and stretched, hungry cunts."[29]

Touching on the queerness underlying Kirstein's aesthetics brings us back to the role of Tooker's own sexual identity in the formation of his art. Comparing his work to Cadmus's, Tooker told Justin Spring that "my work is only implicitly homosexual, not outwardly so."[30] Certainly it is true that after *Children and Spastics* direct references to the oppression of homosexuals largely disappear from Tooker's painting. But Tooker continued to represent the way in which prejudice acted to categorize and compartmentalize people. In a radio interview, he spoke about his most famous painting, *Subway*, as being "about isolation, about people being cut off from their fellow men in this city, even though they're in crowds, and it's my way of protesting it."[31] In the same interview, he recited Langston Hughes's famous poem "I, Too, Sing America," with its lines "I am the darker brother./They send me to eat in the kitchen" and its promise of eventual political and social redemption.[32] As an African American and a homosexual, Hughes was a double outsider in American society. His words are explicitly about the struggle to overcome racism, but they also reverberate with the culture's marginalization of anyone because of race, ethnicity, or sexual orientation. Likewise, Tooker's *Man in the Box* (1967; fig. 17), in which a nude African American male is squeezed into a carton, can be read as an indictment of racism and as an expression of the closet, the central metaphor for the repression of gay identity. I do not mean to suggest that Tooker consciously intended this or any of his paintings directly to reference "closeting," a term that, after all, did not come into vogue in American culture until the 1970s. Rather, I am arguing that Tooker's vision of modern alienation in terms of people trapped in closet-like spaces is a response to the wide-ranging conformist pressures that produce homophobia and prejudice. After all, many of Tooker's most famous paintings were created at the height of the Cold War, amid the paranoia of the McCarthy hearings and the Red Scare. As Hauser points out, the fear of Communist spies everywhere was conflated with a terror of an insidious homosexuality. Yet it would be a mistake to attribute the atmosphere of paranoia of so many of Tooker's pictures solely to political and social forces beyond his control. His aesthetic is deeply conservative, favoring structure, order, and tradition. Ultimately, it is Tooker himself who designs with the utmost geometric precision the alienating spaces his people inhabit and their tendency to act as if they were following some unwritten rule. The figures of *Subway* are watched, even as they watch one

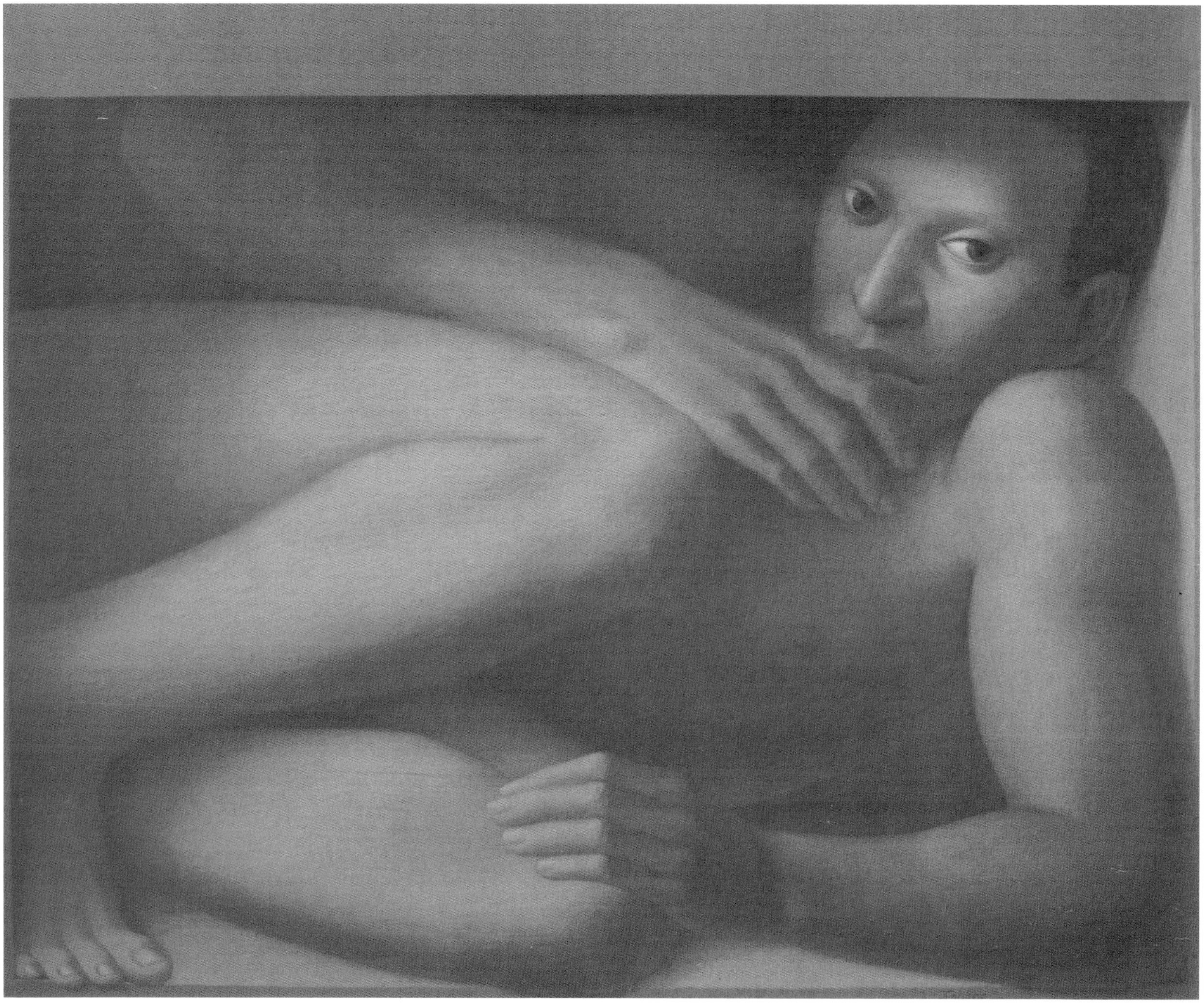



another: we all collude in the policing of desires; we all construct our own particular closets.

In the end, Tooker's statement that his work is "implicitly homosexual" may have less to do with its response to homophobia than its origins in a queer community that was its mainstay and that provided so many of its aesthetic touchstones. In this regard, it is no coincidence that one of the few paintings in which Tooker included likenesses of his friends and family was *Bird Watchers* (1948; plate 9). Cadmus posed for the man who stands at the center of the back row, and Tooker's sister was the basis for one of the androgynous women in the front. If Jared French's face is nowhere to be found in the mix, his influence is registered in the calm monumental figures and the light-blue sky. As in so many of Tooker's paintings, the subject is watchfulness, but no one seems frightened or lost in the crowd. The appreciation of beauty brings men and women together in a manner that Garver relates to religious fervor. Is this exalted meaning negated by mentioning that birds are a traditional symbol of the penis or by identifying the location of the picture as in, or near, the Rambles of New York City's Central Park, a notorious gay cruising ground? No, because, as I have tried to demonstrate in this essay, Tooker's aesthetic arose from a gay milieu for which such potentially camp associations would only further cement the sense of aesthetic community that is the painting's ultimate theme. Recognizing the "implicitly homosexual" in Tooker's art—acknowledging those queer subjects, places, and people that contributed to his formation as an artist—does not limit the meaning of his paintings nor rob them of their essential mystery; rather, it reinforces their fundamental humanity.

fig. 17
George Tooker
*Man in the Box* (1967)
Egg tempera on gesso panel
20 × 24 inches (50.8 × 61 cm)
Location unknown



## Notes

1 George Tooker, letter to the author, postmark August 9, 2007.

2 David Leddick, *Intimate Companions: A Triography of George Platt Lynes, Paul Cadmus, Lincoln Kirstein, and Their Circle* (New York: St. Martin's Press, 2000), 185.

3 George Tooker, unpublished interview with the author, Hartland, Vermont, June 7, 2007.

4 *Ibid.*

5 Paul Cadmus, *George Tooker* (New York: DC Moore Gallery, 1998), n.p.

6 *Ibid.*

7 Thomas H. Garver and George Tooker, *George Tooker* (New York: Rizzoli, 1987), 12.

8 Interview with the author, Hartland, Vermont, June 7, 2007.

9 For my fuller discussion of the controversy surrounding *The Fleet's In!* see Jonathan Weinberg, "Cruising with Cadmus," *Art in America*, 80:11 (1992). See also Richard Meyer, *Outlaw Representation: Censorship and Homosexuality in Twentieth-Century American Art* (Oxford and New York: Oxford University Press, 2002).

10 Garver and Tooker, *George Tooker*, 16.

11 Katherine Hauser, "George Tooker, Surveillance, and Cold War Sexual Politics," *GLQ*, 11:3 (June 2005), 404.

12 William Herbert Sheldon and Stanley Smith Stevens, *The Varieties of Temperament: A Psychology of Constitutional Differences* (New York: Harper, 1942). For a more extensive discussion of the implications of Sheldon's theories for American art, see Jonathan Weinberg, *Male Desire: The Homoerotic in American Art* (New York: Harry N. Abrams, 2005), 85. Tooker mentioned to me that he and Cadmus met Dr. Sheldon and that he had interviewed Cadmus. In the painting, Cadmus gets the book title wrong, and it becomes "Varieties of Physique and Temperament." This was perhaps a conscious conflation with another book by Sheldon, entitled *The Varieties of Human Physique.*

13 George Chauncey, *Gay New York: Gender, Urban Culture, and the Makings of the Gay Male World, 1890–1940* (New York: Basic Books, 1994), 290. The phenomenon of camp has spawned an industry of academic books and articles. An excellent introduction is the anthology *Camp Grounds: Style and Homosexuality*, ed. David Bergman (Amherst, Massachusetts: University of Massachusetts Press, 1994).

14 Martin Duberman, *The Worlds of Lincoln Kirstein* (New York: Alfred A. Knopf, 2007), 291.

15 Chauncey, *Gay New York*, 290.

16 Susan Sontag, "Notes on 'Camp'," in *Against Interpretation and Other Essays* (New York: Farrar, Strauss and Giroux, 1964), 276.

17 Robert Duncan, "The Homosexual in Society, " *Politics*, 1:7 (1944); as reprinted in Ekbert Faas, *Young Robert Duncan: Portrait of the Poet as Homosexual in Society* (Santa Barbara, California: Black Sparrow Press, 1983), 319–20. The repercussions of Duncan admitting his own homosexuality in this essay were severe, including the withdrawal of his "An African Elegy" from an upcoming issue of the prestigious *Kenyon Review* because suddenly the editor, John Crowe Ransom, read it "as an obvious homosexual advertisement, and for that reason not to be eligible for publication" (Faas, *Young Robert Duncan*, 151).

18 Duncan, "The Homosexual in Society," 320.

19 Sontag, "Notes on 'Camp'," 276.

20 Duncan, "The Homosexual in Society," 322.

21 The influential writer Parker Tyler took Duncan's essay to be a direct attack on his artist friends, many of whom, including the painter Pavel Tchelitchew, he shared with Cadmus and Tooker. He was sufficiently angry with Duncan to write a response to his essay, which, though unpublished, is partially quoted in Faas, *Young Robert Duncan*, 151.

22 Cadmus, *George Tooker*, n.p.

23 Justin Spring, "An Interview with George Tooker," *American Art*, 16:1 (spring 2002), 70.

24 Paul Cadmus, interview with Judd Tully, March 22–May 5, 1988, Archives of American Art, Smithsonian Institution, Washington, D.C.

25 Lincoln Kirstein, "The State of Modern Painting," *Harper's Magazine*, 197:1181 (October 1948), 47–48.

26 Interview with the author, June 7, 2007.

27 Lincoln Kirstein, *Nijinsky Dancing* (New York: Alfred A. Knopf, 1975), 18.

28 Lincoln Kirstein, letter to George Tooker, September 20, 1950, George Tooker Papers, Archives of American Art, Smithsonian Institution, Washington, D.C.

29 Quoted in Duberman, *The Worlds of Lincoln Kirstein*, 404.

30 Spring, "An Interview with George Tooker," 77.

31 Interview with Grace G. Alexander and George Kay on "Artists in New York," WNYC Radio transcript, New York City, 1967. George Tooker Papers, Archives of American Art, Smithsonian Institution, Washington, D.C.

32 "I, Too, Sing America," in Langston Hughes, *Selected Poems of Langston Hughes* (New York: Vintage Classics, 1990), 275.

# From anxiety to *agape*: George Tooker and the human condition

Marshall N. Price

**"I believe Art, as painting, is communication of thought by means of design, form, and color. ... I am most interested in people and their relations to each other and the outside world."**

George Tooker, "Artist Statement," Whitney Museum of American Art, New York, 1951[1]

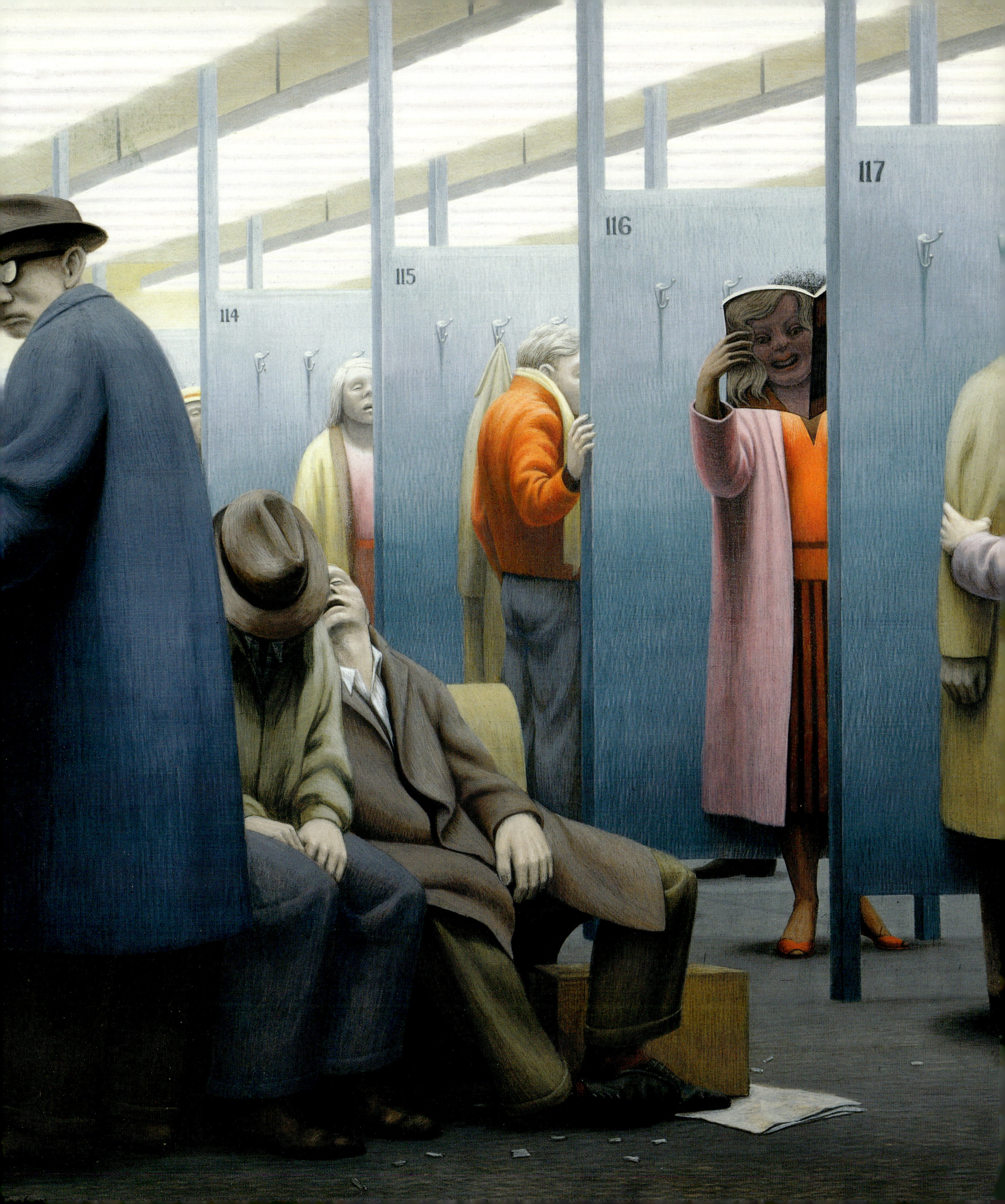
114
115
116
117

Previous page
George Tooker
***Waiting Room*** (1959) (detail)
Egg tempera on wood
24 × 30 inches (61 × 78.4 cm)
Smithsonian American Art Museum, Washington, D.C., Gift of S.C. Johnson & Sons, Inc.
(see page 137)



Until the middle of the twentieth century, the human condition was the *sine qua non* of artistic production. As the art that rose from the ashes of World War II moved further away from representational form, however, work that contained overt humanistic content was often marginalized.[2] While the human condition as subject matter was never eliminated altogether, the rise of Minimalism and Pop art suggested that critics and institutions favored an industrial aesthetic or one that appeared to mock man's plight in the context of popular culture. It was an aesthetic crisis, of sorts, as theologian and philosopher Paul Tillich wrote in his preface to the exhibition catalogue *New Images of Man*: "If we listen to the more profound observers of our period, we hear them speak of the danger in which modern man lives: the danger of losing his humanity and of becoming a thing among the things he produces. Humanity is not something man simply has. He must fight for it anew in every generation, and he may lose his fight."[3]

This fight came at a precipitous cultural juncture. The escalating Cold War created an environment of heightened cultural anxiety, with the very real possibility of an apocalyptic outcome. The very nature of existence was being re-evaluated by such existentialist thinkers as Maurice Merleau-Ponty and Jean-Paul Sartre, who developed ideas antithetical to the previously dominant Cartesian notion that rational consciousness formed the basis for reality.[4] Sartre recognized that "every man [is] in possession of himself as he is, and places the entire responsibility upon his shoulders."[5] Art, like life, Sartre noted, is not determined *a priori* but is created at the moment of invention; the construction of a work of art, therefore, was the equivalent to making moral choices in life.

Many of George Tooker's earliest works possess an overwhelming degree of alienation, dismay, and dehumanization, elements that serve as metonyms for larger existentialist ideas. This did not go unnoticed by the New York cultural impresario and friend of the artist, Lincoln Kirstein, who envisioned Tooker and a number of his contemporaries as descendants of Jan van Eyck (*circa* 1385–1441), Pietro Perugino (*circa* 1445–1524), Nicolas Poussin (1594–1665), and Jean-Antoine Watteau (1684–1721). These predecessors provided inspiration through their methods of painting, which assured them "of permanence as *statements of humane ideas*."[6] Struck by Tooker's *Subway* (1950; plate 15), Kirstein applauded the artist's efforts but voiced the hope that the tenor of his future work would change: "The disgust of your or rather, in your, picture is balanced by its pity or rather beauty. I hope your next picture will relax us from the anxious horror of half your vision. Simply because, since it's almost unbearable, I see no reason why one should attempt to bear it."[7] Interpreted by many as embodying the Zeitgeist of postwar America, Tooker's work has been burdened by an inequitable emphasis on its negative aspects. This essay will consider a greater breadth of the artist's work and chart his progression from a disconcerting visual language that was a larger reflection of cultural anxiety in the 1940s and 1950s to a more compassionate outlook on humanity in the 1960s.

### Anxious beginnings

In addition to being strongly personal statements for the artist, Tooker's earliest paintings, *Audience* (1945; see page 44), *Children and Spastics* (1946; plate 1), *Dance* (1946; plate 3), and *A Game of Chess* (1946–47; plate 5), are often cited as representative examples of the negative aspects of urban life. They incorporate gesture, narrative, and iconographical references to express notions of surveillance, intolerance, and the anxiety of conforming to a life conditioned by society.[8] One of the more powerful statements of man's physical and psychological disembodiment from society, however, is found in a small, albeit anomalous, work from this period. The diminutive painting *The Groping Hand* (*circa* 1947; fig. 1 and plate 7) depicts a man's hand palm-side up against a *trompe l'œil* background of wood paneling. The hand literally hangs in front of the panel, reminiscent of the American nineteenth-century still lifes of William Michael Harnett (1848–1892) and John Frederick Peto (1854–1907). The hanging format of the "object" serves to underscore its disengagement from the body, and, like Tooker's most widely known paintings, it can be read as a personal statement by the artist and a potent cultural signifier.

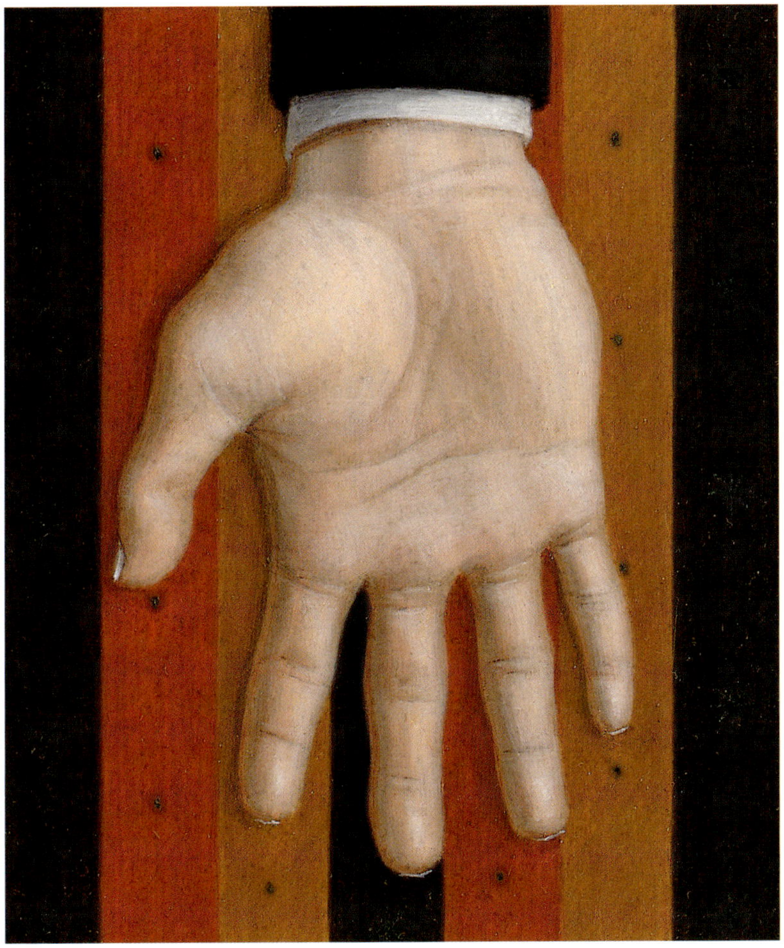

fig. 1
George Tooker
*The Groping Hand* (*circa* 1947)
Egg tempera on watercolor paper
3½ × 2¾ inches (8.9 × 7 cm)
Nicholas Miles Pentecost, Courtesy
DC Moore Gallery, New York



Tooker has acknowledged his anxiety over conforming to society's expectations during this early stage in his career.[9] *The Groping Hand* was completed around 1947, during a period when the burgeoning Cold War rhetoric, couched in such terms as "containment" and "freedom," stoked the fires of cultural anxiety. In this context, examination of the painting's iconography reveals a work rich with cultural associations.[10] The position of the hand, together with the title of the painting, indicates that it is reaching for something—just what, however, is unclear. The hand gropes not for a physical object but for a metaphorical one. During and after times of war, notions of disembodiment are frequent and often transgress disciplinary boundaries. Concurrent with this painting, W. H. Auden, one of Tooker's greatest influences, published *The Age of Anxiety: A Baroque Eclogue*, a narrative poem in which some of the imagery is eerily similar to *The Groping Hand*. Set in a bar during a time of war, the poem focuses on four displaced characters who are helplessly meandering through life. One of the characters, Quant, thinks of the soldiers:

> Their poor hands in a panic of need
> Groping weakly for a gun-butt or
> A friendly fist, as fetched off darkling.
> Many have perished; more will.[11]

In both the painting and the poem, the hand is part of a fragmented body. For existentialist thinkers, the body is essential for determining one's existence and, in a fragmented state, as Jacques Lacan has observed, "regularly manifests itself in dreams when the movement of analysis encounters a certain level of aggressive disintegration in the individual."[12] Corporeal fragmentation is underscored by a subtle allusion to the suggestion of a body. The depiction of the sleeve reveals not the uniform of a serviceman but rather that of an "officer" of contemporary society—a business suit. As a visual metaphor for the painful experience of man at the dawn of the Cold War, the disengaged imagery of *The Groping Hand* elicits an inherently emotional response from the viewer, embodying what art historian Barry Schwartz has identified as an existentialist humanism.[13]

*Bird Watchers* (plate 9) was completed in 1948 and is Tooker's most optimistic early painting. The artist acknowledged that it came about only after he had created a number of unpleasant paintings: "I decided it was high time to paint a pleasant picture about something positive. ... I painted pictures of my friends, my sister, my mother, friends of mine ... Paul Cadmus; just a congregation of my friends, people I cared about."[14] Scholars have noted that religious paintings of the Italian Quattrocento served as the precedent for the subject and the rounded format of *Bird Watchers*. Set in Central Park, with only a hint of the surrounding metropolis in the background, the painting depicts a group of bird watchers standing by a tree in front of a large rock formation. While the figures were based on specific friends and family, their faces were stylized to give them a universal appearance. The tree has been identified as a surrogate for the crucifix, similar to those found in early Renaissance paintings. Standing before it, posed in religiously suggestive ways, some figures cast their gaze upward, while others hold their hands in front of them in a gesture of penance. The foremost figure stands with his hands held out in a manner that suggests either submission before a greater presence or a display of the stigmata.[15] Through the iconography of gesture, the artist has painted "a religious picture without religious subject matter."[16]

Significant gesture has been critical to Tooker's paintings, and he used it in nearly all of his early works to illustrate a strong, often

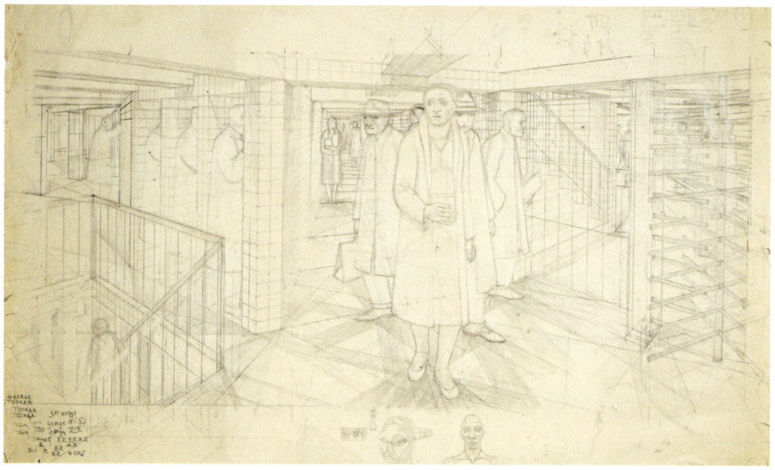

fig. 2
George Tooker
Study for *Subway* (1949)
Graphite on paper
24 × 39⅜ inches (61 × 100 cm)
Gift of the artist (PA 1936) in memory of his parents, George Clair and Angela Montejo Roura Tooker, Addison Gallery of American Art, Phillips Academy, Andover, Massachusetts



mysterious, sense of narrative. When asked about specific content in his paintings, Tooker generally demurs.[17] It is clear in *Bird Watchers*, however, that the picture's theme, whether religious or secular, is one of enlightenment and revelation. While in many early works the artist uses gesture to signify defensiveness, anxiety, or violence, *Bird Watchers* employs it to convey the possibility of awareness and spiritual transcendence. The painting weaves significant gesture, suggestive religiosity, and contemporary subject matter into a complex choreography of modern life, which can thus be understood as an oasis of hope amid the ocean of contemporary urban society.[18] In doing so, *Bird Watchers* is Tooker's earliest realization of a metaphysical humanism—an expression of hope and a lament, and the articulation of an attitude that strives for dignity, justice, beauty, and love.[19] The painting is a prescient indication of the artist's ongoing hopeful and optimistic understanding of humanity, and looks ahead to his work of the 1960s.

*Subway*, Tooker's best-known work, is the first of what would become known as his paintings of social concern, or "protest paintings." An intricate maze of white tiled passages populated by repeated figures who exhibit either obvious dread or callous indifference to the surrounding world, *Subway* is one of the artist's most vociferous statements about the dehumanization of contemporary urban society and the alienation of the individual. It brings to mind art historian Peter Selz's observation that "The revelations and complexities of mid-twentieth-century life have called forth a profound feeling of solitude and anxiety. The imagery of man which has evolved from this reveals sometimes a new dignity, sometimes despair, but always the uniqueness of man as he confronts his fate."[20]

*Subway* was composed using a complex perspective format with multiple vanishing points and orthogonals receding to the center, left, and right of the work. The artist considered the painting "a play of verticals—not so much perspective but the verticals. I think I thought more about rhythms across the canvas at that time."[21] Revealing just how complex these rhythms were, a highly realized preparatory study (fig. 2) illustrates the stage-like setting and the choreography of the figures, whose shadows are akin to the "blocking" of a theatrical production and seem to indicate their directional movements. Tooker has admitted that "at times I think of painting in terms of theater, in terms of putting on a performance."[22] Within this matrix of receding lines and repeated forms, however, the figures seem to shuffle along sluggishly, bearing the weight of the support overhead. The painting is divided into three sections: the center contains figures emerging from a passage; on the left, two figures descend into a darker lower level; while on the right, a slightly obscured set of stairs leads up to a brighter area, or perhaps even street level. Tooker envisioned an urban purgatory when he painted *Subway*: "I was thinking of a large modern city, as a kind of limbo. The subway seemed a good place to represent a denial of the senses and a negation of life itself. Its being underground with great weight overhead was important. I thought of the labyrinth of the Minotaur and the unreal perspectives of a Hall of Mirrors."[23]

Most of the figures seem to be plodding through their quotidian lives with mechanical regularity, but two figures belie this detachment. As an intangible and indefatigable resource, fear was one of the greatest weapons of the Cold War and was exploited by both sides. In addition to the general concern over the spread of Soviet ideology, the fear of being watched was a disconcerting reality as surveillance of private citizens increased exponentially in the 1950s.[24] These fears were popularized and perpetuated in such works as George Orwell's novel *1984*, published only one year before Tooker painted *Subway*, and in which the gaze portrayed is that of the state. In the painting, fear is registered most immediately on the faces of the foremost figure of the woman and a man who is peering out from a phone booth on the left. Use of the gaze operates on a number of levels in this painting. It not only serves to disclose fear on people's faces but also suggests that it is actually they who are being seen by some greater and fearful presence outside the picture.

The relationship between the stare of the subject and that of another seer (and its subsequent implications) was fundamental to Maurice Merleau-Ponty's influential essay *Phenomenology of Perception* (1945). David Mellor has noted that Merleau-Ponty identified the subtext of the look as constituting both body *and*

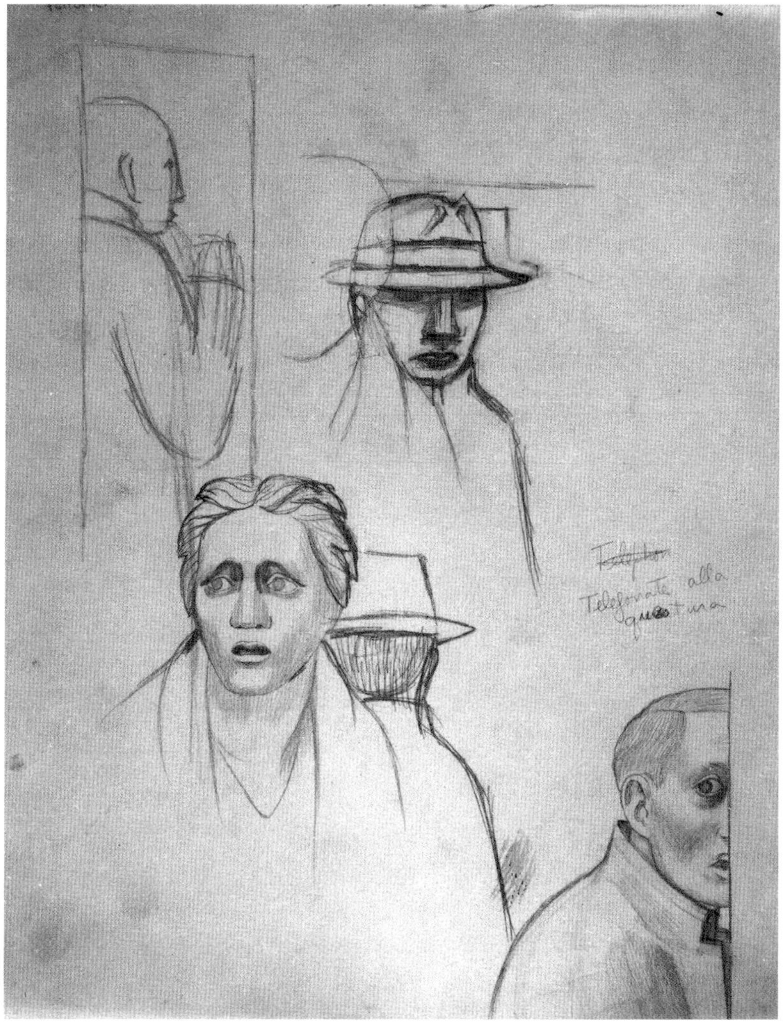


fig. 3
George Tooker
Preparatory study for *Subway* (1950)
Graphite on tracing paper
11 × 8½ inches (27.9 × 21.6 cm)
Location unknown
Image courtesy of the Robert Hill Fleming Museum, University of Vermont



presence, and that this relationship stands over art of the period.[25] The gaze is a critical aspect in Tooker's paintings of the 1950s, and in this instance it serves a phenomenological purpose that constitutes both the physical body of the fearful subjects and an unseen psychological presence of implicit watchers. While the painting has always been identified as displaying mid-century dystopian characteristics, such as paranoia and anxiety, the exact narrative of it, as with most of Tooker's work, is unclear. In addition to the highly realized study for the work, Tooker created a series of smaller studies. In the center right of one particularly revealing study (fig. 3), the artist has written in Italian "Telefonate alla questura" ("Calling police headquarters"). Providing a window into the conception of the painting, it is a study for the face of the man in the phone booth. His expression of alarm indicates that there is more than a mere lurking danger in this urban purgatory.[26] These two figures clearly are distraught and are the only ones in the painting who do not heed Auden's poetic admonition,

> Private faces in public places
> Are wiser and nicer
> Than public faces in private places.[27]

In the second half of the 1950s, Tooker painted *Government Bureau* (1956; plate 27) and *Waiting Room* (1957; plate 31), his most emphatic visual statements against bureaucratic power and the dismay of contemporary life. *Government Bureau* is based on the artist's experience at Brooklyn's Borough Hall during the period when he and his partner, William Christopher, were renovating their recently purchased Brooklyn home. The renovations required various city permits, necessitating a personal visit to Borough Hall. Art historian Thomas H. Garver has described this painting as "a document of anonymous processing, a dumbshow of conditioned response to Kafkaesque bureaucratic demands beyond either comprehension or control of the participants."[28] Composed within the matrix of an overarching grid format, the identical male and female figures appear multiple times, waiting in line before the windows of government officials. Pressed as the workers are into small cubicles, only their eyes, hands, and various ears are visible. Gesture is used in a potent way as each worker caresses his adding machine, denoting it as both a valuable instrument of the state and object of salacious adoration. The multiple eyes and ears indicate visual and aural surveillance of the room and represent a more explicit relationship between the seer and the seen than in *Subway*. The figures in line are repeated over and over, and their faces turn away from our view.

The dehumanizing elements in this painting operate on multiple levels. The workers are reduced to eyes, ears, and hands, disembodying their forms and effectively making them (like their adding machines) merely instruments of the state. Their purpose is to watch over and listen to the waiting citizens and, by association, the viewer of the painting. The citizens are anonymous and exhibit characteristics of automatons. Scholar Katherine Hauser has noted that the painting explicitly connects surveillance with the state and that it is the viewer who is being watched in the painting, not the figures in line.[29] In addition to this reading, however, the painting is about the negation of choice and suggests the destruction of individuality.

*Waiting Room* is a labyrinth of unending waiting stalls illuminated by cold overhead fluorescent lighting and populated by a disadvantaged cast. Painted only one year after *Government Bureau*, the painting, as Hauser has identified, denotes the next stage of some lugubrious narrative.[30] Instead of the repeated figures and emotionless setting of *Government Bureau*, *Waiting Room* reveals the futility of those who wait. Of Tooker's three protest paintings from the decade, this one is the most elusive. The repetition of the stalls and the inclusion of the destitute figures, some of whom seem to be suffering, suggest the environment of Sartre's play *No Exit* (1944), where hell is literally "other people." Surveillance is implied by the figure on the left with glasses but is not, as Hauser posits, the primary theme of the painting. Tooker has described the scene as a kind of purgatory, and the artist's notations on the preparatory drawing again provide a clue to the otherwise hermetic setting. In the center right of the study, he wrote, "Throwing life away for something imagined," suggesting that these characters have chosen to forgo engaging in reality for the hope of a better one. In the center left is a curious notation: "Touch, Taste, Sight, Hearing, Smell." This could indicate either that the picture functions as an allegory of the senses, or that it is these senses on which the characters rely to perceive this strange and dolorous reality.

**Picturing a new awareness**

Two years after painting the dismal reality of a waiting room, Tooker created *Sleepers II* (1959; plate 33), one of his most fantastical works to date. The painting signals a change in direction and attitude for the artist, toward themes of a more overtly humanistic nature. Removed from the familiar setting of everyday life, *Sleepers II* depicts seven heads protruding from a billowing white, cloud-like landscape. This painting is in part a continuation of the artist's interest in the theme of sleep.[31] In the work, Tooker eliminates all trace of a natural landscape and depicts the figures with their eyes staring intently upward, in a transcendent state of being. The theme of spiritual transcendence had been alluded to by the artist in such early works as *Bird Watchers*, but it is now fully realized in *Sleepers II*. Similar transcendental imagery is conjured up in Auden's *Age of Anxiety*, a possible precedent:

> So it was now as they sought that state of prehistoric happiness which, by human beings, can only be imagined in terms of a landscape bearing a symbolic resemblance to the human body. The more completely these four forgot their surroundings and lost their sense of time, the more sensitively aware of each other they became, until they achieved in their dream that rare community which is otherwise only attained in the states of extreme wakefulness.[32]

The "rare community" to which Auden refers is a metaphor for the Jungian notion of the "collective unconscious," or a reservoir of experiences shared among all humanity. Scholars Jeffrey Wechsler and Greta Berman astutely noted that *Sleepers II* "is as close to a visual expression of the term 'collective unconscious' as one is likely to find."[33] The figures in this painting, in contrast to those in *Subway*, *Government Bureau*, and *Waiting Room*, who simply go through the motions of their seemingly pointless existences, exhibit an enlightened state of awareness that surpasses the physical realm to exist on a purely spiritual level. Indeed, the painting shares a startling kinship with Carl Jung's observation that "even in this unconscious social condition there are not a few who are called awake by the summons of the voice, whereupon they are at once set apart from the others, feeling themselves confronted with a problem about which the others know nothing."[34]

The iconography of *Sleepers II* can be interpreted in a host of ways. As a possible visual representation of the seven virtues of Chastity, Temperance, Charity, Diligence, Patience, Kindness, and Humility, it could be interpreted as a counterpart to the seven deadly sins, which were depicted in a well-known series of works by Tooker's close friend Paul Cadmus only ten years earlier. However, by the artist's own admission, the painting is most strongly linked to the religious and mythological iconography of the Christian myth of the Seven Sleepers of Ephesus.[35] This is the tale of seven Christians who retreat to a cave in order to avoid persecution by the Roman emperor. They sleep hundreds of years and awake to a new Christian Roman society, believing they have slept only one day.[36] In its depiction of communal harmony and enlightenment, the painting looks forward to Tooker's work of the succeeding decade.

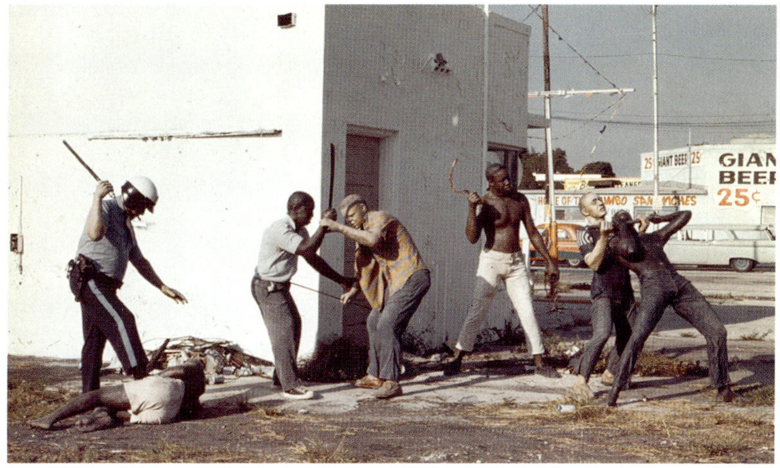


fig. 4
Duane Hanson (1925–1996)
*Race Riot* (1968)
Mixed media
74 × 240 × 144 inches
(188 × 609.6 × 365.6 cm)
© Estate of Duane Hanson/
licensed by VAGA, New York, NY



In the early 1960s, Tooker more frequently embraced universal themes of tranquility and hopeful remedies of social injustices. This trend continued in his works of the 1970s and 1980s.[37] In 1960, the artist moved from New York City to the Vermont countryside and soon became involved in the civil rights movement, which inspired two of his most poignant paintings of the decade. Themes of racial injustice, inequality, and racial harmony were not new to Tooker. He had dealt with these issues in the early 1950s, starting with *Laundress* (1952) and the *Window* series (begun in 1955), which comprises nine variations of figures in a window, and grew out of his admiration for the interracial couples he observed in his Brooklyn neighborhood.[38] Art historian Kymberly N. Pinder has noted that until the mid-twentieth century the historical depiction of mixed-race people in America had been based on the notion of the "tragic mulatto."[39] For Tooker, however, as the descendant of a Cuban Creole family, and one who has always identified with multiracial heritage, these subjects had a deeply personal resonance. On one occasion, when he was asked if some of the African American figures in his paintings were meant to be part white, Tooker responded: "Yes, none of us are pure."[40]

*Supper* (1963; plate 37) and *Lunch* (1964; plate 41) were created as specific responses to segregation and can be understood as visual equivalents to the peaceful demonstrations that took place during the civil rights movement. Both were the result of reactions the artist had to segregated lunch counters. Four college freshmen captured national attention in 1960 by refusing to remove themselves from a Woolworth lunch counter in Greensboro, North Carolina. The protest quickly gained momentum throughout the South and ultimately touched off a national movement.[41] Edward B. King, Jr., administrative secretary of the Student Nonviolent Coordinating Committee, noted, "We once again will dedicate ourselves to purge this country of the rabies of racism. ... Only forthright action can square America's racial practices with the world's changing order of democracy and human rights."[42] Inspired by the message preached by Dr. Martin Luther King, Jr., the artist conceived these works with basic human rights and tolerance at their core. *Supper* features an African American man with one hand on a loaf of bread and the other raised in a gesture of reverence. He is flanked by two men, who resemble Tooker and his partner, William Christopher. The painting is a symbol of universal equality and alludes to the biblical story of the supper at Emmaus.

A similar approach to the issue of equality, this time in a secular context, is taken by Tooker in *Lunch*. Seated among tables too narrow to accommodate them comfortably, the diners are alienated from one another in the shallow space of the lunch room. They are psychologically segregated, as each eats in isolation. A figure seen from behind is repeated along the wall, underscoring the architectural elements and suggesting a recession of space *ad infinitum*. The figure at the far right is depicted in profile, drinking coffee and turning away from the others, so that he stands in complete disengagement. The environment is impersonal, and there is no interaction between people. A central figure, the sole African American in the composition, has downcast eyes like the other figures, but his face is the only one that is not obscured. In an interview with WNYC Radio in 1967, Tooker cited Langston Hughes's poem of realizing racial equality "I, Too, Sing America" as analogous in spirit to much of his work. This poem is particularly relevant to *Supper* and *Lunch*.[43]

While so many of the artist's paintings of the 1950s explore themes of alienation and discord, many of those from the succeeding decade, including the *Window* series and *Supper*, are about concord. "In one kind of painting I'm trying to say 'this is what we are forced to suffer,' while in other paintings I say, 'this is what we should be.'"[44] Many artists in the 1960s addressed themes of segregation, inequality, and racism, but unlike Tooker, they often did so by explicitly illustrating specific actions or events. Among the most powerful examples is Duane Hanson's *Race Riot* (1968; fig. 4). Tooker and Hanson (1925–1996) were close contemporaries, and both artists frequently illustrate themes of human interaction and isolation in contemporary society. Hanson's interpretation of the intolerance of African Americans is literal and brutal, and he depicts them being violently beaten by police officers. Tooker, on the other hand, approaches intolerance with a psychological and visual subtlety that necessitates further reflection.[45] Instead of relying on the forcefulness of the narrative to elicit an emotional response, his images are inherently

fig. 5
George Tooker
*Tree* (1965)
Egg tempera on gesso panel
22 × 22 inches (55.9 × 55.9 cm)
Reis Private Collection



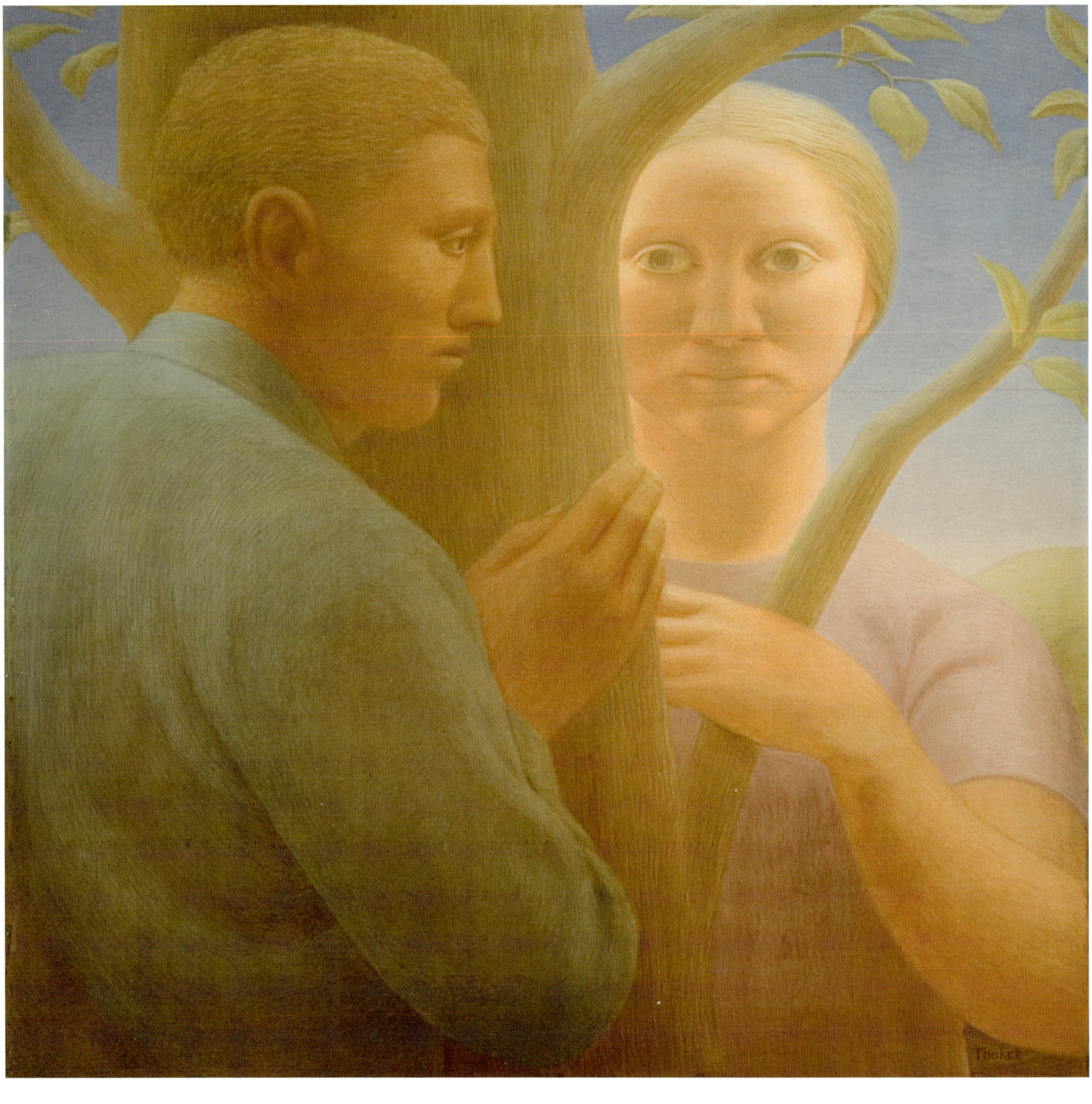

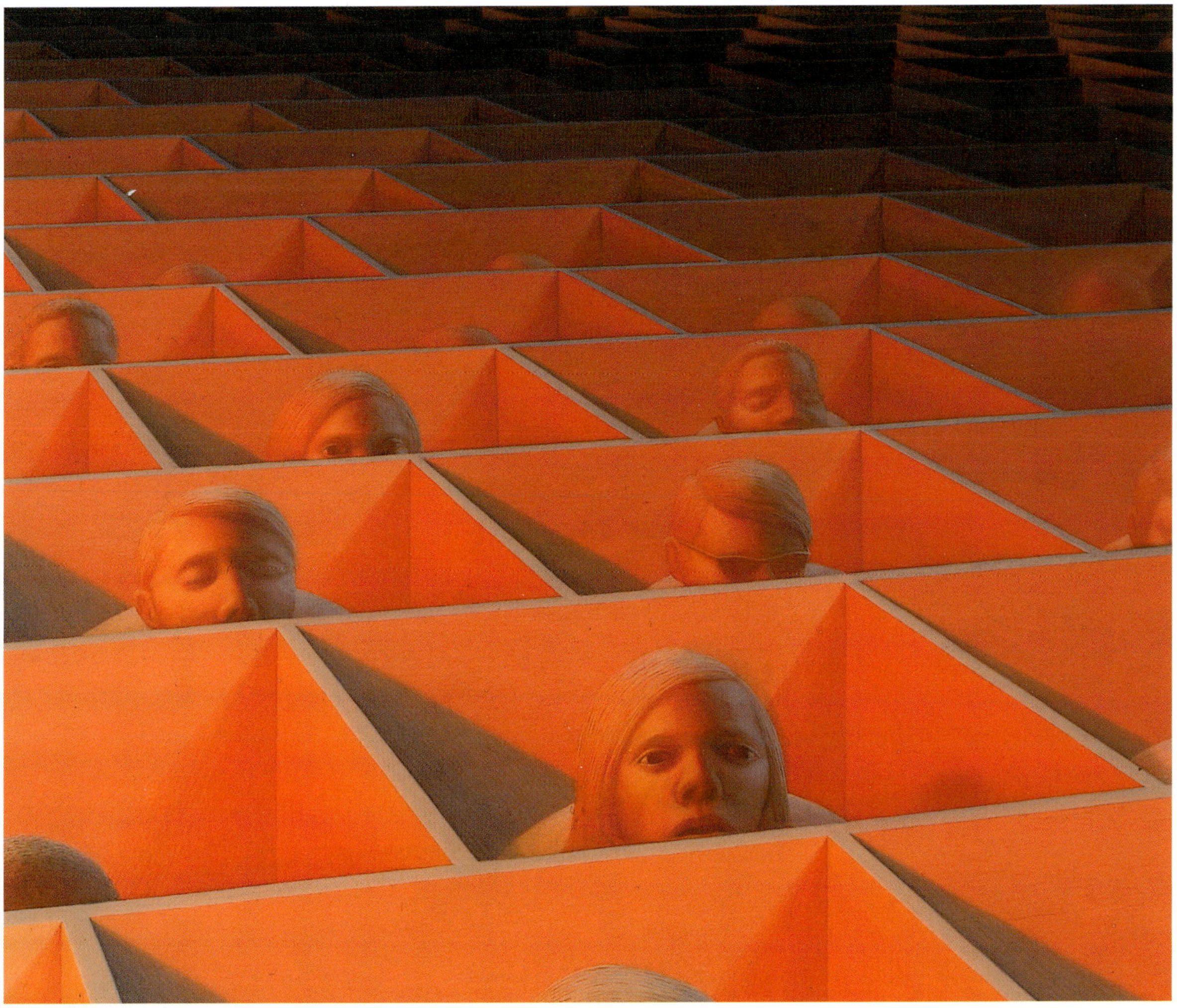

fig. 6
George Tooker
*Landscape with Figures* (1965–66)
Egg tempera on gesso panel
26 × 30 inches (66 × 76.2 cm)
Barbara B. Millhouse



sentient and communicate *sotto voce* the attainable possibility of tolerance and understanding. In contrast to his early works, which often portray a diminished man in society, Tooker's works from the 1960s encourage contemplative reflection and exhibit the metaphysical humanism that first appeared in *Bird Watchers*.[46]

While this awareness had always been manifest in the artist's work, it was in Selma, Alabama, that he "learned the meaning of the Greek word *agape*."[47] References to religion and the notion of *agape*, a universal love of humankind that corresponds to a love of God, also appear in other paintings of the 1960s, such as *Tree* (1965; fig. 5). *Tree* has been linked with Tooker's *Lovers* series (plate 34), which depicts the tender and passionate embrace of a couple. According to Garver, however, *Tree* "shows a different and more ordered aspect of love. The timeless embrace, the desire to be together *always* is replaced by a couple whose relationship to one another is more visual than visceral."[48] I would suggest that in *Tree*, the relationship between the male and female figures, undoubtedly linked to the theme of love, is much more than the visual relationship Garver suggests. All of the elements of the painting, the two figures and the tree, are drawn close to the foreground. The man is in front of the tree in profile, while the woman is behind it, facing the viewer. The man seems to move around the tree toward the woman, but there is no physical contact between them. The potential contact, both physical and psychological, has been held in abeyance and is merely suggested by the overlapping areas of the hands near the center of the painting. *Tree*, like *Bird Watchers*, is a religious painting set in a secular context and suggests Adam and Eve beside the Tree of Life. However, as opposed to rendering the tale of Original Sin, it is a more universal image of hope and optimism for a world of what *might* be possible. The painting lacks the intense visceral qualities identified by Garver in the *Lovers* series and instead exhibits an idyllic tranquility—a hopeful optimism couched in the language of a subtle Edenic paradise.[49]

*Landscape with Figures* (1965–66; fig. 6 and plate 42) is one of Tooker's most powerful statements of the decade, if not of his entire career. Seated within a matrix of cubicles that appear to stretch to infinity are dozens of figures, some of whom look up from their confinement, while others have their eyes closed or keep their heads lowered. Light streams in from the left and right, creating opposing shadows on the backs of cubicles. It is a discomfiting image of confinement and endless repetition. The "landscape" is metaphorical and expresses the artist's feelings toward what he sees as a dystopian society, in which individualism is suppressed and conformity is obligatory. The artist himself stated in *Time* that the painting was his "way of protesting the situation kids are in now. I feel sorry for them with the draft [for the Vietnam War], the pressures to conform."[50] The

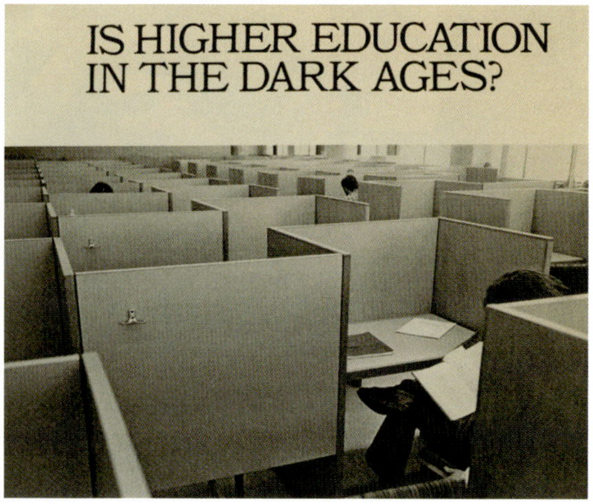


fig. 7
Robert A. Isaacs
"Is Higher Education in the Dark Ages?"
*New York Times Magazine*, November 6, 1983



loss of uniqueness is a principal theme in dystopian literature and art, and as noted by art historian Valerie J. Fletcher, it is often conveyed using the imagery of the "square, the cube, [and] the straight line … [representing] the absolute order imposed by the all-powerful government."[51] A comparable representation of the suppression of individuality for the sake of the larger community is voiced by Auden in his poem "The Unknown Citizen: To JS/07/M/378":

> He was found by the Bureau of Statistics to be
> One against whom there was no official complaint,
> And all the reports on his conduct agree
> That, in the modern sense of an old-fashioned word, he was a saint,
> For in everything he did he served the Greater Community.[52]

The figures in Tooker's cubicles have relinquished their autonomy in order to serve the "Greater Community." The painting specifically relates to the artist's distaste for the military–industrial complex, and when asked by an advertising agency for permission to use the image in an advertising campaign for a steel company, Tooker's response was one of flat denial: "I cannot give my permission for the use of *Landscape with Figures* for any steel company since the subject of the picture is the victimization of our youth by the military–industrial complex and its servant, advertising."[53]

Art historian Ralph Pomeroy has linked *Landscape with Figures* to "isolation wards, [and] solitary confinement—even those 'learning laboratories' wherein each student studies, glassed-off from others, communicating with the instructor only through microphones, earphones and tape recorders."[54] Similarities between the painting and the educational facilities predicted at the time for the future, notably the "learning cubicles" first seen at the World's Fair in 1964, have also been previously identified.[55] Furthermore, similar sentiments of discontent and disaffection over the state of higher education were voiced in 1983 by journalist and political scientist Arnold Beichman, who described the loss of individualism and the conformity manifested in America's colleges and universities as a general reflection of the post-revolutionary years of the 1970s (fig. 7). Beichman viewed this as a systemic, self-perpetuating problem and one that had no apparent solution: "the American university has become an arm of the government to enforce governmental or judicial decrees; that is, when faculty-student cabals aren't enforcing their own decrees by barring 'controversial' speakers and subjects from a once-free campus."[56] Tooker's painting is the visual equivalent of a self-perpetuating system from which there appears to be no escape. The ideological similarities between Beichman's argument and those embedded in *Landscape with Figures* imbue the work with a deep cultural resonance.

There is a striking visual similarity between *Landscape with Figures* and a scene in Jacques Tati's film *Playtime* (1967; fig. 8). These two takes on man's condition within a technological society represent, however, two very different responses. Tooker's painting is a biting critique of the dehumanization of modern society. Tati's film is a more humorous and convivial look at the banality of modern life through the eyes of the main character, the bumbling but affable Monsieur Hulot. Hulot is lost within the immensity of a modern office building and has a bird's-eye view over the workers' cubicles, within which people proceed with mechanical regularity and efficiency. In each row, the figures sit in a similar manner, underscoring their conformity and lack of individuality.

In 1970, Tooker began *Ward* (plate 45), perhaps the most overtly political painting of his career. Depicting the interior of a hospital ward, the artist employs a multiple-point perspective to create a dramatic diagonal recession into space. We immediately notice the *horror vacui* of the room. Four figures are seated in different areas of the room and appear to look off in opposite directions. The monochromaticism of the hospital linen suggests a sterile environment punctuated by the repeated forms of the bed frames, the heads of the patients, and the visible portions of the flags hanging on the wall. The conscious patients are unaware of one another, while the bedridden ones seem to be either unconscious or perhaps dead. The repetition of the headboards in close succession serves to suggest the tombstones of a military graveyard. Garver has identified the painting as addressing the maltreatment of the aged and the wounded,

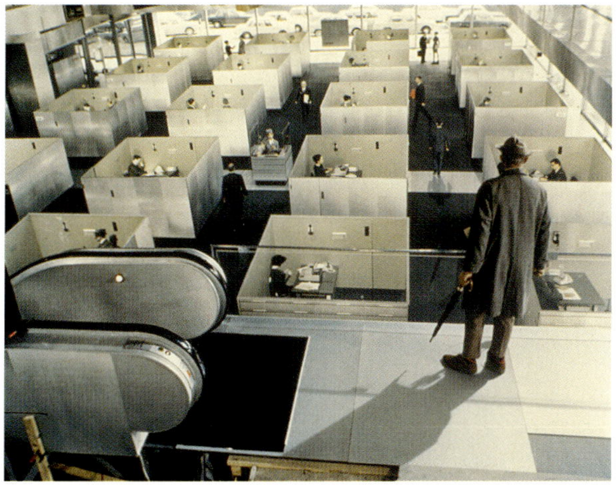

fig. 8
Jacques Tati
Still from the film *Playtime* (1967)
Still courtesy of Janus Films



and he acknowledges that, despite its more universal message, it may be read purely as a polemic against war.[57]

Executed at the height of the Vietnam War, and four years after Tooker completed the potent *Landscape with Figures*, *Ward* is an equally strident "protest" painting. In typical Tooker fashion, the overall composition is relegated to the matrix of a grid structure, and there are numerous repeated forms. The scene does not relate to any specific event of the war but instead serves as a general reflection on the contemporary situation. The artist noted: "I was striking out in a number of directions, and it was intended to shock and jolt people, not depress them."[58] *Ward* is a complex painting, and the artist completed a series of preparatory drawings before undertaking the final work.[59] Two flags are partially obscured by a hanging curtain in such a way that they appear as two parts of a divided single flag. The drawn curtain bisecting the flag implies a lifeless patient and is thus a metaphor for a divided and perhaps deceased American society. Thus, Tooker uses the American flag, a politically charged icon during the war, as an allusion to war's outcome.

The seated figures look off in opposite directions, completely isolated from one another. Despite the company of other people, they are detached and disoriented, conveying the confounding effects of war. Early in the twentieth century, Sigmund Freud recognized the effect that war has on the citizenry of the nation involved. In "Thoughts for the Times on War and Death" (1915), he remarked, "The individual who is not himself a combatant—and so is a cog in the gigantic machine of war—feels bewildered in his orientation, and inhibited in his powers and activities."[60] The bewilderment of the patients is clear, and the inhibitions are manifested in their helplessness. *Ward* is a somber reminder of the physically and psychologically devastating effects of war.

George Tooker is an artist whose primary concern is the effective communication of the human condition. He offers an art that is not only revealing in its outlook on humanity but that also offers hopeful commentaries of reconciliation, understanding, and enlightenment. His is an "art which in its *content* sheds important critical insights on such broad concerns as society and its institutions and ethics, and perhaps even more broadly on the human experience and condition."[61] This essay has examined only a few of the artist's paintings during the first thirty years or so of his career. It has charted a course, however, that begins with work that deals with the very nature of man's existence in a technological world, and its resultant anxieties, and reaches an era of images filled with compassion, tolerance, and understanding. As the cultural landscape of America shifted from international issues of ideological concern in the 1940s and 1950s to more domestic problems of civil rights and divided support for a foreign war, so too did Tooker's work shift. In the 1960s, the artist turned his attention away from the angst-ridden works of the early years toward themes of compassion, equality, and tolerance—progressing from anxiety to *agape*.

## Notes

1 George Tooker, Artist Questionnaire, January 30, 1951, Whitney Museum of American Art, New York.

2 Richard Eitlen has identified this marginalization in his exhaustive study *In Defense of Humanism: Value in the Arts and Letters* (Cambridge: Cambridge University Press, 1996), xiii and *passim*.

3 "A Prefatory Note by Paul Tillich," in Peter Selz, *New Images of Man*, exhib. cat. (New York: The Museum of Modern Art, 1959), 9. See also Paul Moscanyi, *The Humanist Tradition in Contemporary Painting*, exhib. cat. (New York: New School Art Center, 1968), 4.

4 René Descartes, *Discourse on Method*, trans. and ed. Lawrence J. Lafleur (New York and London: Macmillan, 1956), 1 and *passim*.

5 Jean-Paul Sartre, "Existentialism and Humanism," *Art in Theory, 1900–1990: An Anthology of Changing Ideas*, ed. Charles Harrison and Paul Wood (Oxford and Cambridge, Massachusetts: Blackwell Publishers, 1992), 588.

6 Lincoln Kirstein, "The State of Modern Painting," *Harper's Magazine*, 197:118 (October 1948): 47–53. Emphasis mine.

7 Lincoln Kirstein, letter to George Tooker, September 20, 1950, George Tooker Papers, Archives of American Art, Smithsonian Institution, Washington, D.C.

8 Susan Jane Baker, "George Tooker and the Modern Tradition," PhD diss., University of Kansas, 1994, 22. See also Katherine Hauser, "George Tooker, Surveillance, and Cold

War Sexual Politics," *GLQ*, 11:3 (June 2005), 392. While most scholars have identified the anxiety found in Tooker's work as a general reflection of the Zeitgeist of postwar America, Hauser links it to a much more specific source. "The anxiety we see in Tooker's images is not generic but is the product of a keen vigilance about politics and sexuality, manifested partly as an emphasis on the power of scrutiny, which serves as a metonym for state surveillance and pressure to conform." Hauser, 392.

9 Thomas H. Garver, *George Tooker*, rev. edn. (San Francisco, Pomegranate, 2002), 16.

10 An alternative title for this painting is *Helping Hand*. This would indeed drastically change my reading of it. It was listed under this title in Lincoln Kirstein and Jerry L. Thompson, *Quarry: A Collection in Lieu of Memoirs* (Pasadena, California: Twelvetrees Press, 1986). For this essay, I have chosen to rely on Garver, *George Tooker* for titles and dates of works. It is interesting to consider how this alternative title could affect the interpretation of the painting from "negative" to "positive" in the light of this essay. Paul Cadmus recalled that the title of the painting was a reference to Lincoln Kirstein's wandering hand when he was in the company of other men. (Telephone conversation with Ed de Luca, May 15, 2008.)

11 W. H. Auden, *The Age of Anxiety: A Baroque Eclogue* (New York: Random House, 1946), 14. Auden's influence on Tooker is well documented. See Justin Spring, "An Interview with George Tooker," *American Art*, 16:1 (spring 2002), 68. See also Garver, *George Tooker*, 27 and *passim*.

12 Jacques Lacan, "The Mirror-Phase as Formative of the Function of the I," in *Art in Theory, 1900–1990*, ed. Harrison and Wood, 612.

13 Barry Schwartz, *The New Humanism: Art in a Time of Change* (New York: Praeger Publishers, 1974), 61–62. Schwartz identifies four specific types of humanism in contemporary art: metaphysical humanism, existential humanism, political humanism, and humanistic portraiture. Tooker's works relate to each of these designations.

14 Quoted in Gregory M. Hollister-Knepp, "The Sacred and the Profane: Christian and Mythological Imagery within the Œuvre of George Tooker," MA diss., Bloomsburg University, Pennsylvania, 1997, Appendix A: Interview with George Tooker, April 21, 1997.

15 Baker, "George Tooker and the Modern Tradition," 33. Baker has linked the image to Giovanni Bellini's *St. Francis in Ecstasy* (*circa* 1480).

16 Tooker is quoted in Garver, *George Tooker*, 20.

17 Thomas H. Garver, interview with George Tooker, September 11, 1973, Archives of American Art, Smithsonian Institution, Washington, D.C. Tooker has indicated that the explanation of a painter's method of communicating should be solely in visual terms and that the explication of a painting may eliminate the necessity of putting it in visual terms.

18 Gesture played an important role in Tooker's compositions throughout his life. See Alvin H. Reese and Henry Crapo, interview with William Christopher and George Tooker, 1968, New York Public Library, Performing Arts–Dance Division.

19 Schwartz, *The New Humanism*, 38.

20 Selz, *New Images of Man*, 11.

21 Spring, "An Interview with George Tooker," 70.

22 Garver, interview with George Tooker, September 11, 1973.

23 "Artist Statement," Whitney Museum of American Art, 1950.

24 Stephen J. Whitfield, *The Culture of the Cold War* (Baltimore and London: The Johns Hopkins University Press, 1991), 101–26. In 1946, Albert Camus characterized the twentieth century as the century of fear. Albert Camus, "The Century of Fear," in *Between Hell and Reason: Essays from the Resistance Combat, 1944–1947* (Hanover, New Hampshire: Wesleyan University Press; Middletown, Connecticut: University Press of New England, 1991), 117–19. Also Hauser, "George Tooker, Surveillance, and Cold War Sexual Politics," 409 and *passim*. Hauser links the notion of surveillance in Tooker's works to his sexual orientation and the surveillance and persecution of homosexuals during the 1950s. See also Nancy Jachec, *The Philosophy and Politics of Abstract Expressionism, 1940–1960* (Cambridge: Cambridge University Press, 2000), 5.

25 David Mellor, *Paris Post War: Art and Existentialism, 1945–55*, exhib. cat. (London: Tate Gallery, 1993), 59. Merleau-Ponty posited that one experiences the world empirically and that from that experience one's essence is created. This is opposed to the Cartesian notion that one experiences the world through cognition: *cogito ergo sum*. Maurice Merleau-Ponty, *Phenomenonology of Perception*, trans. by Colin Smith (London: Routledge & Kegan Paul, 1967).

26 Ildiko Heffernan, *George Tooker: Working Drawings*, exhib. cat. (Burlington, Vermont: Robert Hull Fleming Museum, University of Vermont, 1987), 13.

27 W. H. Auden, *Collected Shorter Poems, 1927–1957* (New York: Random House, 1966), 43.

28 Garver, *George Tooker*, 30.

29 Hauser, "George Tooker, Surveillance, and Cold War Sexual Politics," 420.

30 *Ibid.*, 417.

31 Tooker completed *Sleepers I*—a tribute to his recently deceased father and inspired by Matthew Arnold's poem "Dover Beach"— in 1951. See Garver, *George Tooker*, 90.

32 Auden, *Age of Anxiety*, 57.

33 Jeffrey Weschler and Greta Berman, *Realism and Realities: The Other Side of American Painting, 1940–1960*, exhib. cat. (Rutgers University Art Gallery, New Brunswick, New Jersey, 1982), 86. See also Baker, "George Tooker and the Modern Tradition," 87.

34 C.G. Jung, *Collected Works*, ed. Herbert Read, Michael Fordham, Gerhard Adler; trans. R.F.C. Hull, Bollingen Series, vol. 20 (New York: Bollingen Foundation and Princeton, New Jersey: Princeton University Press, 1964), 176.

35 Heidi D. Shafranek, "The World of George Tooker: Surreal or Real," MA diss., University of Delaware, 1982, 29, note 72.

36 William Rose Benét, *The Reader's Encyclopedia,* 2nd edn (New York: Thomas Y. Crowell Company, 1965), 918.

37 Shafranek notes this shift beginning in the 1970s, but it clearly begins in the previous decade. Shafranek, "The World of George Tooker," 55.

38 Baker, "George Tooker and the Modern Tradition," 133.

39 Kymberly N. Pinder, "Biraciality and Nationhood in Contemporary American Art," in *Race-ing Art History: Critical Readings in Race and Art History*, ed. Kymberly N. Pinder (New York and London: Routledge, 2002), 393. Pinder identifies recent figures who have broken that stereotype as signifiers of a future racial harmony. Unfortunately, Tooker's work is overlooked in this study.

40 "Contemporary Florentine," *Time,* 89 (April 21, 1967), 72.

41 Miles Wolff, *Lunch at the Five and Ten: The Greensboro Sit-ins, A Contemporary History* (New York: Stein and Day, 1970). See also "Negroes' Sitdown Hits 2 More Cities," *New York Times* (February 19, 1960), 16.

42 Quoted in Claude Sitton, "Sit-in Campaigns Spread in a Year," *New York Times* (January 29, 1961), 64.

43 Arnold Rampersa (ed.), *The Collected Poems of Langston Hughes* (New York: Alfred A. Knopf, 2004), 46.

44 Quoted in Michael Culver, *Reality and Dream: The Art of George Tooker* (Ogunquit, Maine: Ogunquit Museum of American Art, 1996), n.p.

45 *Race Riot* reflects Hanson's early tendency toward depicting figures frozen in action. Soon after, he abandoned these types of scenes in favor of figures at rest or still. Kirk Varnedoe, *Duane Hanson* (New York: Harry N. Abrams, 1985), 20.

46 Schwartz, *The New Humanism*, 38 and *passim*.

47 Ralph Pomeroy, "George Tooker, Really," *Art and Artists* (1967), 27.

48 Garver, *George Tooker*, 113.

49 The painting's iconography can be traced to the artist's student days. While Tooker was at Harvard University, he enrolled in only one art history course, a Florentine sculpture class with the Renaissance sculpture professor Chandler Rathfon Post. Illustrated in Post's seminal study *A History of European and American Sculpture from the Early Christian Period to the Present Day* is Jacopo della Quercia's *Sin of Adam and Eve* from the portal of San Petronio Cathedral, Bologna, Italy. While Jacopo's relief did not serve as a direct model for *Tree*, Tooker would have undoubtedly known of it through Post's class, and it may have inspired him to pursue the subject independently. Despite the absence of the snake and apple, *Tree* is reminiscent of Jacopo's relief in theme and through Tooker's inherently sculptural figures. See Chandler Rathfon Post, *A History of European and American Sculpture from the Early Christian Period to the Present Day* (Cambridge, Massachusetts: Harvard University Press, 1921), fig. 79, n.p.

50 "Contemporary Florentine," 72.

51 Valerie J. Fletcher, *Dreams and Nightmares: Utopian Visions in Modern Art*, exhib. cat. (Hirshhorn Museum and Sculpture Garden, Washington, D.C., 1983), 136.

52 Auden, *Collected Shorter Poems, 1927–1957*, 146.

53 Quoted in Garver, *George Tooker*, 35. Also, George Tooker draft correspondence of a reply to a request from an advertising firm, George Tooker Papers, Archives of American Art, reel 678.

54 Ralph Pomeroy, "A Master of Modern Dismay," *New Lugano Review,* 8–9 (1976), 38.

55 Garver, interview with George Tooker, September 11, 1973.

56 Arnold Beichman, "Is Higher Education in the Dark Ages?" *New York Times Magazine* (November 6, 1983), 46.

57 Garver, *George Tooker*, 43.

58 *Ibid.*

59 The preparatory drawings for *Ward* are in the collection of the Addison Gallery of American Art, accession numbers 1996.80.162–1996.80.174.

60 Sigmund Freud, "Thoughts for the Times on War and Death," in *The Standard Edition of the Complete Psychological Works of Sigmund Freud*, trans. and ed. James Strachey, Vol. XIV (London: The Hogarth Press and The Institute of Psychoanalysis, 1957), 275.

61 Paul von Blum, *The Art of Social Conscience* (New York: Universe Books, 1976), 2.

# Framing imagery: at the intersection of geometry and the social

Anna C. Chave

**"An oyster makes a pearl around an irritant inside a shell, and I think that [my] pictures come frequently from irritants. I hope they're pearls, I don't know."**

George Tooker interview with Grace George Alexander and George Kay, WNYC Radio transcript, 1967

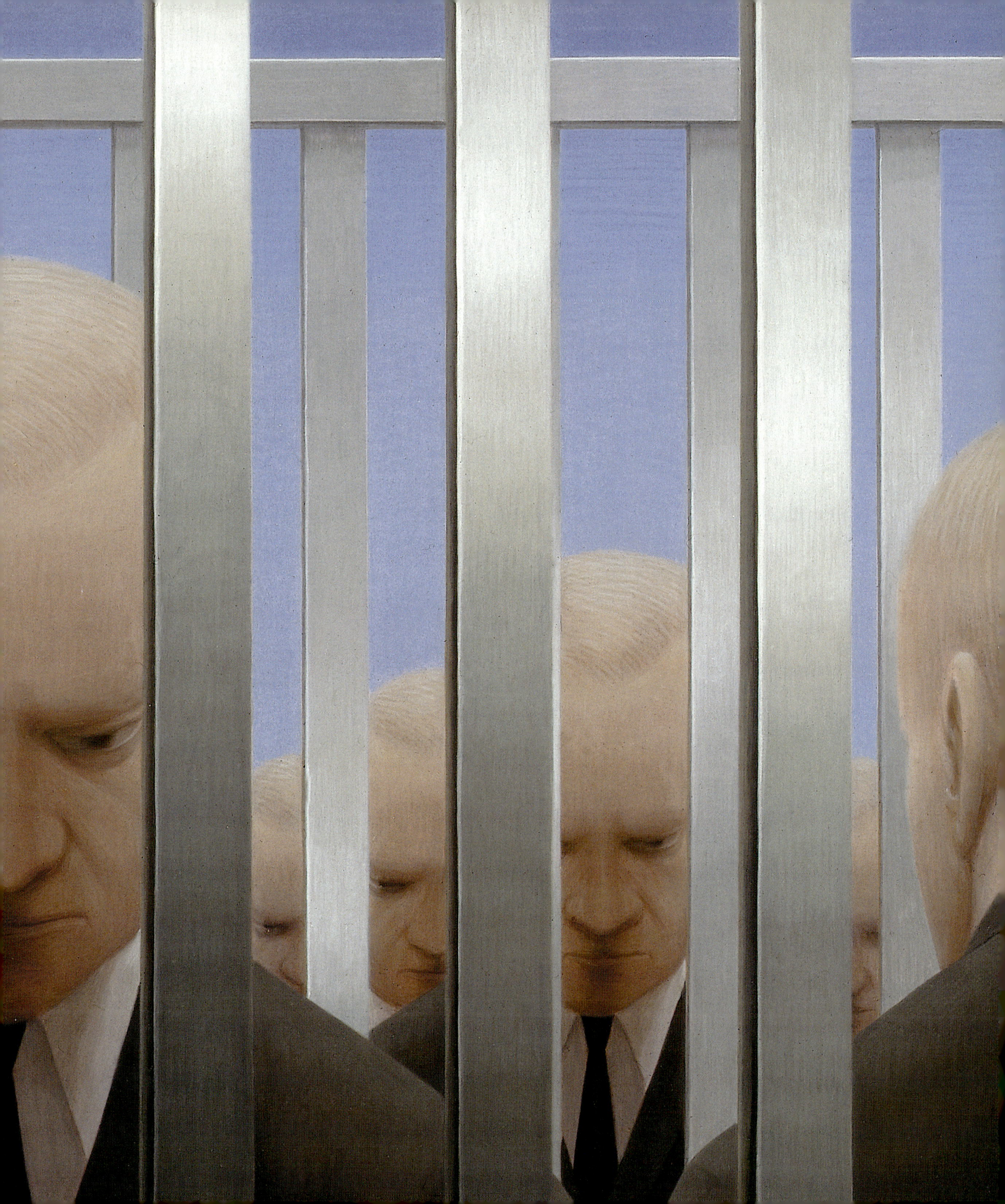

Previous page
George Tooker
***Teller*** (1967) (detail)
Private Collection, courtesy of EKG Art Advisory, New York
(see page 149)



In his haunting "paintings of protest"[1]—such as *Subway* (1950; plate 15), *Government Bureau* (1956; plate 27), *Waiting Room* (1957; plate 31), and *Landscape with Figures* (1965–66; plate 42)—George Tooker conjured the oppressive "social machine"[2] of the modern metropolis, depicting lonely crowds of lookalike drones (and, at times, their sinister overseers) isolated in the closet- or cell-like spaces that proliferate in the ubiquitous architectural grid of urban officialdom. Certain of these images would be sought after as illustrations for sociology and psychology textbooks (even more so than for art publications), following an era when David Riesman's *The Lonely Crowd* (1950) and William H. Whyte's *The Organization Man* (1956) counted as linchpins of sociological study. Over the course of the 1960s and 1970s, Tooker assented to such uses for his protest paintings, while typically instructing that the fees owed him in return be paid directly to the National Association for the Advancement of Colored People (NAACP), whose (all-white) Dartmouth, New Hampshire, chapter counted him as a member.[3] Let us begin, then, with the topic of George Tooker's politics; for here we have the oddball case of a man who emerged from no lesser bastions of élitism than Phillips Academy Andover and Harvard University (BA 1942) as an ally of the oppressed.

As a gay man born in 1920, Tooker might have claimed to belong to the ranks of the oppressed, of course, especially during the persecutory McCarthy era, when his homosexuality, in tandem with his youthful Communist Party ties, placed the artist in double jeopardy. (Even while in college, Tooker suffered a beating at the hands of thugs for distributing Communist literature.[4]) But Tooker understandably saw to his own survival by largely "passing" within mainstream society for a straight white man (that prototypically privileged being), and he left it to a succeeding generation of gay activists to pioneer the struggle against homophobic bias, while pursuing instead the prior civil rights struggle surrounding racial bias. At a moment when segregated Southern lunch counters were being occupied by African American activists, often with violent consequences, Tooker's *Lunch* (1964; plate 41) depicted a black man in business attire quietly devouring a sandwich while closely surrounded by some ten, similarly attired, impassive white diners in what is (pointedly) a non-event for all. And if the black man is notably isolated by his race in this image, his white dining companions nonetheless project an almost comparable sense of isolation. The aim of vanquishing prejudice-driven exclusion and of an equal seat at the table for all would emerge also as the theme of a Langston Hughes poem, "I, Too, Sing America," which Tooker took the time to read when interviewed by WNYC Radio in 1967, characterizing the verses as articulating a "wonderful philosophy" that "relates to what I feel":

> I, too, sing America.
>
> I am the darker brother.
> They send me to eat in the kitchen
> When company comes,
> But I laugh,
> And eat well and grow strong.
>
> Tomorrow,
> I'll be at the table
> When company comes.
> Nobody'll dare
> Say to me,
> "Eat in the kitchen,"
> Then.
>
> Besides,
> They'll see how beautiful I am
> And be ashamed.
>
> I, too, am America.[5]

Tooker was likely sensitized to the scourge of racial discrimination in part by his own family heritage. Notwithstanding that he appears white, Tooker's parentage—his mother, Angela Montejo Roura, was Cuban-born—had marked him as a disparaged "spic" in the

Irish-dominated Catholic communities of New York, where he spent his childhood. Thus, he was reared instead in the Episcopal Church (and converted in 1976 to his family's prior faith, Catholicism). Committed to an ideal of racial harmony, or "the happy mixing of races,"[6] in the early 1960s, Tooker and his partner, William Christopher, traveled to Alabama to attend a memorial service where Martin Luther King eulogized murdered civil rights worker James Reeb, a Unitarian minister. Marching afterward with their fellow congregants to the Selma courthouse to lay a wreath, the two artists thus joined, however briefly, that small contingent of white Northerners who cared enough about the systematic victimization of African Americans in the South of the United States to risk their own safety in that volatile region and time.[7] Tooker went on to salute King indirectly in *Supper* (1963; plate 37), which features two white men flanking a black Jesus-like figure blessing a loaf of bread at table, a characteristic strategy for an artist whose political consciousness was deeply shaped by the moral tenor of his faith:[8] Tooker sympathized with the thinking of Dorothy Day (1887–1930) and the anarchist-oriented Catholic Worker Party, which Day helped to found in 1933.[9] Besides admiring the Reverend King, Tooker also proved—more unusually for someone outside the African American community—receptive to the message of Malcolm X, particularly (Thomas H. Garver reports) after the activist's pilgrimage to Mecca had fired him with a "new sense of universal brotherhood."[10]

Cherishing, as he did, a high ideal for human fellowship and welfare, Tooker felt impelled to address in his art the sorry condition of "isolation" paradoxically endemic in the densely populated urban realm, the problem of "people being cut off from their fellow men in the city even though they're in crowds." And he regarded such paintings as *Subway* as "my way of protesting" such isolation. Though Tooker and his partner would make their principal home in rural or small-town Vermont from 1960, he continued to depict urban scenes because "I think the essential problems of today are shown best by city life."[11] Historically, the metropolis was "at the very center of concern of the avant-garde," some critics have suggested. Manfredo Tafuri, for one, diagnosed a sense of "absolute alienation" and of "shock" endemic in urban experience, while noting that among avant gardists, "The problem now was that of teaching that one is not to 'suffer' that shock, but to absorb it as an inevitable condition of existence." If the city has functioned as a "benchmark" of avant-garde movements, however, George Tooker does not normally count as an avant gardist: not for him the dream of "technological Utopia" that Modernists had advanced, above all following World War I. In Tooker's distinctly anti-Modernist and *dys*topic vision, many of the lookalike urbanites *do* appear to suffer or to be in a state of shock—in *Subway* or *Landscape with Figures*, for example. By the time Tooker came to the topic of the metropolis, however, a second world war had, of course, transpired, and the Modernists' high-flown dreams for the realm of the geometric and the grid, which undergird the city, had been substantially undermined. Thus, Tafuri remarked on "The 'fall' of modern art" that occurs when it emerges that "No 'salvation' is any longer to be found within it: neither wandering restlessly in labyrinths of images so multivalent they end in muteness, nor enclosed in the stubborn silence of geometry content with its own perfection."[12]

Tooker reflected in 1967 that his pictures "come frequently from irritants," just as "an oyster makes a pearl around an irritant."[13] What constituted the optimum visual modality for artists intent on imbuing their practice with critical or political views would prove a lively topic of debate in the hard-pressed, at times radicalized, United States of the 1930s, when Tooker's teacher Reginald Marsh, whom he emulated, was a central figure.[14] In the New York of the 1930s, the Paris-wise, leftist painter Stuart Davis (1894–1964) would argue that Modernist vocabularies tacitly entailed a political moment, for example. But by far the dominant position then—on the left as well as among right-wing, nationalistically minded regionalists—was that representational modes best served political ends generally, by virtue of their presumed transparency to a broad public. The Mexican muralists active in this period were sometimes touted as a case in point, notwithstanding a propensity toward the surreal on the part of some, and they constituted an example that Tooker (who would evince his own bent toward the surreal) reportedly came to admire.[15]

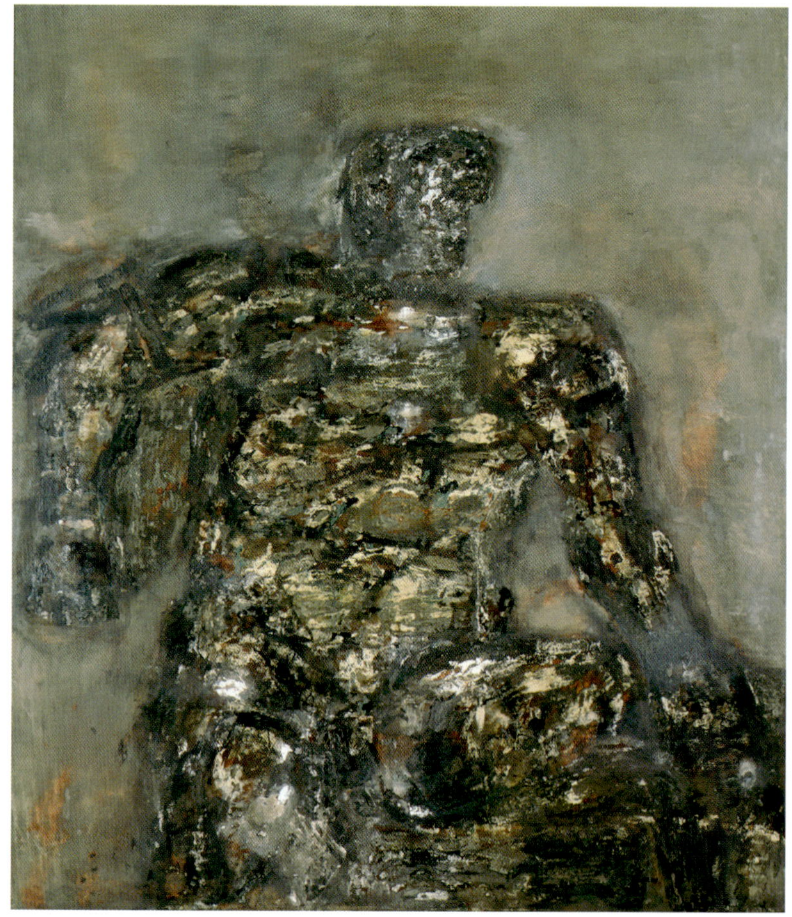



In the inter-war period in the Americas, then, Tooker might have found artistic company of all stripes in his refusal of European avant-garde models. He might further have found some fellow enthusiasts for his archaizing procedures of modeling figures in the round within an illusionistic space meticulously delineated through Renaissance perspective, while deploying egg tempera in a Quattrocento palette of colors on easel-scaled panels. Such like-minded company proved much scarcer, however, during the postwar period, when Tooker in fact emerged as an artist—a period when Modernist abstraction became newly ascendant in the USA, through the emergence of the New York School or Abstract Expressionism, which manifested its practitioners' political (and spiritual) ambitions in necessarily elliptical or inexplicit ways.

Consider as a possible point of comparison to the out-of-step Tooker, then, his likewise maverick contemporary Leon Golub (1922–2004).[16] The politically minded Golub—who eluded the heyday of the New York School to a degree by living in Europe (in Florence 1956–57; in Paris 1959–64)—would devise a representational idiom with explicitly archaizing, classicizing features (fig. 1). Yet Golub's stylizations, the flatness and outsized scale of his compositions, would bespeak withal an awareness of prevalent avant-garde strategies—including Abstract Expressionism, as well as the Art Brut of Jean Dubuffet (1901–1985), who employed deliberately retrogressive, primitivizing devices in his practice. Golub's contradictory, at once conservative and radical, project would eventually capture the attention of some contemporary art critics in a way that Tooker's art did not. But Tooker's visual strategies were not uniformly anachronistic either; his work at times evinced a relation to avant-garde practices, whether historical or contemporary. The oneiric, at once mundane and strange, theater of his protest paintings, with their incongruous interpolation of archaic and contemporary elements, might loosely evoke the proto-surreal vision of urban desolation found in the poetic work of Giorgio de Chirico (1888–1978), for example, and Tooker's sometimes hypnotized-looking personages might evoke the comparably eerie figures of the Belgian Surrealist Paul Delvaux (1879–1994).[17]

From the mid-1960s, shades of Pop art or, to a greater extent and more unexpectedly, Minimalist art may be seen as haunting certain of Tooker's images in their preoccupation with seriality and repetition and in their anomalous conjuring of inhabited, Minimal-looking environs, replete with rows of starkly simple boxes or plinths—as in *Landscape with Figures*, *Standing Figures* (1973; plate 49), or *Waiting Room II* (1982; plate 55). The pronounced differences between that last painting and the more conventionally representational *Waiting Room* of 1957 may conceivably suggest Tooker's intervening awareness of—not to say his affinity for—the gridded, white enameled, semi-architectural sculptures of Sol LeWitt (1928–2007). *Landscape with Figures*, as another example, with its vision of a realm of office dividers run amok, may conjure the fabrication by Robert Morris (b. 1931) of something like steel effigies of nine such divider-units, notwithstanding the artists' radically different premises and means (fig. 2). Although willfully, persistently conservative in his technique, Tooker remained sensitive to, in his words, "the danger of reacting *against* nonobjectivism … the danger of renouncing pattern, design and color."[18] In 1966, he underscored the importance of "keep[ing] a balance between a certain amount of reality and a certain amount of abstract design forms, formal qualities … keep[ing] a balance between these two and not go[ing] off into pure formal escapism and not go[ing] off, on the other hand, into a kind of mindless photographic naturalism." He added, "the form I try to make reinforce the basic meaning of the picture."[19]

fig. 1
Leon Golub (1922–2004)
*Seated Boxer II* (1960)
Oil and lacquer on canvas
96 × 81 inches (243 × 205.8 cm)
Pennsylvania Academy of the Fine Arts, Philadelphia
Alexander Harrison Fund, 2004.10.1

Tooker did employ certain abstracting devices, including a stylized geometry and an elaborate use of pattern, to underscore the Kafkaesque menace of the spaces of officialdom conjured by his protest paintings. The mazelike or labyrinthine spaces and simplified forms of the waiting rooms, subway stations, and the like that Tooker delineated were at once observed and invented. The painter mentioned his trying experiences with Brooklyn's Department of Buildings, for instance, in conjunction with his *Government Bureau*; but the milieu invoked in that painting would seem more generic than specific (as the title suggests) and may equally recall the oppressive environs and dispiriting longueurs of the queues at a driver's license bureau or at passport control, for instance.[20] As for the harsh lighting and the airlessness evinced by Tooker's images, an element of observation combined with a license to invent may again be entailed. Fluorescent lighting was among the "innovations that mobilization for war turned into necessities" in office spaces, James Russell has observed, since "traditional forms of lighting and ventilation," such as windows and skylights, "were sealed to meet wartime blackout requirements." Russell pointed out, too, that under wartime exigencies, "organizations found that people worked efficiently in serried ranks of desks with few traditional amenities or architectural embellishments;" and those same organizations would purposely "'seek the adaptable, interchangeable person,'" Russell noted, citing William Whyte's canonic study from 1956.[21]

In the catalogue to the exhibition *Design and the American Office* (2000), where Russell's findings are published, Donald Albrecht and Chrysanthe Broikos observed that "The office's image as a corporate barrack solidified after World War II. The war's successful military organization was mirrored in postwar America's management model of rigid hierarchies. Khaki-clad soldiers easily morphed into gray-flanneled businessmen."[22] A grim man in a gray flannel suit, sandwiched between rows of steel bars, with five regimented, clone-like figures arrayed behind him, forms the centerpiece of Tooker's *Teller* (1967; plate 43). Whether clad in plain suits, or topcoats and fedoras (suggesting itinerancy and a paucity of heat), Tooker's male figures more often display a degree of difference one from another, although their overall similarity nonetheless speaks to Russell's, Albrecht's, and Broikos's observations. In a study in 2003 of the corporate architecture of the postwar USA, Reinhold Martin also invoked Whyte, as well as David Riesman, in characterizing an "architecture of the lonely crowd," wherein "The organization man and the many secretaries and clerks who surround him ... constitute the units, the modules from which the postwar corporation was constructed. They are the new 'humans,' always already a product of the machine. Their alienation is all that interferes with their full assimilation into the organized social system."[23]

In the USA of the 1950s and 1960s, a sleekly Modernist aesthetic would overtake new office construction, replete with gridded steel and glass curtain walls (figs. 3, 4). "In principle, everything passed through the gridded lines of the curtain wall and projected backward into every square inch of office behind it," notes Martin; "These skins [i.e., the curtain walls], therefore, did more than just impart an image of modernity to the many corporations they serviced. The corporation,

fig. 2
Robert Morris (born 1931)
*Untitled* (1967)
Steel
36 × 180 × 180 inches (91.4 × 457 × 457 cm)
Solomon R. Guggenheim Museum, New York
Purchase Award, Guggenheim International Exhibition, 1967

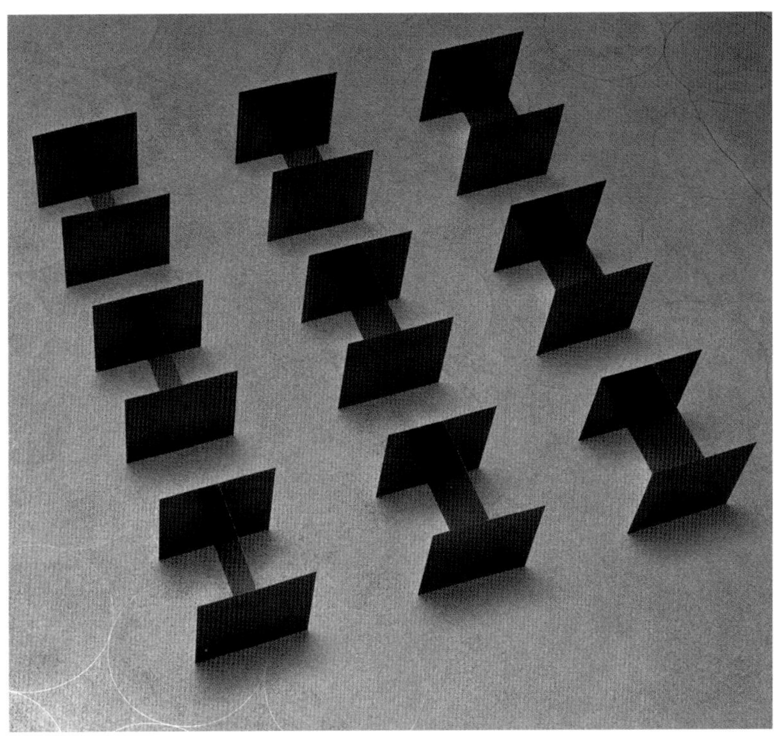

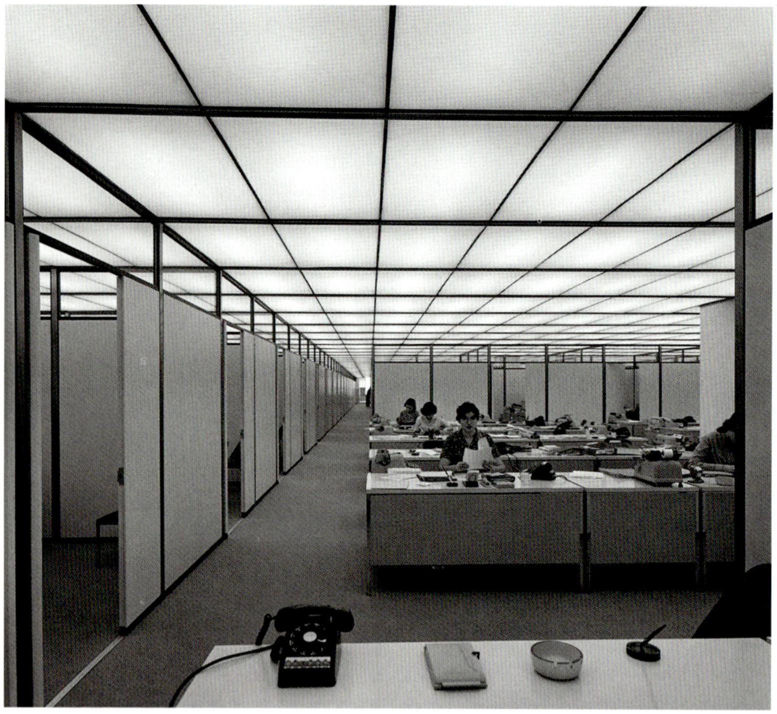

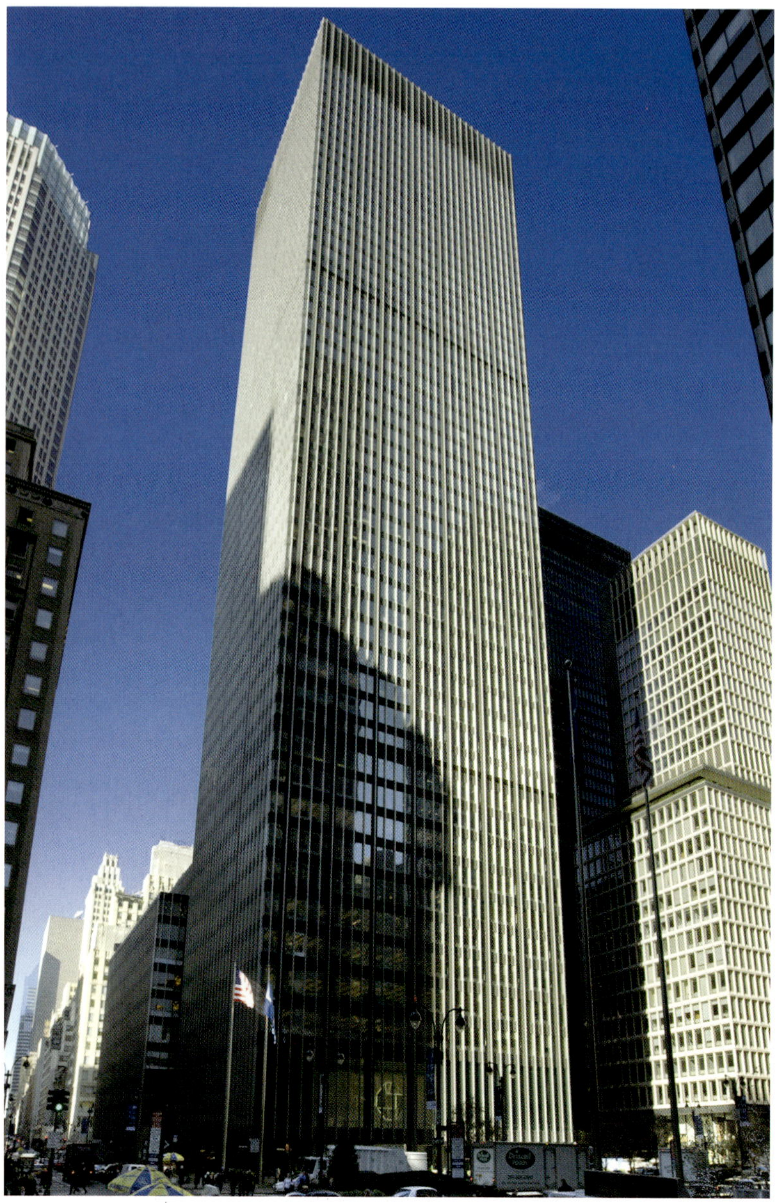

fig. 3
Interior of Union Carbide, New York, 1960
Ezra Stoller © Esto

fig. 4
Union Carbide Building, New York, 1960
Ezra Stoller © Esto

fig. 5
Tom Cheney (born 1954)
*Skeleton in Cubicle* (1997)
© *The New Yorker* Collection 1997
From cartoonbank.com
All rights reserved

well understood by the human relations engineers as a model for society, had opened its densely impacted layers out into the light."[24] In effect, Tooker marked such a shift in his own work through the rows upon rows of desolate workers inhabiting the drastic scheme of office space delineated in *Landscape with Figures*—although the closest actual equivalents to the sea of open cubicles conjured by that painting did not in fact become commonplace in the USA until the 1970s, when offices broadly migrated to "open plans" organized by lightweight, moveable "systems furniture" comprising the "regimented ranks of cubicles" familiar, still, to office workers today.[25] *Landscape with Figures* at once foreshadowed the all-out realization of the cubicled office layout and took it to its logical, though patently unrealistic extreme—an extreme that eventually became fodder for cartoonists (fig. 5). Tooker's painting further offered a pointedly panoptical (all-seeing) view of the uniformly boxed "organization men" and women who have nowhere to hide and "no exit" or escape.[26]

Corporate architecture of the mid-century USA constituted an "organizational complex" that encompassed "the aesthetic and technological extension of what has been known since the early 1960s as the 'military–industrial complex,'" by Reinhold Martin's account. Through its postwar adoption of an increasingly standardized Modernist building vocabulary, corporate architecture may appear to "mark the apotheosis of the alienated, modernized 'mass'," Martin noted.[27] Certain of Tooker's images conjure a demoralized vision of just such a mass: a rote, penitentiary- or assembly-line-like mode of urban life at once dictated and enforced by the cell-like, gridded environments provided by industry and government.[28] Indeed, Tooker spelled out that the subject of *Landscape with Figures* was "conceived with the victimization of our youth by the military–industrial complex and its servant advertising" in mind when, in 1968, he denied permission to an advertising firm hoping to reproduce the painting in recruitment material for the Republic Steel corporation.[29] Although an occasional misfit animates Tooker's scenes (the man in the short jacket loitering by the stairs in *Subway*, for example—pinpointed by one critic as a possible gay subject), such figures serve largely as a foil for the otherwise similarly clad and barbered drones who populate his

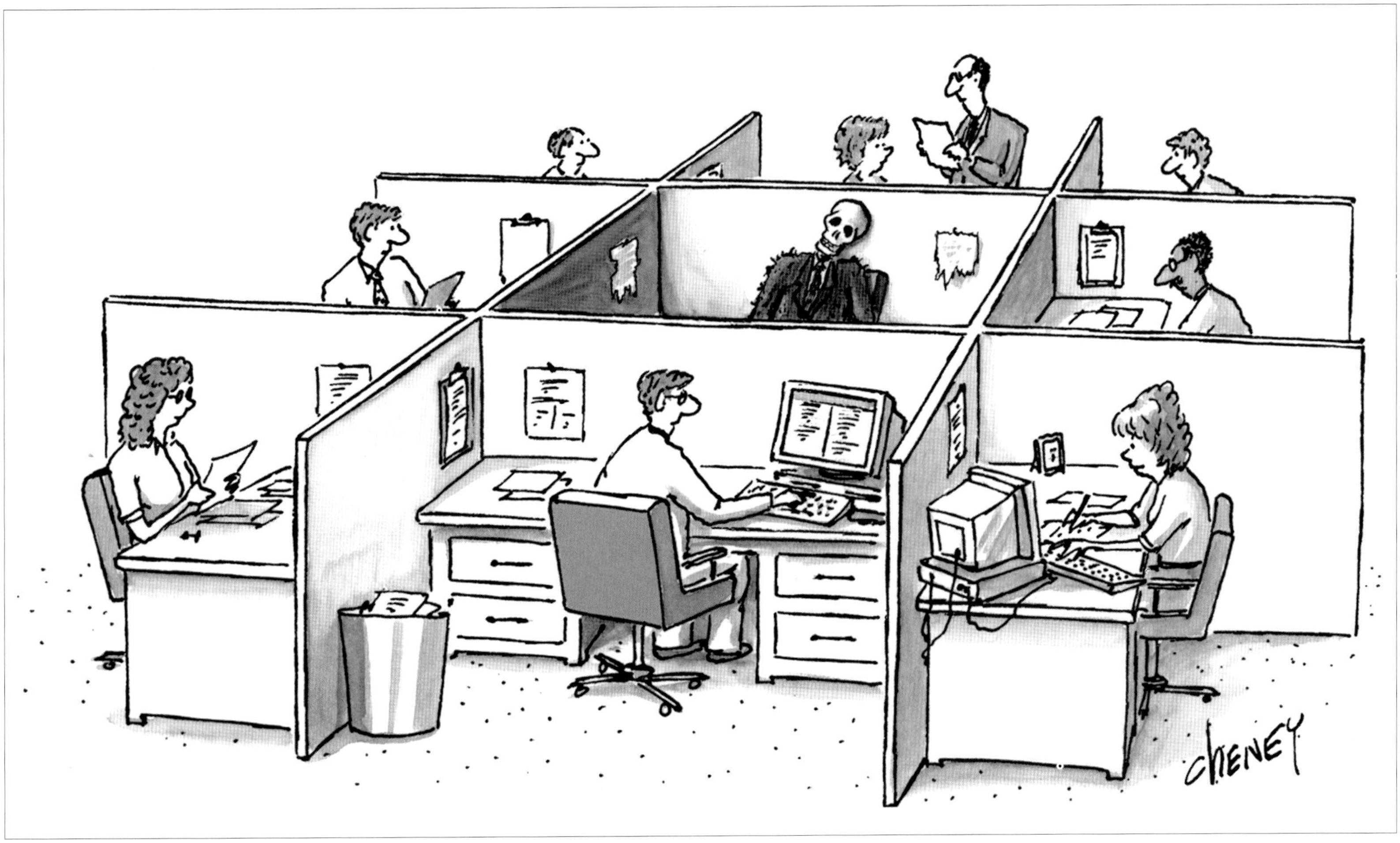




paintings of protest.[30] A nominal variety emerges within this vision of relentless sameness, as Tooker's standard-issue topcoats may be orange, tan, blue, or brown for the male figures, for example, and pink or blue for the females. But, for that matter, Martin traces an emergent social "vector" entailed in the broader "reconditioning of the modern subject" following the war, namely the constructing of that subject as a consumer who is compelled to make 'individual' choices "within a system that was designed to offer variety by providing interchangeable elements in standardized formats. Architects would call these elements *modules*." By the 1950s, "modularity ... became the very image—and the instrument—of the organizational complex," both architecturally and, in a sense, humanly; for "A comparable module likewise appeared in the social life of the postwar corporations, in the form of the figure designated by William H. Whyte as the 'organization man,'" a figure who was not merely conformist, but who "brought together the twin imperatives of variety and standardization"[31]—imperatives illustrated, in his own way, by Tooker.

The marketing to the consumer of a kind of ostensible choice that masks an ineluctable, banal sameness was also targeted by the Conceptual artist Dan Graham (b. 1942), especially in *Homes for America* (1965–70), his sardonic photographic and text project concerning postwar tract housing. Within such residential subdivisions, Graham noted, "The standard unit is a box or a series of boxes ... When the box has a sharply oblique roof, it is called a 'Cape Cod.' When it is longer than wide, it is a 'ranch.' A two-story house is usually called 'colonial,'" and so forth.[32] To illustrate his text, Graham took low-grade photographs of mass-production housing as well as of sundry other mundane sights, such as stacks of pink plastic bins glaring biliously under fluorescent lights inside a New Jersey discount store—an image that he would also pair with a photograph of a high-rise, low-income housing project in the Bronx, replete with bin-like balconies for its "stacked" apartments. Around the same time as Tooker painted his despairing view of scores of regulation pink bins or cells, each for a single (at once crowded and isolated) inhabitant, then, Graham was bringing into pointed juxtapositions his crude photographs of "Quasi-Discrete Cells" or "found" Minimalist forms in his own deadpan form of social critique.[33] That critique functioned also as a subtle commentary on, for instance, the series of sculptural "stacks" (fig. 7) begun in 1965 by the Minimalist artist Donald Judd (1928–1994). While some Minimalists would suggest that their radically materialist, or "literal," and desubjectivized work entailed critical and political valences, in its abstractly blunt reiterations of materials and forms signal to the corporate and industrial sphere, Minimalism could at times more easily be read as affirming the "organizational complex."[34] Thus Melanie Mariño, for one, could

fig. 6
Peter Halley (born 1953)
*Two Cells with Conduit* (1987)
Day-Glo, acrylic, and Roll-a-Tex on canvas
78⅝ × 155⅛ inches (990.1 × 3940 cm)
Solomon R. Guggenheim Museum, New York
Purchased with funds contributed by Denise and Andrew Saul and Ellyn and Saul Dennison, 1987 (87.3550)



describe Graham's *Homes for America* as having "effectively placed Minimal art in context—where its decentering of subjective expression reads less as a 'liberating' aesthetic procedure than as a naive idealization of a penitentiary, 'one-dimensional' culture."[35]

"The deployment of the geometric dominates the landscape. Space is divided into discrete, isolated cells, explicitly determined as to extent and function. Cells are reached through complex networks of corridors and roadways that must be traveled at prescribed speeds and at prescribed times. The constant increase in the complexity and scale of these geometries continuously transforms the landscape," observed Peter Halley (b. 1953) in 1986. Further:

> Geometric art has been made to justify the deployment of the geometric. It has linked the modern deployment of geometry to the wisdom of the ancients, to the tradition of religious truth, and to the esoteric meditative practices of non-Western cultures … Geometric art has sought to convince us, despite all the evidence to the contrary, that the progress of geometry is humanistic, that it is part of the "march of civilization," that it embodies continuity with the past.[36]

At the same time as Halley was theorizing about "The Crisis in Geometry,"[37] in the mid-1980s, he was painting large-scale acrylic, DayGlo- and Roll-a-Tex-covered abstract paintings that deployed geometric forms, including (sometimes barred) squares rhetorically framed as "cells" that he associated with "the apartment house, the hospital bed, the school desk—the isolated endpoints of industrial structure" (fig. 6).[38] The self-consciously Post-modernist Halley explained: "Informed by [Michel] Foucault, I see in the square a prison; behind the mythologies of contemporary society, a veiled network of cells and conduits."[39] While he deployed geometric form in a deliberately quotational way, with a view to exposing geometry's identity with "confinement" in a "critique of idealist modernism,"[40] Halley would face a similar stumbling block to the Minimalists, namely that the would-be criticality of his project could be mistaken by viewers (especially those not privy to his extensive writings).

Whereas Peter Halley and some of the Minimalists would risk having their work misread—as reaffirming rather than interrogating the consequences of the overtaking of the social by the geometric—Tooker's illustrational approach largely circumvented such risk. Consonant with the dominant strategies for a political art practice framed in the USA of the 1930s, Tooker's art was "literal" in quite another sense, namely that of being explicitly literary or narrative. What *his* art would risk was being too literal or pointed, achieving bathos—especially once he reprised in the 1980s, in more overtly nightmarish terms, the themes of some of his prior paintings, as in *Waiting Room II* or *Terminal* (1986). Even as Tooker remained implacably aloof from dominant modes of contemporary art production, however, from the 1950s through the 1980s, certain of his concerns nonetheless anticipated or intersected with those of more prominent, younger artists. Like Graham in the 1960s, and Halley in the 1980s, for example, Tooker would make a point of rejecting the Utopianism that the Modernist avant garde had historically attached to the geometric, while further interrogating the lingering conceit of geometry as ideally neutral or content-less (a conceit underwriting key accounts of the Minimalist project). While Graham and Tooker both implicated the tyranny of the grid over the social in the contemporary realm, Graham did so via eminently contemporary means, with a conceptual strategy whose integration of text and mass-market photographic technology rendered his criticality fairly transparent. From a certain perspective, it was Tooker who carried his protest to the furthest extreme, however, not merely by refusing Modernism's tenacious attachment to the geometric, but also—through his stubbornly archaizing craft—by refusing the avant garde's lingering credence in the possible progress of technology itself.

fig. 7
Donald Judd (1928–1994)
*Untitled* (1969)
Brass and colored plexiglass on steel brackets
116½ × 24 × 27 inches
(294.4 × 60.9 × 68.6 cm)
Hirshhorn Museum and Sculpture Garden, Smithsonian Institution, Washington, D.C.,
Gift of Joseph H. Hirshhorn, 1972

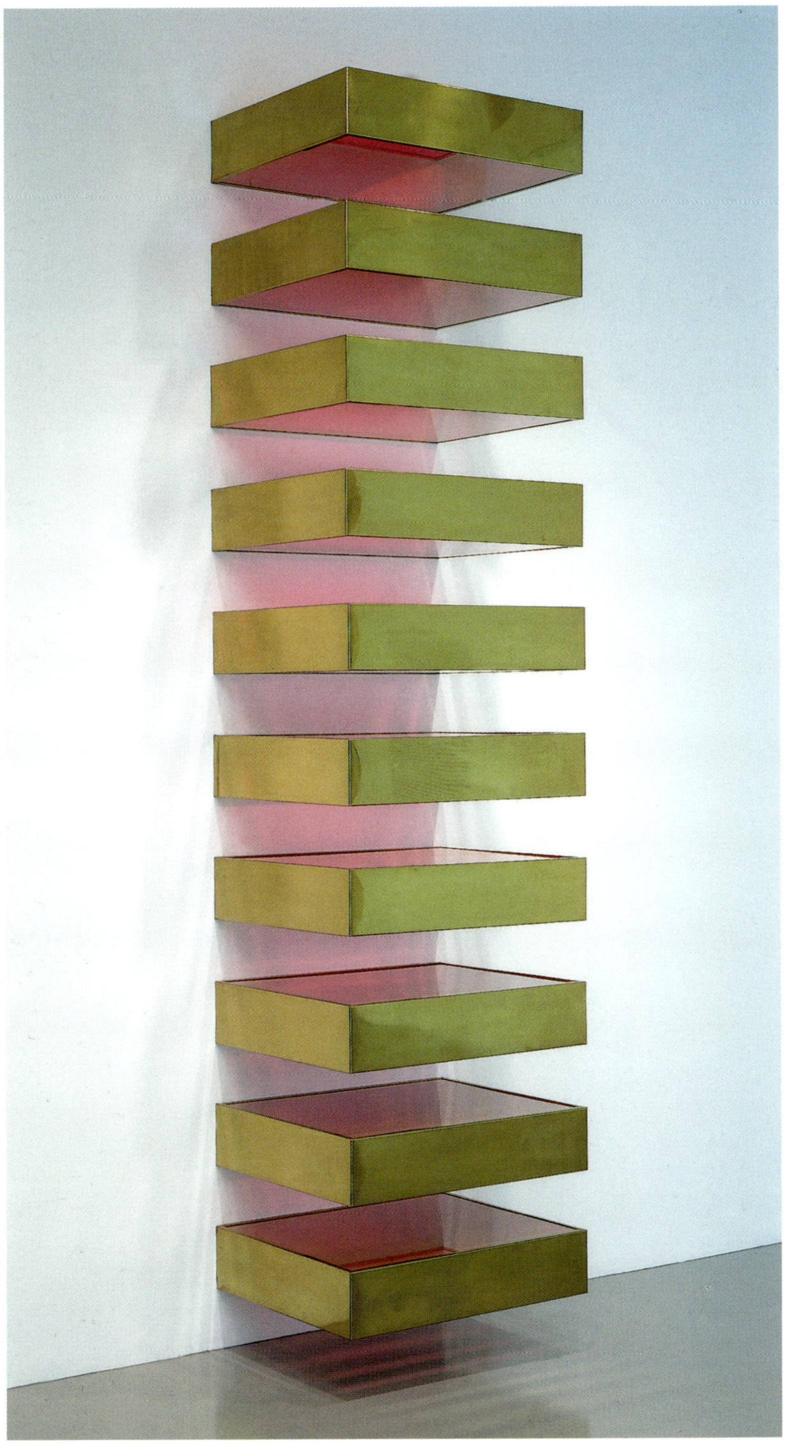



## Notes

1 David Tunkl, "An Interview with George Tooker," in Merry A. Foresta and David Tunkl, *George Tooker*, exhib. cat. (Los Angeles: David Tunkl Gallery, 1980), n.p. "I think the rebellion in everyone is at its apex during one's younger years," Tooker stated; "I painted the world as I saw it, and in many cases I didn't like what I saw" (*ibid.*). Tooker was generally in his thirties and older when he produced his critically minded paintings, however, and the most iconic of those paintings emerged well before a culture of protest galvanized the youth of the USA during the later 1960s. For an incisive reading of the protest paintings as implicit commentary on the insidious, pervasive tactics of surveillance intrinsic to the McCarthy era, see Katherine Hauser, "George Tooker, Surveillance, and Cold War Sexual Politics," *GLQ*, 11:3 (June 2005), 391–425. Oddly, however, Hauser does not mention the closet-like spaces rife in Tooker's work. Regarding the crucial trope of the closet within gay subcultures, see the canonical work of Eve Kosofsky Sedgwick, *Epistemology of the Closet* (Berkeley, California: University of California Press, 1990).

2 Ludwig Hilberseimer, *Grosstadtarchitektur* (1927), as cited in Manfredo Tafuri, *Architecture and Utopia: Design and Capitalist Development*, trans. Barbara Luigia La Penta (Cambridge, Massachusetts: The MIT Press, 1976), 104. Hilberseimer argued that "The architecture of the large city depends essentially on the solution given to two factors: the elementary cell and the urban organism as a whole" (*ibid.*). Added Tafuri: "The cell is not only the prime element of the continuous production line that concludes with the city, but it is also the element that conditions the dynamics of the aggregations of building structures … The building cell understood in this sense represents the basic structure of a production program, from which is excluded any other standard component … Since these cells are elements reproducible *ad infinitum*, they conceptually embody the prime structures of a production line that excludes the old concepts of 'place' or 'space' … The conformation of the cells predisposes the coordinates of the planning of the whole city" (*ibid.*, 105).

3 Tooker and his partner, William Christopher, made their primary home in Vermont from 1960, hence the Dartmouth affiliation, likely the closest chapter to them in the New England region: Justin Spring, "An Interview with George Tooker," *American Art*, 16:1 (spring 2002), 61, 76. Tooker sometimes more specifically directed the monies owed him to be paid to the NAACP's legal fund (see, for example, the Archives of American Art [hereafter AAA] roll 678, frame 0475). On an occasion in 1970, Tooker also directed such monies to be paid to the National Center for Afro-American Artists (AAA roll 678, frame 0534). He and Christopher donated as well to the Mississippi Freedom

Democratic Party, per an acknowledgment from that organization of January 28, 1966 (AAA roll 678, frame 0235). Further, among the correspondence in Tooker's archive is a letter written in 1964 by the director of a Birmingham, Alabama, museum in response to a query from Tooker as to policies of racial equality in admissions to the museum, a query meant as a litmus test by the artist prior to the lending of a painting (AAA roll 678, frame 0165).

4 Although he became a card-carrying member of the Young Communist League at Harvard, Tooker eventually quit the group because "I found the meetings dreadfully boring!" Spring, "An Interview with George Tooker," 63.

5 Interview with Grace George Alexander and George Kay on "Artists in New York," WNYC Radio transcript, New York City, 1967, 7. George Tooker Papers, Archives of American Art, Smithsonian Institution, Washington, D.C. "I, Too" is transcribed with incorrect orthography and spacing in this source. For the correct form, as cited here, see Langston Hughes, *The Collected Poems of Langston Hughes*, ed. Arnold Rampersad (New York: Vintage Books/Random House, 1995), 46.

6 Spring, "An Interview with George Tooker," 62, 77–79, 73. To the question, "Do you consider yourself a person of mixed race?" Tooker answered, "Yes, I think so. In one of the recent censuses I was given the opportunity to list myself as Anglo-Hispanic, and I did." *Ibid.*, 62.

7 Thomas H. Garver, *George Tooker*, rev. edn. (San Francisco: Pomegranate, 2002), 122. Also Spring, "An Interview with George Tooker," 76.

8 Tooker explained that *Supper* was "not a depiction of—but an allusion to—the supper at Emmaus and was painted because I was very moved by Dr. King." Cited in Garver, *George Tooker,* 122. Tooker's painted remembrances of politically charged figures are highly oblique in their content, depicting figures with features distinct from those being subliminally or surreptitiously honored, as in the case of *Supper*, as well as (the equally blandly titled) *Window VIII* (1965–66; plate 39), a half-length image of a black man, wherein Malcolm X's "name in Arabic is carved into the window sash framing the upper part of the picture" (*ibid.*, 64); and *Man in a Tree* (1998; plate 61), which commemorates Reinaldo Arenas (1943–1990), the Cuban poet and novelist arrested for homosexuality, who eluded capture by the police for several days by hiding in a tree in a Havana park; see Grace Glueck, "Art in Review," *New York Times* (December 22, 2000).

9 "I read Dorothy Day and the *Catholic Worker*. And her ideas are ones I agree with," Tooker affirmed in Spring, "An Interview with George Tooker," 78; he does not specify when he began such reading.

10 Garver, *George Tooker*, 64.

11 Interview with Grace George Alexander and George Kay, WNYC Radio transcript, 3, 4.

12 Tafuri, *Architecture and Utopia*, 1, 86, 92, 153, 181.

13 Interview with Grace George Alexander and George Kay, WNYC Radio transcript, 7.

14 "I wanted to be just like him," Tooker said of Marsh, with whom he studied at the Art Students League, where he enrolled in 1943–44: Spring, "An Interview with George Tooker," 65. Marsh had worked in egg tempera, though at a faster, sketchier rate than the deliberate Tooker (*ibid.*).

15 Tooker "was especially interested in the political and emotional content of the Mexican painters," particularly David Alfaro Siqueiros (1896–1974) and José Clemente Orozco (1883–1949), according to Garver, *George Tooker*, 159.

16 Tooker and Golub were not, to my knowledge, acquainted. With a view to the fact that other authors in the present volume would be locating Tooker in relation to his circle of acquaintance and affinity, the present essay takes a different, more experimental tack, positioning him in relation to certain figures with whom he had no particular connection—or whom he actually disdained—but whose endeavors may nonetheless provide a useful foil for Tooker's art.

17 "We all admired de Chirico," Tooker recalled, while recounting his own formation as an artist. Spring, "An Interview with George Tooker," 66.

18 Quoted in Selden Rodman, *Conversations with Artists* (New York: Devin-Adair, 1957), 210.

19 Interview with Grace George Alexander and George Kay, WNYC Radio transcript, 2.

20 Garver, *George Tooker*, 30. With respect to *Waiting Room*, Tooker has said that he was thinking generally, of "all sorts of waiting rooms, prison waiting rooms, hospital waiting rooms." Spring, "An Interview with George Tooker," 77.

21 James S. Russell, "Form Follows Fad: The Troubled Love Affair of Architectural Style and Management Ideal," in *On the Job: Design and the American Office*, ed. Donald Albrecht and Chrysanthe B. Broikos, exhib. cat. (Washington, D.C.: National Building Museum, 2000), 55, 56, 59.

22 Donald Albrecht and Chrysanthe B. Broikos, "Introduction," *On the Job*, 25.

23 Reinhold Martin, *The Organizational Complex: Architecture, Media, and Corporate Space* (Cambridge, Massachusetts: The MIT Press, 2003), 121. (I thank my colleague Rosemarie Bletter for referring me to the text by Martin, as well as to *On the Job*.)

24 *Ibid.*, 103. Martin argues that "the colonization of modern architecture after the war by the corporations represented not simply a corruption of a socially conscious modernist utopianism but rather the logical conclusion of an organicist project written into the very curriculum of modernism." *Ibid.*, 186.

25 Russell, "Form Follows Fad," 60. In fact, the "open-plan" office floor became increasingly standard in corporate real estate from the time of the high-rise office building boom of the 1920s; by that time, "experience showed that prebuilt spaces would often be substantially modified upon occupancy in any case." Martin, *The Organizational Complex*, 87. The open office space of the 1920s (and later) was generally outfitted by corporate tenants not with cubicles, however, but with rows of desks for low-level employees, while effectively permanent, room-like offices were mostly provided for managerial staff.

26 The panoptic model, as Michel Foucault famously described it in *Discipline and Punish: The Birth of the Prison*, trans. Alan Sheridan (New York: Pantheon, 1977), was ingrained in nineteenth-century prisons and in disciplinary systems more broadly. In her study of the theme of surveillance endemic in Tooker's art, Hauser suggests that Foucault's concept "that modern disciplinary power is exercised best through a mutually reinforcing relationship between its invisibility and its subjects' visibility" is effectively played out in certain of Tooker's paintings, such as *Government Bureau*, where "the bureaucrats' obscured position reinforces their power over the exposed, waiting population." Hauser, "George Tooker, Surveillance, and Cold War Sexual Politics," 415.

27 Martin, *The Organizational Complex*, 3–4. Martin refers, for example, to an "aesthetics of dead neutrality" characterizing the Bell Telephone Laboratories designed by Eero Saarinen at Holmdel, New Jersey (1962–66), noting that, "The dullness of the interiors reflected the institutional grayness of the nondescript laboratories being built by the military–industrial complex in suburbs across the country, tinted only … by the colored light of the computer screens mapping new informatic landscapes." *Ibid.*, 208.

28 The concept of "environment" as an "arrangement of objects and events which coerce behavior in accordance with their own dynamic patterns" was framed by Roger G. Barber's study *Ecological Psychology* (1968). Mildred Hall and Edward Hall, in turn, summarized Barber's finding, that "the environment provides a setting which elicits standard behavior according to binding but as yet unverbalized rules," in their study of the modular, Saarinen-designed headquarters of John Deere and Company in Moline, Illinois, *The Fourth Dimension in Architecture: The Impact of Building on Man's Behavior* (1975), as noted in Martin, *The Organizational Complex*, 222.

29 Tooker, draft of a reply to a request (dated September 6, 1968) from an advertising firm, AAA roll 678, frames 0464, 0463.

30 Re the misfit, see Hauser, "George Tooker, Surveillance, and Cold War Sexual Politics," 405–8. Citing, and building on, the theories of Georg Simmel (specifically his *Die Grossstadt und das Geistesleben* [1903]), Tafuri would frame the urban or "'metropolitan man'" as a "*blasé* … 'man without quality,'" his powers of discrimination blunted by his internalization of an economy wherein, "*All things float with equal gravity in the constantly moving stream of money. All things lie on the same level.*" Tafuri, *Architecture and Utopia*, 86–88 (emphasis added by Tafuri; English translation from *The Sociology of Georg Simmel*, trans. and ed. Kurt H. Wolff [New York: Free Press, 1950]).

31 Martin, *The Organizational Complex*, 4–5. By the mid-1950s, US offices would often be organized around an "abstract module … ranging from 4′ 6″ to 5′ square" that "was distributed in a virtual, organizational matrix—a grid—capable of accommodating office partitions, ceiling tiles, lighting fixtures, and furniture, in any number of combinations." *Ibid.*, 94–95.

32 Dan Graham, "Homes for America," in Dan Graham, *Rock My Religion: Writings and Art Projects, 1965–1990*, ed. Brian Wallis (Cambridge, Massachusetts: The MIT Press, 1993), 14.

33 An illustration of Graham's work can be found in John Alan Farmer, ed., *Urban Mythologies: The Bronx Represented Since the 1960s* , exhib. cat. (Bronx, NY: Bronx Museum of the Arts, 1999), 38, plate 6.

34 For the canonical argument to this effect, see Anna C. Chave, "Minimalism and the Rhetoric of Power," *Arts*, 64:5 (January 1990), 44–63.

35 Melanie Mariño, "Disposable Matter: Photoconceptual Magazine Work of the 1960s," in Douglas Fogle, *The Last Picture Show: Artists Using Photography 1960–1982*, exhib. cat. (Minneapolis: Walker Art Center, 2003), 199. Mariño adds, with a view to the operations of Pop art, that Graham's "'Homes' duplicates the everyday logic of enforced consumption that packages our 'quasi-discrete cells' into morbid uniformity. This quotidian rationalization withers the very possibility of aesthetic expression. Ultimately, it is this grim dynamic of depletion that Graham's article mimes, offering up to its readers a spectacle of the deep banality of everyday experience." *Ibid.*, 199–200.

36 Peter Halley, "The Deployment of the Geometric" (1986), in *Collected Essays, 1981–87* (Zurich: Bruno Bischofberger Gallery, 1988), 128–29.

37 Peter Halley, "The Crisis in Geometry" (1984), in *Collected Essays*, 74–105. The essay commences: "Where once geometry provided a sign of stability, order, and proportion, today it offers an array of shifting signifieds and images of confinement and deterrence." *Ibid.*, 75.

38 Peter Halley, "Notes on the Paintings" (1982), in *Collected Essays*, 23.

39 Peter Halley, "Statement" (1983), in *Collected Essays*, 25.

40 Halley, "Notes on the Paintings," 23.

# Between Paradise and Purgatory: George Tooker's modern icons

Robert Cozzolino

"In some of my paintings I am saying that 'this is what we are forced to suffer in life,' while in other paintings I say 'this is what we should be.' I oscillate between the earthly state and a concept of paradise."

George Tooker to Thomas H. Garver, letter, 1983

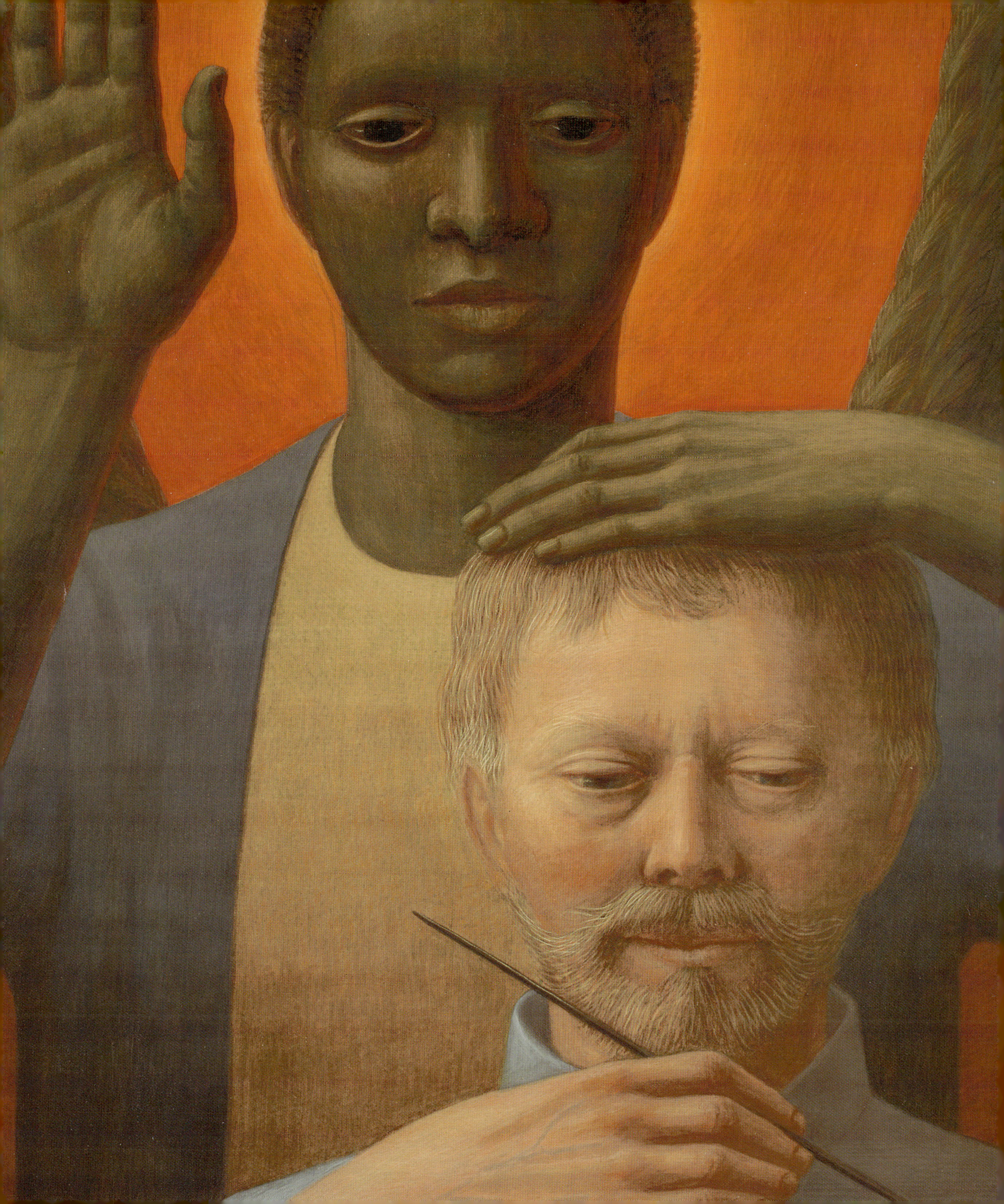

Previous page
George Tooker
***Dark Angel*** (1996) (detail)
Pennsylvania Academy of the Fine Arts, Philadelphia, Henry C. Gibson Fund, 2007.7
(see page 166)

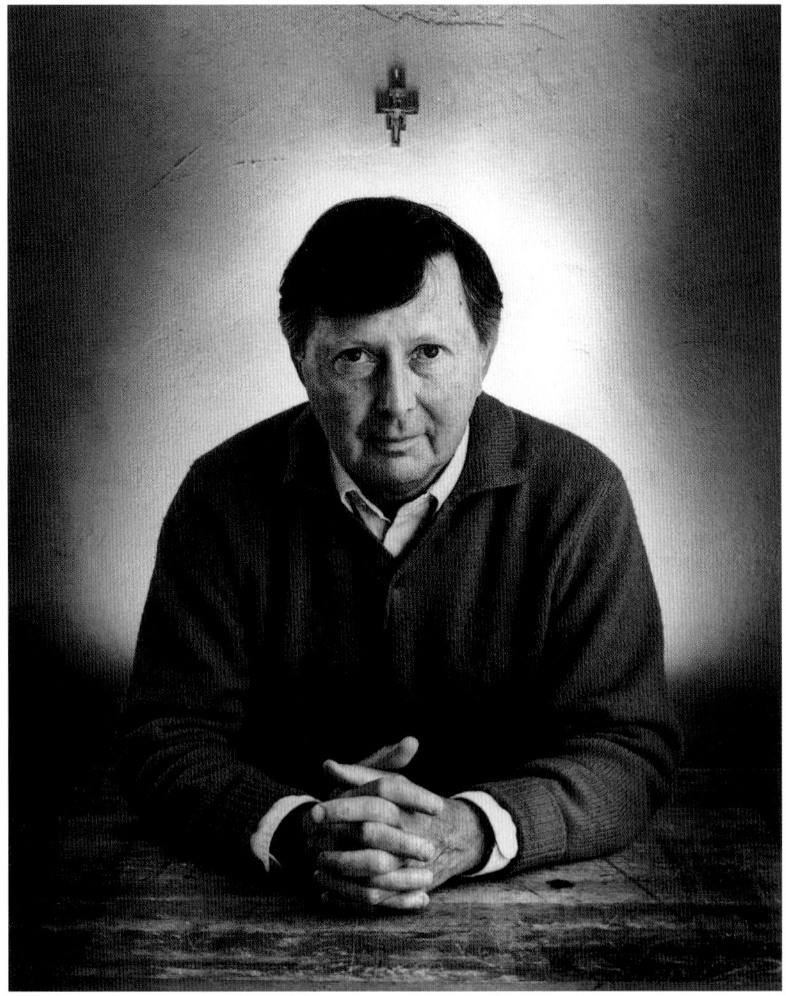

Right
fig. 1
David J. Teplica (born 1959)
*George Tooker* (1985)
Selenium toned silver gelatin print
10½ × 7¾ inches (26.7 × 19.7 cm)
Hood Museum of Art, Dartmouth College, Hanover, New Hampshire, Gift of the artist



In 1976, following the death of his life partner, William Christopher, George Tooker converted to Catholicism, and he has emphasized this aspect of his identity ever since. He has repeatedly connected these events in interviews, stating that the profound experience of losing Christopher precipitated a crisis that his conversion helped resolve. Faith and the community that came with it provided Tooker with, as he put it, the "kind of happiness and spiritual fulfillment I needed to become whole again."[1] Rather than simply convert from one faith (Episcopalian) to another, Tooker became engaged in the life and mission of the Church by administering the Eucharist at Mass, bringing Communion to the sick, and accepting three major commissions for communal devotional practice.[2]

Tooker's conversion, together with what visitors to the house that he and Christopher built describe as his humble, even "Franciscan," lifestyle, has affected how many see the artist and his work.[3] When the photographer David Teplica visited Tooker in 1985, he composed a portrait of the artist seated at an austere wooden table with hands clasped and fingers interwoven as if in prayer (fig. 1). A powerful white light flares up at his back like a nimbus, outlining his body and drawing attention to the tiny reproduction of a thirteenth-century monumental crucifix by Cimabue (*circa* 1240–1302) that punctuates an otherwise bare studio wall. Teplica set his exposure to emphasize lights and darks in such a way that the contrast of Tooker's white shirt beneath a dark sweater alludes to a priest's collar. Leaning into the picture to look directly at the viewer, Tooker's firm gaze and attentive demeanor suggest those of a confessor.

Some critics and interviewers have suggested that Tooker's artistic interests changed after his conversion, to stress the private and spiritual over works of public outrage. When pressed, the artist has asserted continuity in his art and life.[4] "I think I've always been religious but in a very undirected way," he reflected in 1981. "When I was a child, I used to go to church every Sunday. Then, for a long while, I just didn't ... my conversion is not a sudden reversal. It was gradual."[5] Tooker has often rejected suggestions that his engagement with spirituality arose only with his Catholic identity. He told an interviewer in 1989, "Religion was always implicit in my work ... with age it has become more explicit. My conversion to Catholicism has had a great effect on my life, so I guess it has had a great effect on my art."[6] Tooker's appeal that viewers see an underlying spiritual dimension to his work is provocative and urges an examination of the religious implications of subject matter throughout his career.

It is instructive to consider the ways in which Tooker intimately linked artistic and spiritual aspects of his identity in a self-portrait titled *Dark Angel* (1996; fig. 2 and plate 60). It is one of only four formal self-portraits he has painted and is notable for its inclusion of a supernatural figure—the angel referred to in the title.[7] This unusually frank self-image is remarkable in the work of a man who, despite having been interviewed by a wide array of admirers and scholars, remains consistently reticent about the meaning, inspiration, and personal implications of his work. *Dark Angel* celebrates belief and vocation through allusions to earlier devotional art and by imagining physical contact between a messenger of God and the mortal artist. As a guardian figure, the angel is an anthropomorphic manifestation of resilient faith itself, a spiritual version of the artistic muse, which grants vision and rekindles creative force.

As Tooker works contemplatively on a painting, the solemn angel rises behind him with its right hand held up in benediction or to profess guardianship. Rather than guide Tooker's paintbrush, the

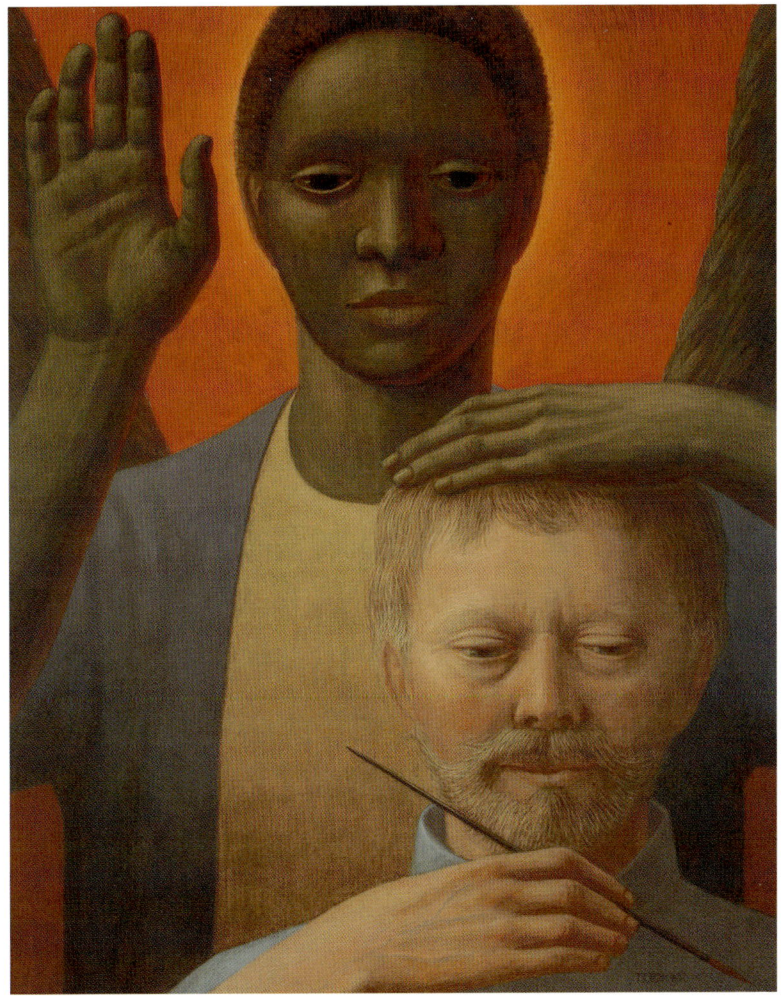

fig. 2
George Tooker
*Dark Angel* (1996)
Egg tempera on gesso panel
24 × 19 inches (61 × 48.3 cm)
Pennsylvania Academy of the Fine Arts, Philadelphia, Henry C. Gibson Fund, 2007.7

angel lays its left hand on Tooker's head, reflecting the artist's frequent explanation that his subject matter arises from his subconscious and proceeds through intuition.[8] Although the guardian provides inspiration and serves as a protector, it may also be a celestial messenger who has arrived to call the aging artist home. Tooker's self-portrait could thus be eschatological, envisioning a future moment of visitation by the Angel of Death, who comes quietly and peacefully into the studio to guide him beyond his body to the afterlife. Its close relationship to a *Self-Portrait* lithograph made the same year (fig. 3), showing a skeletal Death lurking behind an anxious Tooker, suggests that mortality is implicit in the relationship between the artist and his muse. Tooker's acknowledgment of his own proximity to the grave therefore has a spiritual dimension and is a hopeful event that leads to resurrection in his faith.[9]

*Dark Angel* also alludes to the legend of St. Luke, evangelist and patron saint of painters, said to have produced the first miraculous images of the Virgin Mary and the Christ child.[10] Scholars have discussed the significance of this subject for artists in the fifteenth and sixteenth centuries in terms of a new assertion of professional identity, as an argument against iconoclasm, and as a model for image-based devotional practice.[11] Such images as *St. Luke Painting the Madonna* (1520–25; fig. 4) by Jan Gossaert (*circa* 1478–1532) portray the evangelist rendering the holy icon from life or from a vision positing the truth of Luke's gospel and the piety of the painter's craft. Like Gossaert's vision of *St. Luke*, Tooker's self-portrait imagines the artist guided to image-making by the sure presence of a spiritual intercessor. This grounds Tooker's vocation and body of work in moral purpose and connects him to a long tradition of devotional art.[12]

Whereas Gossaert and others traditionally depicted St. Luke in profile transcribing a vision that we also witness, Tooker faces us and the world beyond the picture plane, contemplating contemporary life, from which he will draw spiritual lessons. Never comfortable depicting subjects with a fixed iconography, Tooker slips imaginatively into an echo of St. Luke, who was an extraordinarily descriptive chronicler of the life of Christ. So too, Tooker has been a perceptive observer of contemporary experience and human nature.

*Dark Angel* emerged at the end of a period in which Tooker had accepted commissions to paint ecclesiastical subjects, including an altarpiece of *The Seven Sacraments* (1980), the *Stations of the Cross* (1983–84), and a banner of the *Resurrection* (1995). It made sense that he would eventually reflect on his transformed, now explicit role as a religious painter and on the relationship between spirituality and art.

Tooker was raised by a devout Episcopalian father and a mother who, though devoted to social issues, was "almost an agnostic."[13] As a young man, he was aware of the intolerant atmosphere that had led his historically Catholic family to turn to the Episcopal Church. Whereas one community rejected what it perceived as his family's unworkable difference, another welcomed them. He recalled: "When [my Catholic Cuban family] came to New York, they didn't get treated very well by the Catholic Church, because they were … Spanish-speaking. And the Catholic Church in New York was largely Irish, who were enduring some prejudice themselves, and in a way, I guess they kind of took it out on the Spanish … so my Cuban family … found that the Episcopal Church was much more friendly to them."[14] It is significant that this confrontation between creed and action took place in the context of religious practice. This experience likely strengthened Tooker's sensitivity to the importance of community and to how a community's willingness to uphold or contradict beliefs can affect others.

fig. 3
George Tooker
*Self-Portrait* (1996)
Lithograph on Somerset Soft White paper
12 × 18 inches (30.5 × 45.7 cm) (image),
Edition of 50
Photo courtesy DC Moore Gallery,
New York



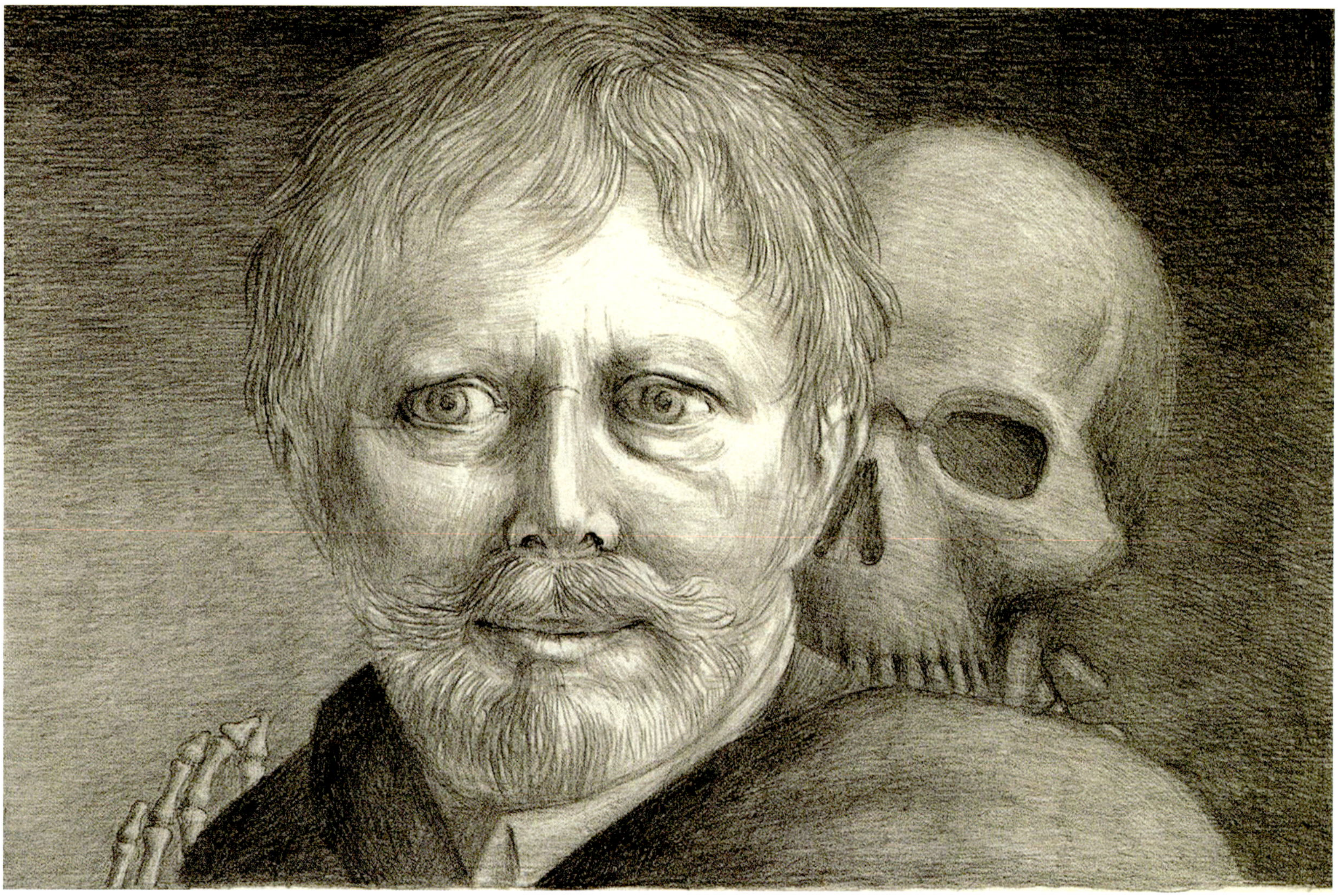

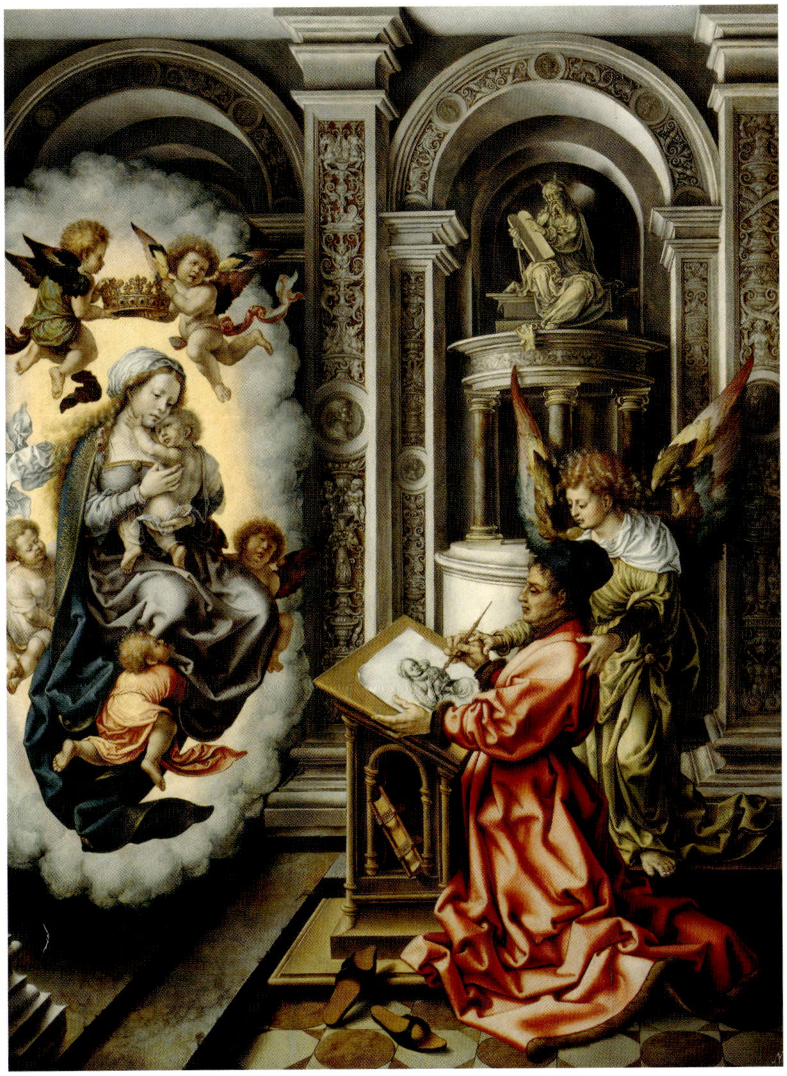

fig. 4
Jan Gossaert (called Mabuse)
(*circa* 1478–1532)
*St. Luke Painting the Madonna* (1520–25)
Oil on wood
43 × 32¼ inches (109.2 × 82 cm)
Kunsthistorisches Museum, Vienna

Tooker also read the writings of Dorothy Day and agreed with the viewpoint of the *Catholic Worker*, which she founded in 1933.[15] Day described the *Catholic Worker* and its staff as "propagandists for Catholic Action."[16] Over the course of extremely turbulent decades and contrary to the political views of some Catholics, she upheld an anti-Fascist, anti-Communist, and anti-capitalist viewpoint, promoting community through private action, personal responsibility, and "the creation of order out of chaos."[17] The *Catholic Worker* tirelessly drew attention to human rights issues and reported on topics that the American mainstream press would not touch, including lynching and other domestic horrors.[18]

Day consistently grounded her moral stance in spirituality, arguing that it is crucial to love and to be devoted to Christ in his humanity—not just in his mystical form. She explained that "It is because we love Christ in His Humanity that we can love our brothers. It is because we see Christ in the least of God's creatures that we can talk to them of the love of God and know that what we write will reach their hearts."[19] This empathetic strain of spiritually motivated activism was compatible with Tooker's evolving attitude to politics and society.

Tooker has often revealed his belief that an artistic calling carries moral responsibility.[20] In an interview in 1967, he maintained that *Subway* (1950; plate 15) and *Lunch* (1964; plate 41) were "about isolation. About people being cut off from their fellow men in the city even though they're in crowds." He then placed this theme in the context of personal action. "It's my way of protesting ... something I think is wrong, that's why it's unpleasant." Ultimately he hoped that the pictures would provoke viewers to "do something about making things better."[21]

Tooker's comments came at the height of his involvement with the civil rights movement, and they convey the urgency that he and Christopher felt about opposing inequality and injustice. Two years earlier, they had traveled to Alabama to join the momentous Montgomery–Selma march led by Dr. Martin Luther King, Jr., and to attend memorial services for murdered civil rights supporters. Christopher's handwritten daily account of their trip shows how faith and action were intertwined among participants. One particular entry reveals the great emotional effect a Montgomery church service had on him and on Tooker:

> The ABC [television] cameras are on, they grind away at the candles, the cross, the faces, the congregation. We sing, we pray, the feeling is utterly beautiful and the spiritual depth in the church is profound. We sing, "We Shall Overcome," the negro ladies next to me, we join hands. We move out into the aisle so George can join hands with the man across the way. The effect is stunning. Tears are on our cheeks, the singing is marvelous. When it stops the strength that we have gathered from this service is a strength that will stay with us for years.[22]

Tooker's immersion in a community dedicated to spiritual action resurfaced—as Christopher surmised it would—in such works as *Embrace of Peace II* (1988; plate 62). Ostensibly an image based on the communal greeting of love and friendship made before Communion in the Catholic Mass, this scene of harmony and acceptance echoes Tooker's experience in Alabama. *Supper* (1963; plate 37), Tooker's contemporary meditation on racial harmony, was inspired by Dr. King and alludes to the Supper at Emmaus.[23] This biblical story describes

fig. 5
Meister Francke (*circa* 1380–*circa* 1436)
*The Man of Sorrows* (*circa* 1430)
Tempera on oak panel with designed frame
16¾ × 12⅛ inches (42.5 × 30.8 cm)
Museum der Bildenden Kunst, Leipzig

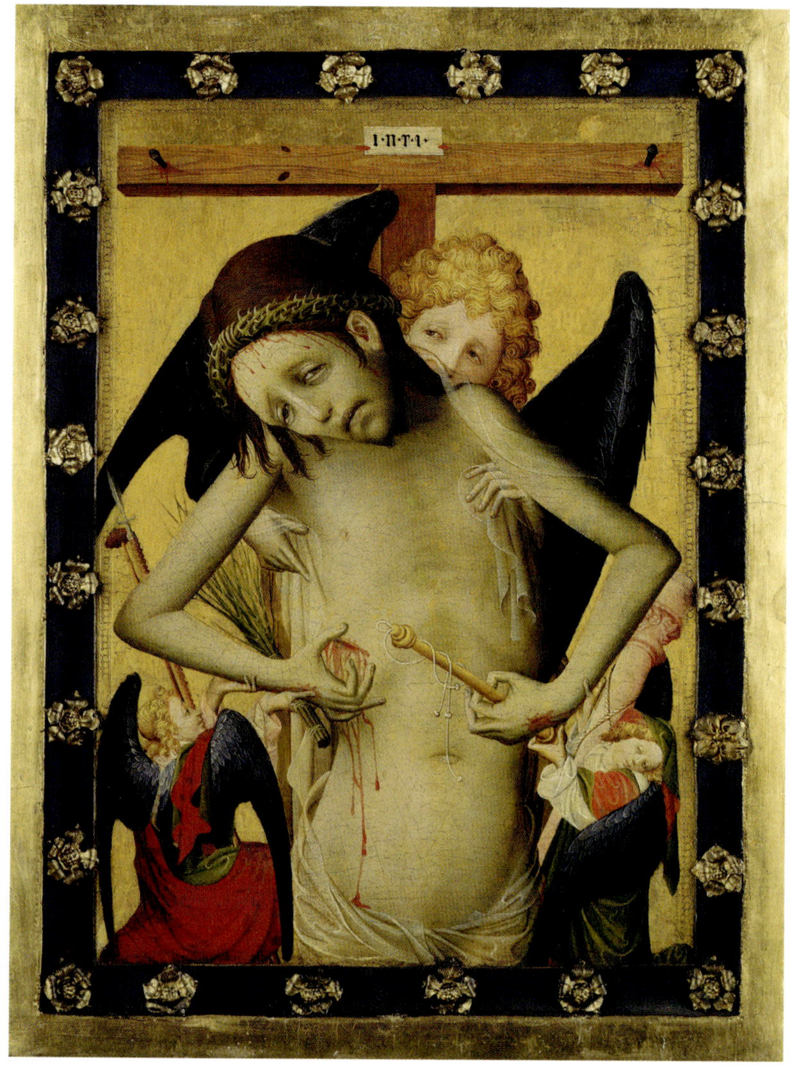



Christ's appearance to two grieving apostles three days after his Crucifixion. Believing him a wandering stranger, they invite him home to share a meal. When, during supper, Jesus moves to bless and break bread, the men realize that he is the risen Christ, and he vanishes. *Supper* depicts the hushed moment just before their recognition of the Savior. Like an apparition, the central figure emanates light as he moves to bless the meal. This daring and compassionate homage, with an allusion to King as the Resurrected Christ unrecognized by his disciples, now appears to foreshadow King's martyrdom and suggests Tooker's awareness of skeptics within the cause.

Tooker's appeal for his pictures to affect the ethical decisions and morality of viewers also corresponds with how images function in Catholic piety. Meditation on what is pictured in a panel painting, altarpiece, or prayer book is a devotional practice that brings one closer to God. In some instances, it brings a promise of reducing the duration of one's suffering in Purgatory, binding the act of looking directly to the soul's redemption.[24] *Andachtsbilder* (or devotional images), such as *The Man of Sorrows* (*circa* 1430; fig. 5), by Meister Francke (*circa* 1380–*circa* 1436), present images of Christ in his earthly suffering as a means to encourage empathy and compassion. Contemplation of Christ's bloody, wounded body (or of images of the saints enduring grisly tortures) was thought to bring viewers closer to an understanding of the physical and spiritual depths of sacrifice and the power of Resurrection. Francke, who may have been a Dominican monk, includes scourges in his vision of Christ, suggesting that this picture was made for another monk who engaged in self-flagellation to heighten his devotional practice. A passage from St. Paul in Romans (8:17) provides a basis for this relationship between vision, meditation, and pain: "We are … joint heirs with Christ if so be that we suffer with Him, that we may be glorified together."

Tooker had access to a wide range of Christian iconography, having studied the collections of the Fogg Art Museum, the Museum of Fine Arts, Boston, and the Metropolitan Museum of Art in New York as a complement to his training. He also traveled to the Philadelphia Museum of Art to see Italian and Flemish paintings in the John G. Johnson Collection.[25] In 1949, Tooker traveled in Europe for six months with Paul Cadmus in order to see major works of art *in situ* and in the collections of the Uffizi, the Louvre, and the National Gallery in London. Cadmus and Tooker spent most of their time in Italy, where they sought out monuments in towns that still require much effort to visit. Works by Piero della Francesca in Arezzo and Sansepolcro, by Giotto in Padua, by Luca Signorelli (*circa* 1445–1523) in Orvieto, and by Agostino di Duccio (1418–*circa* 1481) in Rimini were particular targets.[26]

Tooker's close attention to this material had a strong effect on the development of his imagery and benefited his own church commissions later in life.[27] As he put it, the "directness and simplicity of early Italian [and Flemish] painting appealed to me."[28] When he began designing what he considered his first "professional" paintings in 1945, Tooker used narrative predella panels as a point of reference.[29] These intimate pictures appear beneath the central panel of an altarpiece and usually depict incidents from the life of Christ or the saint to whom the polyptych is dedicated. Among the pictures that made a great impression on Tooker at this time was a series of four predella panels by Sandro Botticelli (*circa* 1445–1510) that shows scenes from the life of Mary Magdalene (*circa* 1484–91; fig. 6). Originally part of an altarpiece painted for the Augustinian convent

fig. 6
Sandro Botticelli (Alessandro di Mariano Filipepi; 1445–1510)
*Saint Mary Magdalene Listening to Christ Preach* (*circa* 1484–91)
Tempera on panel
7⅞ × 17¼ inches (20 × 43.8 cm)
Predella panel—one of four—from an altarpiece from the convent of Sant'Elisabetta delle Convertite, Florence
John G. Johnson Collection, Philadelphia Museum of Art

of Sant'Elisabetta delle Convertite in Florence, founded in 1329 to house penitent prostitutes and courtesans, the panels are now in Philadelphia.[30] Tooker found the narrative structure, emphatic incorporation of architecture, and atmosphere of mystery evoked by relationships of figures to be an important model for such Modernist compositions as *Subway*.[31]

While he denies that there is a direct relationship between any particular historical picture and his own, Tooker acknowledges that compositional elements slip in unconsciously as he develops his work. His description of *Subway* as a picture that envisions "a large modern city, as a kind of limbo," reflects his consideration of art and theological issues, which are dissolved into the form and narrative structure of the picture. As he explained, "The subway seemed a good place to represent a denial of the senses and a negation of life itself. Its being underground with great weight overhead was important."[32] Commenting on his own picture of a subway, made twenty-five years later, Paul Cadmus reflected that Tooker had painted this space "as Purgatorio ... its architect was Lucifer."[33]

Such analogies were deliberate on the part of the artists and underscore an important meaning that Tooker's paintings bear. His carefully designed, beautifully illuminated pictures compel close looking and meditation, despite their visualization of tension and despair. His method encourages viewers to become psychologically, emotionally and spiritually involved in what is depicted. Father Forrest Rouelle, who converted Tooker, once observed that he "has always painted in parables."[34] The artist once explained his aims to Thomas H. Garver in precisely this manner. "In some of my paintings," he said, "I am saying that 'this is what we are forced to suffer in life,' while in other paintings I say 'this is what we should be.' I oscillate between the earthly state and a concept of paradise."[35] Because his work depicts the familiar with great clarity and tangibility, we are able to identify and merge our own experiences with what is shown. In this way, Tooker's most "unpleasant" works are entreaties for intercession by sympathetic viewers to effect change in a world that can be frightening, hateful, or dangerous. This binds his "public" paintings to an underlying religious impulse born of empathy and compassion.

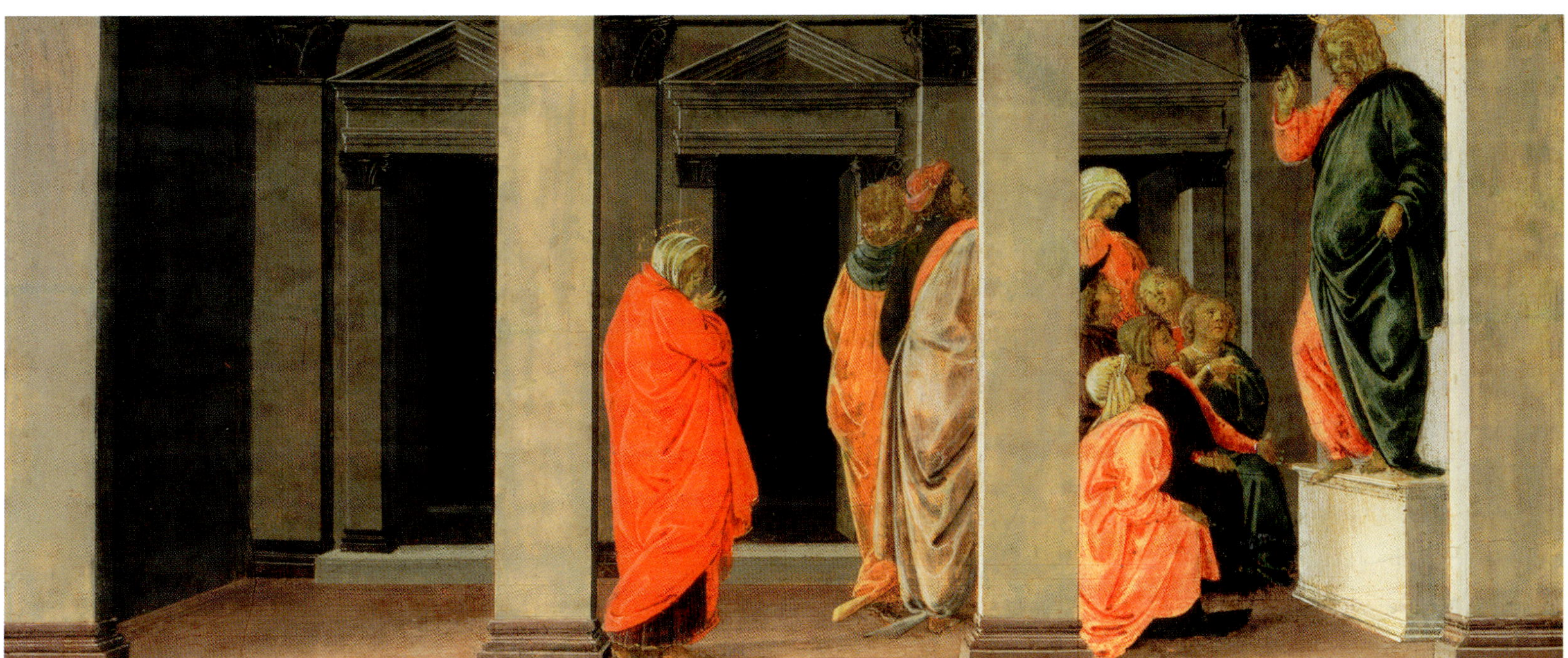

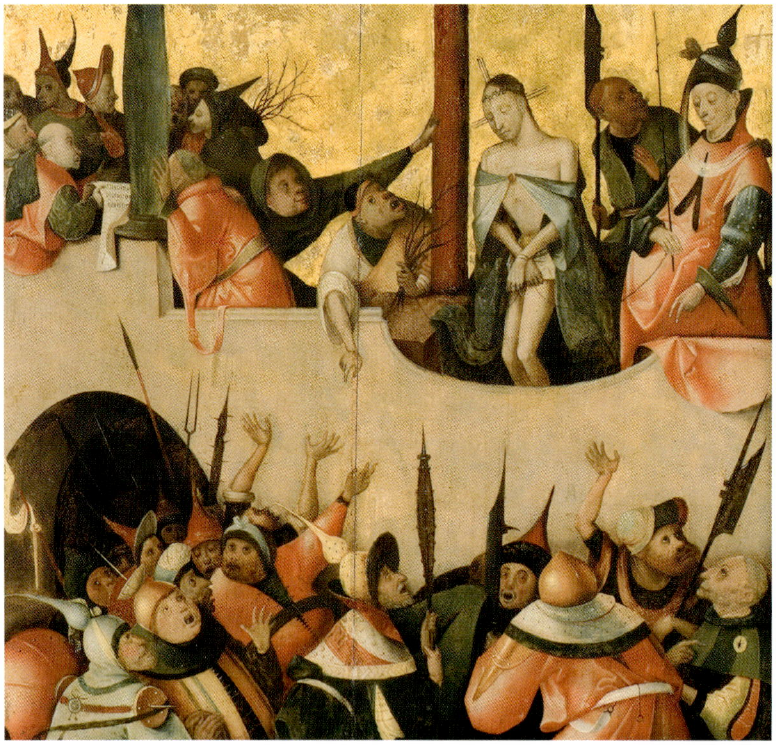

fig. 7
Attributed to Hieronymus Bosch
(*circa* 1450–1516)
*Ecce Homo* (sixteenth century)
Oil and gold leaf on panel
20½ × 21¼ inches (52 × 54 cm)
John G. Johnson Collection,
Philadelphia Museum of Art

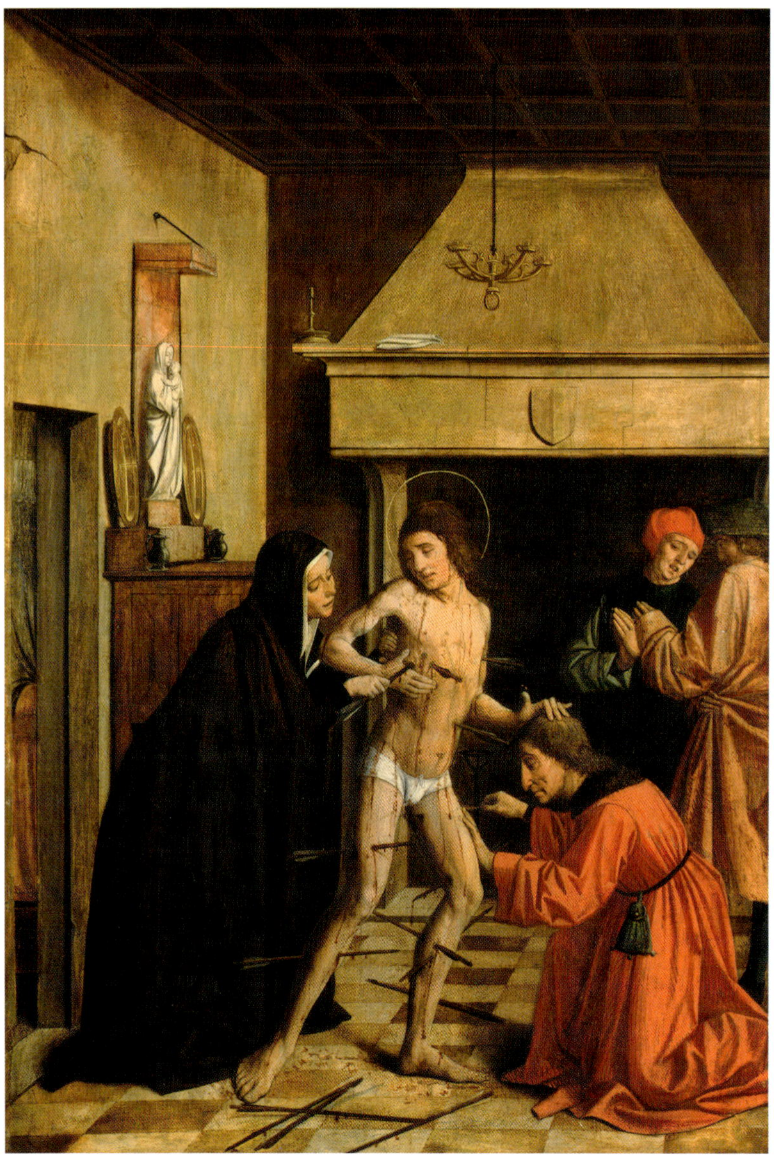

fig. 8
Josse Lieferinxe (documented
1493–1505/8)
*Saint Sebastian Cured by Irene*
(*circa* 1497)
Oil on walnut panel
32 × 21⁹⁄₁₆ inches (81.2 × 54.8 cm)
Panel from the altarpiece of the Saint Sebastian chapel of Notre-Dame-des-Accoules, Marseilles, done in collaboration with Bernardo Simondi (died 1498)
John G. Johnson Collection,
Philadelphia Museum of Art

Tooker characterized *Children and Spastics* (1946; plate 1), *Bird Watchers* (1948; plate 9), and other early works as opportunities to "reconsider religious concepts in a modern context without painting a specific religious narrative."[36] *Children and Spastics* presents a scene of "spiritual violence" perpetrated by a menacing band of bullies.[37] *Dance* (1946; plate 3) imagines Tooker and his contemporaries, ready or not, stalked by Death, who appears literally around every corner visible in the painting. *Bird Watchers* was Tooker's attempt to paint "a religious picture without religious subject matter."[38] In these and other cases, Tooker imbued observations of contemporary life with spiritual weight through a delicate balance of religious and art-historical references.

In *Children and Spastics,* a trio of men gesture and recoil in exaggerated, even grotesque, poses as they are cornered by five boys and a dog. The children menace the men with brooms and poles, jeer and cackle while the dog snarls at their feet. Tooker noted that he composed the picture "thinking of [Hieronymus] Bosch and the cruelty of children. And they were half cruel children and half Bosch monsters."[39] One scholar has interpreted the painting as Tooker's youthful expression of anxiety over authoritarian surveillance, his sexuality, and societal expectations.[40]

*Children and Spastics* draws on violent martyrial imagery and the tradition of depicting crowds of cruel spectators mocking Christ.[41] Depicting scenes of psychological persecution or violent physical torment was an opportunity to teach about ideal behavior. Tooker's aggressive children may call to mind Mussolini's blackshirts or the Ku-Klux-Klan, but they also model their demeanor on the bloodthirsty audience shown in such images as *Ecce Homo* (sixteenth century; fig. 7), by a follower of Bosch. The agitated, tortured state of the bodies of the "spastics" recalls the bloody and pained body of St. Sebastian in a prominent altarpiece in the Philadelphia Museum of Art (fig. 8). *Children and Spastics* relies on a long and meaningful tradition in Catholic piety to establish the relationship between tormenter and tormented.[42] Whatever its inspiration, the painting is a parable about enduring hate and violence in the world.

fig. 9
Hans Holbein (*circa* 1497–1543)
*Plate XI: The Queen* from *Dance of Death*, Lyons Edition, 1538
Harvard University Art Museums, Fogg Art Museum, Gift of William Gray from the collection of Francis Calley Gray, G375
Photo: Imaging Department © President and Fellows of Harvard College



*Dance* shows unwitting New Yorkers confronted by Death in the midst of nighttime sidewalk traffic. In this painting, Tooker reinterpreted a popular theme of late medieval art that concerns the soul's readiness for and placement in the afterlife.[43] The subject is best known through the woodcut variations (1523/1525) of Hans Holbein (*circa* 1497–1543), published in book form in 1538.[44] In Holbein's woodcuts, Death appears suddenly to claim individuals, regardless of class, vocation, piety, or age. In one of the book's more terrifying visions, a queen out for a stroll with her courtiers is assaulted by Death in the guise of a court jester, carrying aloft an hourglass that has run out (fig. 9). She and her attendants cry out and struggle violently to resist his lead. Tooker clearly studied the narrative nuances of Holbein's woodcuts. Like the events in *Dance*, Holbein's incidents occur during daily routines, heightening the horror of an unexpected death. The unfortunate couple at the center of Tooker's painting gesture and howl, in close correspondence to the struggles of the queen in Holbein's plate. Their bony hands press against the fabric of black and red gloves, revealing their rapid degeneration into skeletons before our eyes. A growing crack in the pavement suggests that they are destined for the underworld.

*Bird Watchers* arose from Tooker's weariness of painting "unpleasant pictures." It was an attempt to design a picture about "people living together harmoniously. I wanted to paint a harmonious picture because I painted so many unpleasant pictures ... of people being beaten down by the subway and the city."[45] Although not ready to paint a specific religious theme, Tooker thought that the slow, contemplative adoration of nature together with companions would be "a good subject which could get close to a religious picture."[46] He noted that he went on an actual birdwatching excursion into New York's Central Park and that, ironically, the birders were jealously competitive and horrible to one another.

Tooker removed any discord in his rendition of birders alert and open to the wonders of nature. In composing the picture, he incorporated memories from thirteenth- and fourteenth-century Italian paintings, including works by Giovanni Bellini (*circa* 1430–1516), Botticelli, and Sassetta (*circa* 1390–*circa* 1450). Most prominently, the curved top and several aspects of the composition recall Piero della Francesca's *Baptism of Christ* altarpiece (1450s; fig. 10). In the center, a man in a light-brown coat appears in a transfigured state; he has opened his arms and turned his palms up, as though receiving stigmata or awake to a vision. As in Piero's *Baptism*, witnesses gather around a tree, while a path winds back through the landscape to reveal a brief view of the city. While it avoids any trace of dogma, *Bird Watchers* shows an ideal community on earth and is a good example of Tooker's desire to "express man's relation to the world and to himself—and to some spiritual force outside himself."[47]

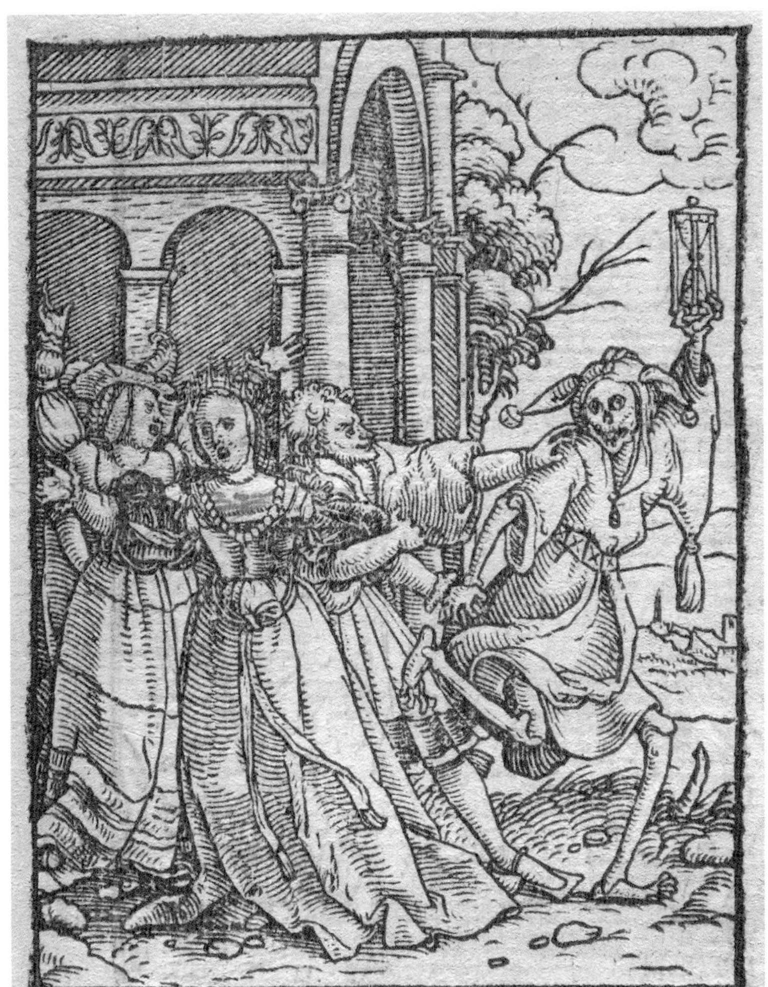

92

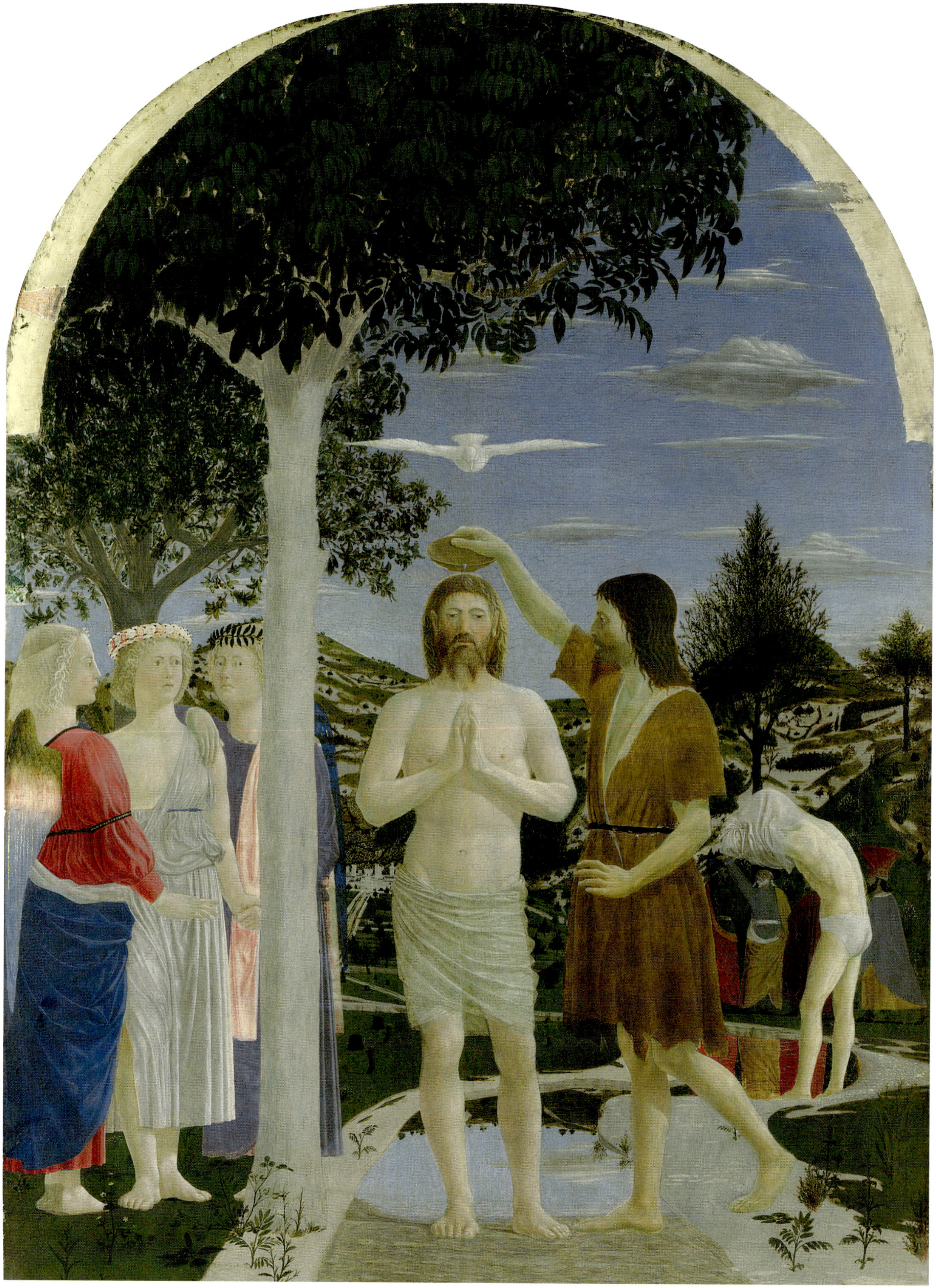

fig. 10
Piero della Francesca (1416?–1492)
*Baptism of Christ* (*circa* 1452)
Tempera and oil (?) on panel
65½ × 45½ inches (165.2 × 114.2 cm)
© National Gallery of Art, London

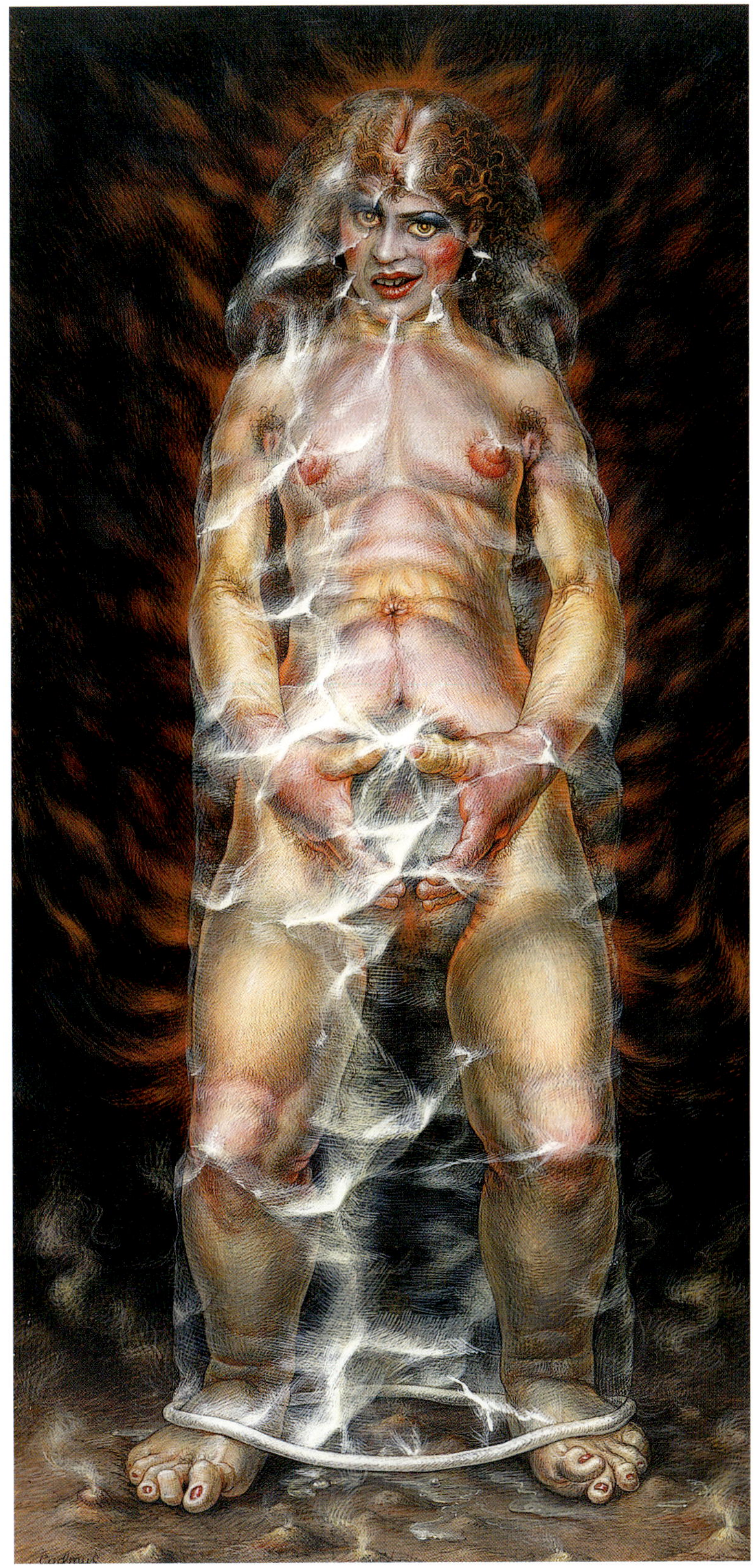

fig. 11
Paul Cadmus (1904–1999)
*The Seven Deadly Sins: Lust* (1945)
Egg tempera on Masonite
24½ × 11¾ inches (62.2 × 29.9 cm)
The Metropolitan Museum of Art, New York, Gift of Lincoln Kirstein, 1993 (1993.87.1)
Photograph © 1994 The Metropolitan Museum of Art, New York

Tooker's implicit allusions to religious art contrast with his contemporaries' explicit confrontation with religion, which often resulted in grotesque interpretations of traditional subjects. One prominent example that Tooker knew well was Paul Cadmus's *Seven Deadly Sins* (1945–49; fig. 11), which functions as an elaborately savage critique of humanity in its darkest incarnation. Cadmus, following earlier examples, invented personifications of the vices, including his own features among the seven horrors. Cadmus implied thus that we each bear all sins within ourselves and have the capacity to poison every fiber of our existence and pollute our surroundings. When they were first shown, one reviewer responded with the disgust that the artist intended, dismayed that Cadmus revealed "so little sympathy with, and so much contempt for people."[48]

In the years following World War II, artists invoked Christ's Passion and other biblical tales as a way of coping with and addressing global suffering. Artists working in a wide range of styles from diverse ideological viewpoints employed Christian symbols or depicted specific biblical stories to draw comparisons between ancient tragedy and the contemporary situation.[49] For instance, Philip Evergood (1901–1973) used the tortured body of Christ in a complex and accusatory painting called *The New Lazarus* (1927–54; fig. 12). Rotting, emaciated, and wounded American GIs, allusions to lynching, and anxious little figures hover around the edges of a scene that features a mystical vision of the crucified Christ. Although the newly risen Lazarus emerges from a sarcophagus, the world he has returned to implies hatred and fear. Evergood explained that he borrowed the "crucified and thorn-pierced" Christ from Matthias Grünewald (*circa* 1475–1528), "to say that man is inhuman to man and why can't he change?" He further emphasized that "Christ, with all his generosity, his goodness, his love for people" is here imagined put to death again, "drained of his blood, and left for the vultures to devour" as an analogy to contemporary barbarism embodied in "unnecessary wars for lust, opportunism and hate, racial violence, the result of bigotry, arrogance and suppression."[50]

Other artists deployed religion enigmatically as extensions of personal iconography. *The Arcades* (1950; fig. 13), by Henry Koerner (1915–1991), was inspired by Coney Island sideshow exhibits. It relates to a short story called "The Rosebush," in which Koerner imagined himself as barker and show attendant. While the scene appears to include a suspended body of Christ and an encased Virgin Mary, these represent the sideshow attractions Abdullah the Hanging Corpse and Fatima the Fortune Teller. Their appearance is transformed through the hallucinations of a mentally ill protagonist

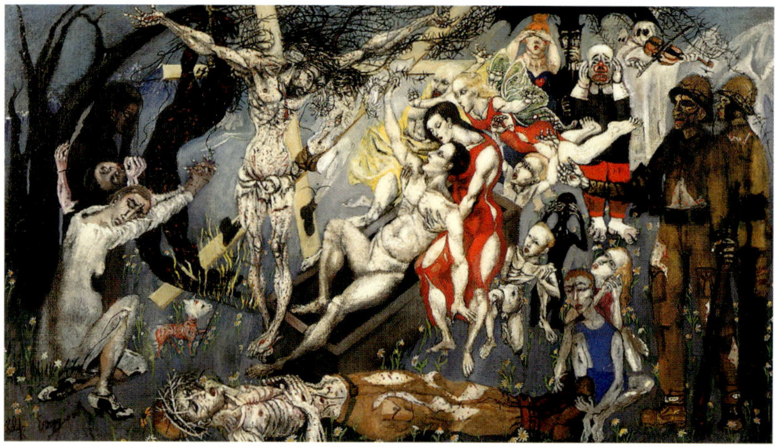

fig. 12
Philip Evergood (1901–1973)
*The New Lazarus* (1927/1940/1954)
Oil on plywood
48 × 83¼ inches (122 × 208 cm)
Whitney Museum of American Art, New York, Gift of Joseph H. Hirshhorn 54.60
Photograph by Geoffrey Clements

fig. 13
Henry Koerner (1915–1991)
*The Arcades* (1950)
Oil on Masonite panel
30 × 37¾ inches (76.2 × 95.9 cm)
Courtesy of the Michael Rosenfeld Gallery, LLC, New York, New York



who believes they are Jesus and Mary. The man prays on his knees before the Giottoesque arcade, treating the entire edifice as a shrine.[51] His obsessive faith can be read as Koerner's skeptical critique of belief and a challenge to the viewer to find the marvelous and spiritual in one's surroundings.

Also enigmatic is *The Flagellants* (1957; fig. 14), by Jules Kirschenbaum (1930–2000). Painted in Florence, Italy, it depicts three men practicing mortification of the flesh amid urban decay on the banks of a river, simultaneously to deny and to assert the body. Denying flesh represents a triumph over sin; asserting it binds them with Christ's suffering. Their profound focus on pain asserts spiritual continuity with medieval Christian confraternities despite their contemporary existence. Figures in the distance creep slowly towards the men in order to get a better look at the spectacle or to join in.[52] Koerner and Kirschenbaum each employed religious imagery in order to draw attention to the fissures in society between belief and practice. *The Arcades* and *The Flagellants* suggest, in a very different way from Tooker, that devotion is never by half-measures. Koerner and Kirschenbaum suggest that giving oneself over completely to devotion leads to the edge of what society considers rational. Tooker's lesson may be that the courage to maintain one's beliefs in the face of physical or emotional persecution has a price—but its reward transcends earthly existence.

What distinguishes Tooker from his contemporaries is the way he assimilates meaningful religious references into his work without revealing a particular source or committing to programmed iconography. His pictures' meaning is complicated by the memory trace of earlier narratives that lie embedded, like a palimpsest, beneath transformed, modern scenes. This causes the viewer to puzzle over the predicament of iconography that slips back and forth between fixed and fluid meaning to suggest multiple interpretations. In this way, Tooker is able to incorporate the emotional, spiritual, and transcendent potential of religious art without being bound to tradition or obvious symbols. Cultural theorist and critic Mieke Bal has observed that visual images by their nature not only translate but also overwrite the narratives they illustrate. This produces new narratives, which have the capacity to represent and critically engage the old. She remarks that

> Images are readings, and the rewritings they give rise to, through their ideological choices, function in the same way as sermons: They are not a retelling of the text but a use of it; not an illustration but, ultimately, a new text … [Therefore] the image does not replace a text; it *is* one. Working through the visual, iconographic, and literary traditions that produced it, these images propose for the viewer's consideration a propositional content, an argument, an idea, inscribed in line and color, by means of representation. They function by means, also, of an appeal to the already established knowledge that enables recognition of the scene depicted. And paradoxically, this recognition of what is already known is an indispensable step in the communication of a new, alternative propositional content of what is not yet known.[53]

In Tooker's work, the trace of the significant gesture or reference to a familiar narrative haunts the new composition and suggests extraordinary situations. Thus the couple in the foreground of *Coney*

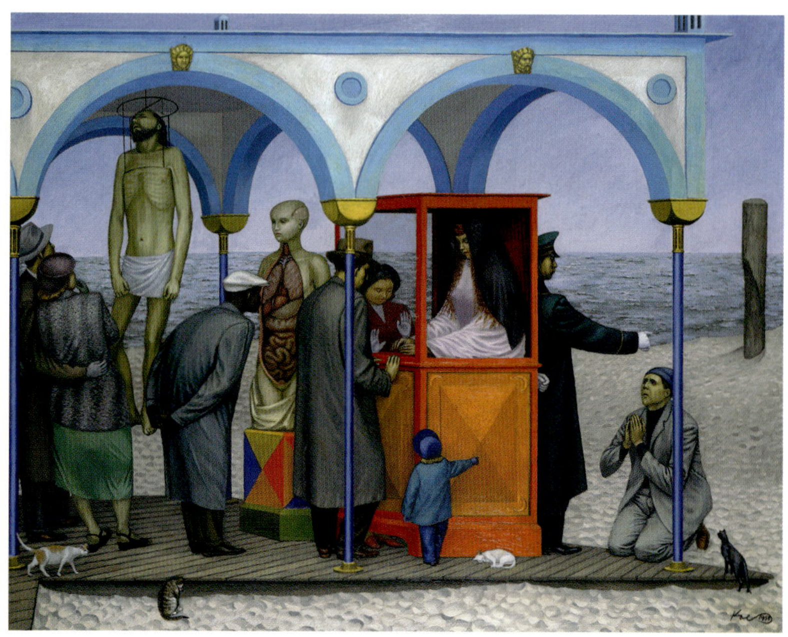

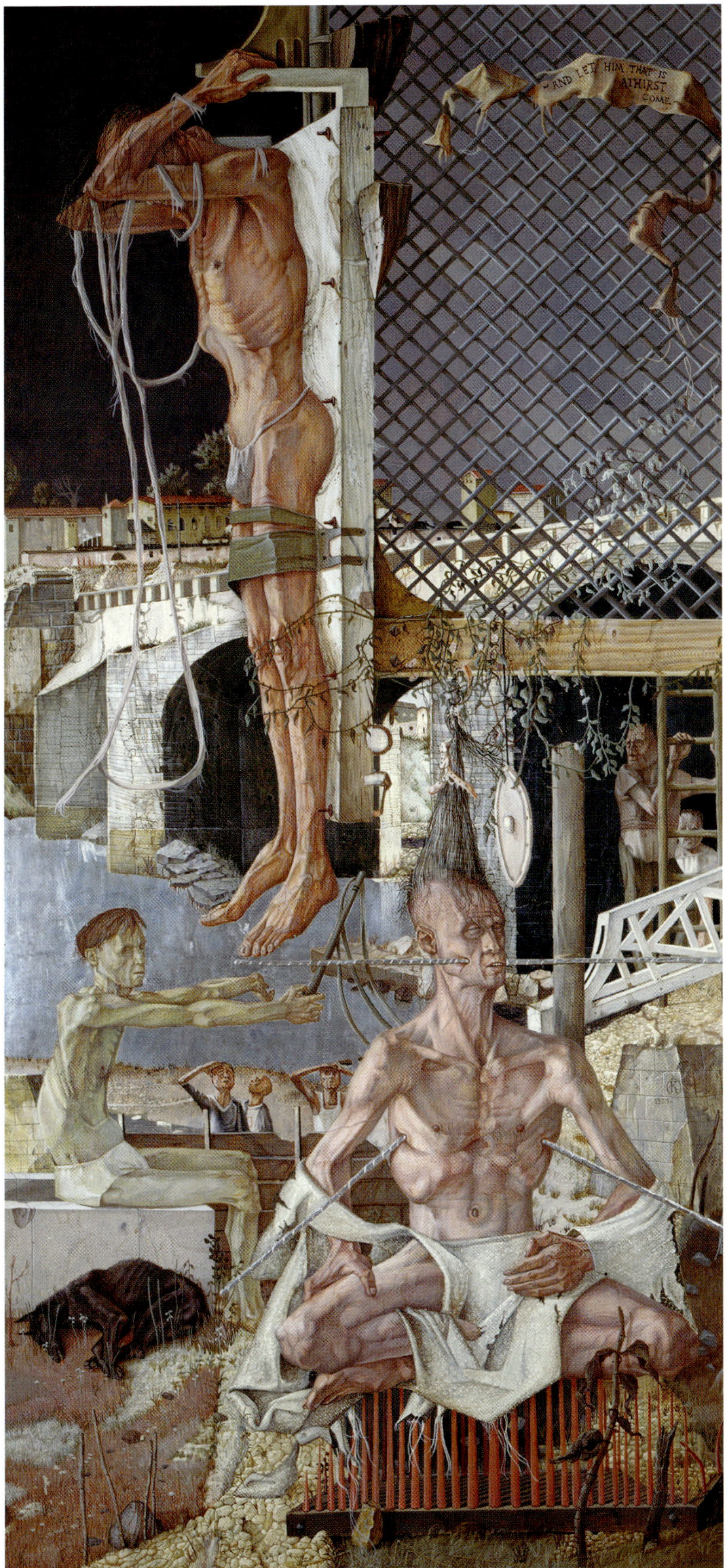


fig. 14
Jules Kirschenbaum (1930–2000)
*The Flagellants* (1957)
Tempera on panel
58 × 27 inches (147.4 × 68.6 cm)
Estate of Jules Kirschenbaum

*Island* (1947–48; plate 11) has been viewed not as a warm, affectionate genre detail but as a tragic echo of the *Pietà*—Mary mourning over the dead Christ.[54] Separated from the beach activity in a quiet, dark place under the boardwalk, they focus the viewer's attention and provoke thoughts on their meaning. Attendant figures who appear to bear witness to a lamentation frame them, further suggesting that their significance transcends that of a casually observed couple. In this way, Tooker's reliance on allusion heightens the mystery of his early work and gives his depiction of contemporary life the weight of biblical lessons and parables. 

Later in life, Tooker's close friendship with the parish priest who converted him, Father Forrest Rouelle, led to two commissions for St. Francis of Assisi Church in Windsor, Vermont, which he considered his first explicitly religious works.[55] A dynamic and charismatic presence in Vermont, Rouelle was much admired by his parishioners and fellow priests for his dedication to improving the lives of families, the elderly, and the disabled. Before arriving at Windsor, he attained a reputation as "activist priest" for founding Faith, Hope, and Charity, a low-income advocacy group, and Art Vermont, a cooperative that helped low-income women improve their situations. He had been instrumental in guiding the relocation of a mission to the church in which he had previously served and had initiated local nursing home and transportation services.[56]

After a fire destroyed St. Francis's Church in December 1977, Rouelle motivated his community to rebuild and became involved in the design of the new building. Over supper one evening in October 1979, Rouelle asked Tooker, who had already contributed to the reconstruction fund, whether he would paint something for the church. Tooker agreed, and the two decided together on the subject of the seven holy sacraments of the Catholic faith.[57] They are represented on individual panels in the following order: Baptism, Confirmation, Reconciliation, the Eucharist, Matrimony, the Anointing of the Sick, and Holy Orders (1980; fig. 15).[58] As Tooker developed preliminary sketches, he conferred with Rouelle to "make sure that the design was in accordance with church doctrine."[59] "I wanted Father Rouelle to approve before I started to work," he noted.[60] Excited by what he saw,

fig. 15
George Tooker
*The Seven Sacraments* (1980)
Egg tempera and gold leaf on seven gesso panels
42 × 132 inches overall (106.6 × 335.2 cm)
Church of Saint Francis of Assisi, Windsor, Vermont
Photography by Jeffrey Nintzel



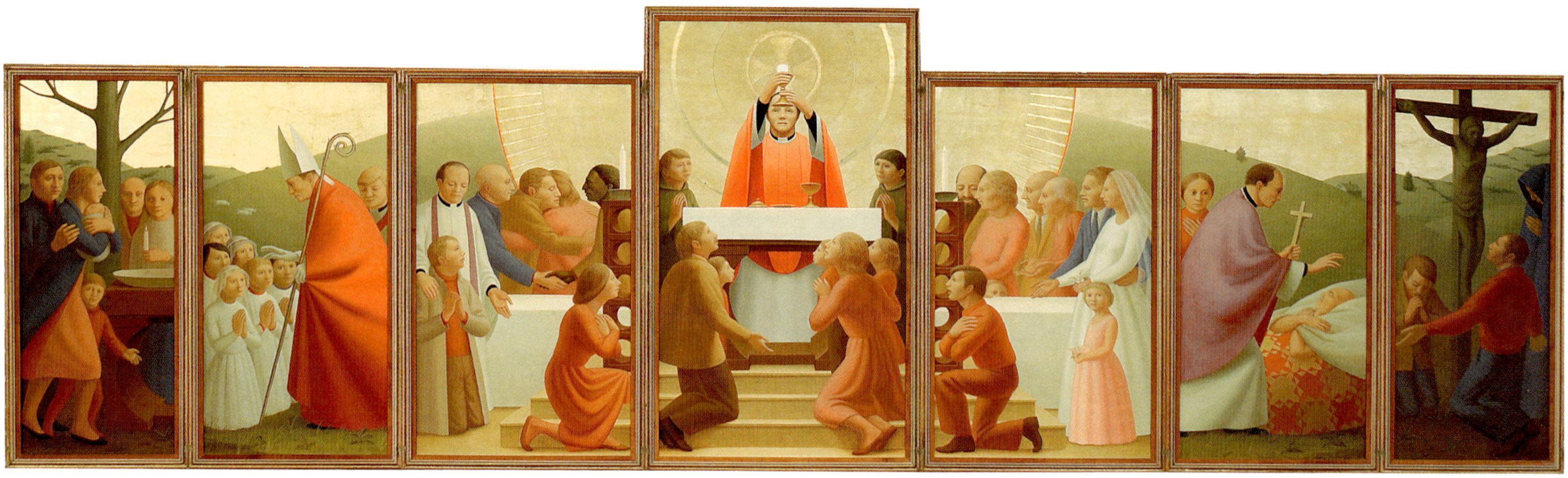

Rouelle urged Tooker to proceed with the polyptych, exclaiming, "George, your theology is fantastic."[61]

Rouelle's enthusiasm for Tooker's altarpiece was a response to the meaningful format, historical resonance, and personal dimension that he perceived in the work. He planned the new church as a place for his community to "celebrate life" through prayer, participation in the sacraments, and communal activities meant to strengthen faith and friendship. Tooker's arrangement is centered on a depiction of St. Francis's altar, with Rouelle as the community's spiritual leader. The sacraments flow outward from the central panel against a hilly Vermont landscape. The absence of walls defining a new building emphasizes that "the church" is its people, who carry their faith to the world beyond their parish through action and commitment.

As Tooker explained, the altarpiece honors "the centrality of the Eucharist among the sacraments and in the Church."[62] The ritual focus of Mass, the Eucharist embodies Christ's Incarnation, the Passion story, and its redemptive purpose. As it is raised and lowered above the altar by the priest, the Eucharistic bread symbolizes the body of Christ as elevated on the cross, taken down after death, and then glorified in the Resurrection. Tooker painted Rouelle dramatically consecrating the communion bread and wine. This depicts the moment of transubstantiation—the miracle in which, Catholics believe, the bread and wine become the flesh and blood of Christ during Mass. By ingesting this physical and spiritual nutriment, Catholics show their willingness to accept God as a part of the self and to be an instrument of His love and good works.[63]

Tooker placed the sacraments of Baptism and Holy Orders at either end of the ensemble. This arrangement meaningfully alters the traditional order in which the sacraments are shown relative to their appearance in life, beginning with Baptism and ending with the Anointing of the Sick. Each of these sacraments represents renewal in the Church through the introduction of new life into the parish and new clergy to a life of prayer and service. These panels also provide doctrinal support for the redemptive properties of the Eucharist. A bare tree in the Baptism panel alludes to the Tree of Knowledge, from which Adam and Eve ate the forbidden fruit of original sin. It is paired with a large wooden crucifix in the final panel, which symbolizes the Tree of Life, upon which Jesus died to secure humanity's salvation.

Although Tooker was aware that Rogier van der Weyden (1399/1400–1464) had painted the seven sacraments (*circa* 1445–50; fig. 16), he resisted consulting historical examples until his own version was under way.[64] Despite this, Tooker's instinct for placing the rituals in a meaningful setting and celebrating the Eucharist corresponds with this important precedent. Van der Weyden's triptych shows the sacraments within a Gothic church similar to examples near his workshop. They are arranged forward to back and forward

fig. 16
Rogier van der Weyden (1399/1400–1464)
*Triptych of the Seven Sacraments, "Chevrot Altarpiece,"* (*circa* 1445–50)
Oil on oak panel
78¾ × 38¼ inches (200 × 97.1 cm) (central panel), 46⅞ × 24¾ inches (119 × 62.9 cm) (side panels)
Koninlijk Museum voor Schone Kunsten, Antwerp, image courtesy of Reproductiefronds–Lukas



again in a semicircle from left panel to the right. Their appearance commences with infancy and ends with old age, showing the soul's progression on the journey of faith. The Baptism of an infant is the first ritual shown, while a dying man receives the Anointing of the Sick at far right. The large central panel in Van der Weyden's painting celebrates the primacy of the Eucharist by depicting a priest raising the consecrated host up to the heavens. This point is emphasized by a vision of Christ on the cross in the church foreground, attended by St. John, the Virgin Mary, and St. Mary Magdalene and others in lamentation.[65]

*The Seven Sacraments* is a celebration of Tooker's faith and the happiness he found in the Catholic community at St. Francis. It also expresses his love and respect for Father Rouelle, emphasizing his ability to keep a congregation united during its time of loss. It honors Rouelle's presence in Tooker's life, as the man who helped him embrace faith and inspired him to paint his first "explicitly religious" images. While Tooker did not consciously paint a self-portrait in *The Seven Sacraments*, he has acknowledged being identified with

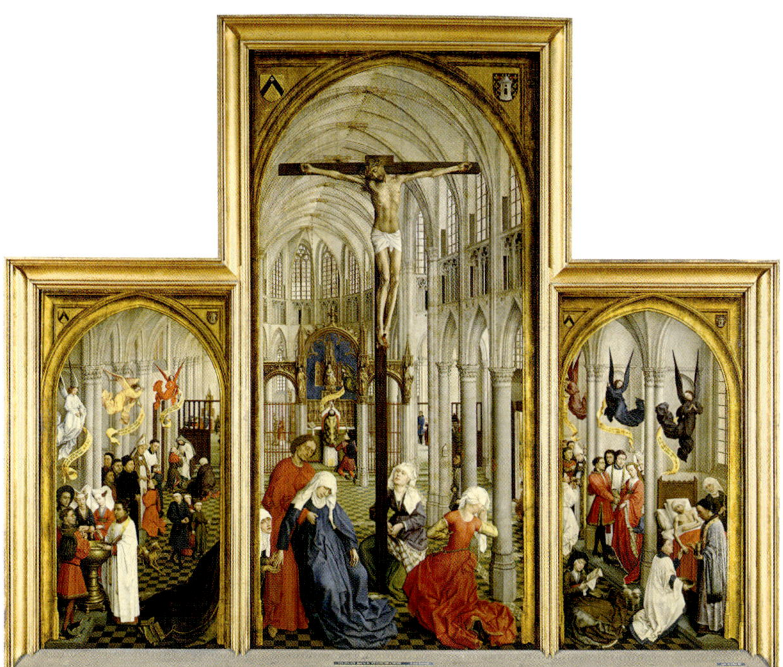

"the kneeling figure in the Reconciliation panel."[66] This penitent figure does resemble Tooker, and the priest behind him, Rouelle. Rouelle places a reassuring hand upon the kneeling man's right shoulder, and extends his left hand in a welcoming gesture, as though re-enacting Tooker's conversion before a radiant vision of the Eucharist.

Shortly after *The Seven Sacraments* was dedicated, Rouelle asked Tooker to paint the *Stations of the Cross* (fig. 17), a subject that was developed by the Franciscan order in the late thirteenth century and thus particularly appropriate to the church of St. Francis of Assisi. The Franciscans conceived of the "way of the cross" as a Jerusalem pilgrimage route to trace Christ's procession to the site of his Crucifixion. The Stations of the Cross involve the devotee's entire body in a ritual of remembrance, reflection, and meditation on Christ's suffering. Each of the fourteen Stations represents an event in Christ's progression to Calvary and afterward, from Pilate's pronouncement of a crucifixion sentence to the entombment.

During an interview in 1981, Tooker expressed anxiety about his readiness to undertake this important subject. "I have certain problems," he explained. "It's a matter of painting Our Lord. That's a problem I haven't resolved at this point."[67] Rouelle later recalled that Tooker said he felt "unworthy to paint the body of Christ."[68] The artist invented an unusual solution, in which he focused all narrative expression on gestures of hands. Tooker recently reflected on this strategy: "I think that everybody has an image in their head of Christ," he explained. "I didn't want to interfere with the image that's already in somebody's head … I felt that hands could be expressive and not interfere with anybody's image of Christ. Because I've been … put off by images of Christ. And I didn't want to do that. And hands are more universal."[69]

In the period immediately following his conversion, Tooker had painted two intimate studies of figures completely absorbed in prayer. *Orant* (1977; plate 52) shows a figure in dialogue with the infinite, bathed in a sonorous light that suggests the mysterious presence of God. Animated hands—precursors to the *Stations*—and an open mouth evoke an intense experience of prayer in which the entire being is active and given over to devotion. *Girl Praying* (1977; fig. 18) shows a

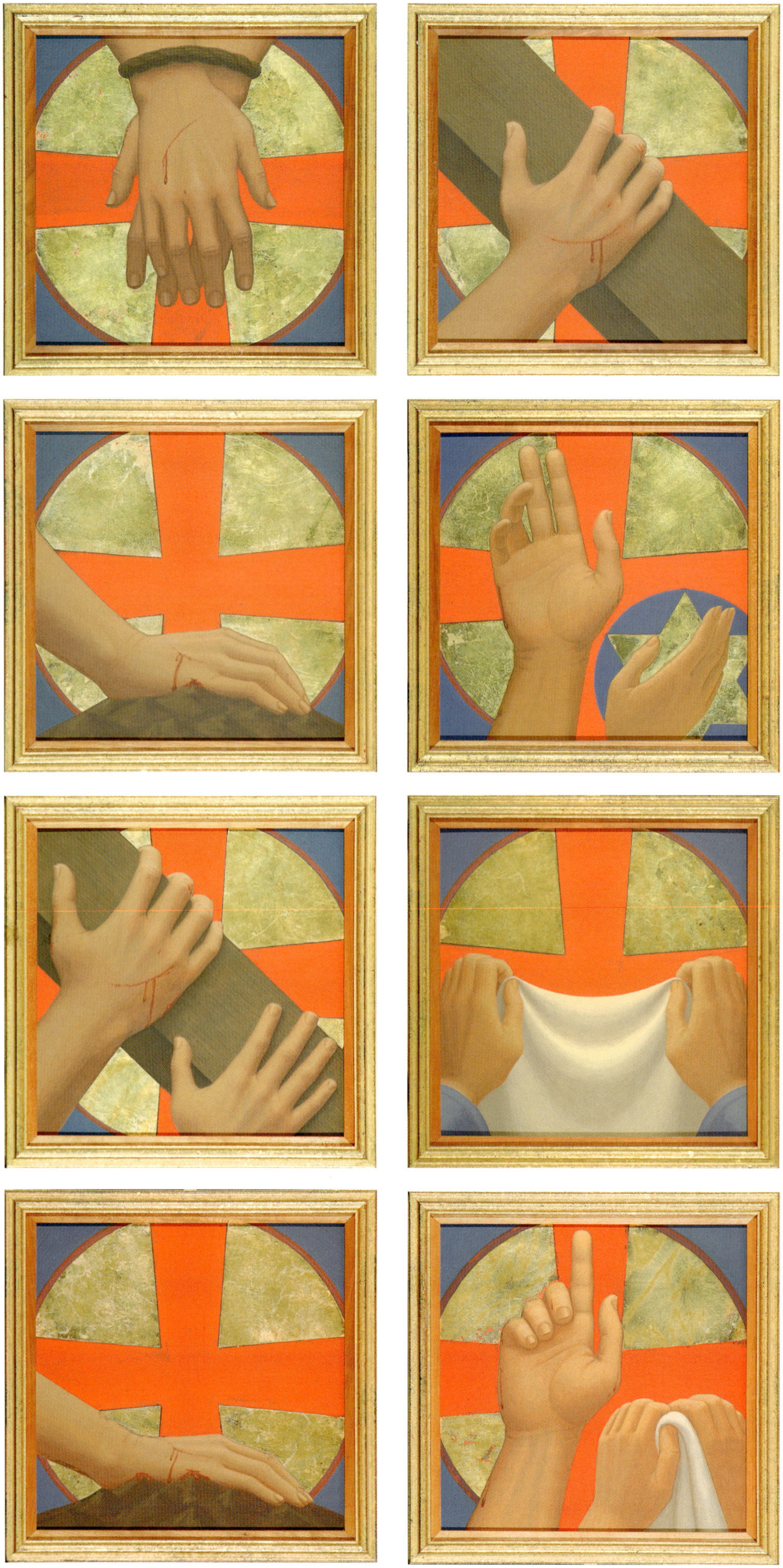

fig. 17
George Tooker
*Stations of the Cross* (1983–84)
Egg tempera and gold leaf on fourteen gesso panels
12 × 12 inches (30.5 × 30.5 cm) each
Church of Saint Francis of Assisi, Windsor, Vermont
Photography by Jeffrey Nintzel

Row 1, left: Christ is condemned to death by Pilate
Row 1, right: Christ is laden with his cross

Row 2, left: Christ falls for the first time
Row 2, right: Christ encounters his sorrowing mother

Row 3, left: Simon of Cyrene is forced to help Christ with the cross
Row 3, right: Veronica wipes Christ's face with her veil

Row 4, left: Christ falls for the second time
Row 4, right: Christ meets the women of Jerusalem

fig. 17 (continued)

Row 1, left: Christ falls for the third time
Row 1, right: Christ is stripped of his garments

Row 2, left: Christ is nailed to the cross
Row 2, right: Christ dies on the cross

Row 3, left: Christ's body is taken down from the cross
Row 3, right: Christ is laid in the sepulchre

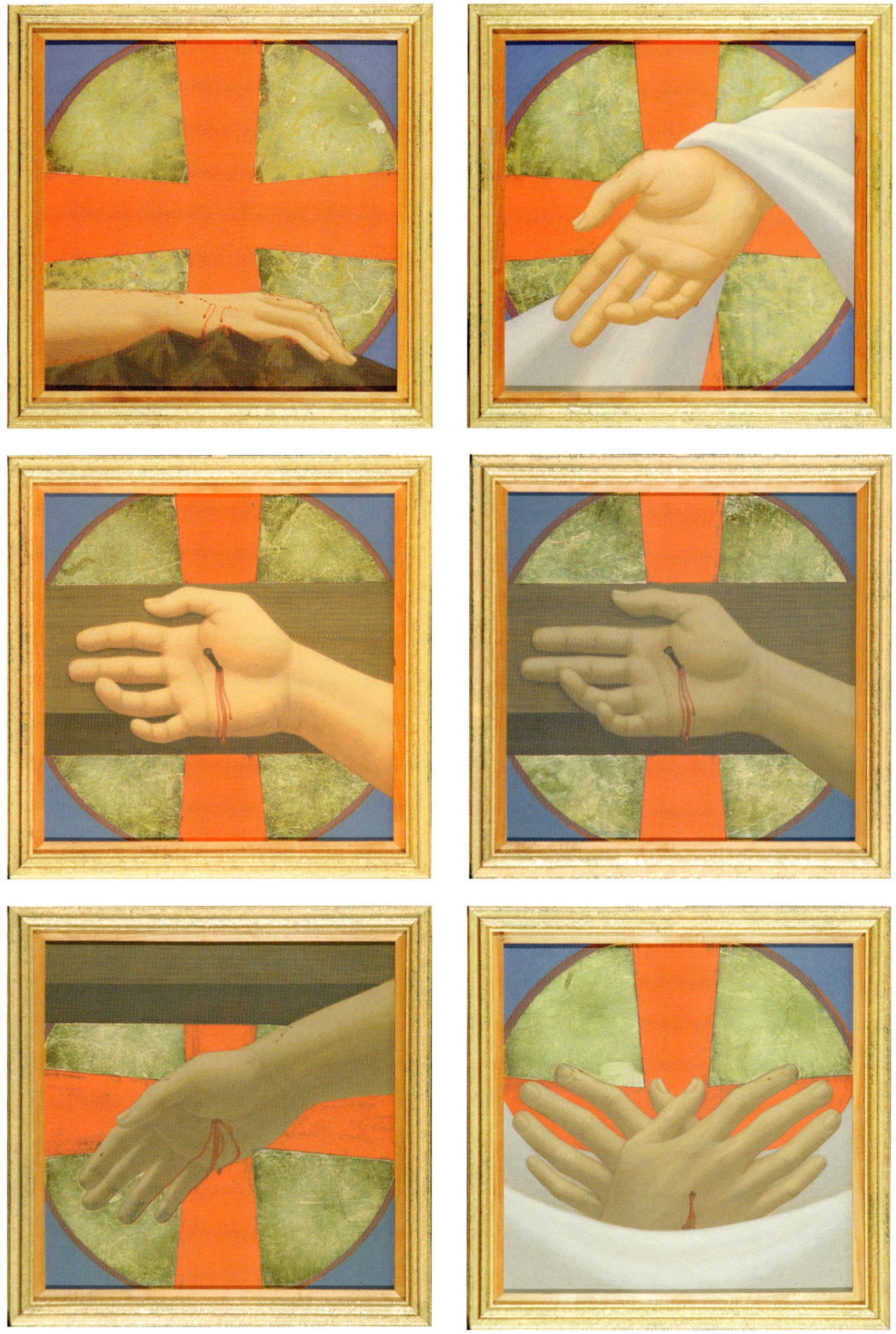

fig. 18
George Tooker
*Girl Praying* (1977)
Egg tempera on gesso panel
17 × 15 inches (43.2 × 38.1 cm)
Location unknown



woman at peace with herself in quiet meditation. She focuses inward on a mental image, object, or phrase to facilitate her communion with God. Each of these images enabled Tooker to contemplate God's presence within the self and in the surrounding world—two inseparable aspects of the divine accessed through prayer.

The *Stations of the Cross* gave Tooker an opportunity to design images that would be the focus of prayer and meditation. His focused narrative engages believers with Christ's suffering and encourages them to enter imaginatively into the scenes to picture the Passion. Each of the panels reveals hands that bleed from deep cuts, which drip and run down to the wrist or wet the stones that receive Christ's fall. As the panels progress, the bleeding becomes more intense, the imagined pain more acute, and Rouelle, recognizing the intense concentration and compassion embodied in the completed pictures, called them "truly devotional images."[70]

A decade later, Tooker reconsidered his relationship to the imagined body of Christ at the request of another priest at St. Francis of Assisi. Father Robert Campbell asked the artist–parishioner to consider making an image of the Resurrection, to be displayed behind the altar during Easter celebrations (1995; fig. 19). Initially Tooker resisted, presenting Campbell with the same reasons that led him to visualize the *Stations of the Cross* through expressive hands. Father Campbell explained:

> Every Easter I like to decorate the altar. In other parishes I had a big poster of the Resurrected Christ or paintings done by the women's guild. But here I was with an uncommon, inspired artist and one whose work I had marveled at in the church. For two years I asked him to paint a banner of the Resurrection. He said, "Father I'm not equipped to paint or even draw an image of our Lord." But eventually he agreed and said, "I'll give it a try." And one day he showed up quietly with this enormous drawing. I was astonished.[71]

Tooker reasoned that he was finally able to depict Christ's body simply because "Father Campbell asked for a figure of the Resurrection."[72] However, it is significant that he resolved his anxiety about depicting Christ through this particular subject. The *Resurrection* completed a cycle of ecclesiastical images in which he publicly revealed his engagement with faith. *The Seven Sacraments* celebrated his place in Catholicism and devotion to the community that accepted him. The *Stations of the Cross* enabled him to make a specific set of devotional images firmly in a venerable tradition of meditation and empathy. *Resurrection* forced Tooker to imagine the Passion story's glorious conclusion by representing Christ in triumph over sin and death, which is a mystery that lies at the center of the Catholic faith. Tooker rendered the risen Christ in graphite with slight touches of white on unprimed linen—a reference to the burial shroud that some venerate as a cult relic bearing the image of Jesus. Christ appears newly awake, neither spirit nor body, in a state of grace as he raises his arms in a celebratory gesture of hope preparing to ascend to Heaven.

Theologian Paul Tillich wrote that aspiring toward the fulfillment of humanity's possibilities "is a continuous task. It is never completely reached and will never be completely missed." Citing an array of examples from the past, including Piero della Francesca and Hieronymus Bosch, he suggested that artists had reflected the degree to which their culture approached or struggled against spiritual fulfillment. In defense of modern art that emphasized existential struggle, Tillich appealed to its humanistic purpose: "The very fact that a great work of art depicts the negative side in the fight for humanity is in itself a fulfillment of a high human possibility. The courage and the honesty which underlie such works, and the creative power which is able to grasp the negativity of the content by the positivity of the form, is a triumph of humanity." Some artists expressed fear of being possessed by "demonic forces" within the self, anxiety about living, and "feelings of emptiness, meaninglessness, and despair." But to Tillich, the admission and recognition of spiritual vulnerability signaled "courage, longing and hope, a reaching out into the unknown."[73]

Tillich's remarks are relevant to Tooker's exploration of our moral and spiritual predicament. Throughout his career, Tooker made pictures that confront anxiety, social fragmentation, and the pervasive

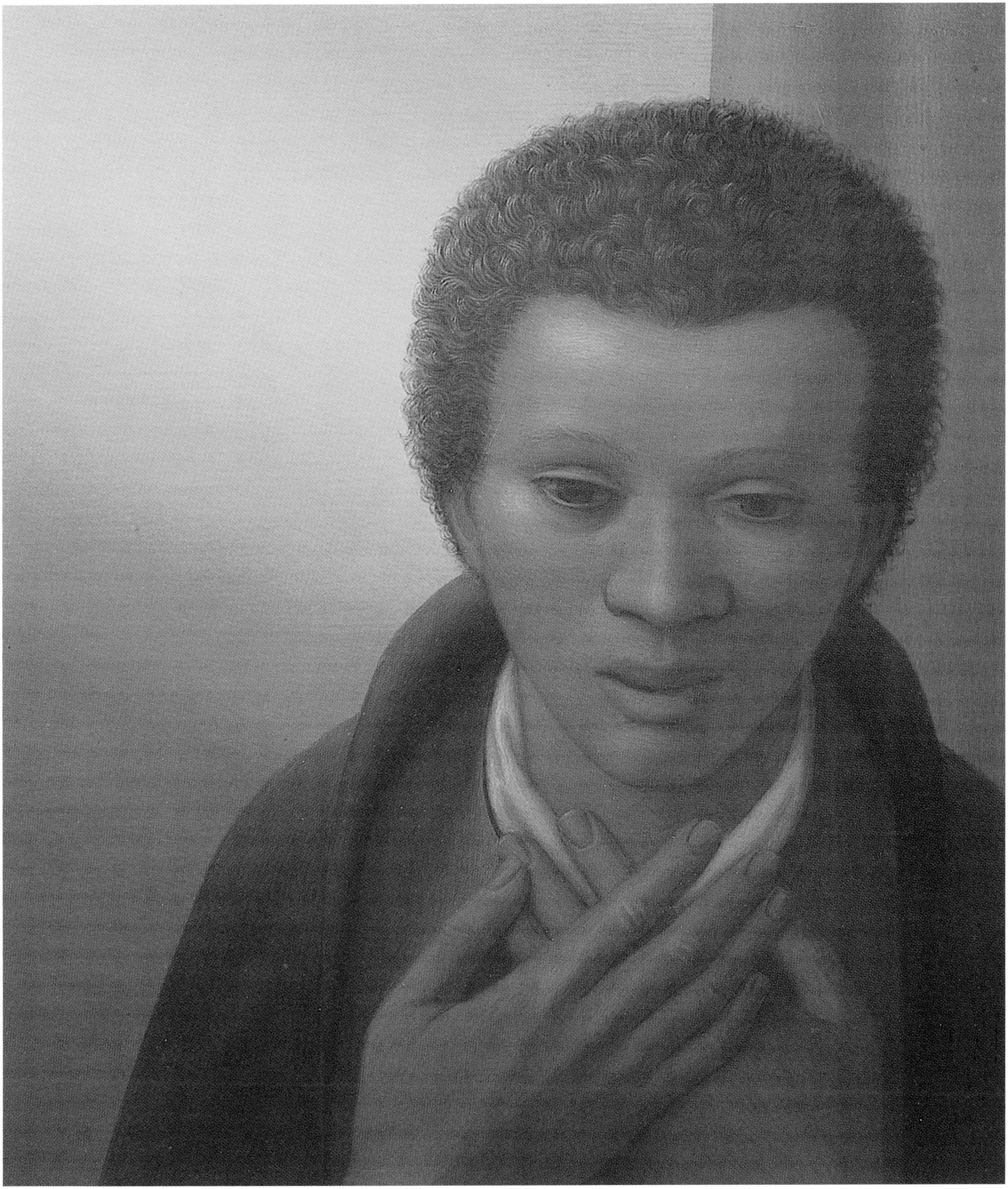

102

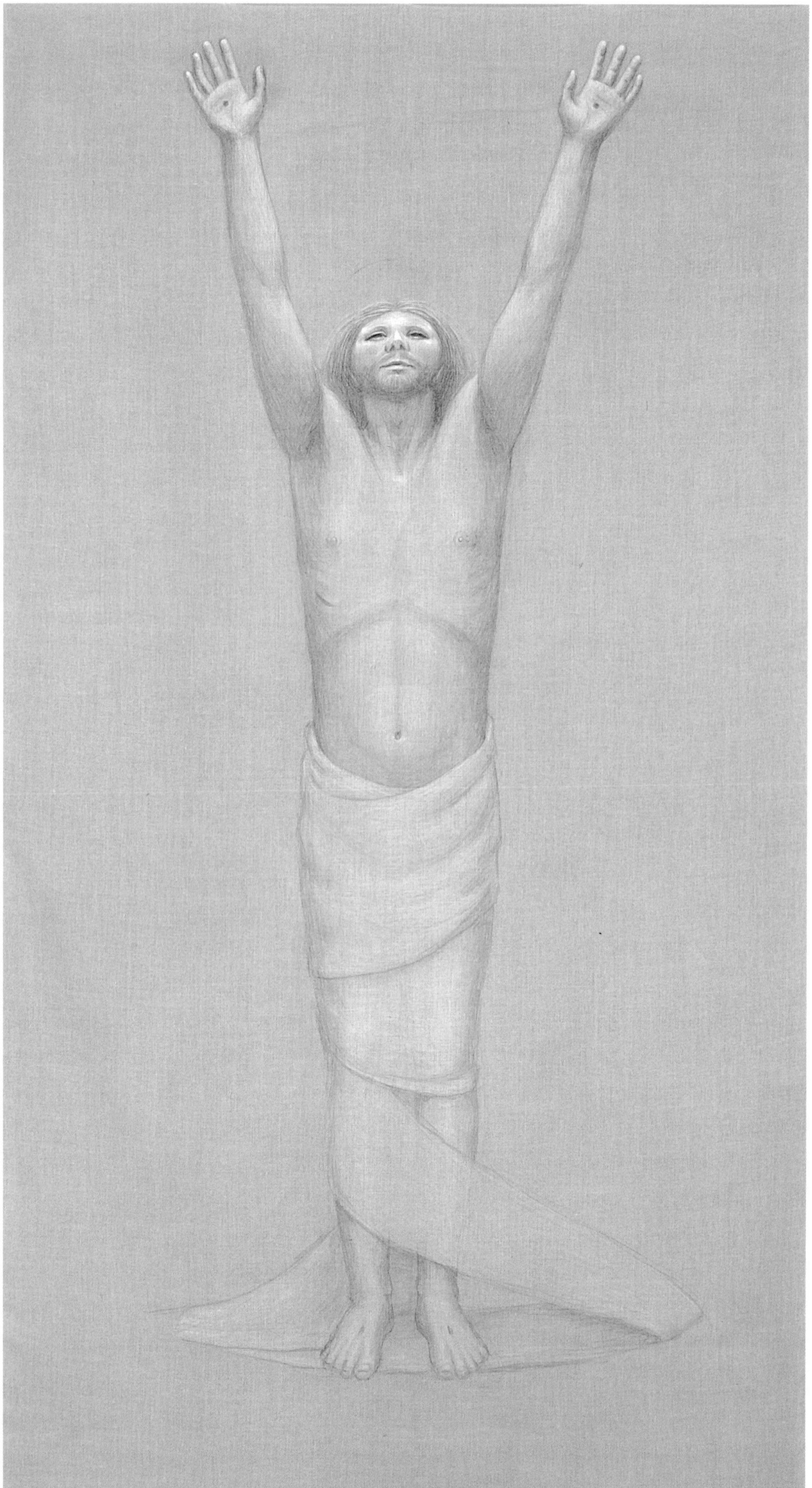

fig. 19
George Tooker
*Resurrection* (1995)
Graphite and egg tempera on linen
96 × 42 inches (243.9 × 106.6 cm)
Father Robert Campbell, Shrine of LaSalette, Enfield, New Hampshire
Photography by Jeffrey Nintzel



sense of loss that can infect troubled communities. He situated this within the framework of New York since, as he put it, "I think the essential problems of today are shown best by city life."[74] By merging his examination of human relationships with allusions to religious art, he suggested that our actions have implications that transcend this life and affect the state of the soul.

Tooker's work posits that the absence of community, communication, empathy, or kindness is the source of, and path to, human suffering. The so-called public paintings envision suspended states of despair, anxiety, and terror, representing a terrestrial purgatory that reflects a lack of harmony. Tooker also imagined how humanity can share in joy and sympathy, enacting a version of Paradise. If *Children and Spastics* and *Waiting Room* (1957; plate 31) portray what we must suffer, *Bird Watchers* and *Embrace of Peace II* (1988; plate 62) show what we should be. Through an exploration of both aspects of humanity, Tooker pictures a world in which our actions decide its position between Purgatory and Paradise.

## Notes

1 David Tunkl, "An Interview with George Tooker," in Merry A. Foresta and David Tunkl, *George Tooker*, exhib. cat. (Los Angeles: David Tunkl Gallery, 1980), n.p. See also Justin Spring, "An Interview with George Tooker," *American Art*, 16:1 (spring 2002), 78–80.

2 Information about Tooker's participation in the church comes from telephone interviews with the artist and with Father Robert Campbell, formerly of Tooker's parish of St. Francis of Assisi, Windsor, Vermont, now part of the community at the La Salette Shrine, Enfield, New Hampshire; both interviews, August 24, 2007.

3 As characterized by Spring, "An Interview with George Tooker," 61.

4 See, for instance, Tunkl, "An Interview with George Tooker," n.p., and Spring, "An Interview with George Tooker," 80.

5 Heidi D. Shafranek, "An Interview with George Tooker," June 5, 1981, in "The World of George Tooker: Surreal or Real," MA diss., University of Delaware, 1982, 165.

6 Victoria Robinson, "Interview with George Tooker," in Elizabeth Langhorne-Reeve, *George Tooker: Paintings and Working Drawings, 1947–1988* (Richmond: Modlin Fine Arts Center, University of Richmond, 1989), 8.

7 The others were done in 1947, 1969, and 1994 (see plates 8, 44, and 59). Apart from these formal self-portraits, Tooker has made two self-portrait lithographs (in 1984 and 1996) and one self-portrait drawing (1992; plate 58). Tooker appears amid other figures in several paintings, including *Dance* (plate 3), discussed later in this essay. Scholars and critics have repeatedly remarked on the close resemblance between Tooker's facial features and those of his imagined characters throughout his œuvre. This is the origin of the term "the Tooker man."

8 Shafranek, "An Interview with George Tooker," 157, 160; Melissa Wolfe, "Interview with George Tooker," July 28, 2007, 20.

9 See his comments regarding death in Tunkl, "An Interview with George Tooker," n.p.

10 Tooker has acknowledged that he composed the picture with the icon tradition in mind. Telephone interview with the author, August 24, 2007.

11 For more on this tradition, see the volume devoted to the best-known example of the subject, painted by Rogier van der Weyden (Museum of Fine Arts, Boston): Carol J. Purtle *et al.*, *Rogier van der Weyden: St. Luke Drawing the Virgin, Selected Essays in Context* (Turnhout: Brepols, 1997).

12 Tooker betrays modesty regarding his achievements, yet consistently positions himself within a specific tradition dominated by painters synonymous with religious art. See, for instance, Selden Rodman, *Conversations with Artists* (New York: Devin-Adair, 1957), 210.

13 Thomas H. Garver, interview with George Tooker, tape 1, 1973, Archives of American Art, Smithsonian Institution, Washington, D.C.; and Gregory M. Hollister-Knepp, "The Sacred and the Profane: Christian and Mythological Imagery within the Œuvre of George Tooker," MA diss., Bloomsburg University, Pennsylvania, 1997. "Appendix A: An Interview with George Tooker," April 21, 1997, 67.

14 Wolfe, "Interview with George Tooker," 14; see also Spring, "An Interview with George Tooker," 62.

15 Spring, "An Interview with George Tooker," 78.

16 Dorothy Day, "Technique of Agitation," *Catholic Worker* (December 1933), 2.

17 Dorothy Day, "For the New Reader," *Catholic Worker* (December 1936), 6.

18 The examples are plentiful, but see Dorothy Day, "On Pilgrimage—March 1965," *Catholic Worker* (March 1965), 1–2, 6.

19 Dorothy Day, "Wealth, The Humanity of Christ, Class War," *Catholic Worker* (June 1935), 5.

20 Amusingly, Tooker recalled that his first teacher, Malcolm Fraser, once wrote to him, "I fear the gods have willed that you are going to be an artist." Spring, "An Interview with George Tooker," 63.

21 Interview with Grace George Alexander and George Kay on "Artists in New York," WNYC Radio transcript, New York City, 1967. George Tooker Papers, Archives of American Art, Smithsonian Institution, Washington, D.C., 3.

22 William Christopher, journal of trip to Montgomery and Selma, March 15, 1965, William Christopher Papers, box 1, folder 2, "King File," Archives of American Art, Smithsonian Institution, Washington, D.C.

23 Wolfe, "Interview with George Tooker," 20.

24 For considerations of these concepts, see David Morgan, *Visual Piety: A History and Theory of Popular Religious Images* (Berkeley, California: University of California Press, 1998), 60–73; and Henk van Os *et al.*, *The Art of Devotion in the Late Middle Ages in Europe 1300–1500* (Princeton: Princeton University Press, 1994).

25 Telephone interview with George Tooker, August 24, 2007. For Tooker's emphasis of the importance of the Johnson Collection, see also Hollister-Knepp, "An Interview with George Tooker," 61; and Richard Boyle and Hilton Brown, "Interview with George Tooker," January 14, 1993, Archives of the Brandywine River Museum, Chadds Ford, Pennsylvania, research files for the exhibition *Milk and Eggs: The American Revival of Tempera Painting, 1930–1950*, 3–4, 14.

26 Jonathan Weinberg, "Interview with George Tooker," June 7, 2007, 12. See also Spring, "An Interview with George Tooker," 67; and Hollister-Knepp, "An Interview with George Tooker," 61–63.

27 For an analysis of the medieval precedent for *A Game of Chess* (1946–47; plate 5), see Charles Brock, "George Tooker, *The Chess Game (The Chessman)* [*sic*], 1947," in Bruce Robertson *et al.*, *Twentieth-Century American Art: The Ebsworth Collection*, exhib. cat. (Washington, D.C.: National Gallery of Art, 2000), 263–65.

28 Robinson, "Interview with George Tooker," 5.

29 Telephone interview with George Tooker, August 24, 2007; see also Boyle and Brown, "Interview with George Tooker," 14.

30 Ronald Lightbrown, *Sandro Botticelli: Complete Catalogue*, 2 vols. (Berkeley and Los Angeles: University of California Press, 1978), Vol. 1, 109–12; Vol. 2, 74–78.

31 Telephone interview with George Tooker, August 24, 2007.

32 George Tooker, Artist Questionnaire, January 30, 1951, Whitney Museum of American Art, New York.

33 Paul Cadmus, "Broadside [regarding *Subway Symphony*, 1976–77]," Midtown Galleries, 1977, quoted in Lincoln Kirstein, *Paul Cadmus*, rev. edn (New York: Chameleon Books, 1996), 105.

34 Thomas H. Garver, *George Tooker*, rev. edn (San Francisco: Pomegranate, 2002), 130.

35 Tooker in conversation with Thomas H. Garver, 1983.

36 Tooker, quoted in Susan Jane Baker, "George Tooker and the Modern Tradition," PhD diss., University of Kansas, 1994, 26; also discussed in a telephone interview with the author, August 24, 2007.

37 Garver, *George Tooker*, 15.

38 *Ibid.*, 20.

39 Hollister-Knepp, "An Interview with George Tooker," 72.

40 Katherine Hauser, "George Tooker, Surveillance, and Cold War Sexual Politics," *GLQ*, 11: 3 (June 2005), 391–425.

41 Hauser notes this, although she does not use the examples that I give.

42 The literature on this topic is extensive and complex. For a good introduction to the subject, see Caroline Walker Bynum, "Violent Imagery in Late Medieval Piety," *German Historical Institute Bulletin*, 30 (spring 2002), 3–36. See also Mitchell B. Merback's response, "Reverberations of Guilt and Violence, Resonances of Peace: A Comment on Caroline Walker Bynum's Lecture," *German Historical Institute Bulletin*, 30 (spring 2002), 37–50.

43 For more on this subject, see Paul Binski, *Medieval Death: Ritual and Representation* (Ithaca, New York, and New York: Cornell University Press, 1996).

44 *The Dance of Death by Hans Holbein the Younger: A Complete Facsimile of the Original 1538 Edition of "Les simulachres & historiées faces de la mort,"* intro. by Werner L. Gundersheimer (New York: Dover Publications, 1971). See also Peter Parshall, "Hans Holbein's Pictures of Death," in *Hans Holbein: Paintings, Prints, and Reception*, ed. Mark Roskill and John Oliver Hand (Washington, D.C.: National Gallery of Art and Yale University Press, 2001), 83–95.

45 Hollister-Knepp, "An Interview with George Tooker," 69–71.

46 Garver, *George Tooker*, 20.

47 Rodman, *Conversations with Artists*, 210.

48 Belle Krasne, "Cadmus' Deadly Sins," *The Art Digest*, 24:5 (December 1, 1949), 15. For an analysis of these paintings, see Kirstein, *Paul Cadmus*, 53–61.

49 The examples are plentiful. For instance, Mark Rothko titled paintings of the 1940s *Gethsemane* and *Entombment* for this reason. Stephen Greene reinterpreted numerous scenes from the New Testament, including the carrying of the cross, as a way to explore human suffering. Rico LeBrun embarked on an enormous body of work exploring the brutality of the Crucifixion. An international competition initiated by the filmmaker Albert Lewin to select a painting for his film, *The Private Affairs of Bel Ami* (1947), dictated the theme of the Temptation of St. Anthony as the quintessential struggle

between good and evil. For more on this general topic, see Jeffrey Wechsler and Greta Berman, *Realism and Realities: The Other Side of American Painting, 1940–1960*, exhib. cat. (Rutgers University Art Gallery, New Brunswick, New Jersey, 1982), 55, 73, 101, and 108; for the Lewin competition, see Albert Lewin *et al.*, *The Temptation of Saint Anthony* (Washington, D.C.: American Federation of Arts, 1947), and Robert Cozzolino, "Every Picture Should Be a Prayer: The Art of Ivan Albright," PhD diss., University of Wisconsin-Madison, 2006, 192–209.

50 Evergood, quoted in Kendall Taylor, *Philip Evergood: Never Separate from the Heart* (London and Toronto: Associated University Presses, 1987), 167. Evergood's comments are from a letter written in 1966.

51 Gail Stavitsky, *From Vienna to Pittsburgh: The Art of Henry Koerner* (Pittsburgh: Museum of Art, Carnegie Institute, 1983), 18, 53. Regarding Giotto and the function of modern narrative pictures, see Koerner's statement in *Paintings and Drawings by Henry Koerner* (New York: Midtown Galleries, 1951).

52 For more on this picture, see Thomas Worthen, *Jules Kirschenbaum: The Need to Dream of Some Transcendent Meaning*, exhib. cat. (Iowa City, Iowa: University of Iowa Museum of Art, 2006), 20.

53 Mieke Bal, *Reading "Rembrandt": Beyond the Word–Image Opposition* (Cambridge: Cambridge University Press, 1991), 34–35.

54 See Hollister-Knepp, "The Sacred and the Profane;" Shafranek, "An Interview with George Tooker;"and Dana Simpson, "George Tooker, *Self-Portrait*, 1947," in Elizabeth Armstrong *et al., Villa America: American Moderns 1900–1950* , exhib. cat. (Newport Beach, California: Orange County Museum of Art, 2005), 109–110.

55 Mark D. Lombard, "Artist–Convert Paints Celebration of Joy," *Vermont Catholic Tribune* (January 23, 1981), 24. See also Spring, "An Interview with George Tooker," 79–80; and Wolfe, "An Interview with George Tooker," 14.

56 This is a short list of Rouelle's various activities. Sandy Cooch, "Crafts Co-op Delivers Support and Savings," *The Herald (Randolph Vermont)* (September 28, 2000), and "Historic Catholic Church to Close after Services on Sunday," *The Herald (Randolph Vermont)* (June 28, 2001).

57 Tooker agreed to undertake each commission as a contribution to the church; no payment was made.

58 "It was Father Rouelle who suggested that I paint something for the church." Telephone conversation with the artist, August 24, 2007. See also Lombard, "Artist–Convert Paints Celebration of Joy," 24. Garver (*George Tooker*, 129) explains that Rouelle asked Tooker whether he would consider making a painting that could be sold to benefit the reconstruction and that Tooker responded that he would rather make a painting specifically for the church. This accords with Tooker's attitude to art and commerce (see, for instance, his contemporary comments about just this issue in Tunkl, "An Interview with George Tooker," n.p.); see also Wolfe, "Interview with George Tooker," 21.

59 Spring, "An Interview with George Tooker," 80.

60 Shafranek, "An Interview with George Tooker," 160.

61 Lombard, "Artist–Convert Paints Celebration of Joy," 24.

62 *Ibid.*

63 For literature on theological debates regarding the Eucharist, see Caroline Walker Bynum, *Holy Feast and Holy Fast: The Religious Significance of Food to Medieval Women* (Berkeley, California: University of California Press, 1987); Miri Rubin, *Corpus Christi: The Eucharist in Late Medieval Culture* (Cambridge: Cambridge University Press, 1991); and Ann W. Astell, *Eating Beauty: The Eucharist and the Spiritual Arts of the Middle Ages* (Ithaca, New York, and London: Cornell University Press, 2006).

64 Tooker says that the art historian Greta Berman drew his attention to Van der Weyden's triptych, but he avoided looking at precedents until his design was complete, afraid that the memory of the example would have, as he put it, "torn" him up. Shafranek, "An Interview with George Tooker," 160.

65 For this altarpiece, see Dirk de Vos, *Rogier van der Weyden: The Complete Works* (New York: Harry N. Abrams, 1999), 217–25.

66 Shafranek, "An Interview with George Tooker," 161.

67 *Ibid.*, 165–66.

68 Nancy Walker, "Church Receives Tooker Paintings," *Rutland Herald* (January 27, 1984).

69 Wolfe, "Interview with George Tooker," 21.

70 Walker, "Church Receives Tooker Paintings."

71 Telephone interview with Father Robert Campbell, August 24, 2007.

72 George Tooker, letter to the author, July 24, 2007.

73 Paul Tillich, "A Prefatory Note by Paul Tillich," in Peter Selz, *New Images of Man*, exhib. cat. (New York: Museum of Modern Art, 1959), 10.

74 Interview with Grace George Alexander and George Kay, WNYC Radio transcript, 4.

# Plates

plate 1
***Children and Spastics*** (1946)
Egg tempera on gesso panel
24½ × 18½ inches (62.2 × 47 cm)
Collection Museum of Contemporary Art, Chicago
Gift of Mary and Earle Ludgin Collection
Photography © Museum of Contemporary Art, Chicago



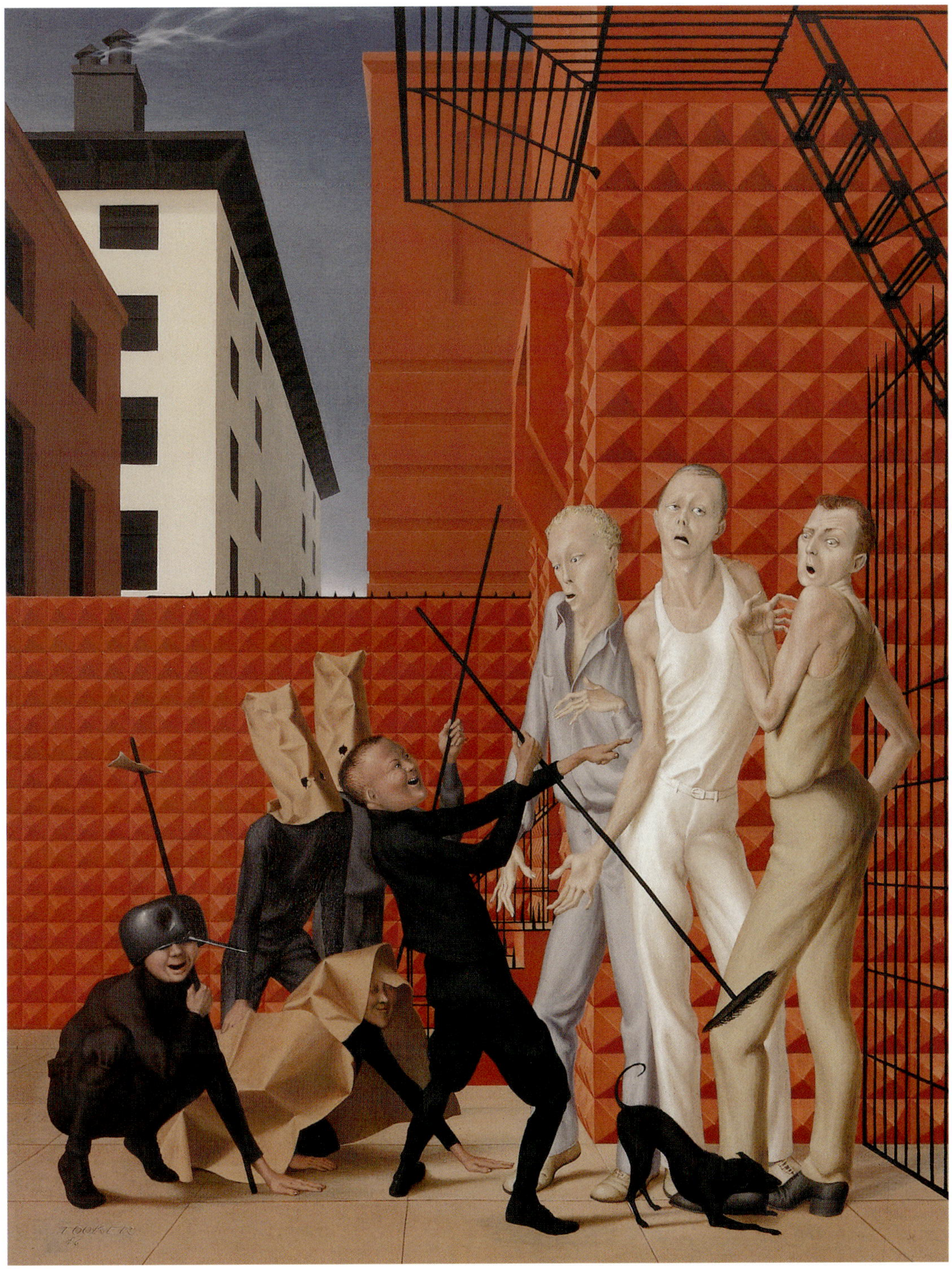

plate 2
**Study for *Dance*** (*circa* 1946)
Graphite, chalk, wash, and ink on paper
13 × 20⁷⁄₁₆ inches (33 × 51.9 cm)
Gift of the artist (PA 1936) in memory of his parents, George Clair and Angela Montejo Roura Tooker, Addison Gallery of American Art, Phillips Academy, Andover, Massachusetts



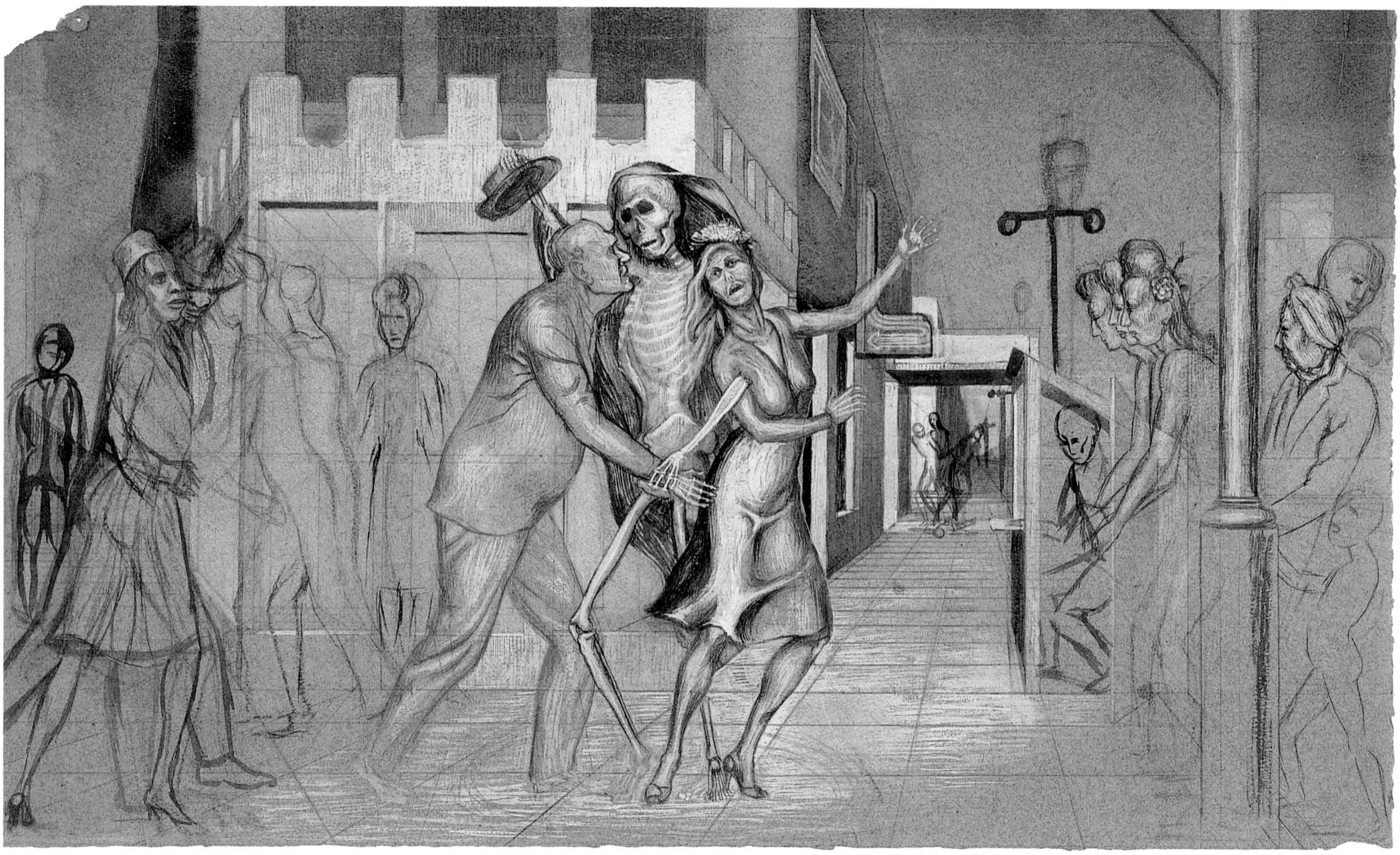

plate 3
*Dance* (1946)
Egg tempera on gesso panel
13¼ × 20½ inches (33 × 52 cm)
Collection of Andrew Nelson

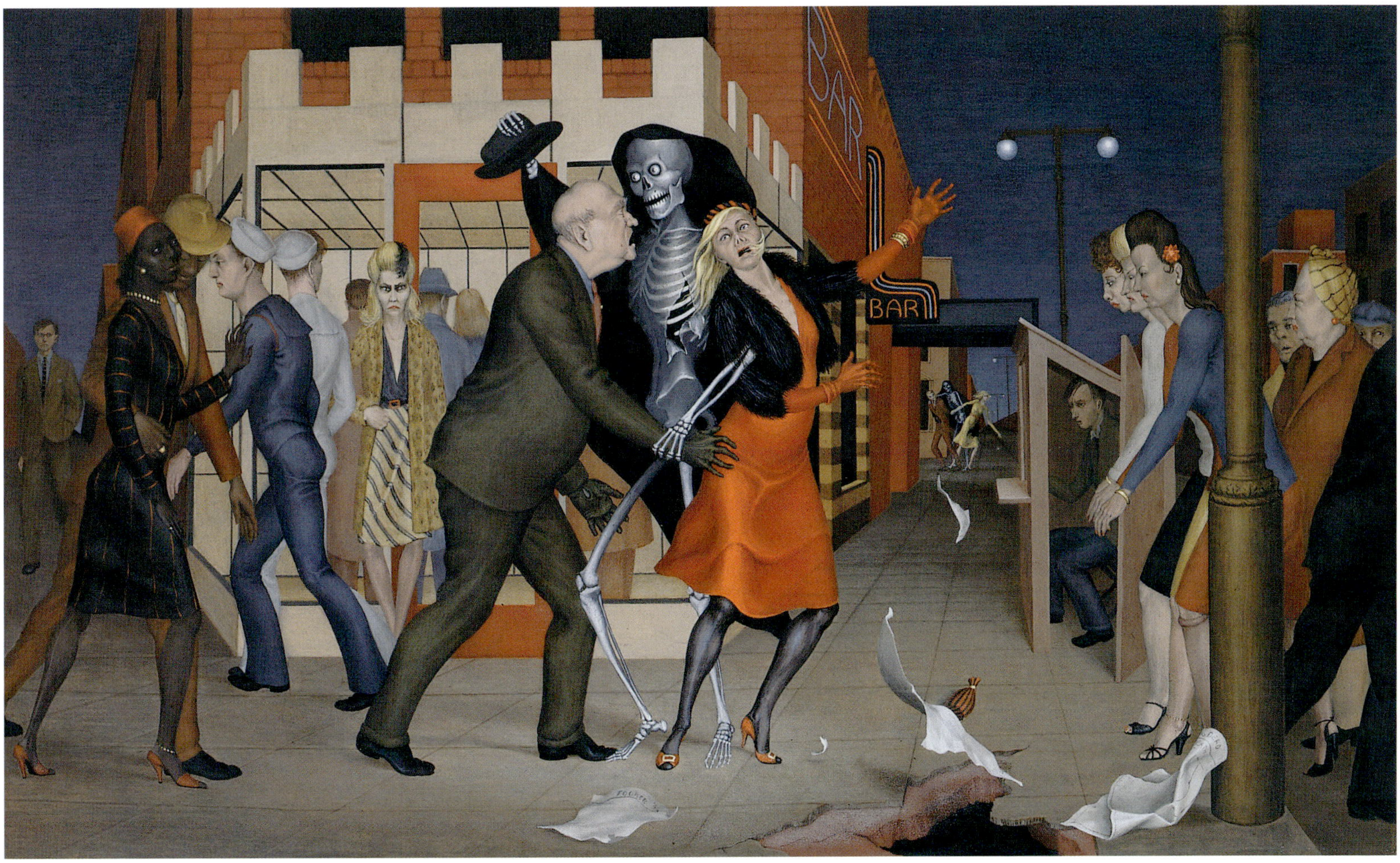

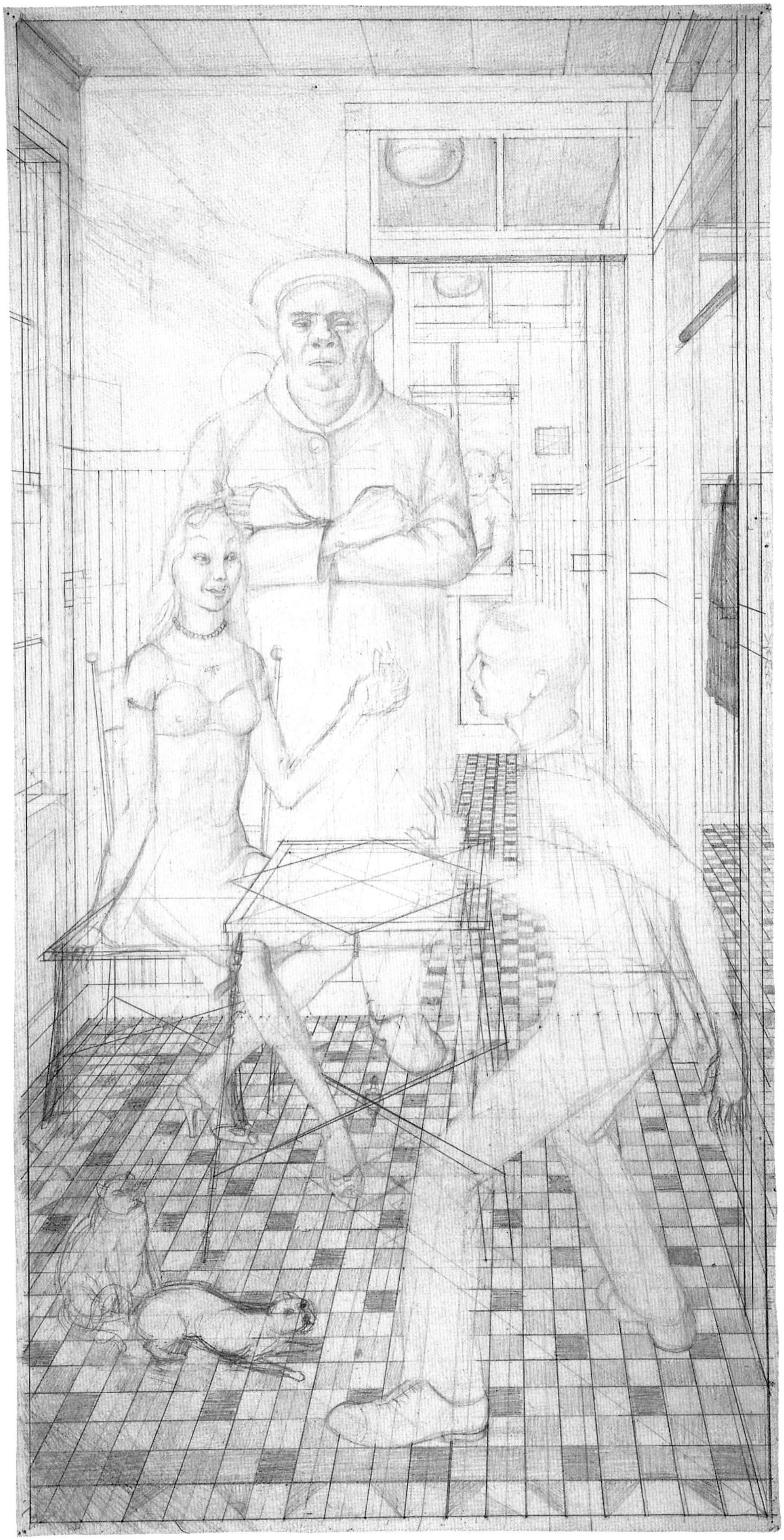

plate 4
**Study for *A Game of Chess*** (1946)
Graphite on paper
$29^{15}/_{16}$ × 15 inches (76 × 38.1 cm)
Gift of the artist (PA 1936) in memory of his parents, George Clair and Angela Montejo Roura Tooker, Addison Gallery of American Art, Phillips Academy, Andover, Massachusetts

plate 5
*A Game of Chess* (1946–47)
Egg tempera on gesso panel
30 × 15 inches (76.2 × 38.1 cm)
Collection of Barney A. Ebsworth

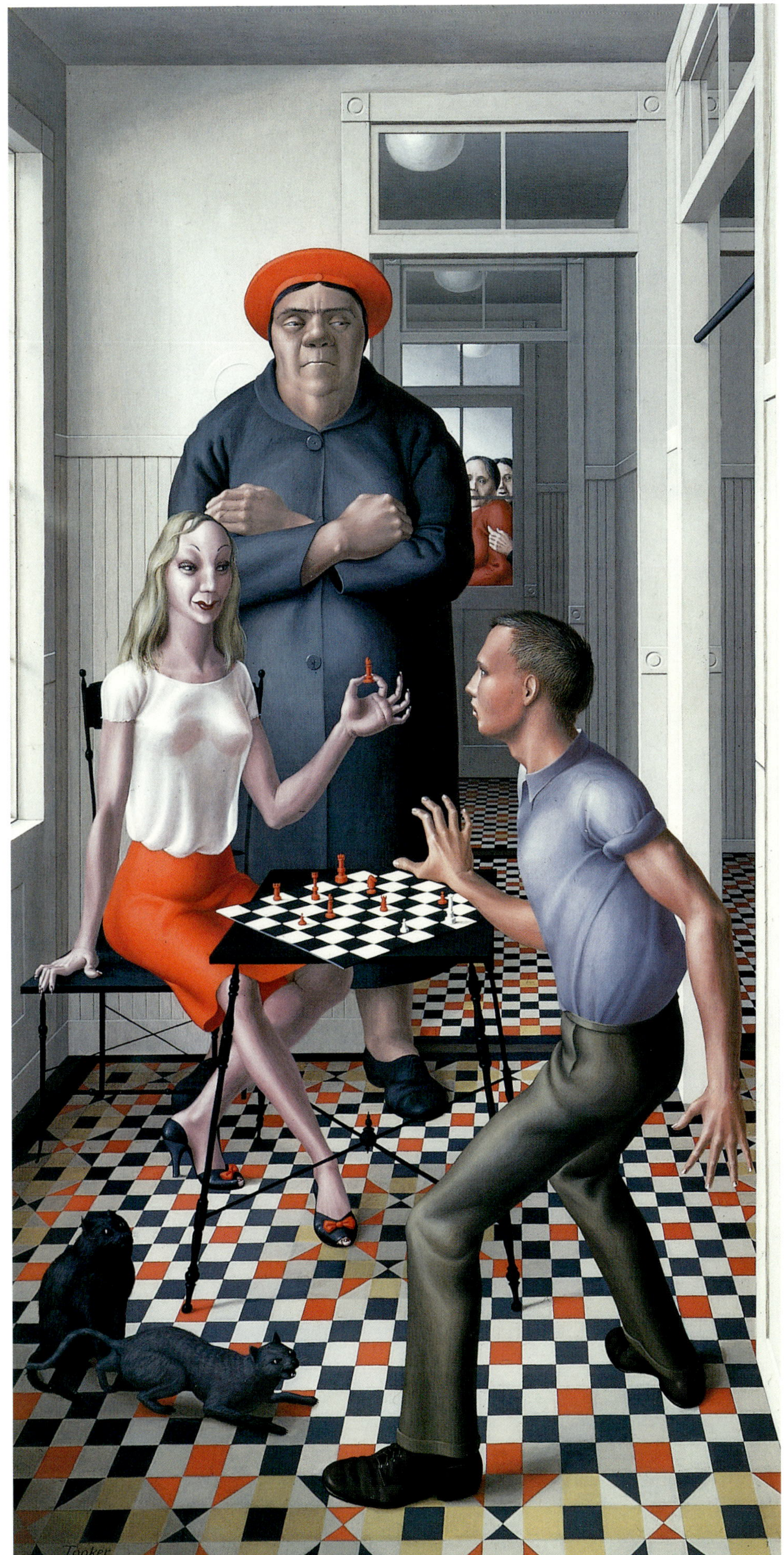

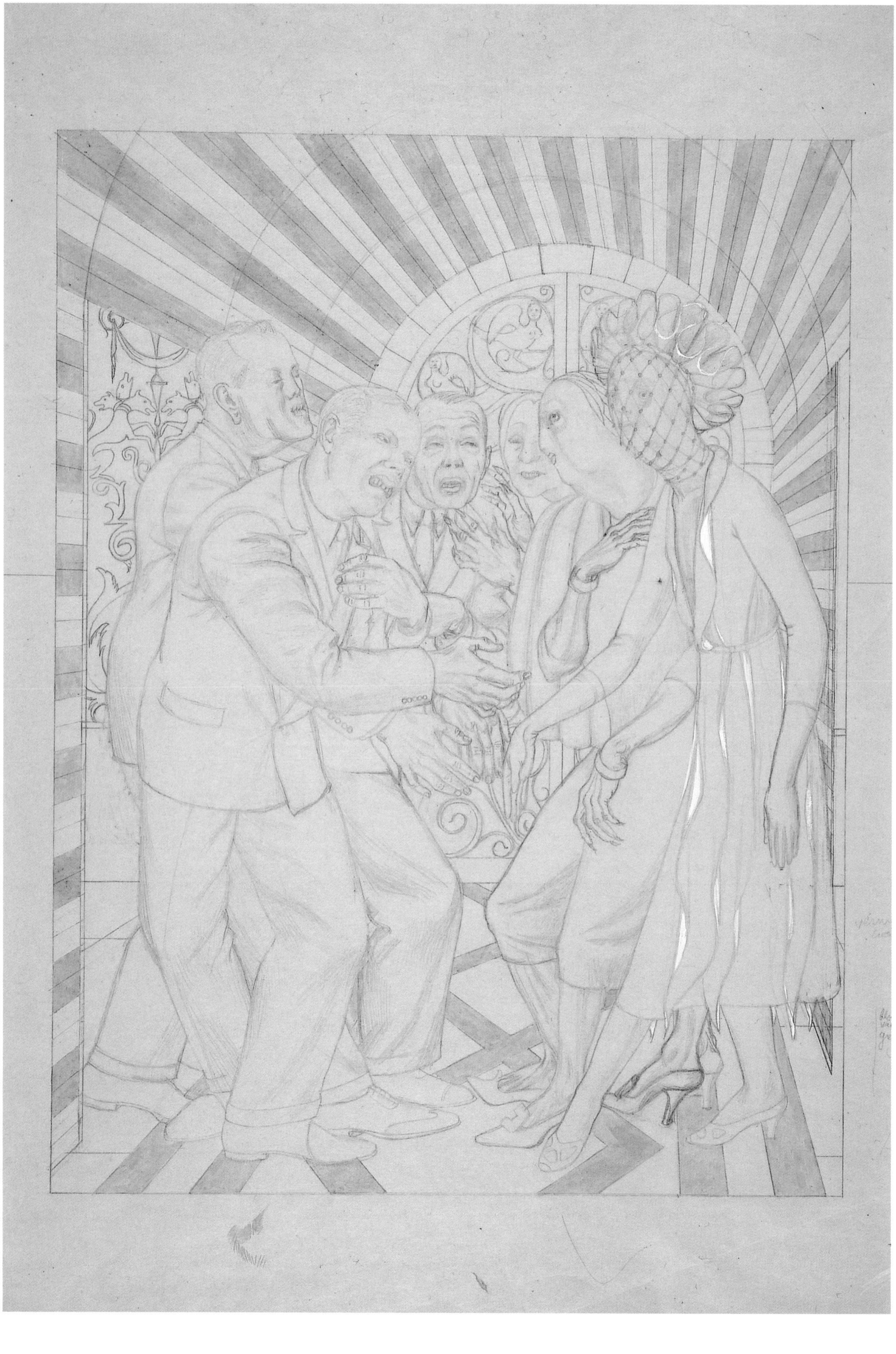

plate 6
**Study for *How Do You Do?*** (*circa* 1947)
Colored pencil, graphite, and wash on paper
26 1/16 × 19 inches (66.2 × 48.3 cm)
Gift of the artist (PA 1936) in memory of his parents, George Clair and Angela Montejo Roura Tooker, Addison Gallery of American Art, Phillips Academy, Andover, Massachusetts

plate 7
***The Groping Hand*** (*circa* 1947)
Egg tempera on watercolor paper
3 1/2 × 2 3/4 inches (8.9 × 7 cm)
Nicholas Miles Pentecost, Courtesy DC Moore Gallery, New York



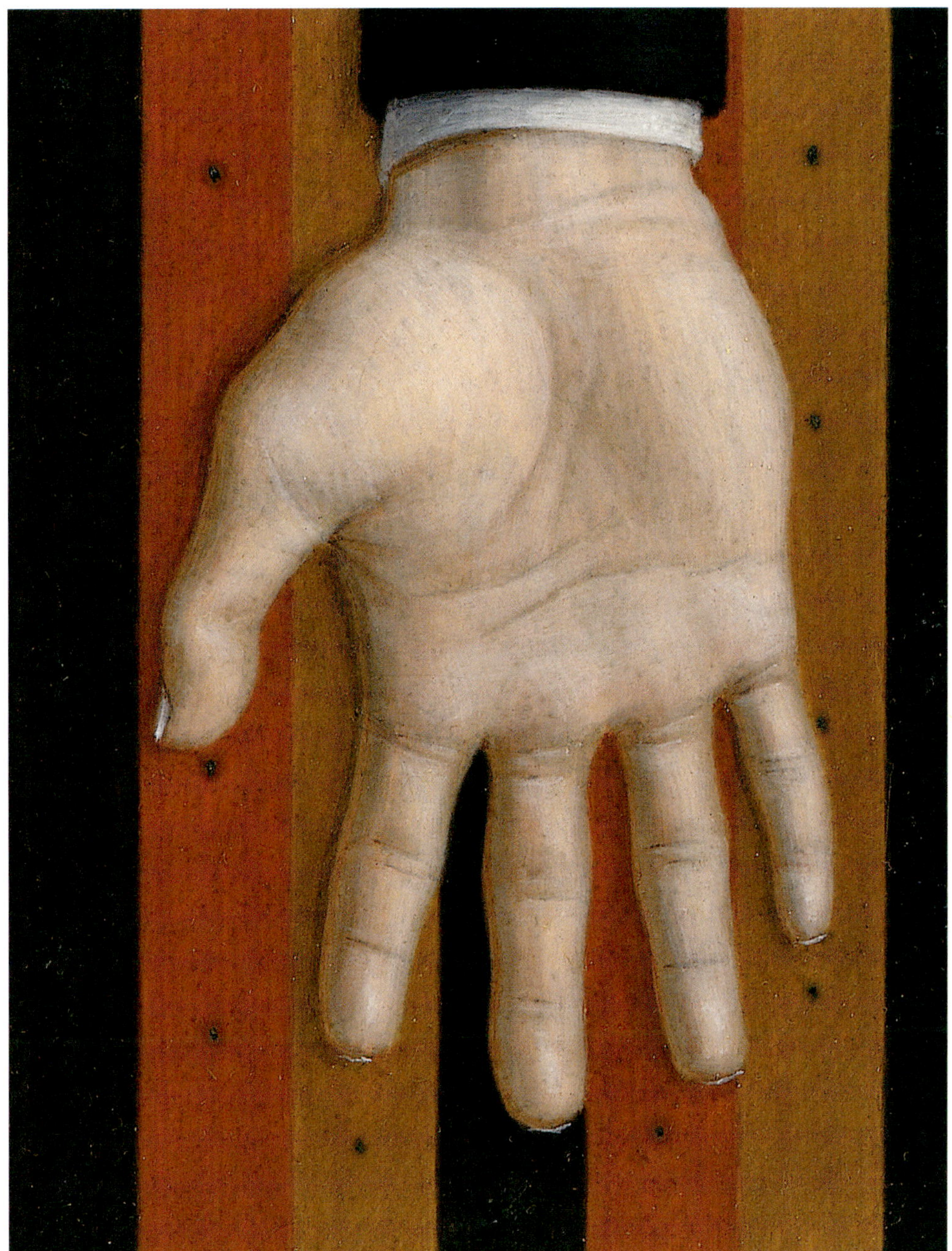

plate 8
***Self-Portrait*** (1947)
Egg tempera on gesso panel
$18\frac{3}{4}$ inches (47.6 cm) diameter
Curtis Galleries, Minneapolis, Minnesota



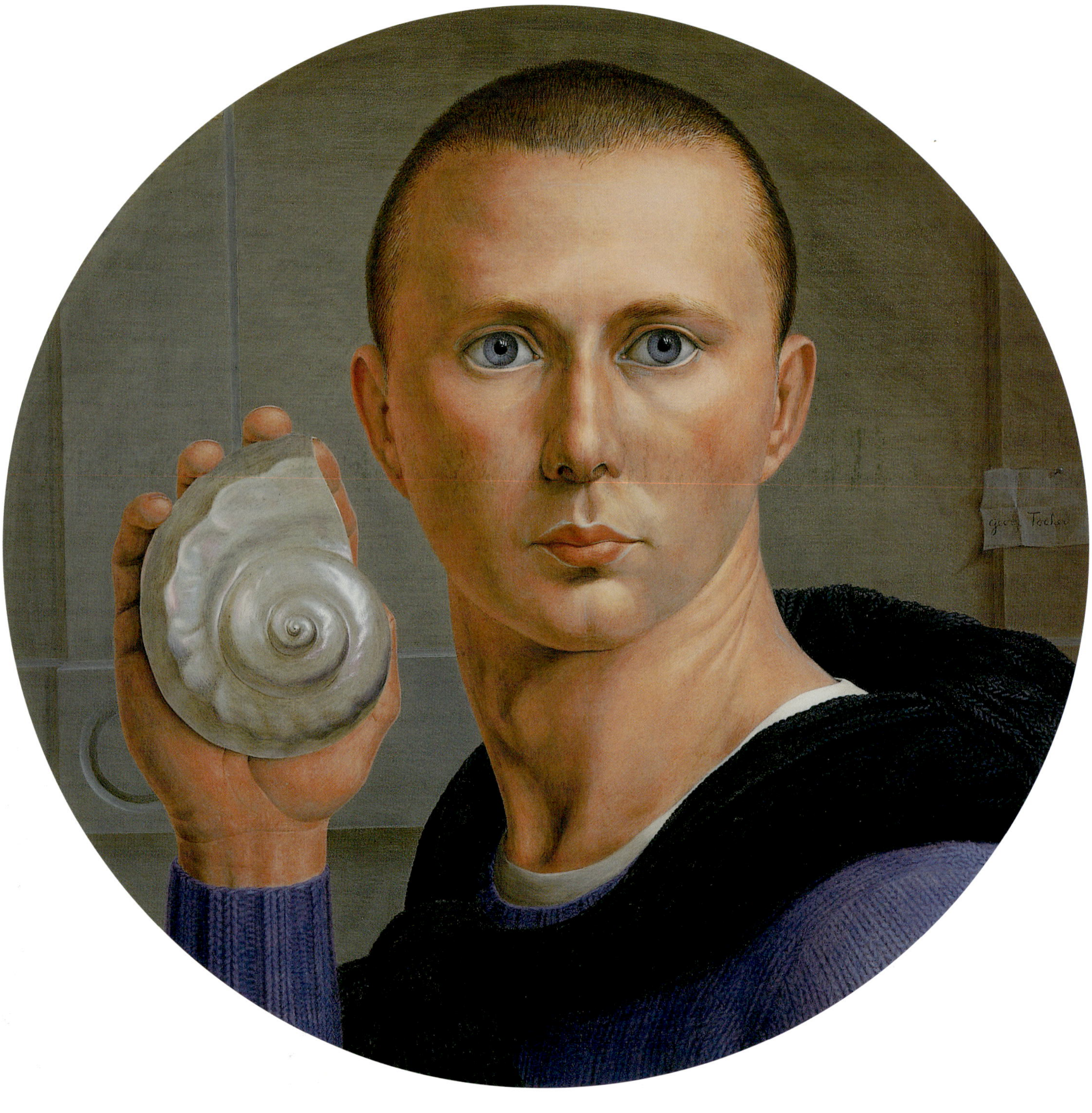

plate 9
*Bird Watchers* (1948)
Egg tempera on gessoed board
26¾ × 32¾ inches (67.9 × 83.2 cm)
New Britain Museum of American Art, Connecticut, Gift of Olga H. Knoepke, 1992.33



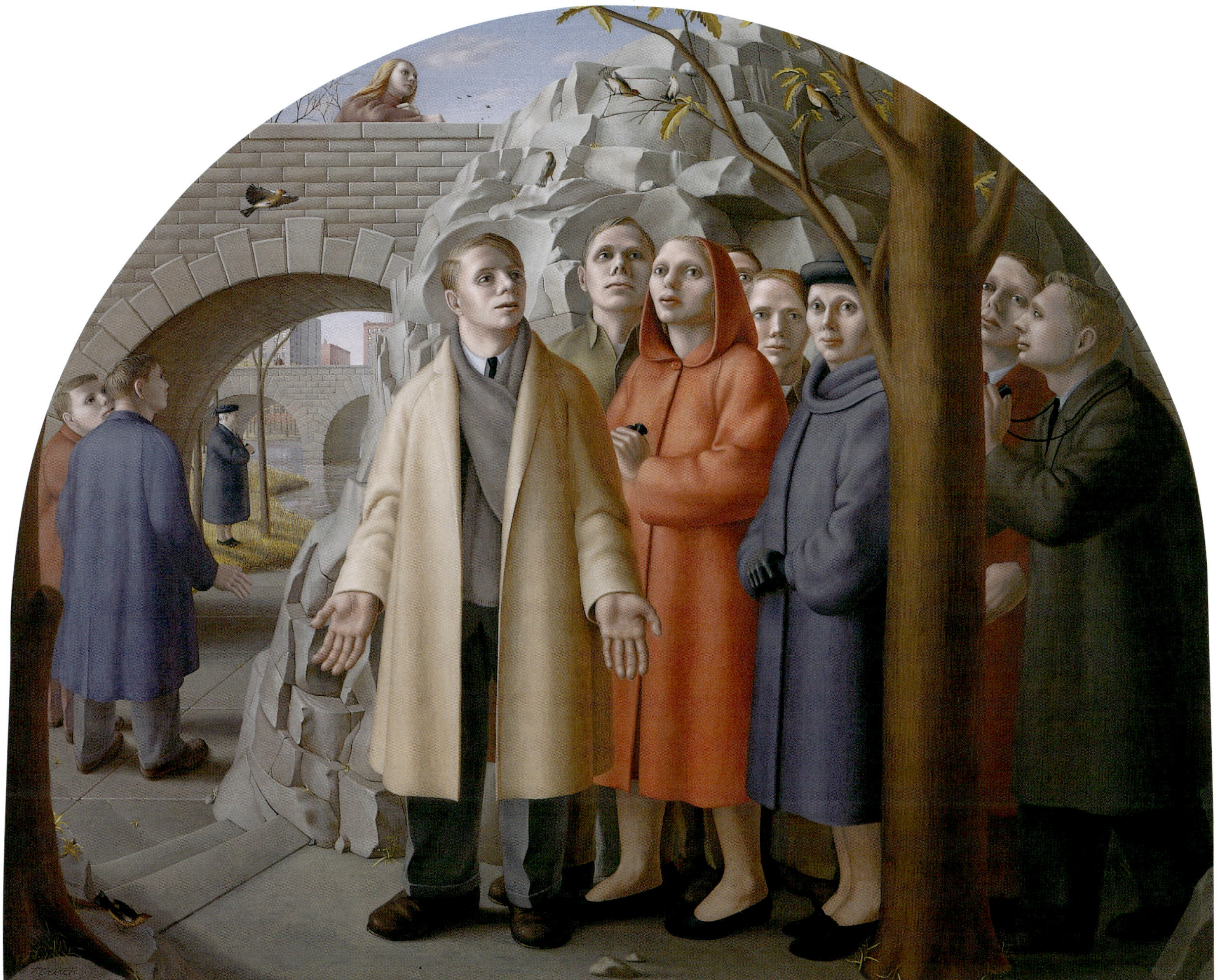

plate 10
**Study for *Coney Island*** (1947)
Graphite on paper
22½ × 30⅞ inches (57.1 × 78.4 cm)
Gift of the artist (PA 1936) in memory of his parents, George Clair and Angela Montejo Roura Tooker, Addison Gallery of American Art, Phillips Academy, Andover, Massachusetts



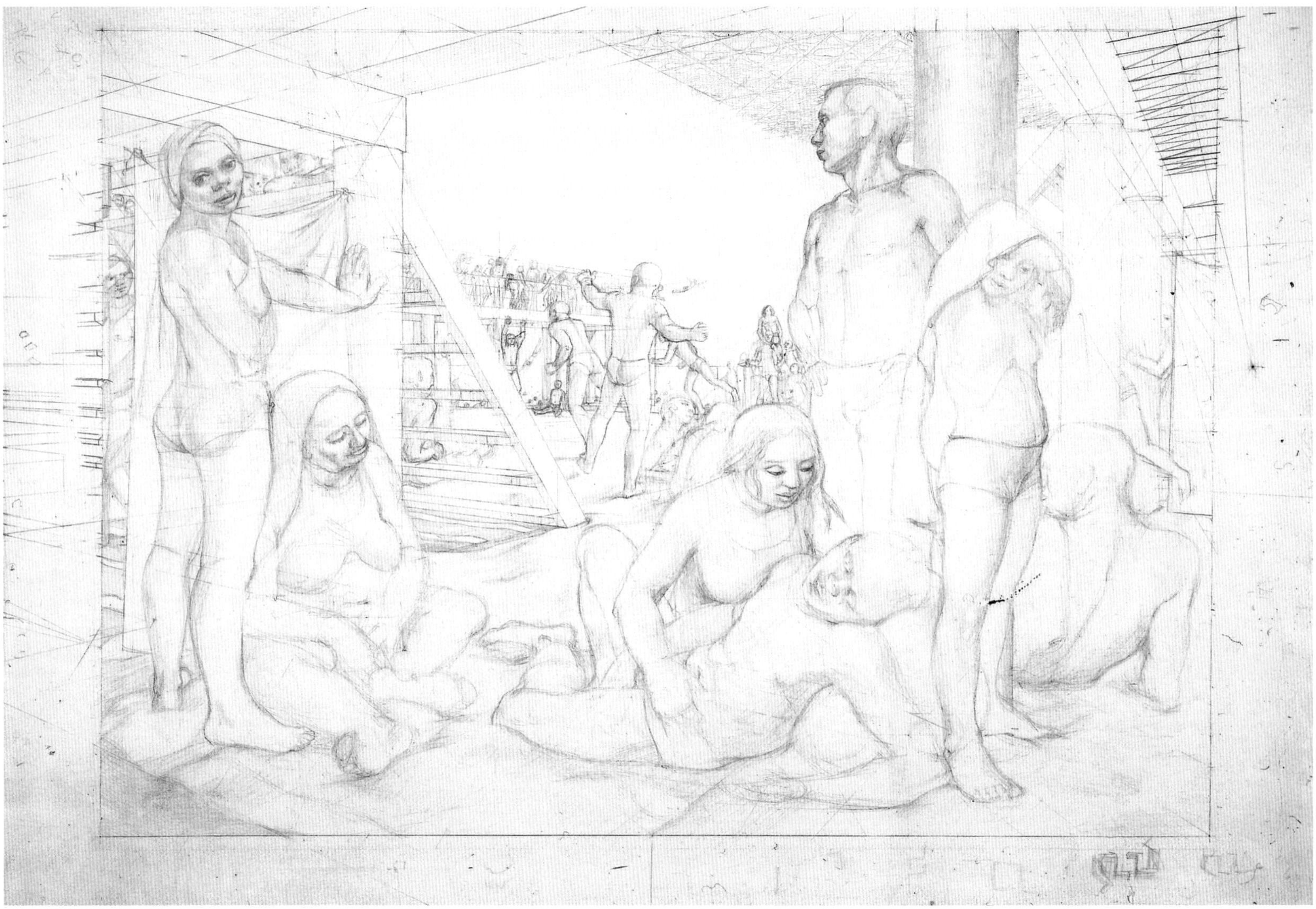

plate 11
***Coney Island*** (1947–48)
Egg tempera on gesso panel
19 × 26 inches (48.3 × 66 cm)
Curtis Galleries, Minneapolis, Minnesota



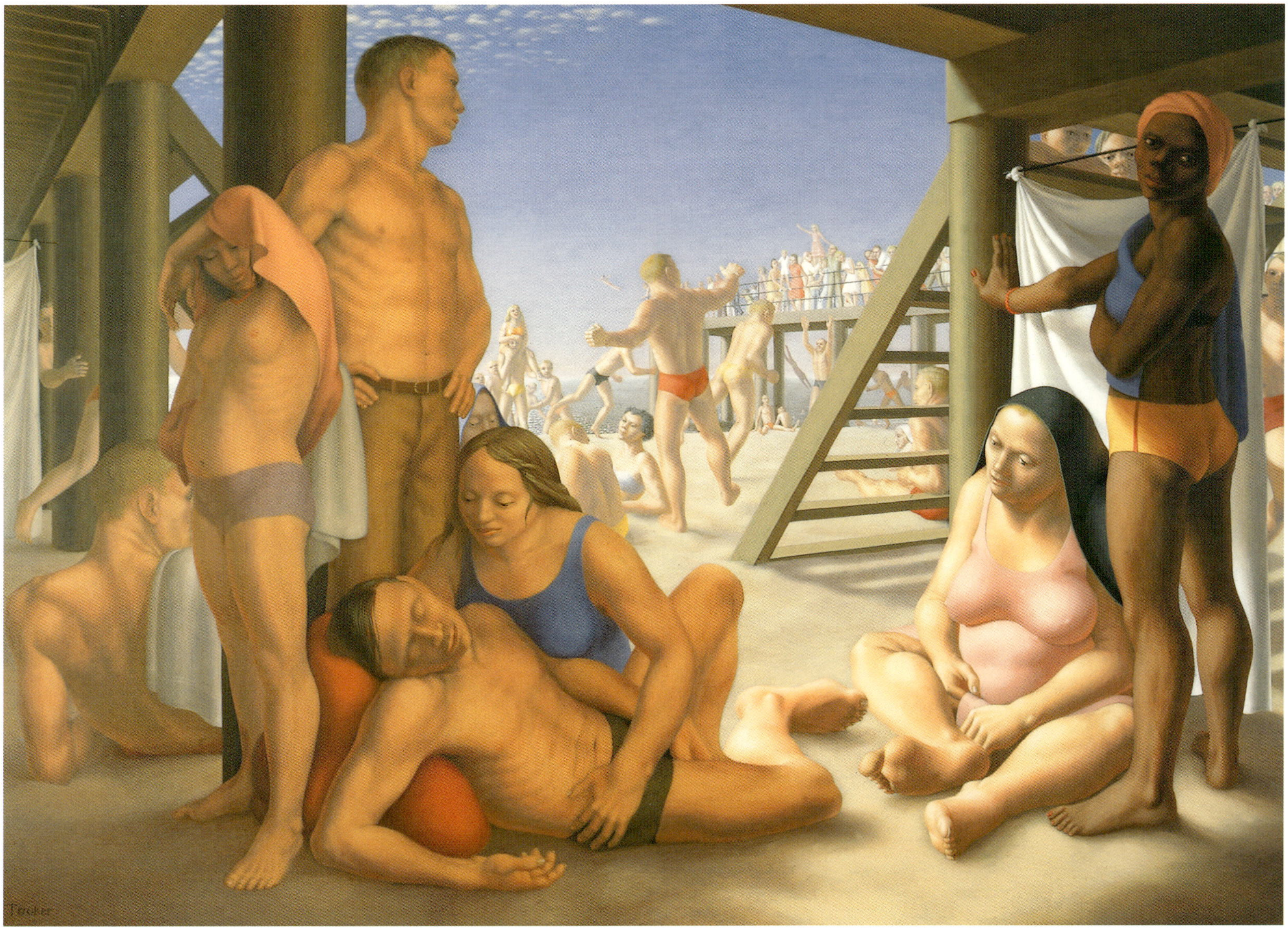

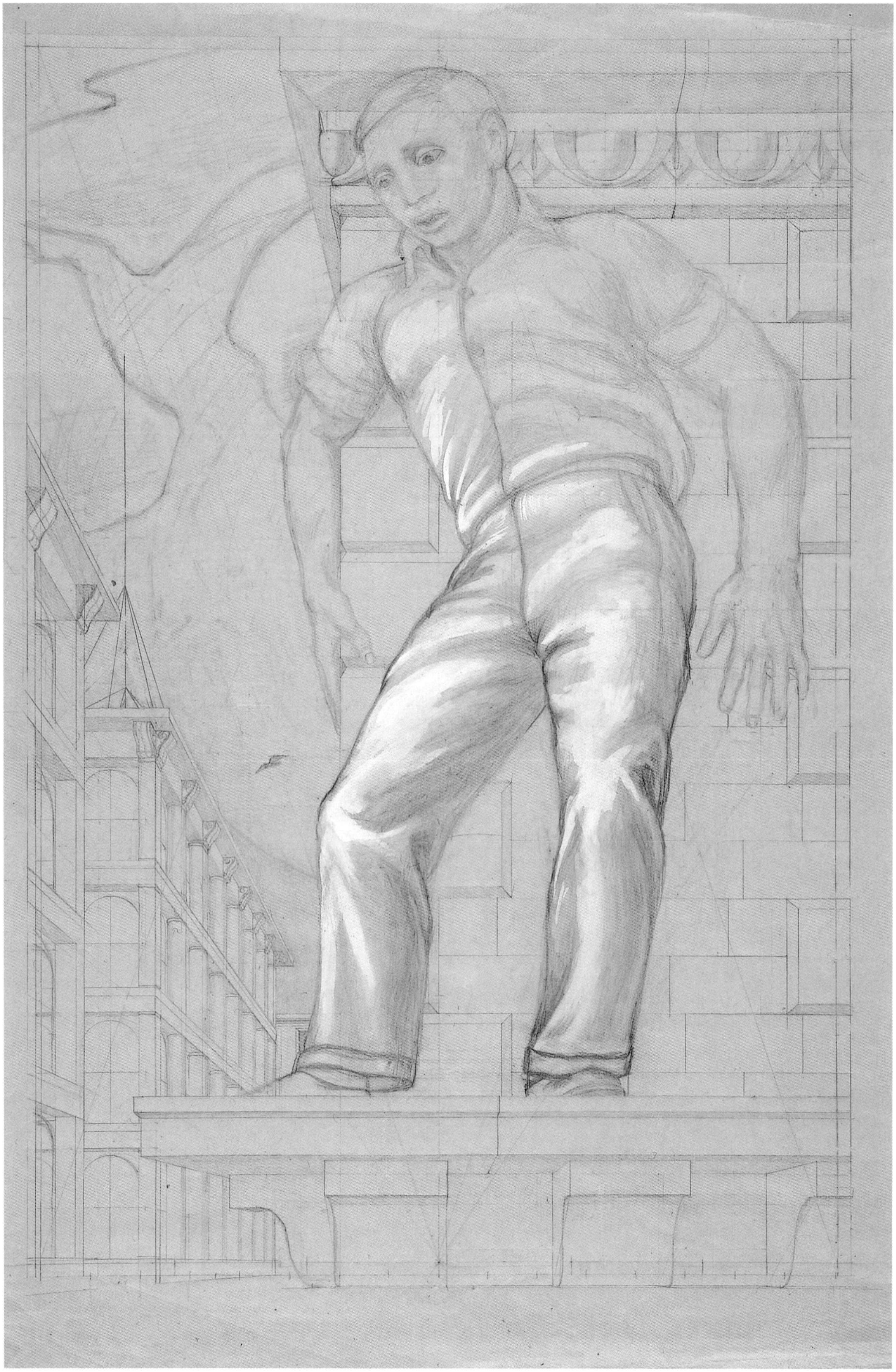

plate 12
**Study for *Cornice*** (1949)
Graphite and wash on paper
27 11/16 × 18 1/8 inches (70.4 × 46 cm)
Gift of the artist (PA 1936) in memory of his parents, George Clair and Angela Montejo Roura Tooker, Addison Gallery of American Art, Phillips Academy, Andover, Massachusetts

plate 13
***Cornice*** (*circa* 1949)
Egg tempera on gesso panel
24 × 15 1/2 inches (61 × 39.4 cm)
Columbus Museum of Art, Ohio: Museum Purchase, Howald Fund II

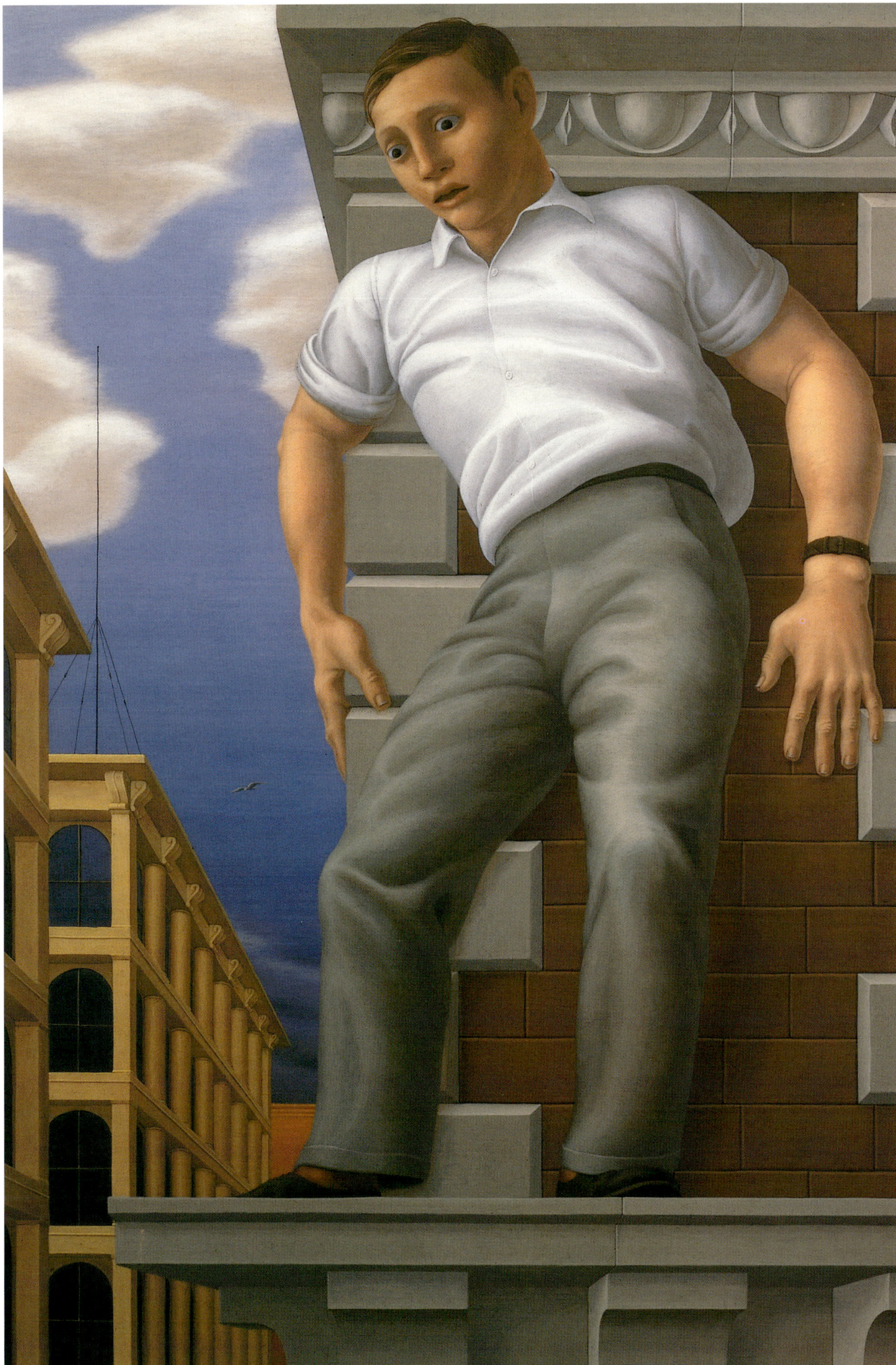

plate 14
**Study for *Subway*** (1949)
Graphite on paper
24 × 39⅜ inches (61 × 100 cm)
Gift of the artist (PA 1936) in memory of his parents, George Clair and Angela Montejo Roura Tooker, Addison Gallery of American Art, Phillips Academy, Andover, Massachusetts



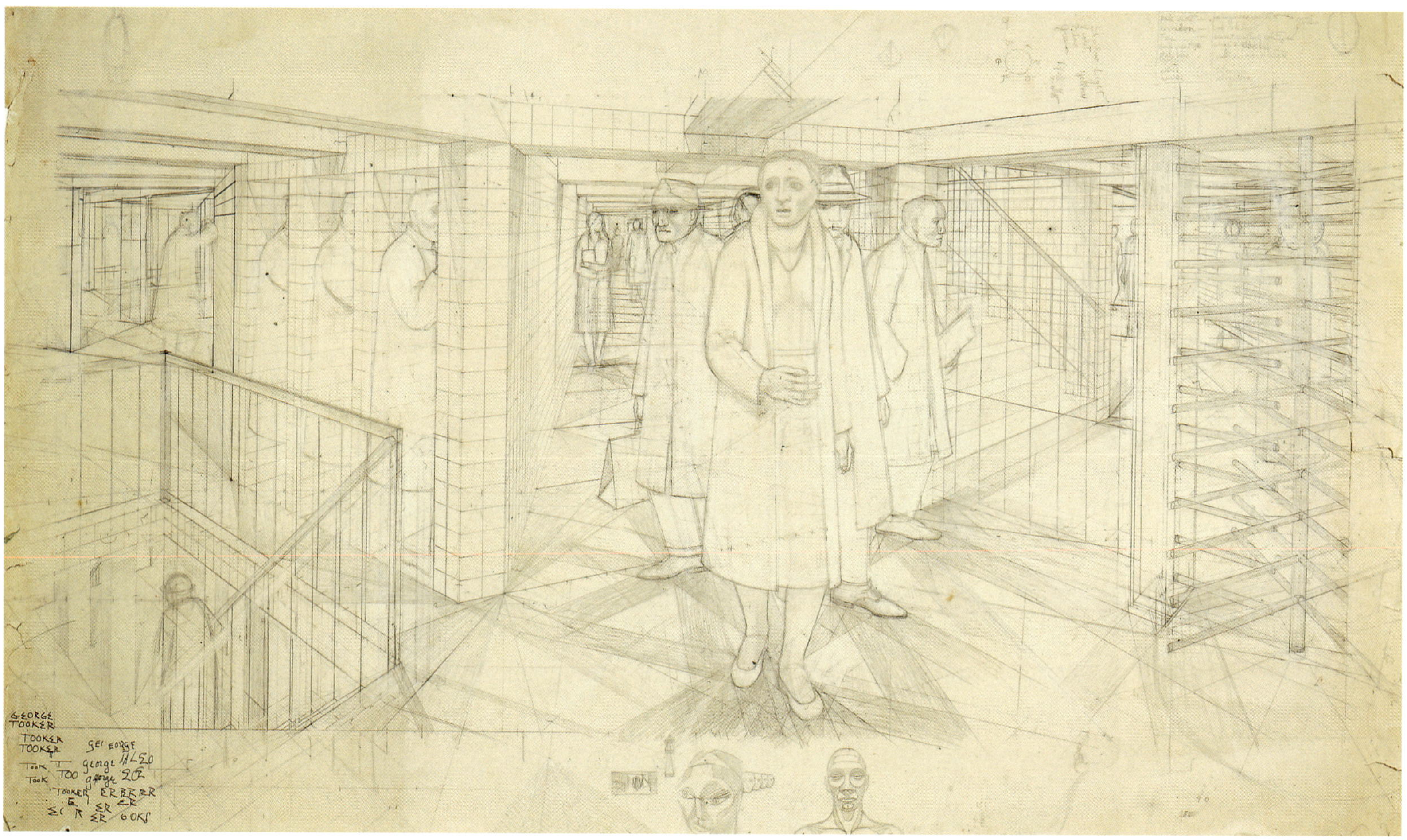

plate 15
*Subway* (1950)
Egg tempera on composition board
18⅛ × 36⅛ inches (46 × 91.8 cm)
Whitney Museum of American Art,
New York
Purchase, with funds from the Juliana
Force Purchase Award
Photography by Sheldon C. Collins



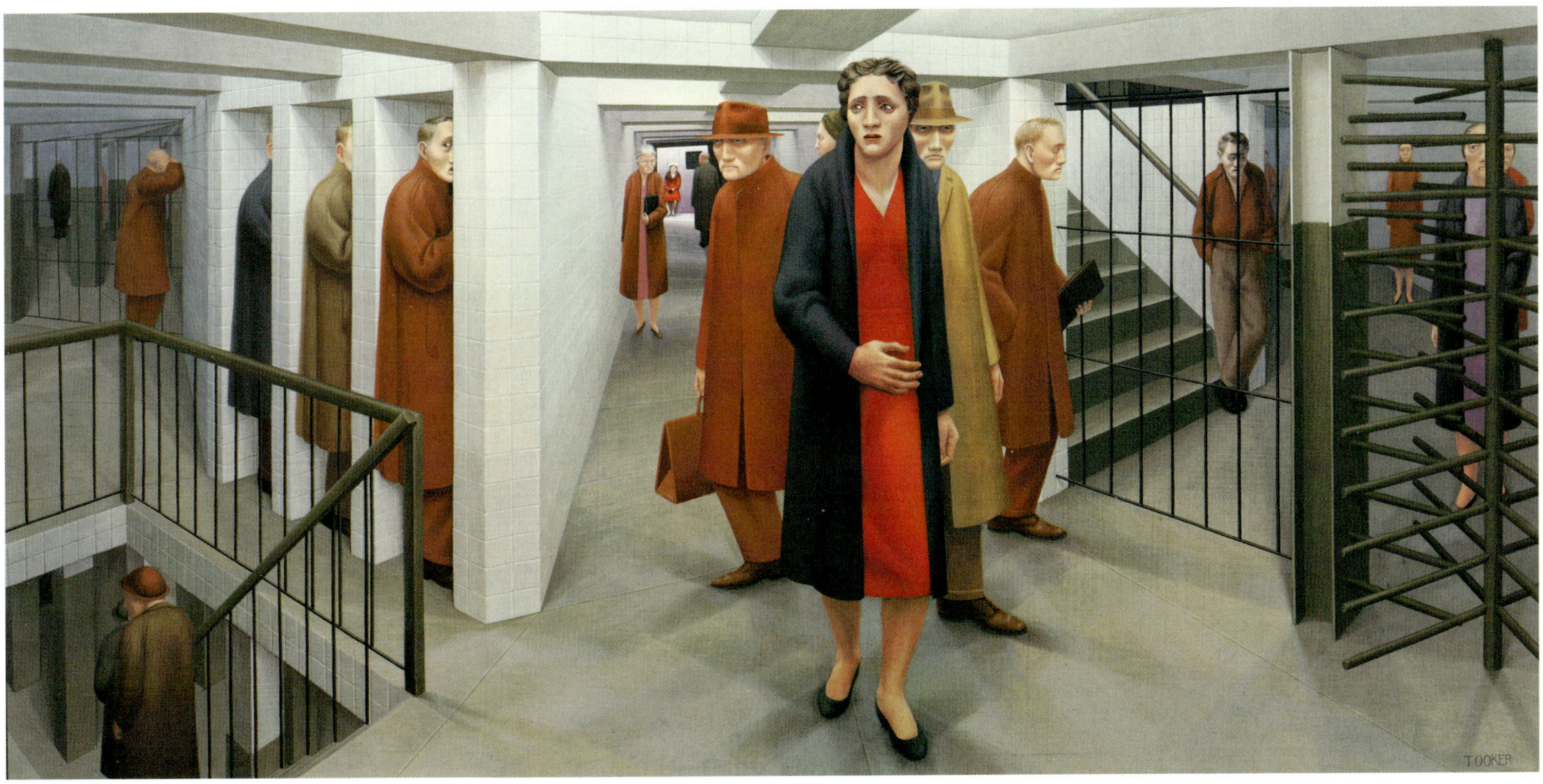

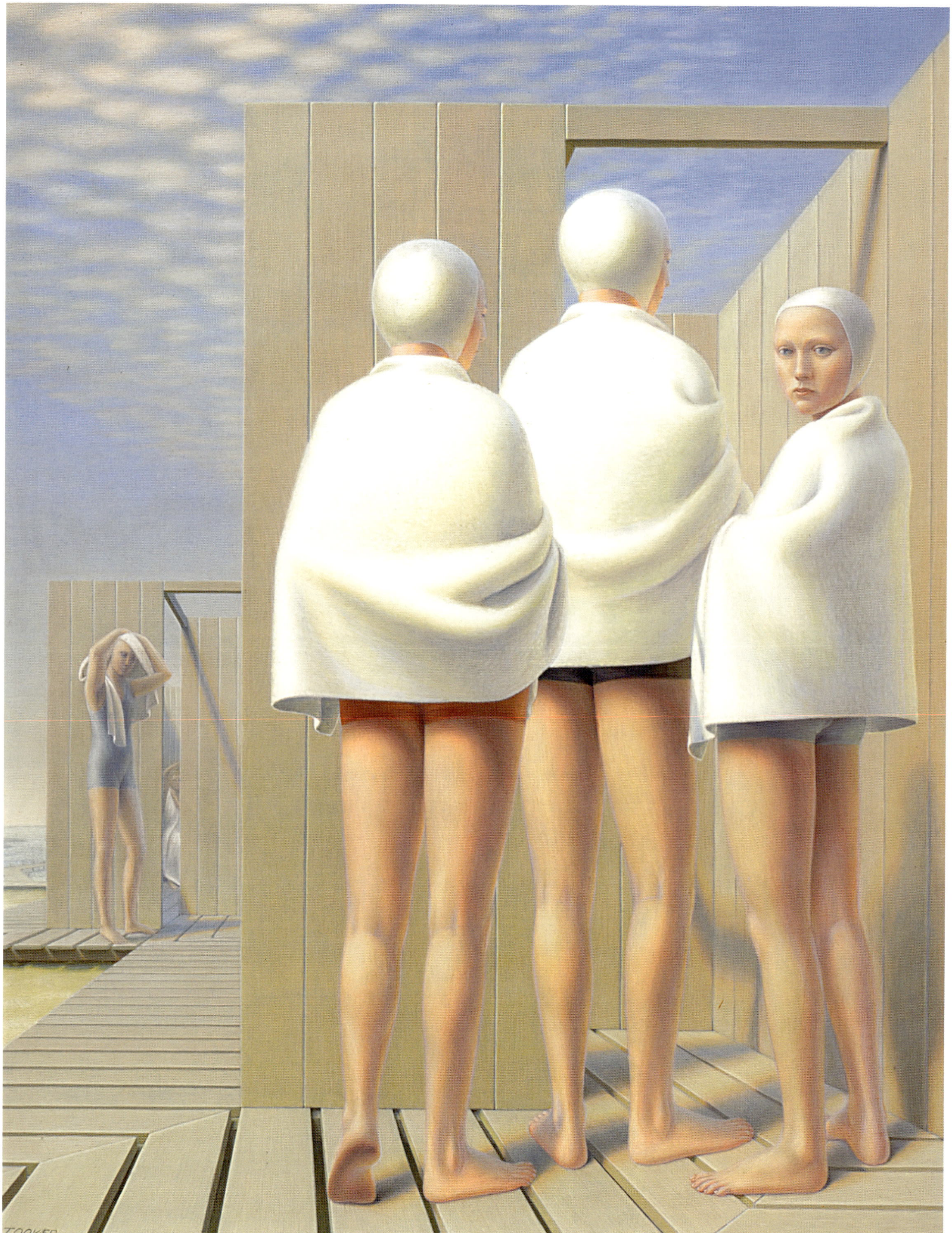
TOOKER

plate 16
***Bathhouses*** (1950)
Egg tempera on gesso panel
20¼ × 15¼ inches (51.4 × 38.7 cm)
Private Collection

plate 17
**Study for *Laundress*** (1952)
Graphite and chalk on paper
26⅝ × 26 inches (67.6 × 66 cm)
Gift of the artist (PA 1936) in memory of his parents, George Clair and Angela Montejo Roura Tooker, Addison Gallery of American Art, Phillips Academy, Andover, Massachusetts



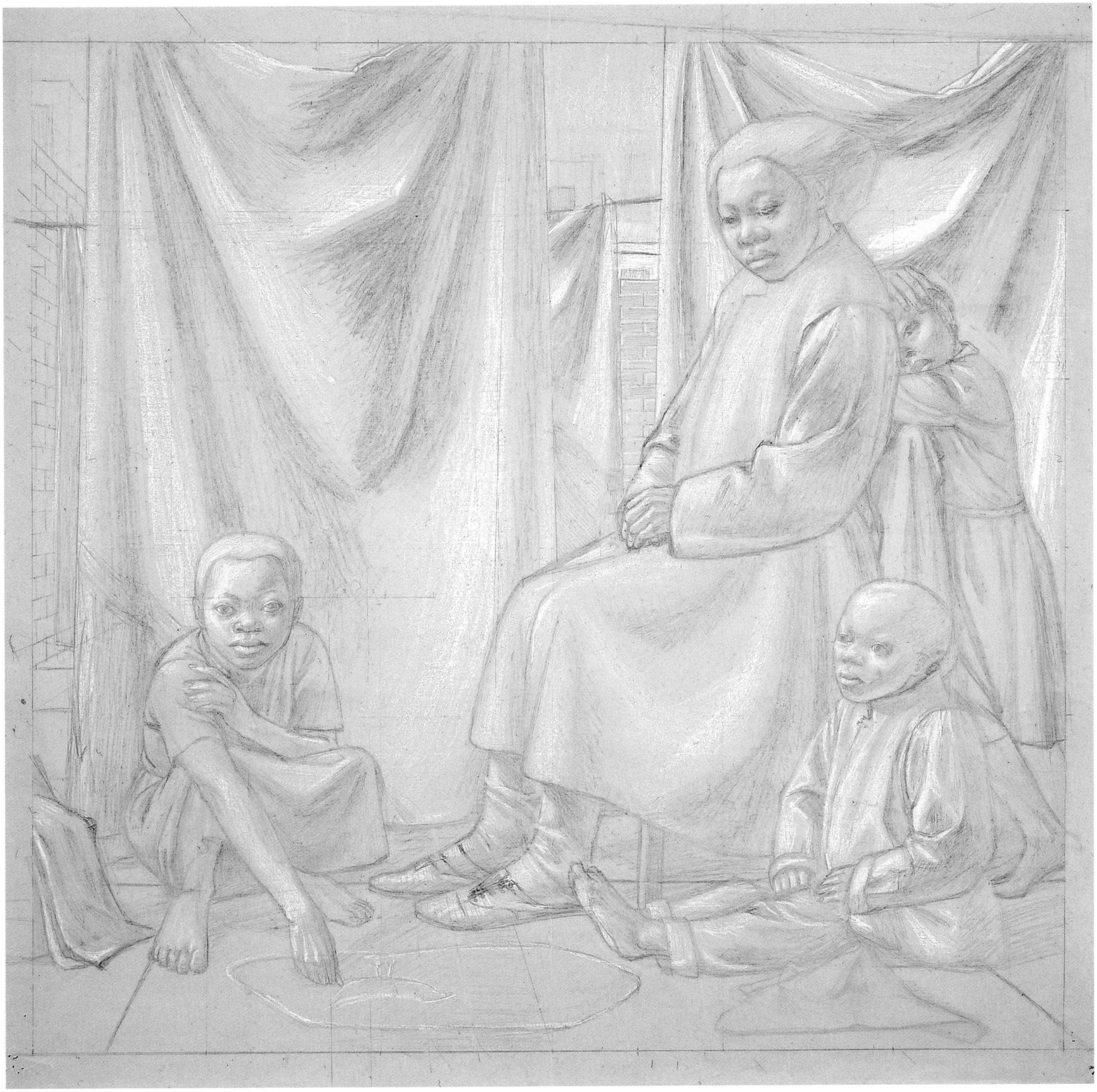

plate 18
***Letterbox*** (1953)
Egg tempera on fiberboard
18⅛ × 24 inches (46 × 61 cm)
Hirshhorn Museum and Sculpture Garden, Smithsonian Institution, Washington, D.C.,
Museum Purchase, 1993



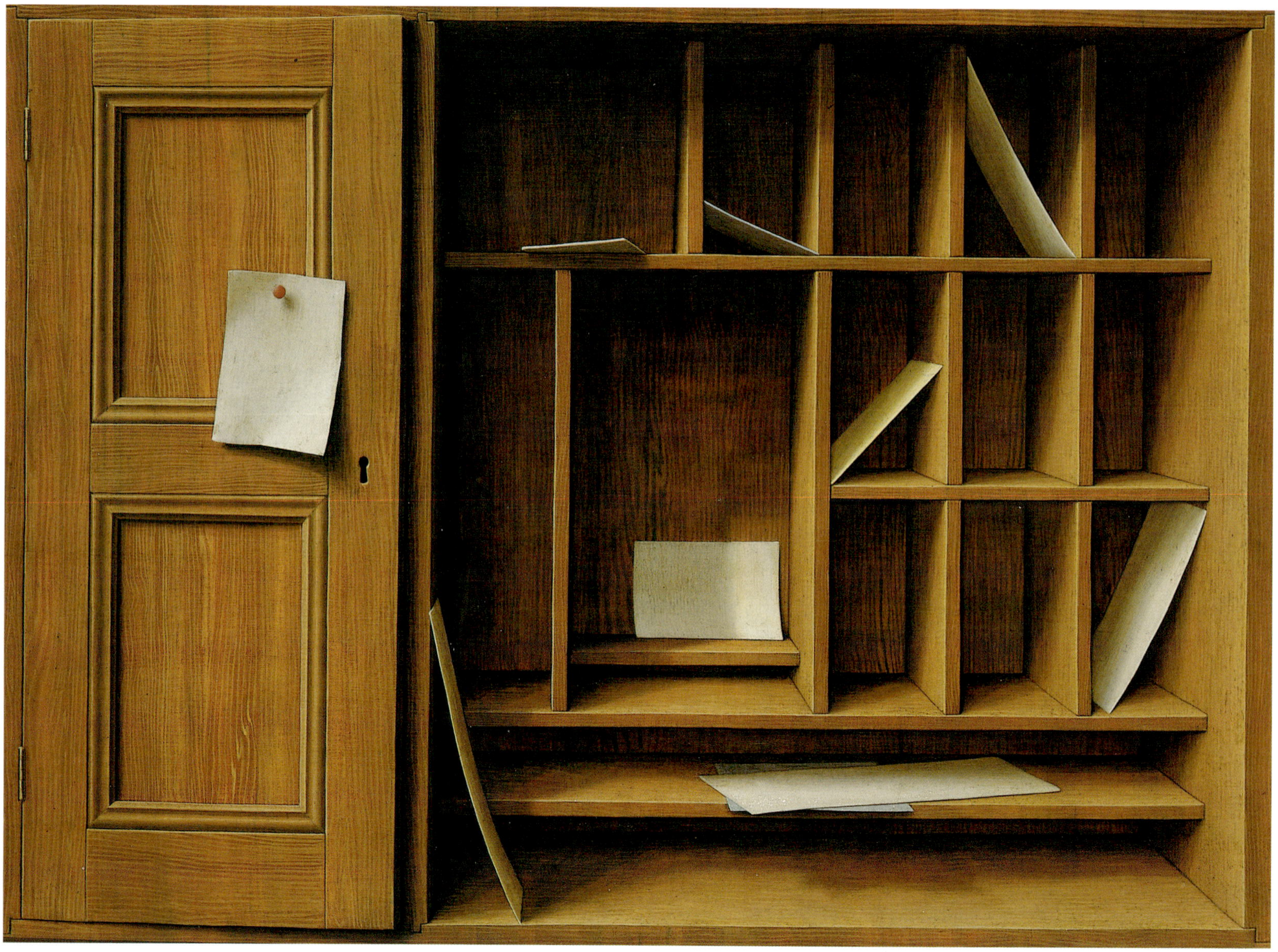

plate 19
***Builders*** (1952)
Egg tempera on gesso panel
16 × 16 inches (40.6 × 40.6 cm)
Wayne County Public Library, Inc.



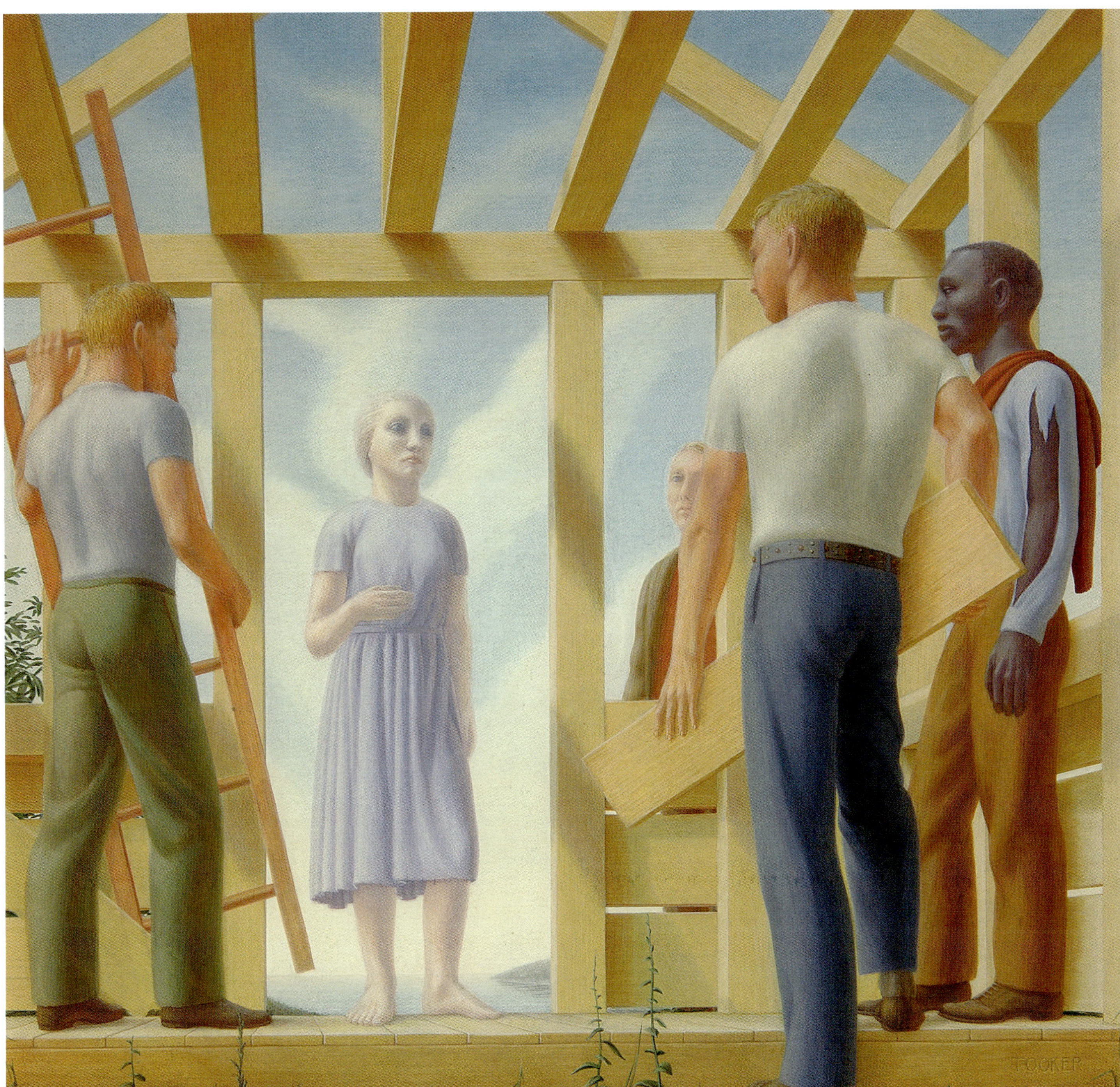

plate 20
*Garden Party* (1952)
Egg tempera on gesso panel
18 × 11¾ inches (45.7 × 29.8 cm)
Private Collection, courtesy Debra Force Fine Art, New York

plate 21
*Juke Box* (1953)
Egg tempera on gesso panel
21 × 14 inches (53.3 × 35.6 cm)
Mr. and Mrs. James C. Biddle



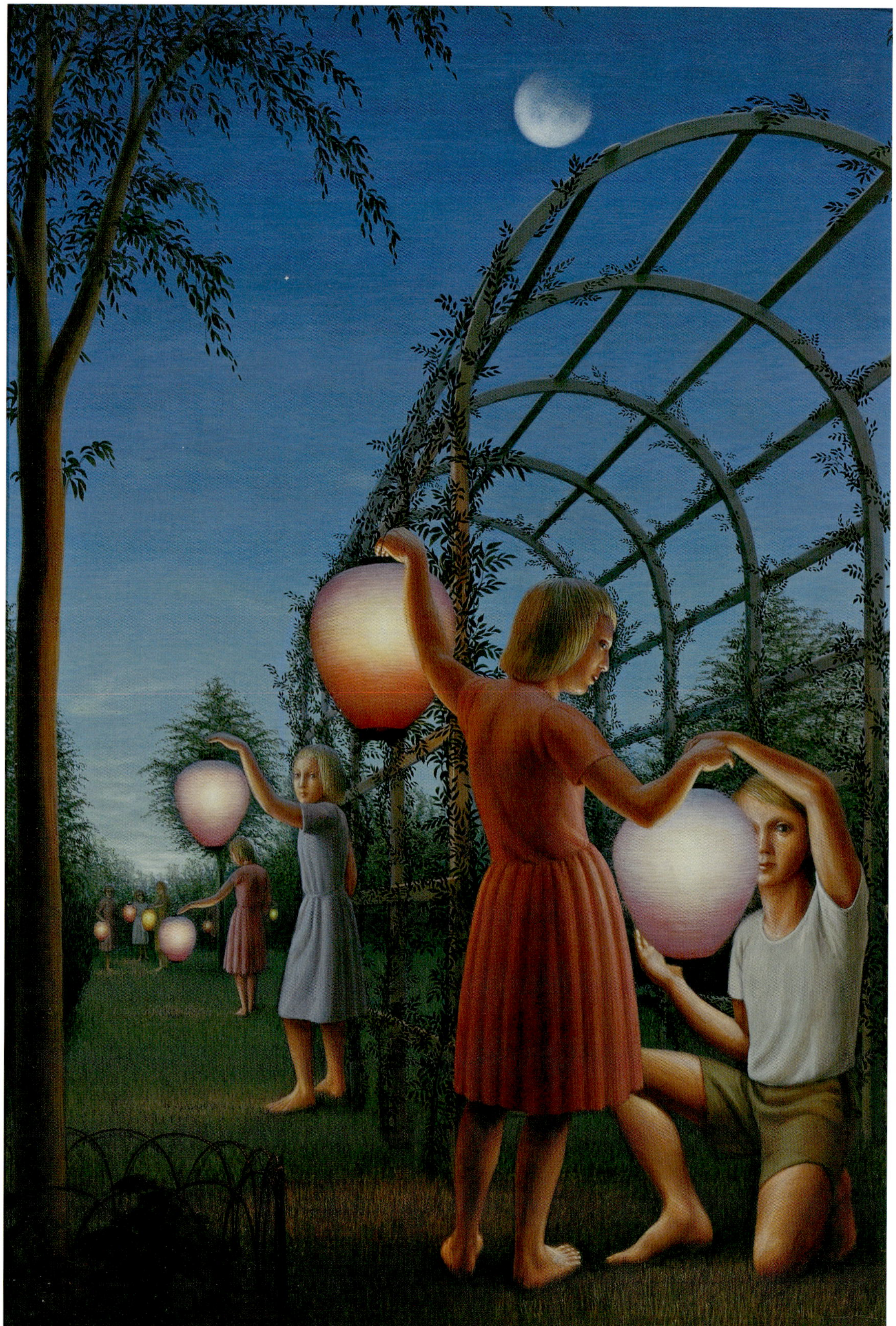

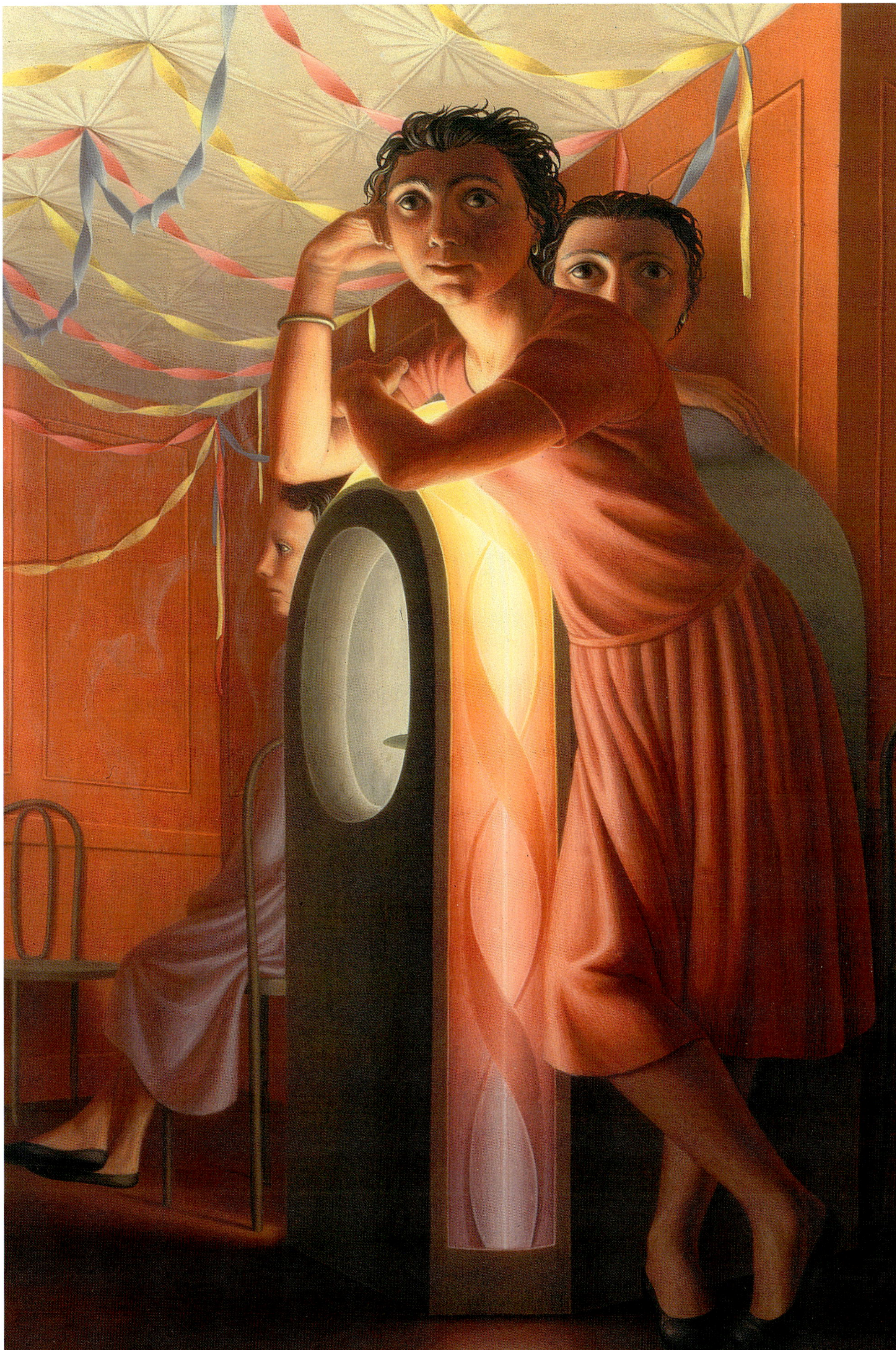

plate 22
*Red Carpet* (1953/1954)
Egg tempera on gesso panel
16 × 20¼ inches (40.6 × 51.4 cm)
Reis Private Collection

plate 23
*Highway* (1953)
Tempera on gesso panel
22⅞ × 17⅞ inches (58.1 × 45.4 cm)
Terra Foundation for American Art,
Daniel J. Terra Collection, 1992.134



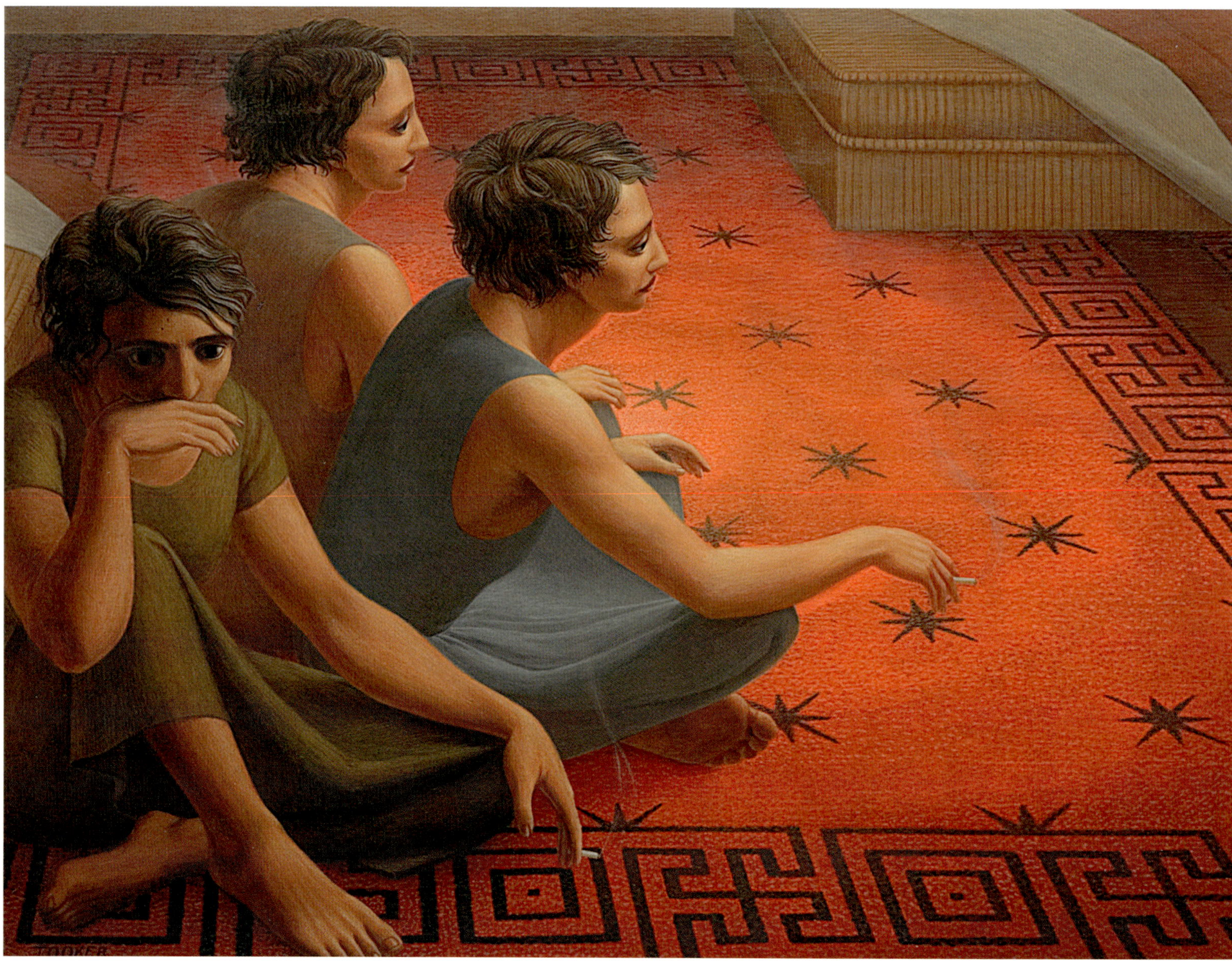

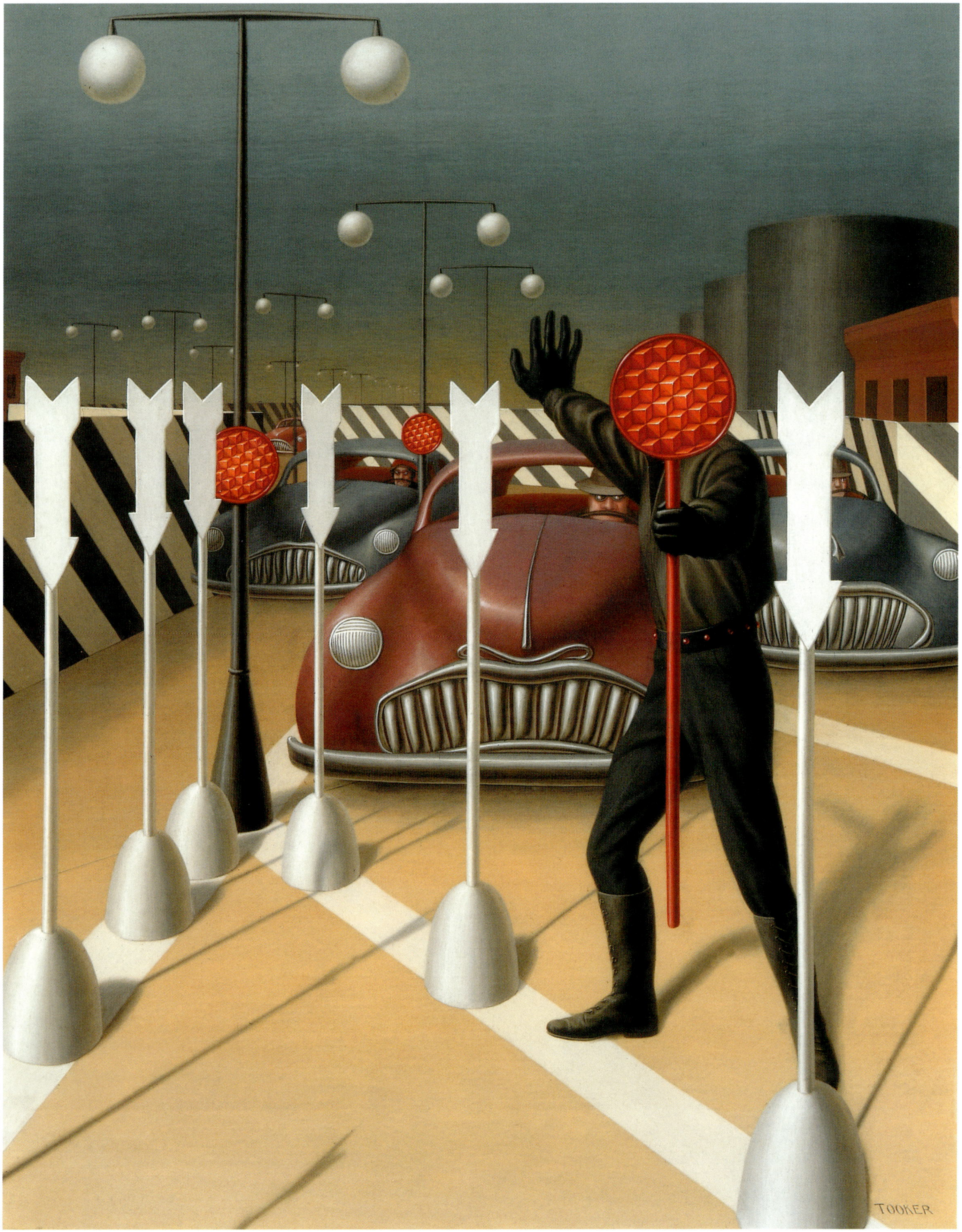
TOOKER

plate 24
***Fig Tree*** (1955)
Egg tempera on gesso panel
18 × 24 inches (45.7 × 61 cm)
Private Collection



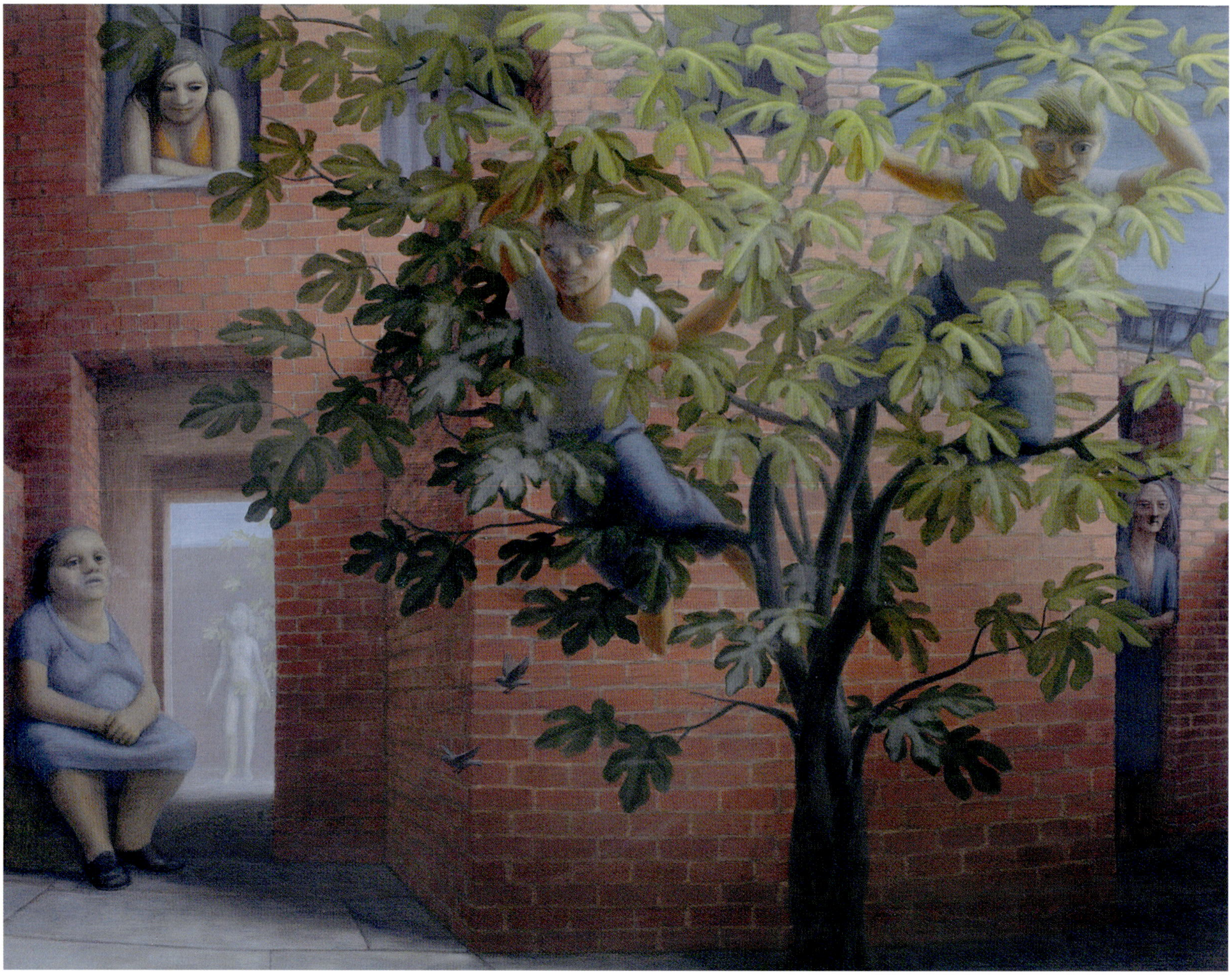

plate 25
*The Artist's Daughter* (1955)
Egg tempera on gesso panel
24 × 12½ inches (61 × 31.7 cm)
Private Collection

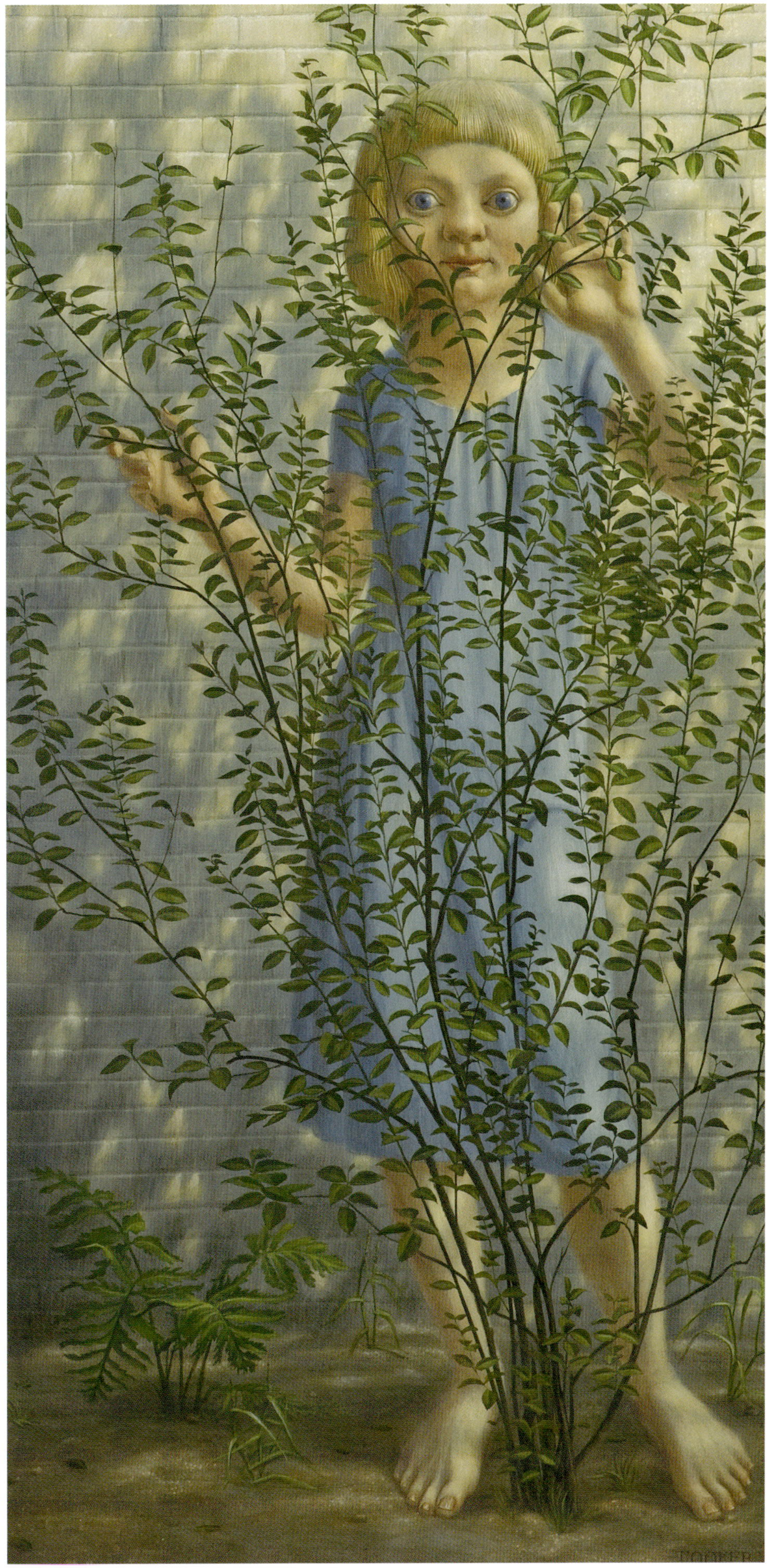

plate 26
**Study for *Government Bureau*** (1956)
Graphite, chalk, and wash on paper
25¾ × 32^13/16 inches (65.4 × 83.4 cm)
Gift of the artist (PA 1936) in memory of his parents, George Clair and Angela Montejo Roura Tooker, Addison Gallery of American Art, Phillips Academy, Andover, Massachusetts



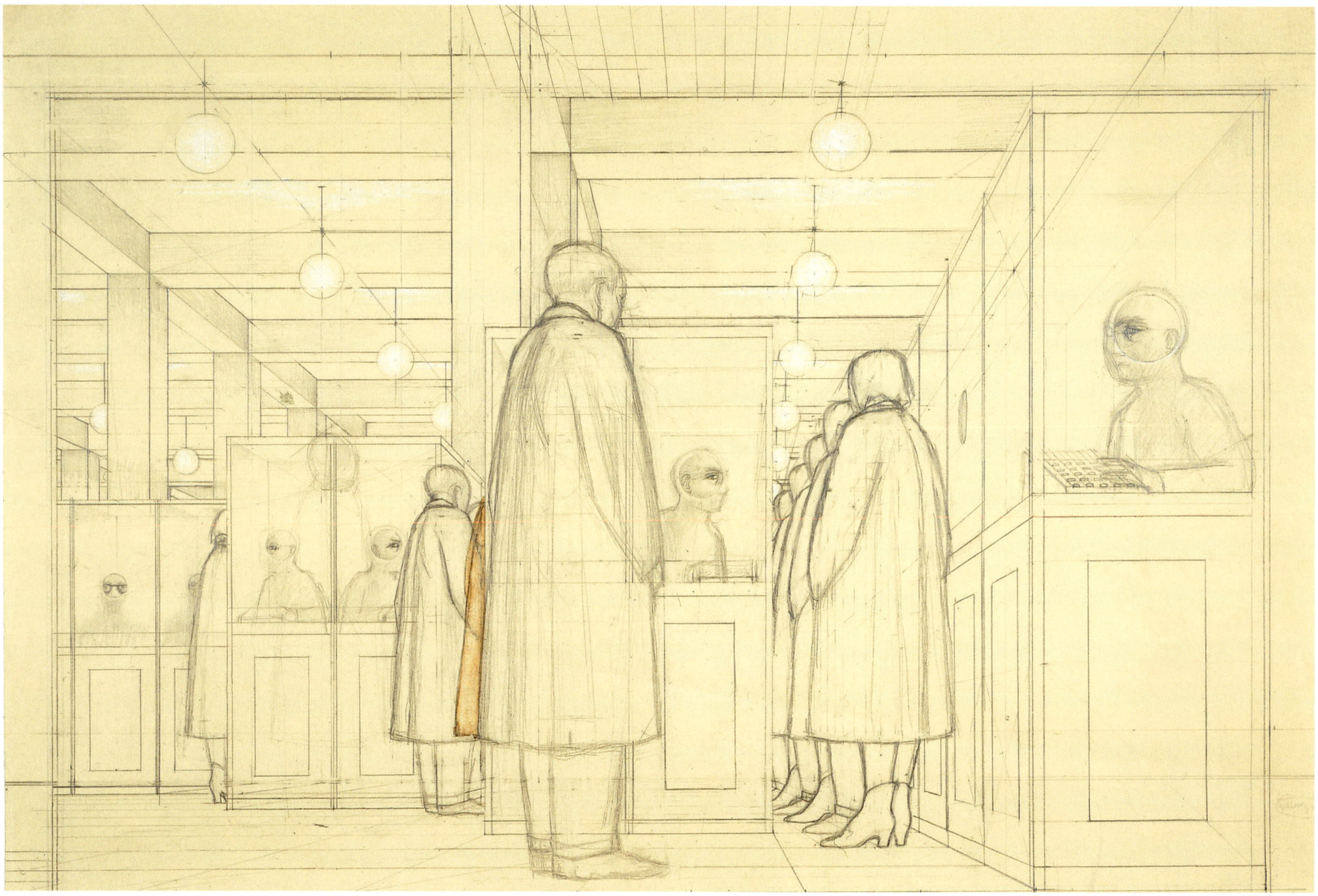

plate 27
*Government Bureau* (1956)
Egg tempera on gesso panel
19⅝ × 29⅝ inches (49.8 × 75.3 cm)
The Metropolitan Museum of Art,
New York, George A. Hearn Fund, 1956
(56.78)




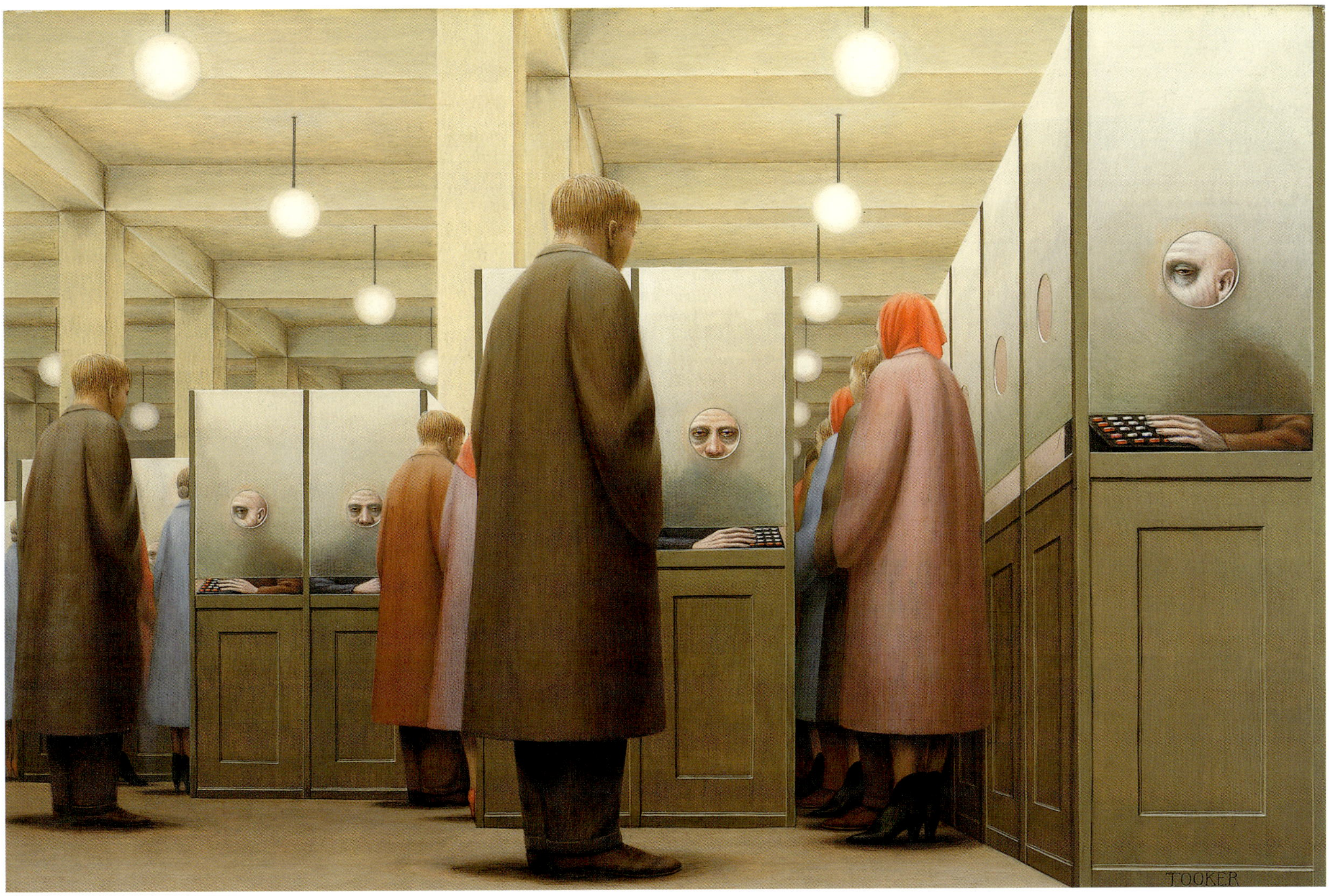

plate 28
***Window II*** (1956)
Egg tempera on gesso panel
24 × 18 inches (61 × 45.7 cm)
Collection of James and Barbara Palmer



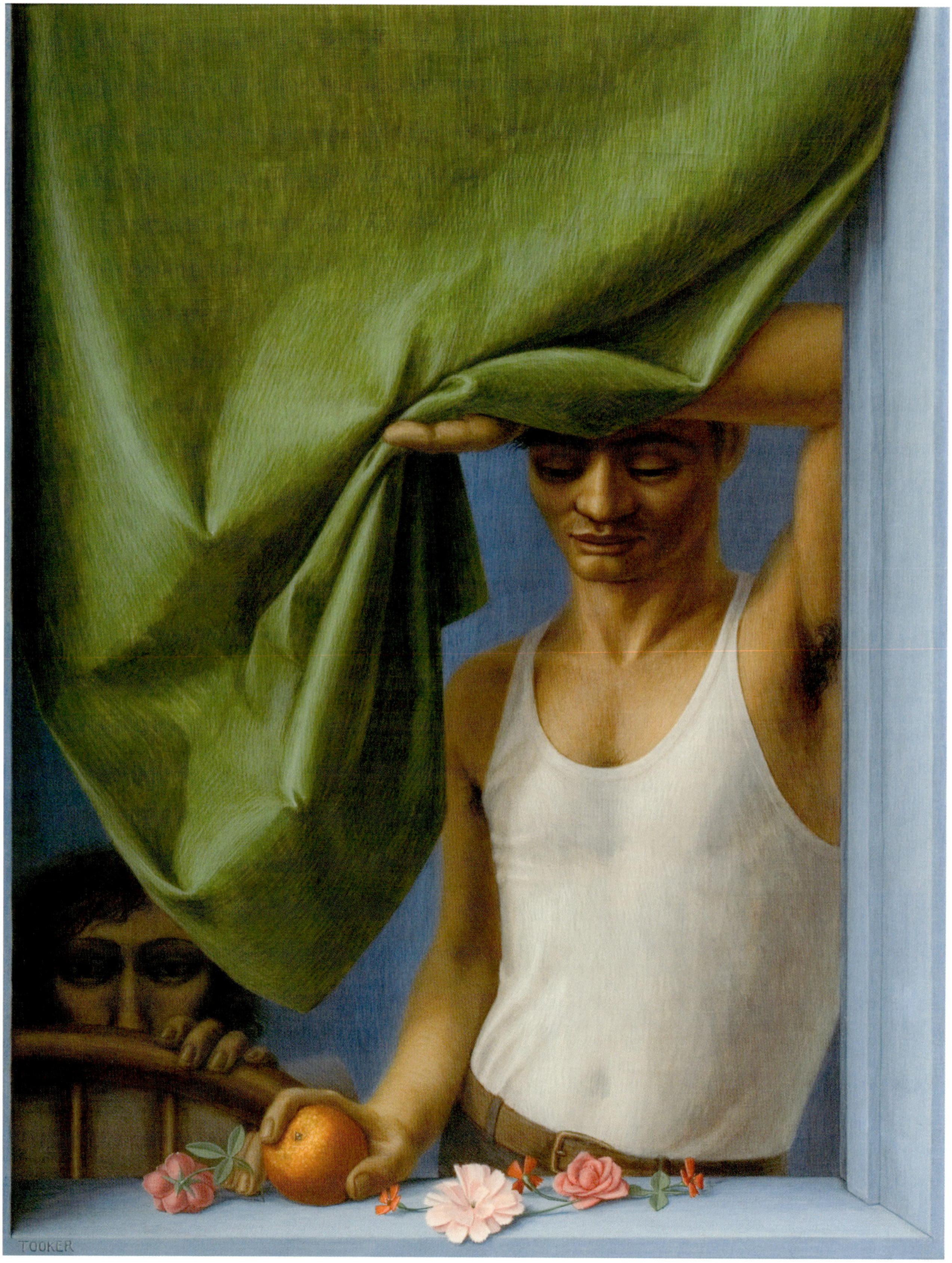

plate 29
*Guitar* (1957)
Egg tempera on gesso panel
18 × 24 inches (45.7 × 61 cm)
Private Collection



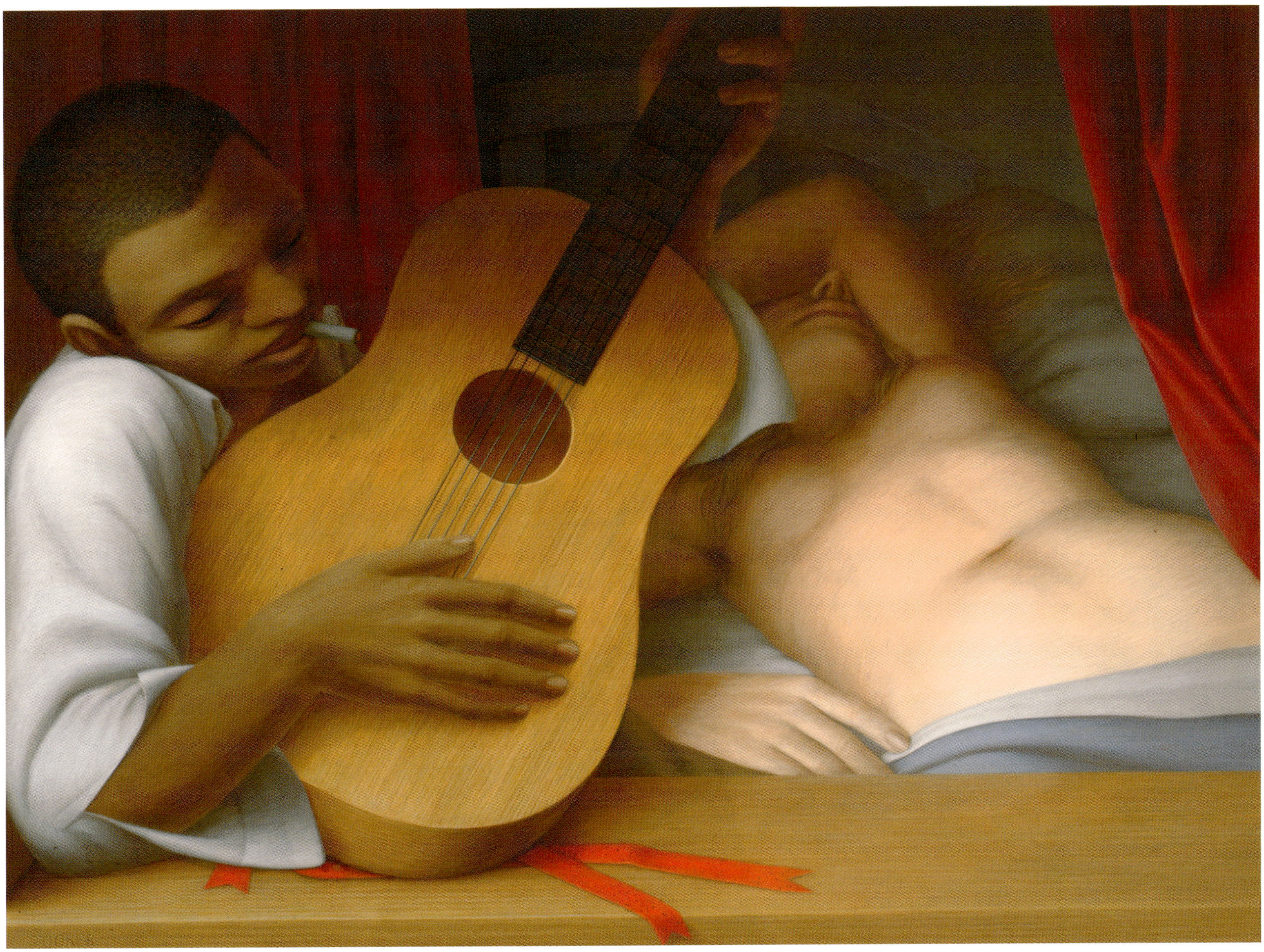

plate 30
**Study for *Waiting Room*** (1957)
Graphite on paper
27⅜ × 35⅞ inches (69.5 × 91.1 cm)
Gift of the artist (PA 1936) in memory of his parents, George Clair and Angela Montejo Roura Tooker, Addison Gallery of American Art, Phillips Academy, Andover, Massachusetts



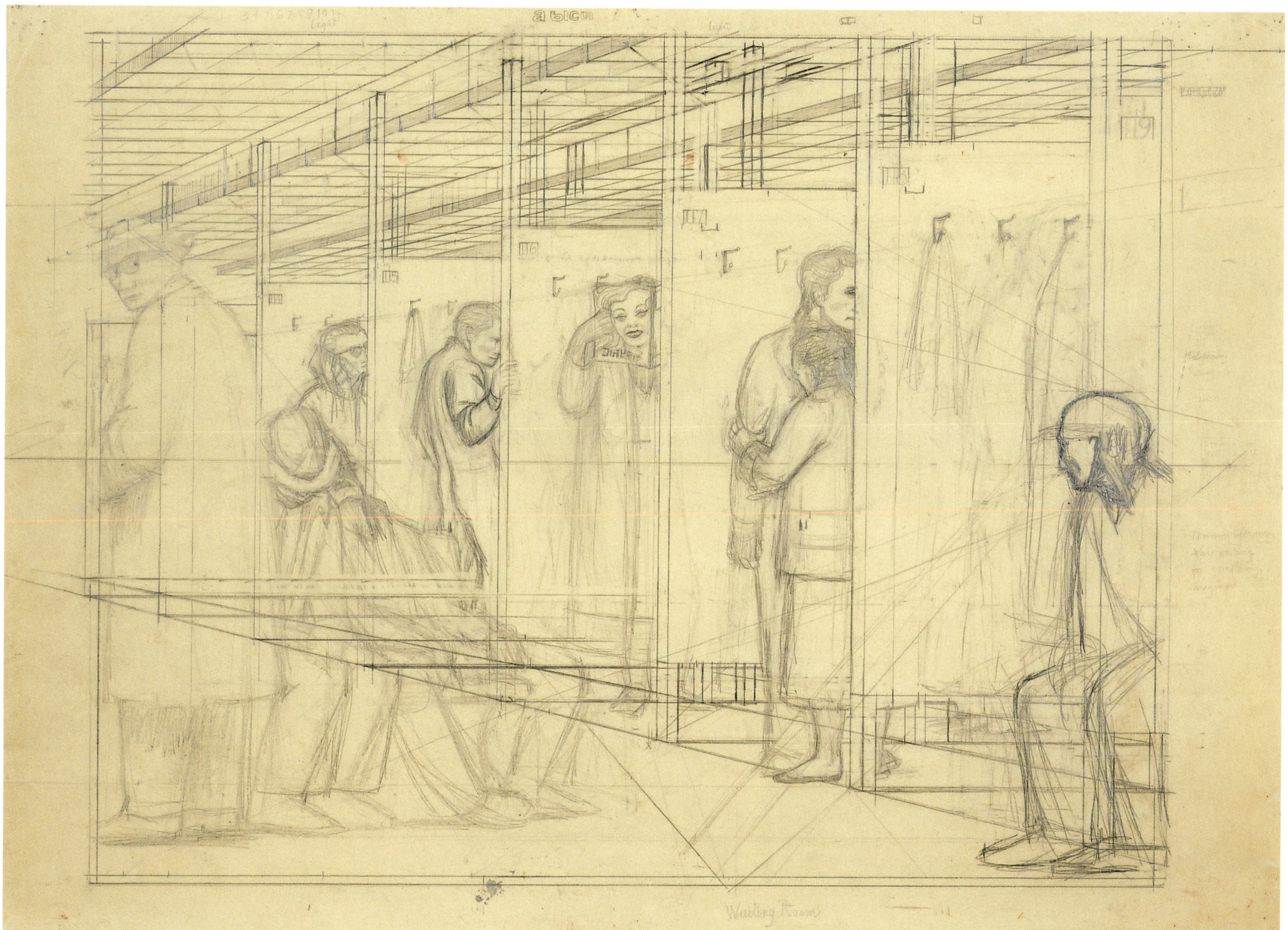

plate 31
***Waiting Room*** (1957)
Egg tempera on wood
24 × 30 inches (61 × 78.4 cm)
Smithsonian American Art Museum, Washington, D.C., Gift of S.C. Johnson & Sons, Inc.

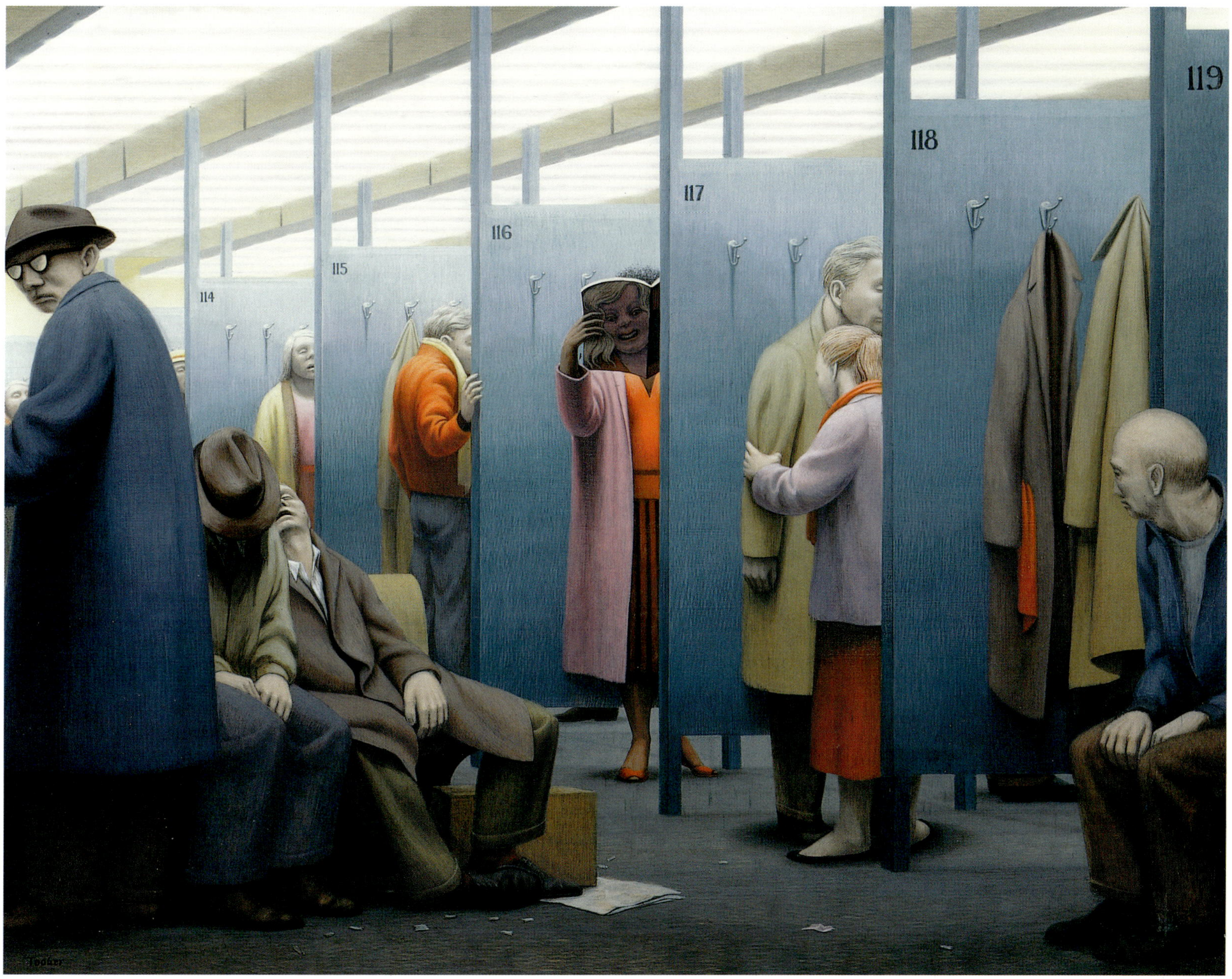

plate 32
*In the Summer House* (1958)
Egg tempera on fiberboard
24 × 24 inches (61 × 61 cm)
Smithsonian American Art Museum,
Washington, D.C., Gift of the Sara
Roby Foundation



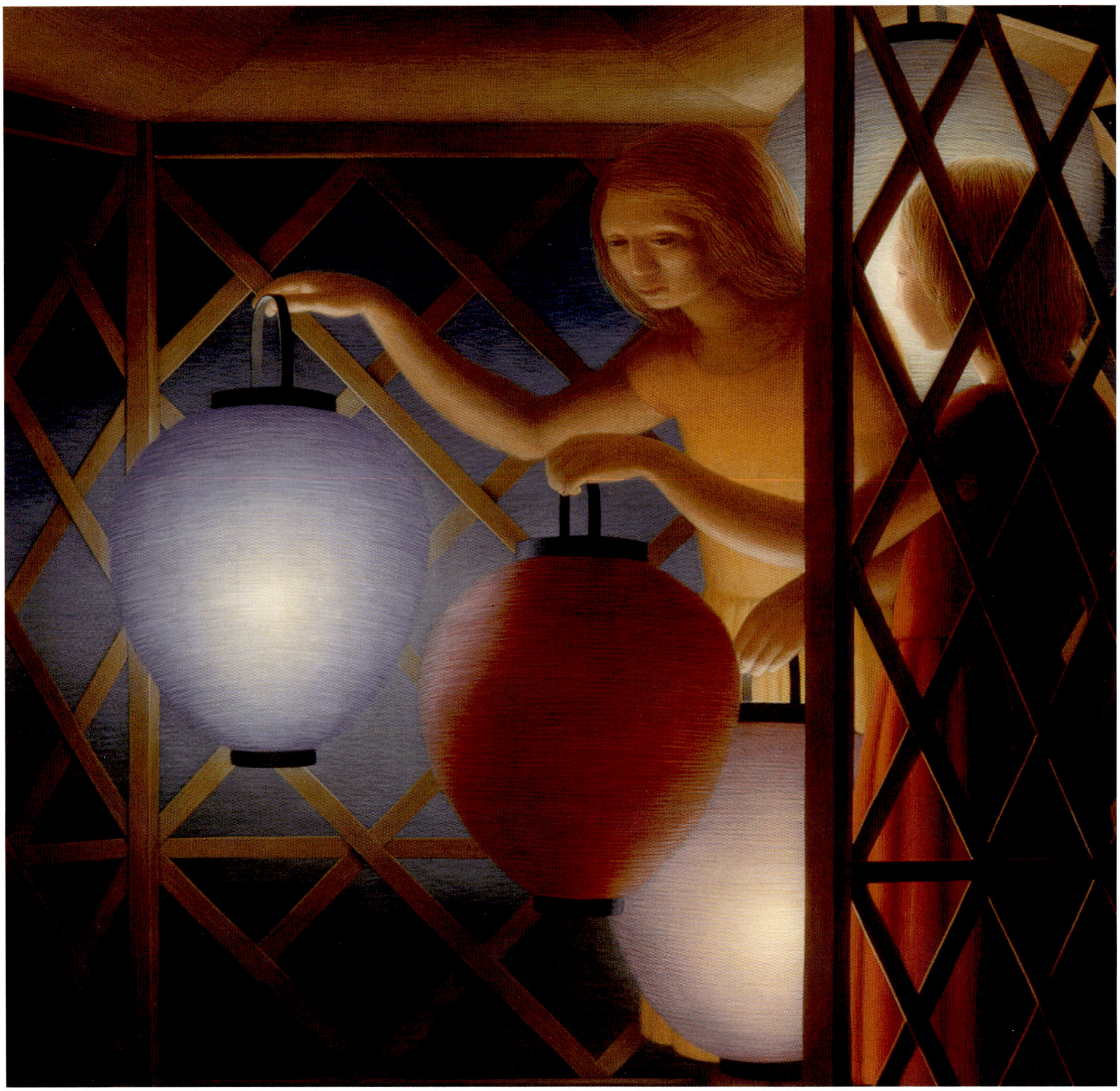

plate 33
***Sleepers II*** (1959)
Tempera on wood panel
16⅛ × 28 inches (41.2 × 71.1 cm)
The Museum of Modern Art, New York, New York, USA
Larry Aldrich Foundation Fund




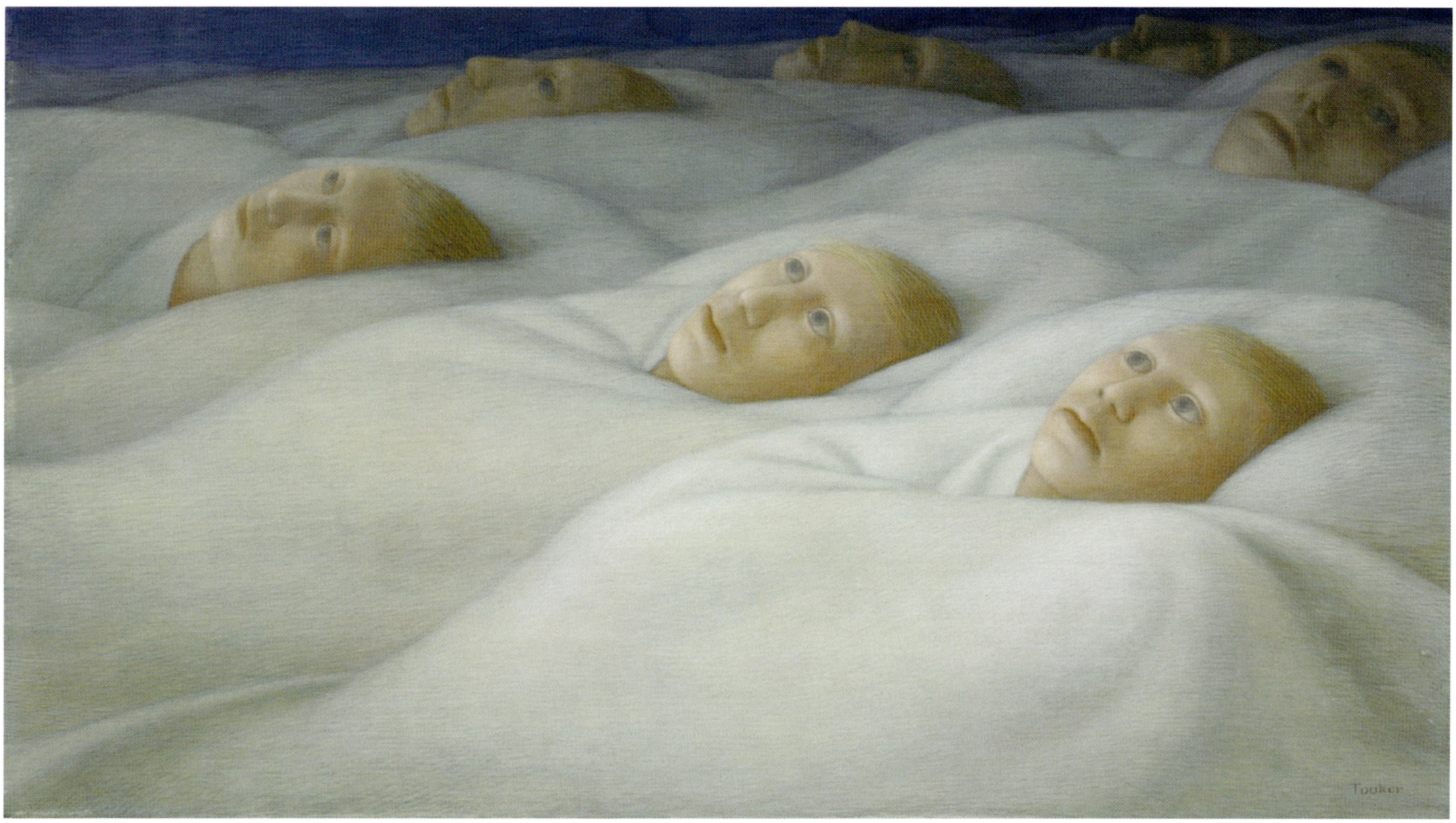

plate 34
***Lovers I*** (1959)
Egg tempera on gesso panel
18 × 24 inches (45.7 × 61 cm)
Collection of William T. Hillman



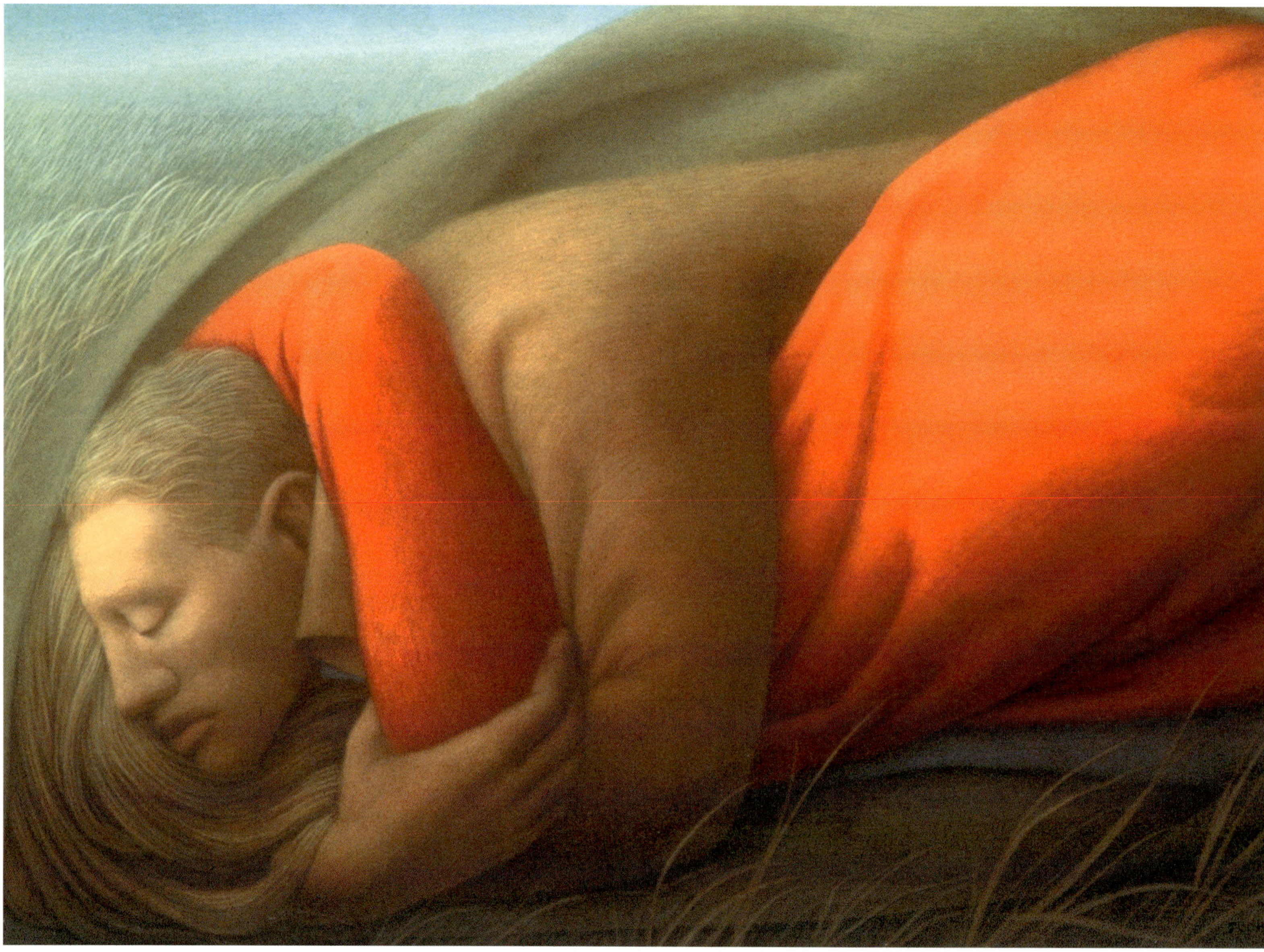

plate 35
*Toilette* (1962)
Egg tempera on gesso panel
20½ × 17½ inches (52.1 × 44.4 cm)
Linda Lichtenberg Kaplan



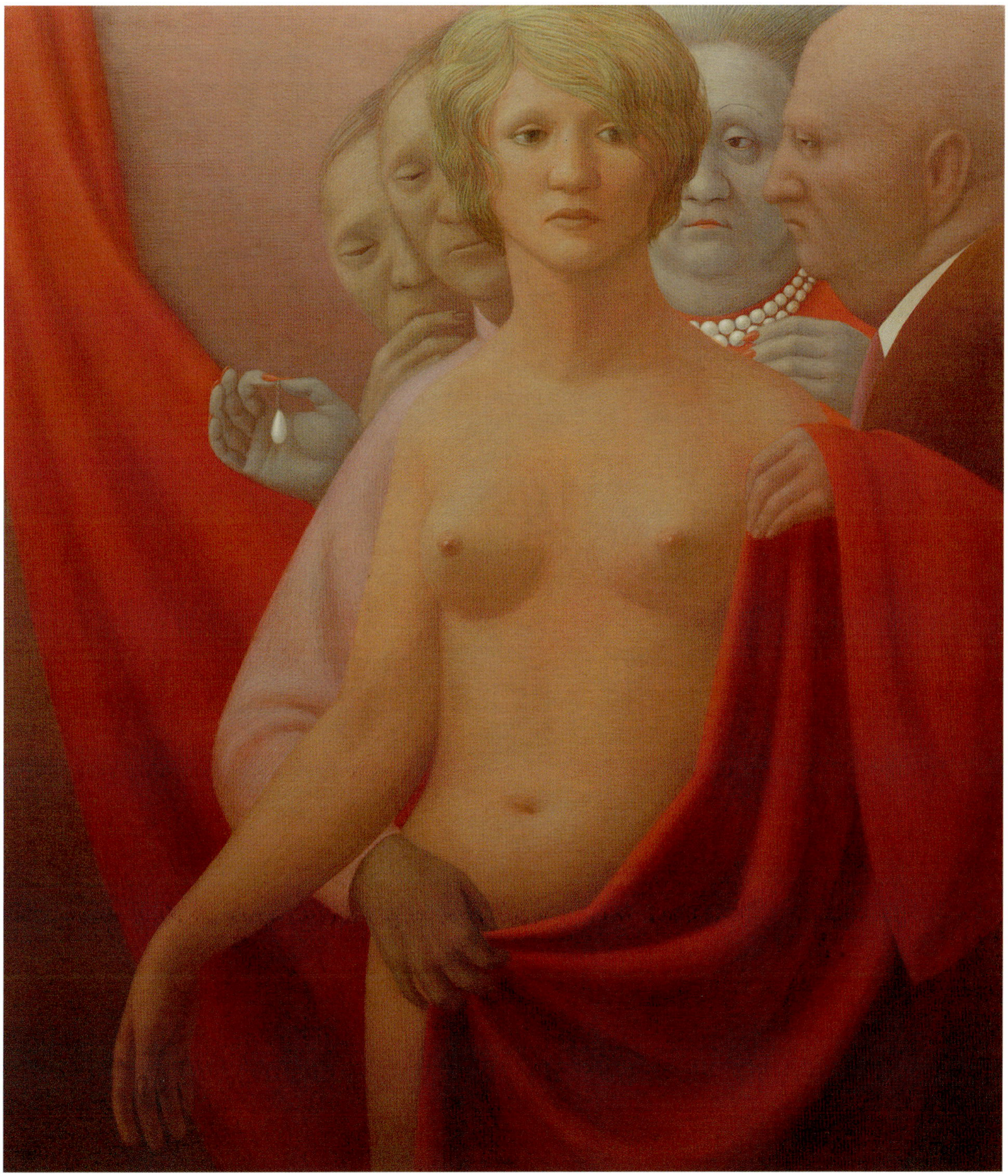

plate 36
***Meadow I*** (1960–61)
Egg tempera on gesso panel
20 × 28 inches (50.8 × 71.1 cm)
Toledo Art Museum: Gift of the Woodward Foundation and purchased with funds from the Libbey Endowment, Gift of Edward Drummond Libbey, by exchange, 2007.47



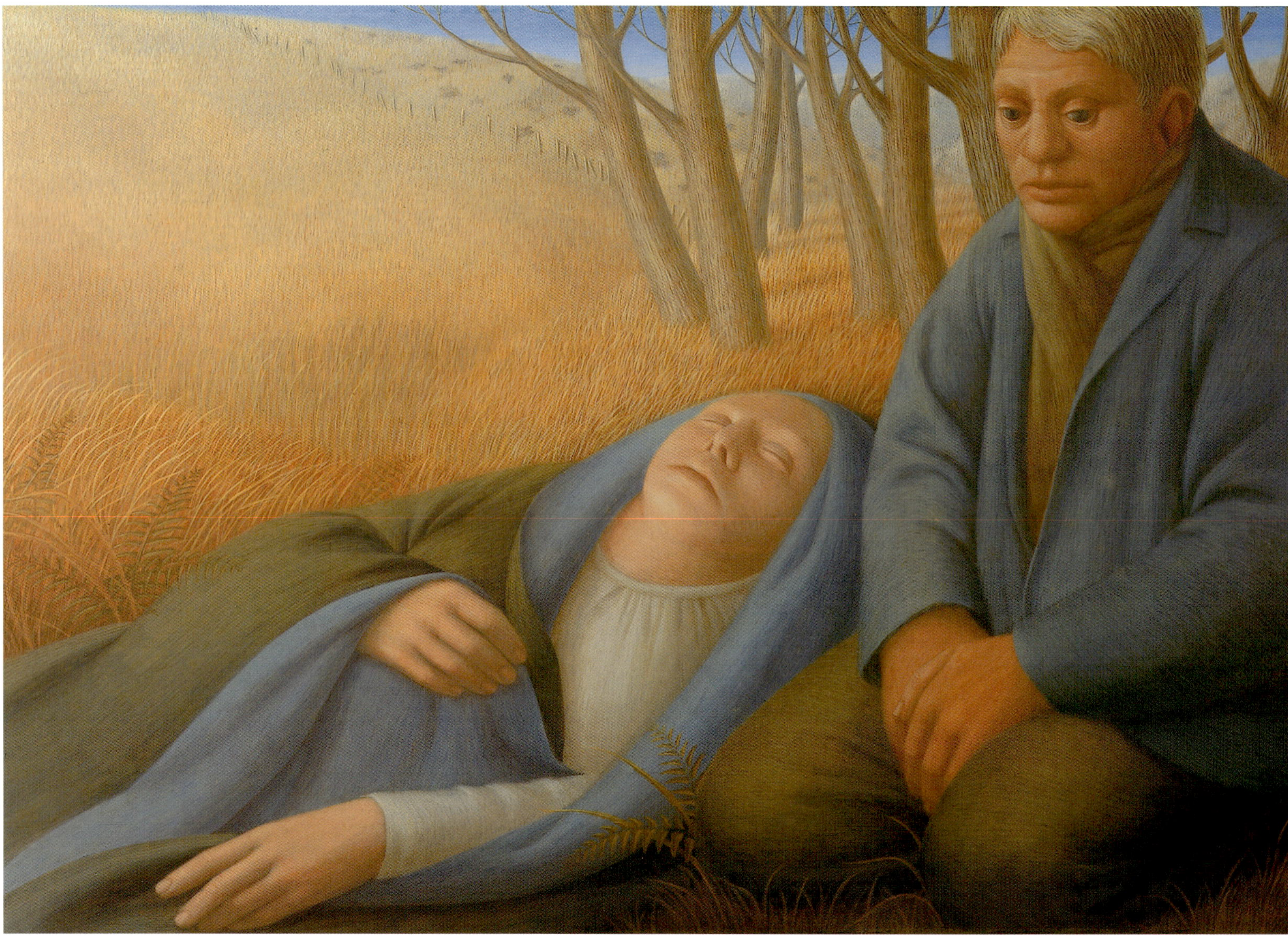

plate 37
***Supper*** (1963)
Tempera on board
20 × 24 inches (50.8 × 61 cm)
Memorial Art Gallery of the University of
Rochester, Marion Stratton Gould Fund



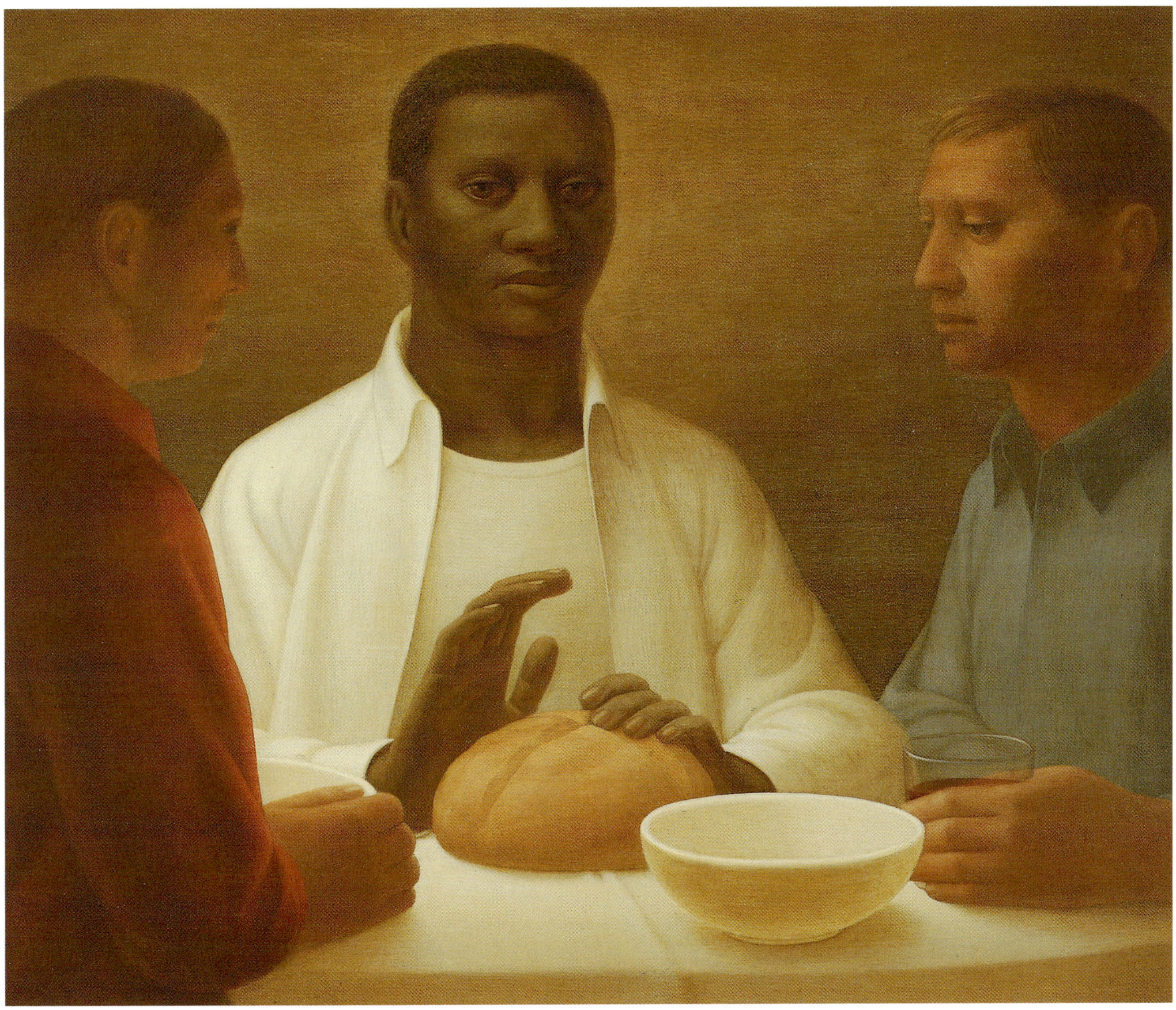

plate 38
***Window VII*** (1963)
Egg tempera on gesso panel
24⅛ × 21⅛ inches (61.3 × 53.7 cm)
Terra Foundation for American Art,
Daniel J. Terra Collection,
1992.168



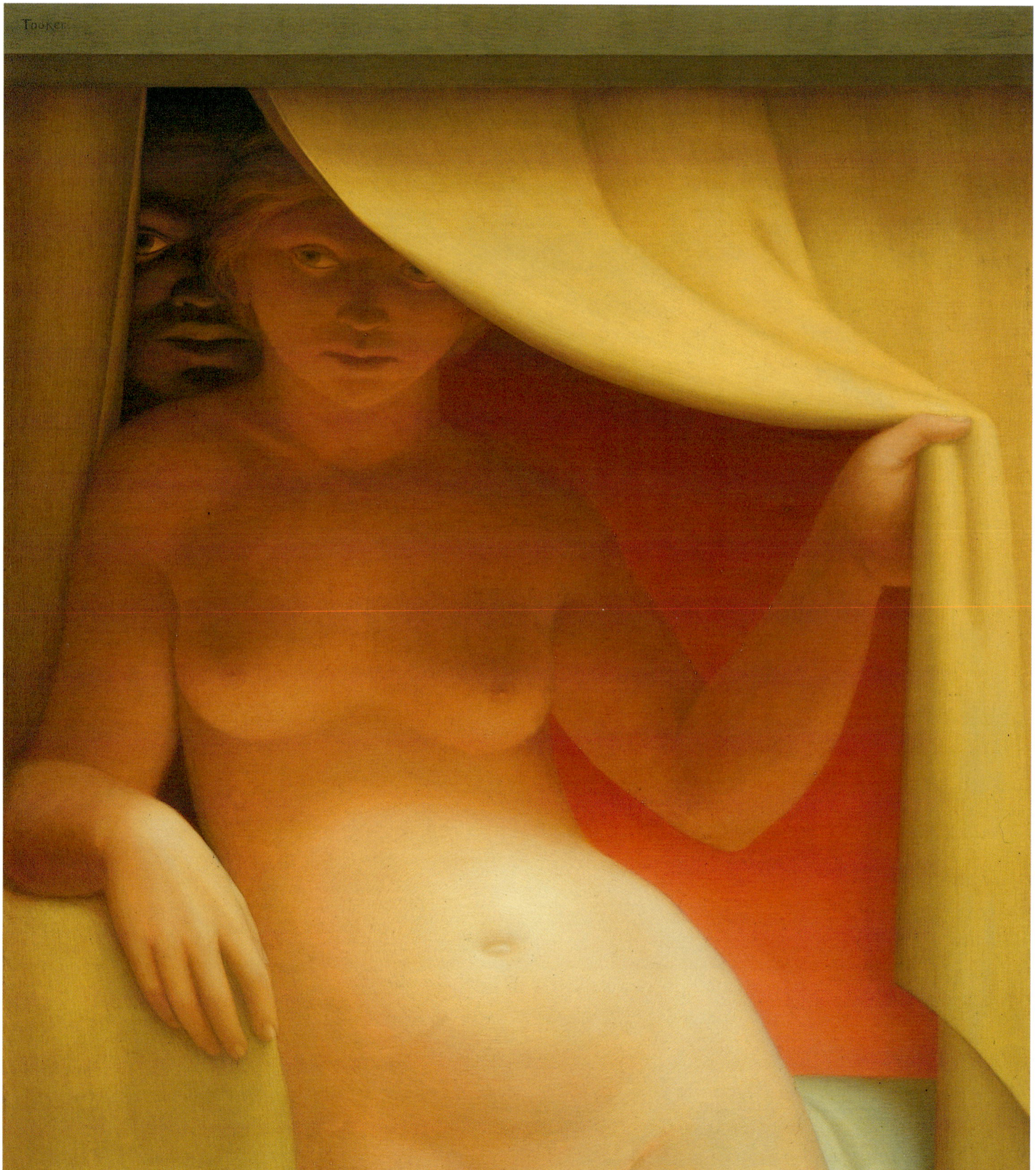

plate 39
***Window VIII*** (1966)
Egg tempera on gesso panel
24 × 20 inches (61 × 50.8 cm)
Private Collection

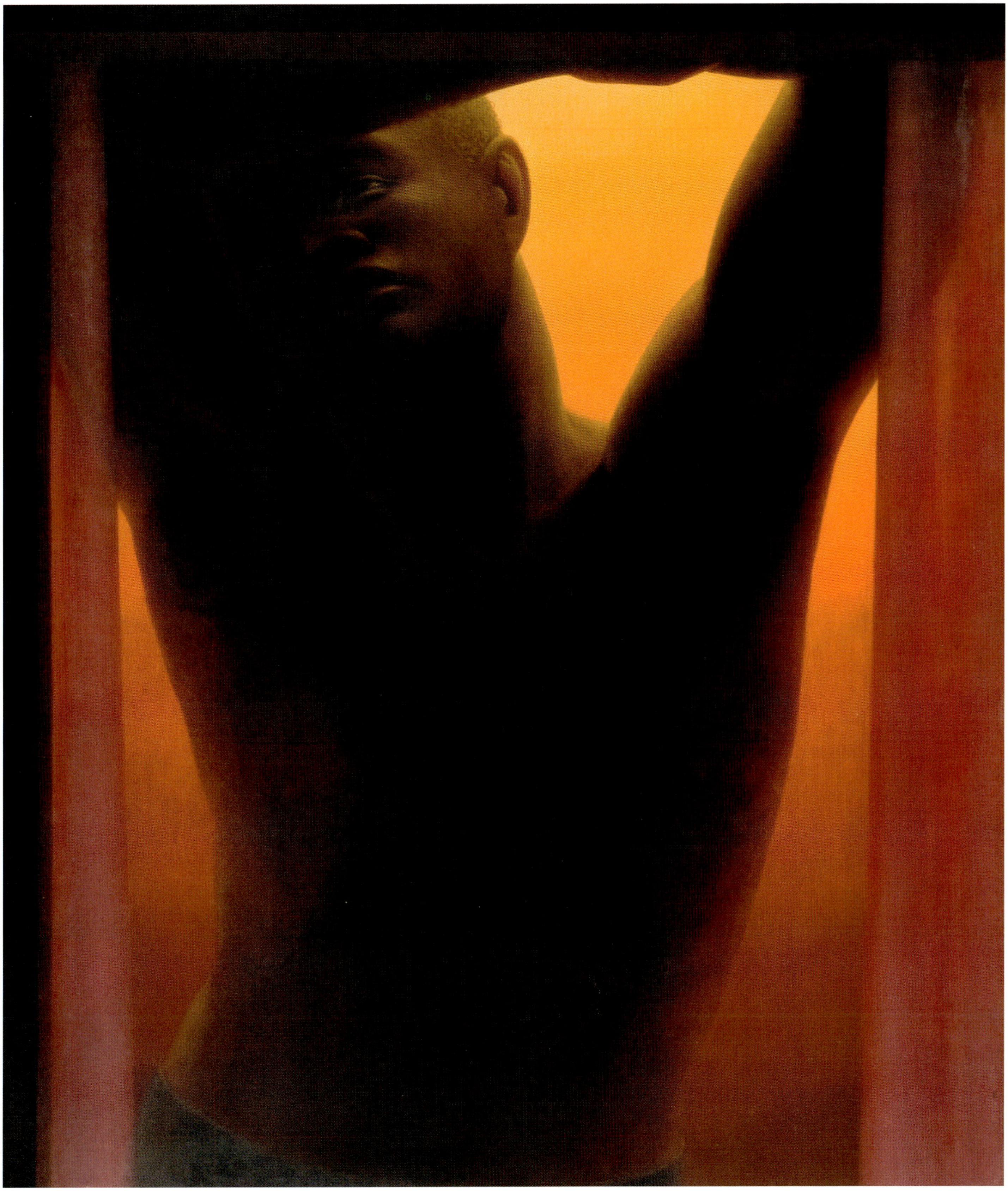

plate 40
**Study for *Lunch*** (1964)
Graphite, chalk, and wash on paper
20⅞ × 26¹³⁄₁₆ inches (53 × 68.1 cm)
Gift of the artist (PA 1936) in memory of his parents, George Clair and Angela Montejo Roura Tooker, Addison Gallery of American Art, Phillips Academy, Andover, Massachusetts



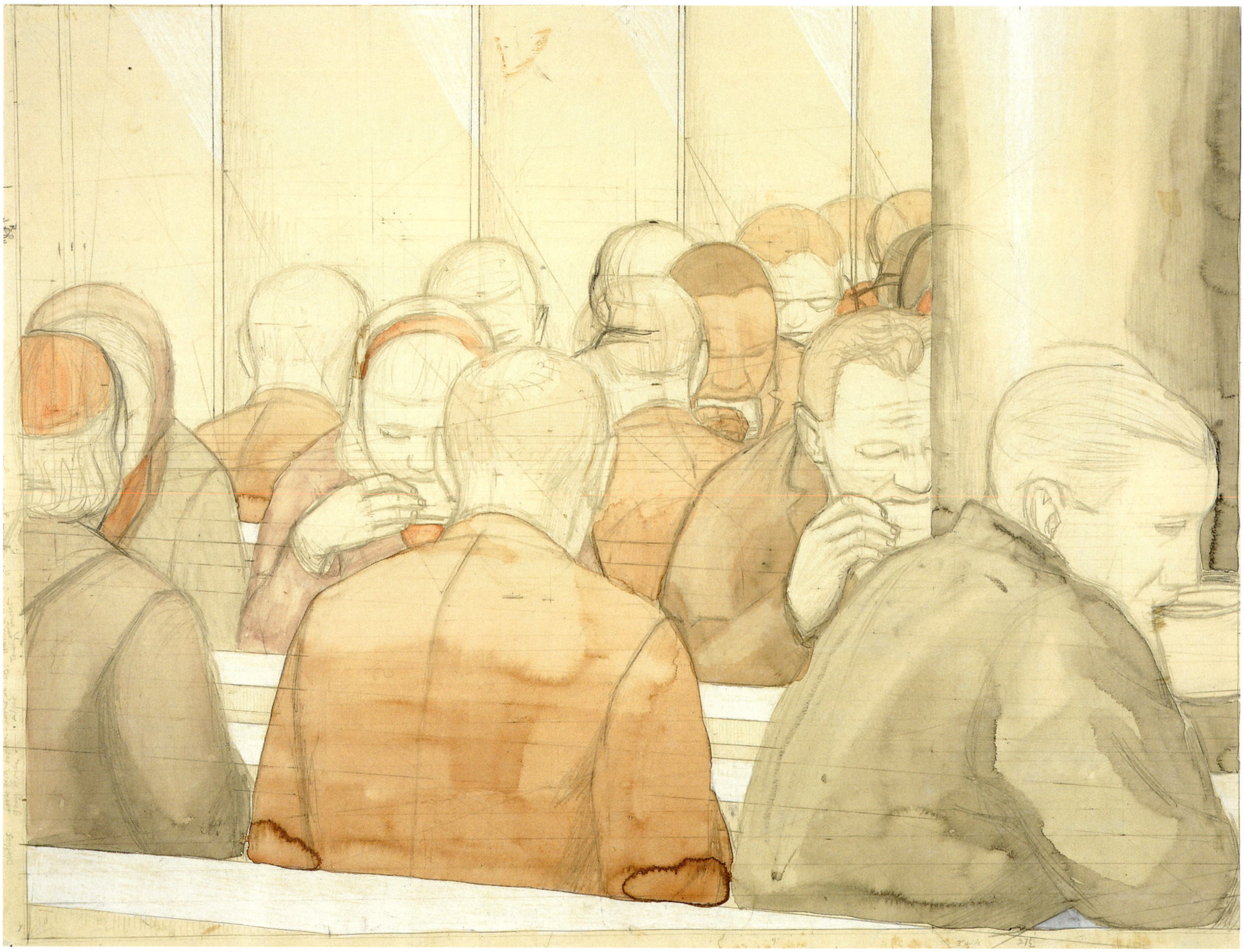

plate 41
***Lunch*** (1964)
Egg tempera on gesso panel
20 × 26 inches (50.8 × 66 cm)
Columbus Museum of Art, Ohio:
Museum Purchase, Derby Fund, from the
Philip J. and Suzanne Schiller Collection
of American Social Commentary Art
1930–1970



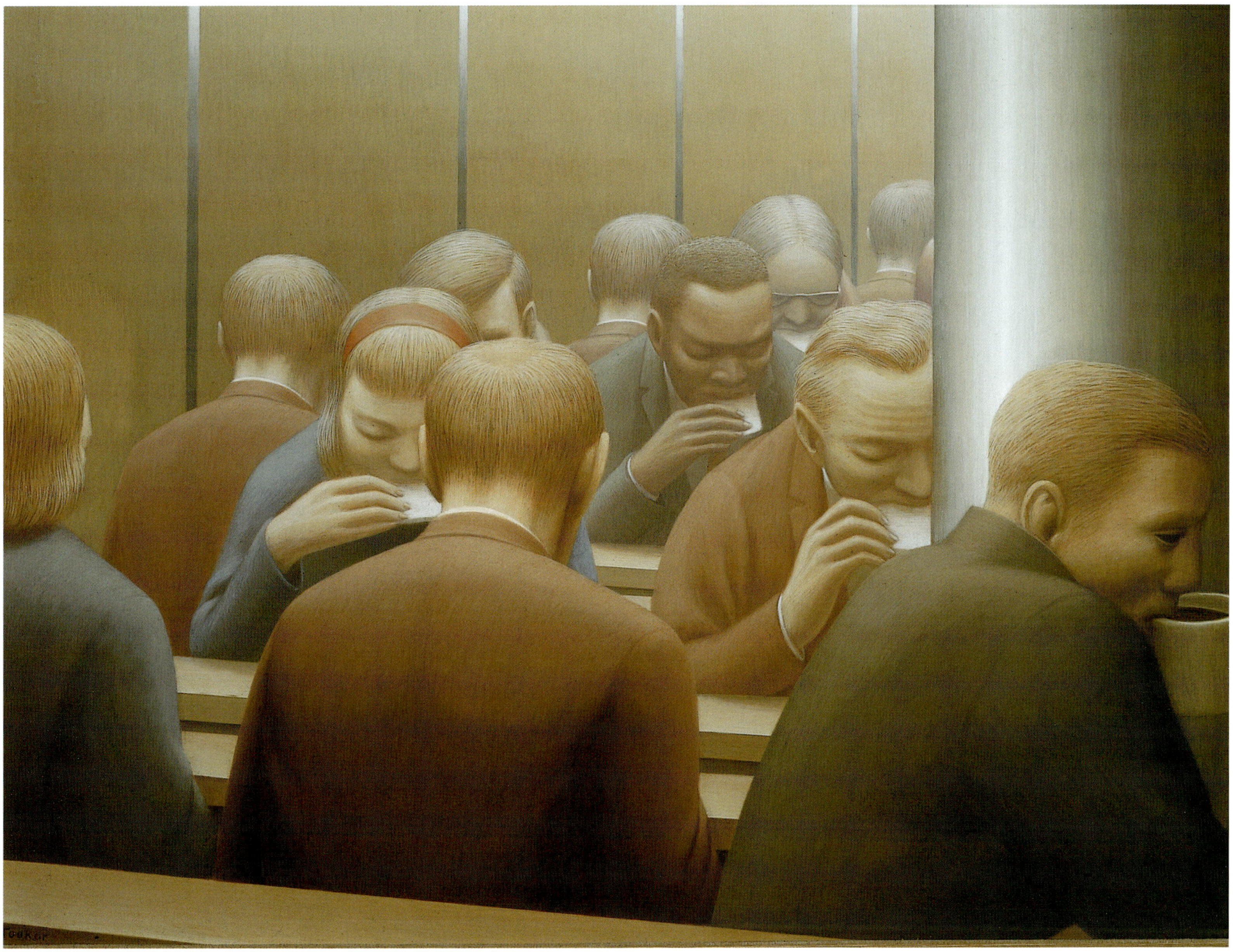

plate 42
***Landscape with Figures*** (1965–66)
Egg tempera on gesso panel
26 × 30 inches (66 × 76.2 cm)
Barbara B. Millhouse

plate 43
***Teller*** (1967)
Egg tempera on gesso panel
23½ × 15½ inches (59.7 × 39.4 cm)
Private Collection, courtesy of EKG Art Advisory, New York



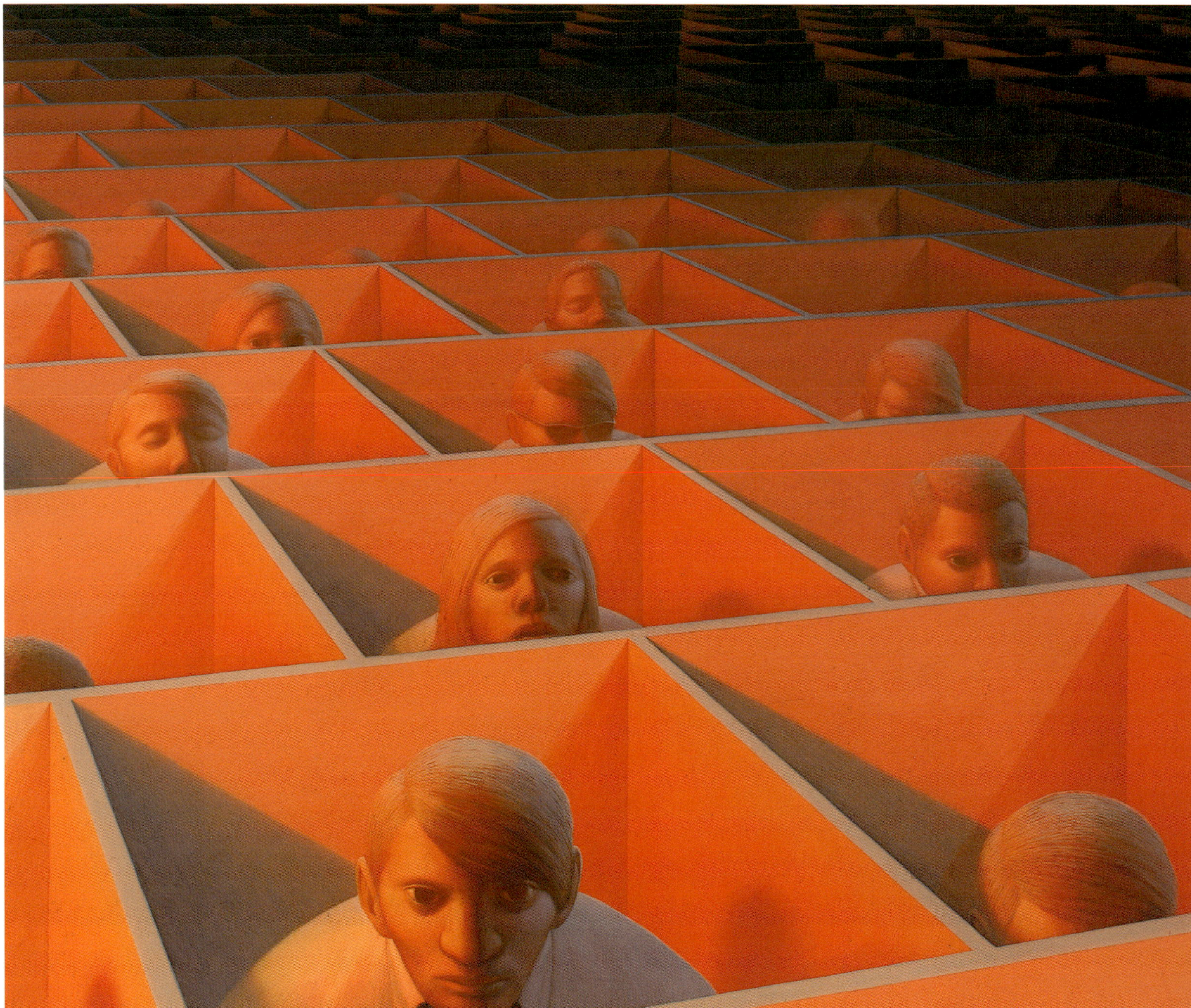

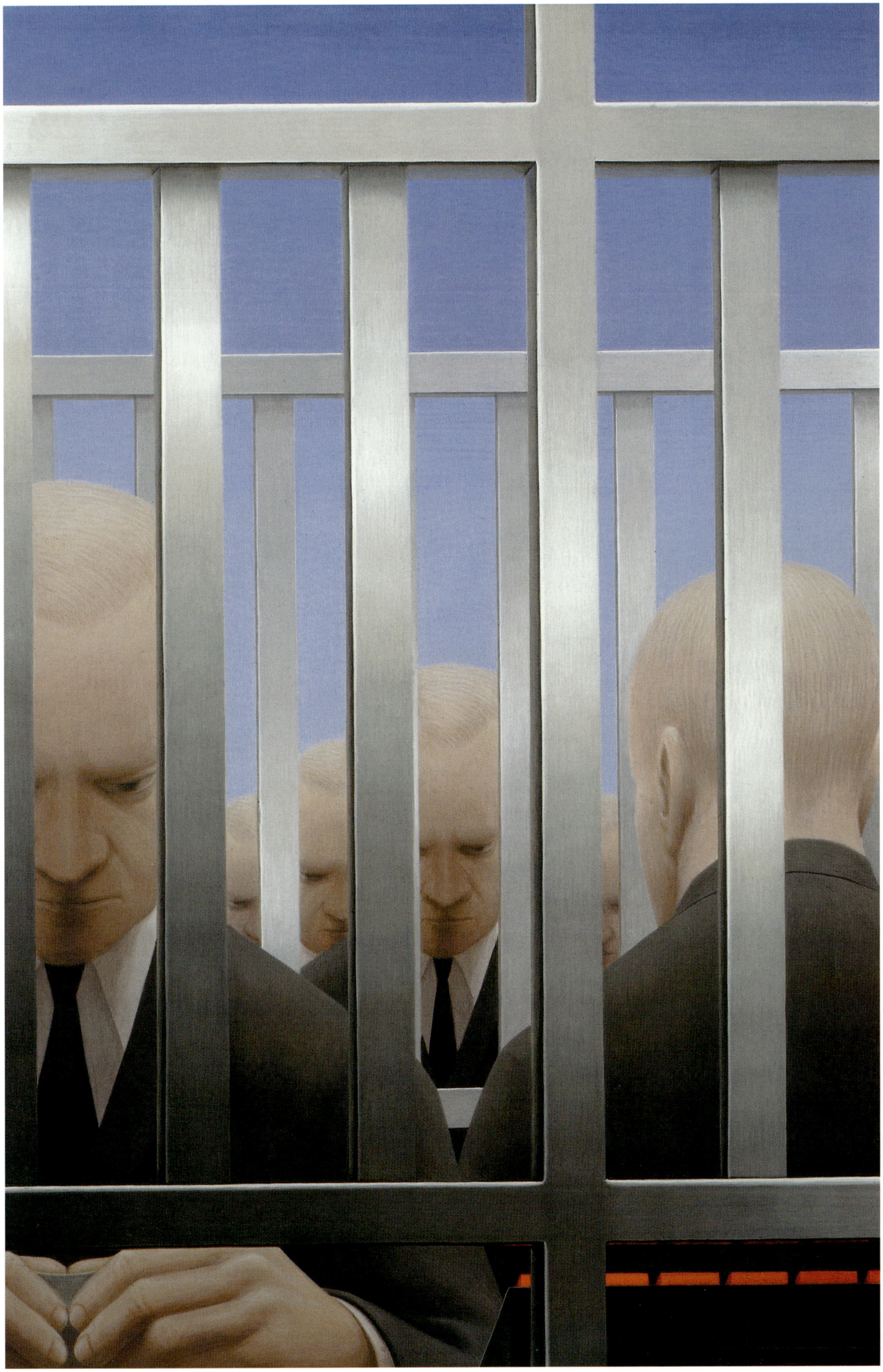

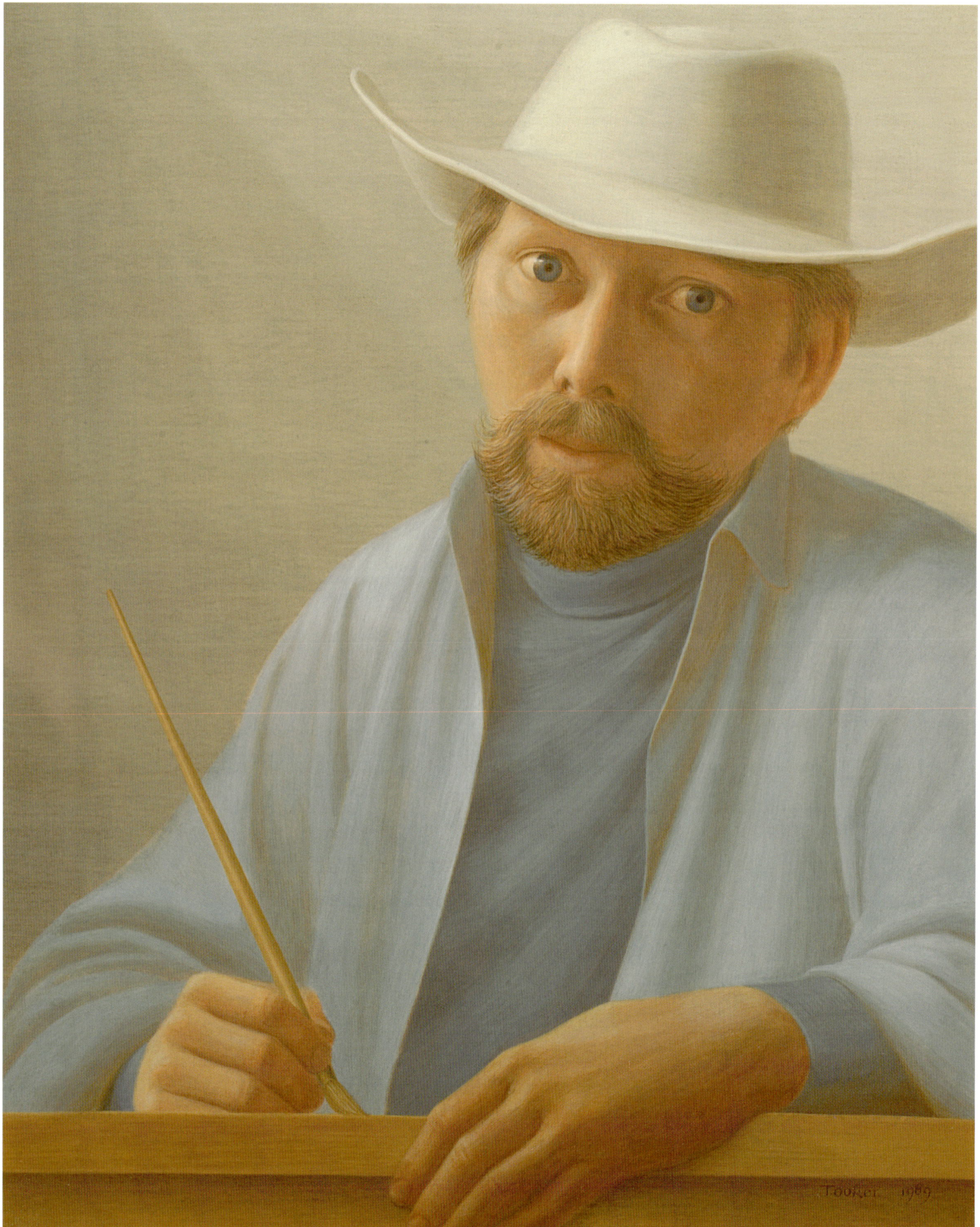
Tooker 1969

plate 44
***Self-Portrait*** (1969)
Egg tempera on gesso panel
24 × 19½ inches (61 × 49.5 cm)
National Academy Museum, New York, 1706-P

plate 45
***Ward*** (1970–71)
Egg tempera on gesso panel
20 × 30 inches (50.8 × 76.2 cm)
Private Collection



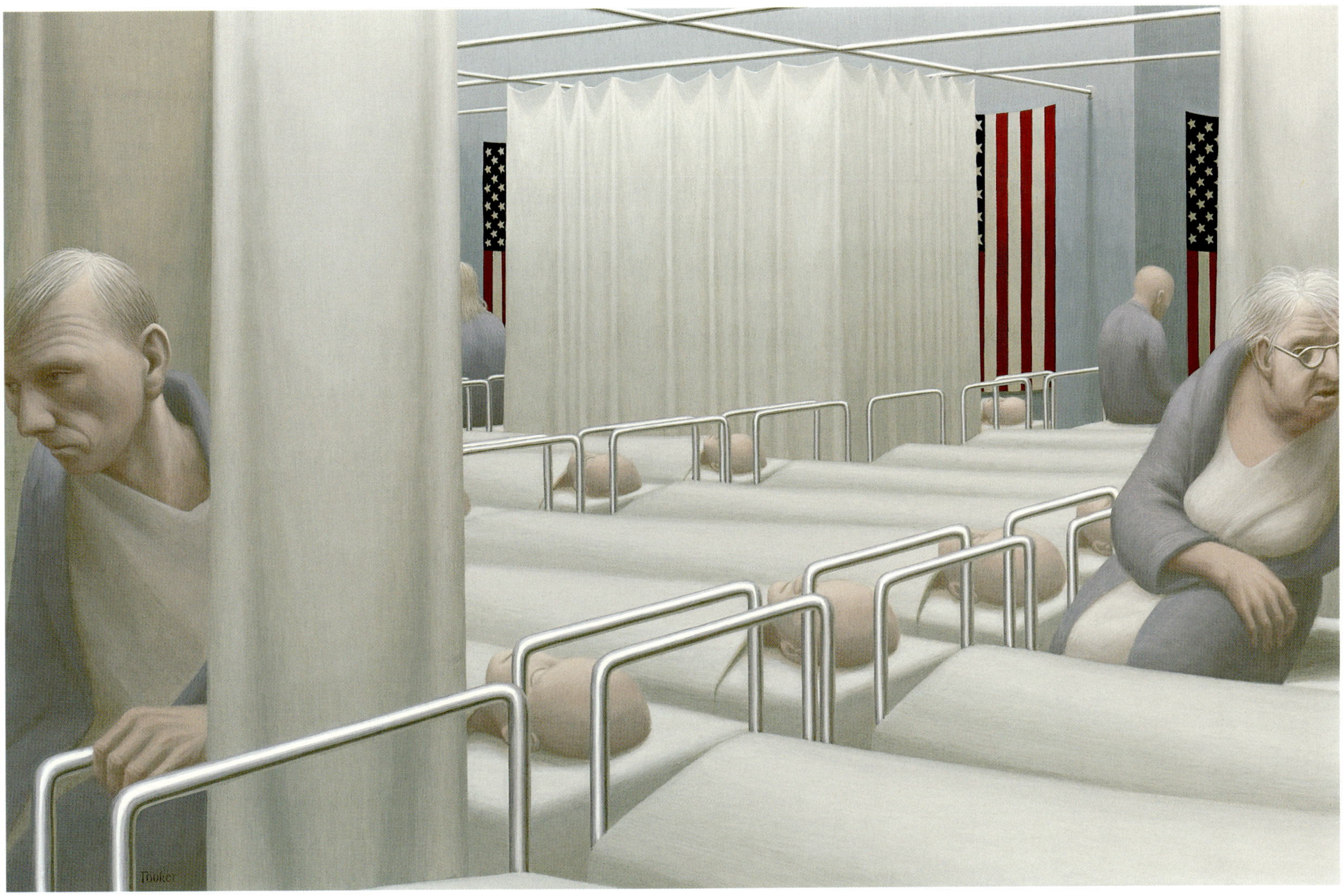

plate 46
*Voice II* (1972)
Egg tempera on gesso panel
17½ × 11½ inches (44.5 × 29 cm)
National Academy Museum, New York,
1758-P



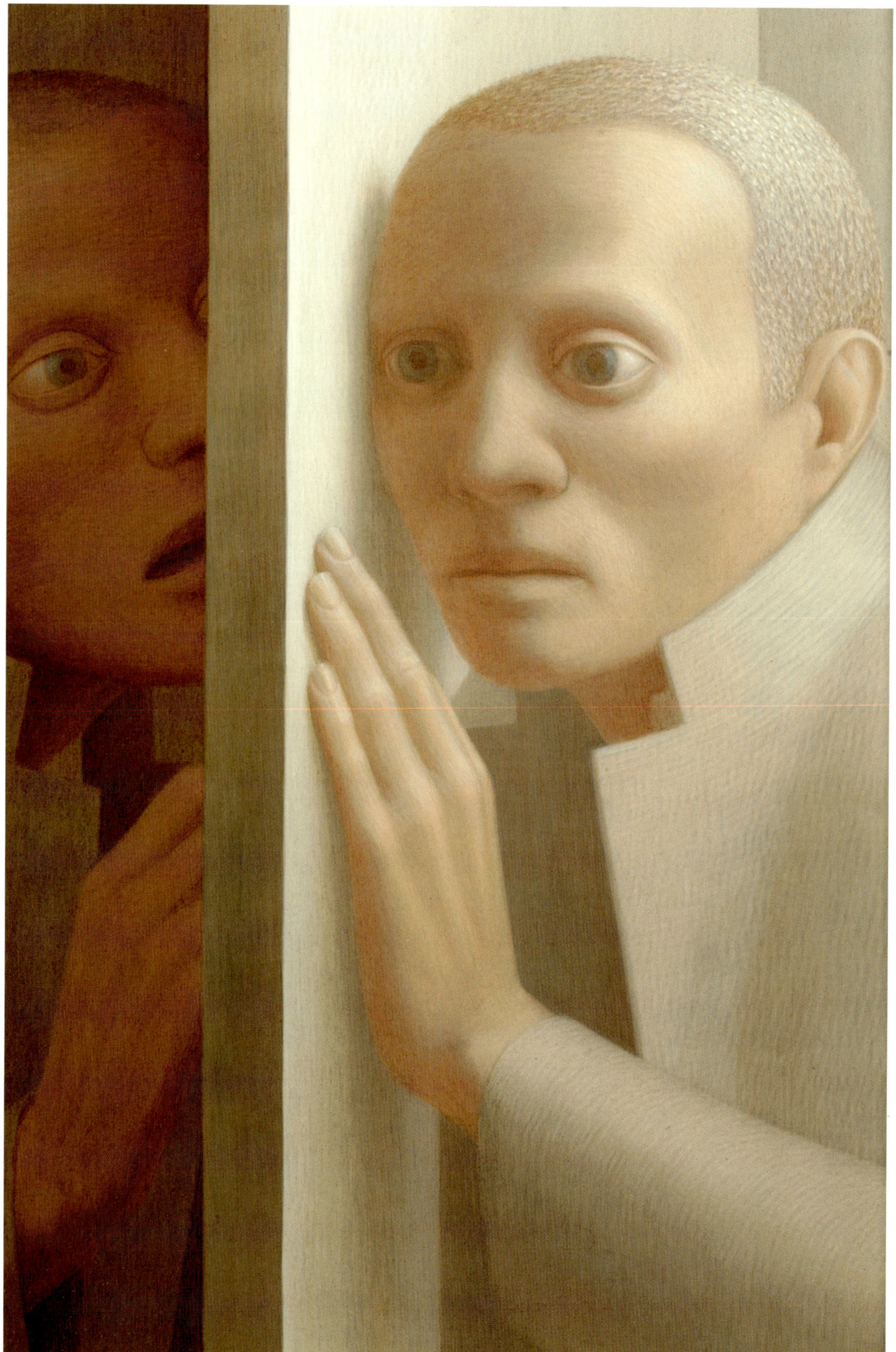

plate 47
***Mirror III*** (*circa* 1970–71)
Egg tempera on gesso panel
22 × 19¾ inches (55.9 × 50.2 cm)
Indianapolis Museum of Art,
Gift of Edwin F. Koch, Jr., M.D.,
2006.66



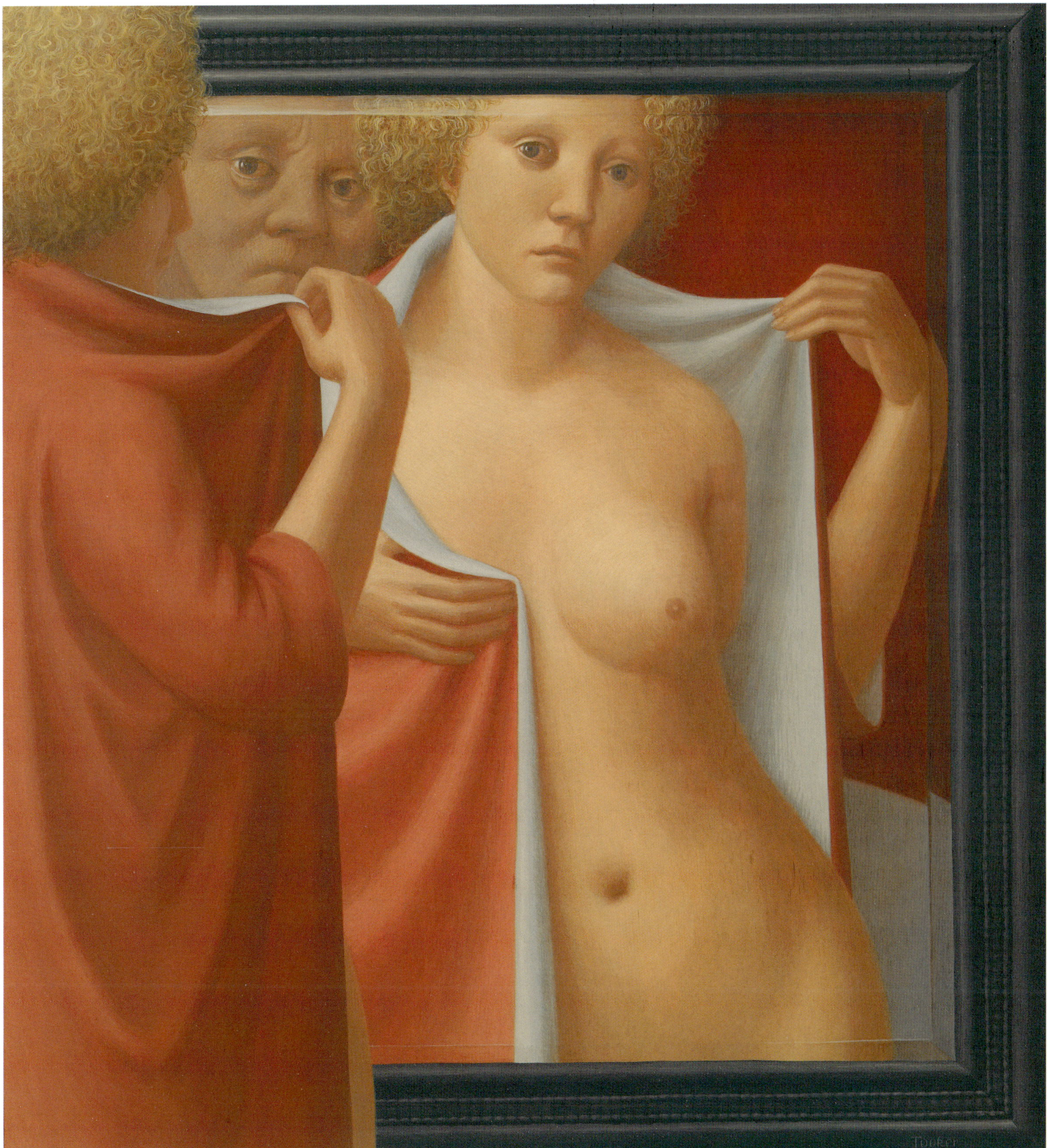

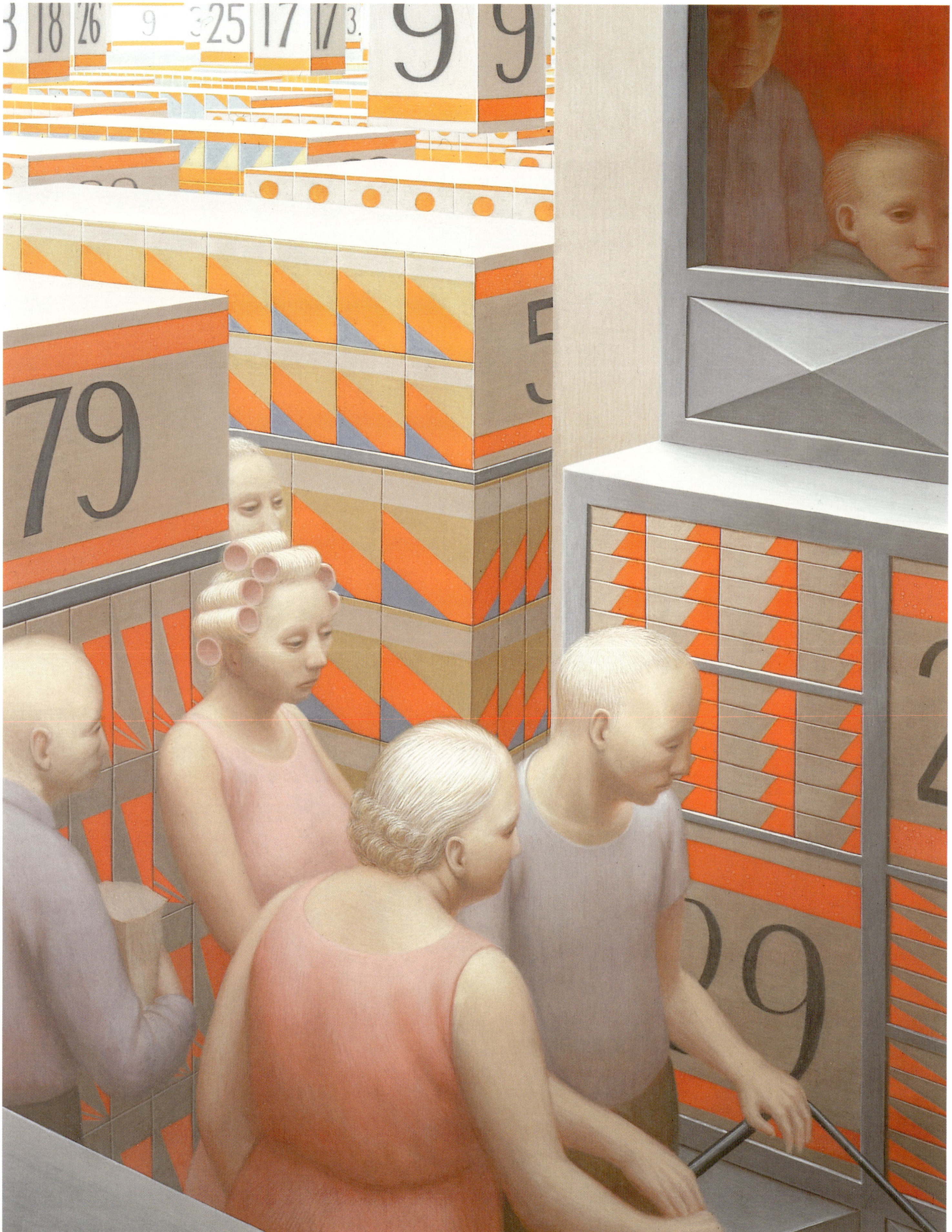

plate 48
***Supermarket*** (1973)
Egg tempera on gesso panel
23 × 17¼ inches (58.4 × 43.8 cm)
Curtis Galleries, Minneapolis, Minnesota

plate 49
***Standing Figures*** (1973)
Egg tempera on gesso panel
18 × 24 inches (45.7 × 61 cm)
Private Collection



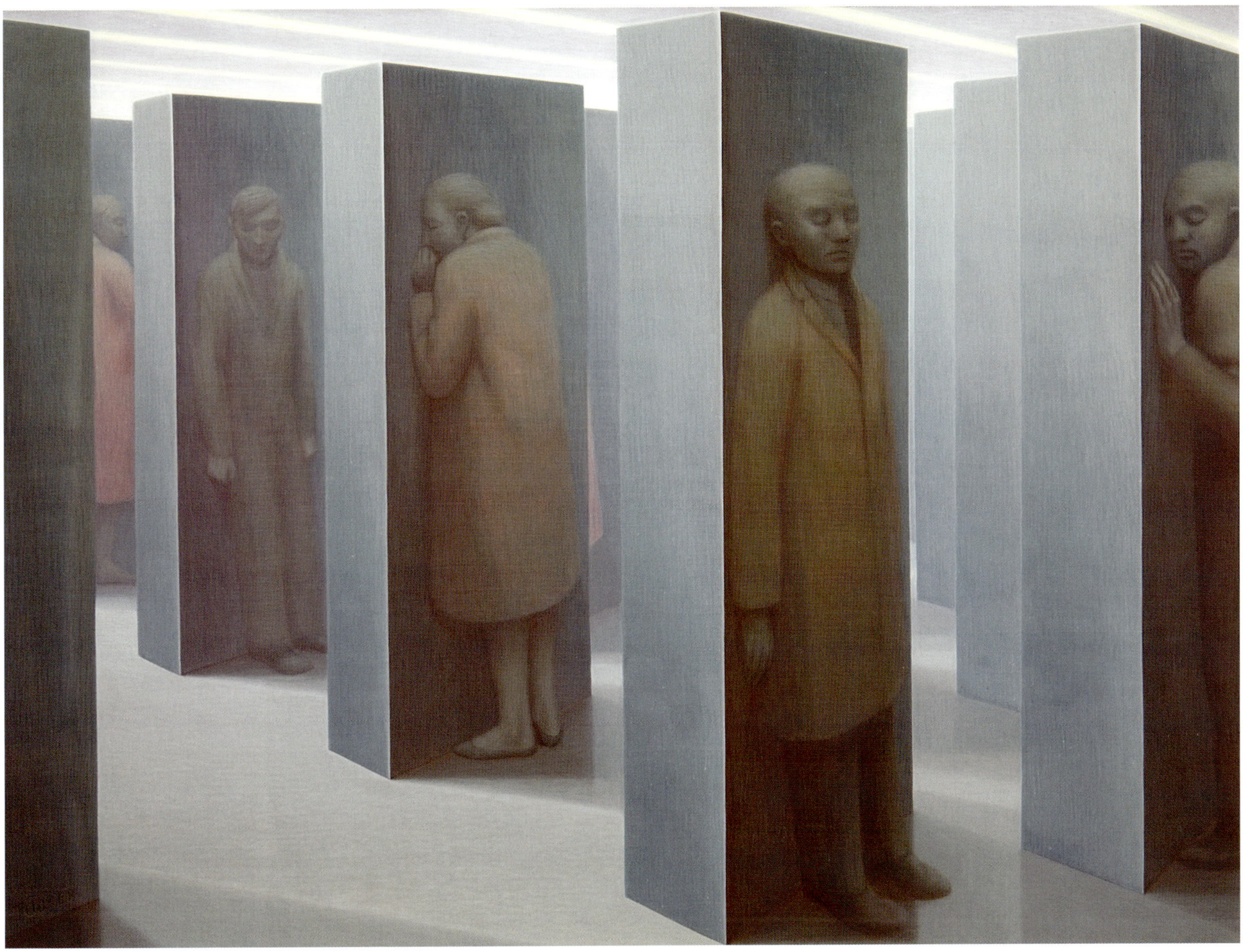

plate 50
*Pot of Aloes* (1974)
Egg tempera on gesso panel
24 × 18 inches (61 × 45.7 cm)
Private Lender

plate 51
*Woman with Oranges* (1977)
Egg tempera on gesso panel
23½ × 15½ inches (59.7 × 39.3 cm)
Courtesy DC Moore Gallery, New York



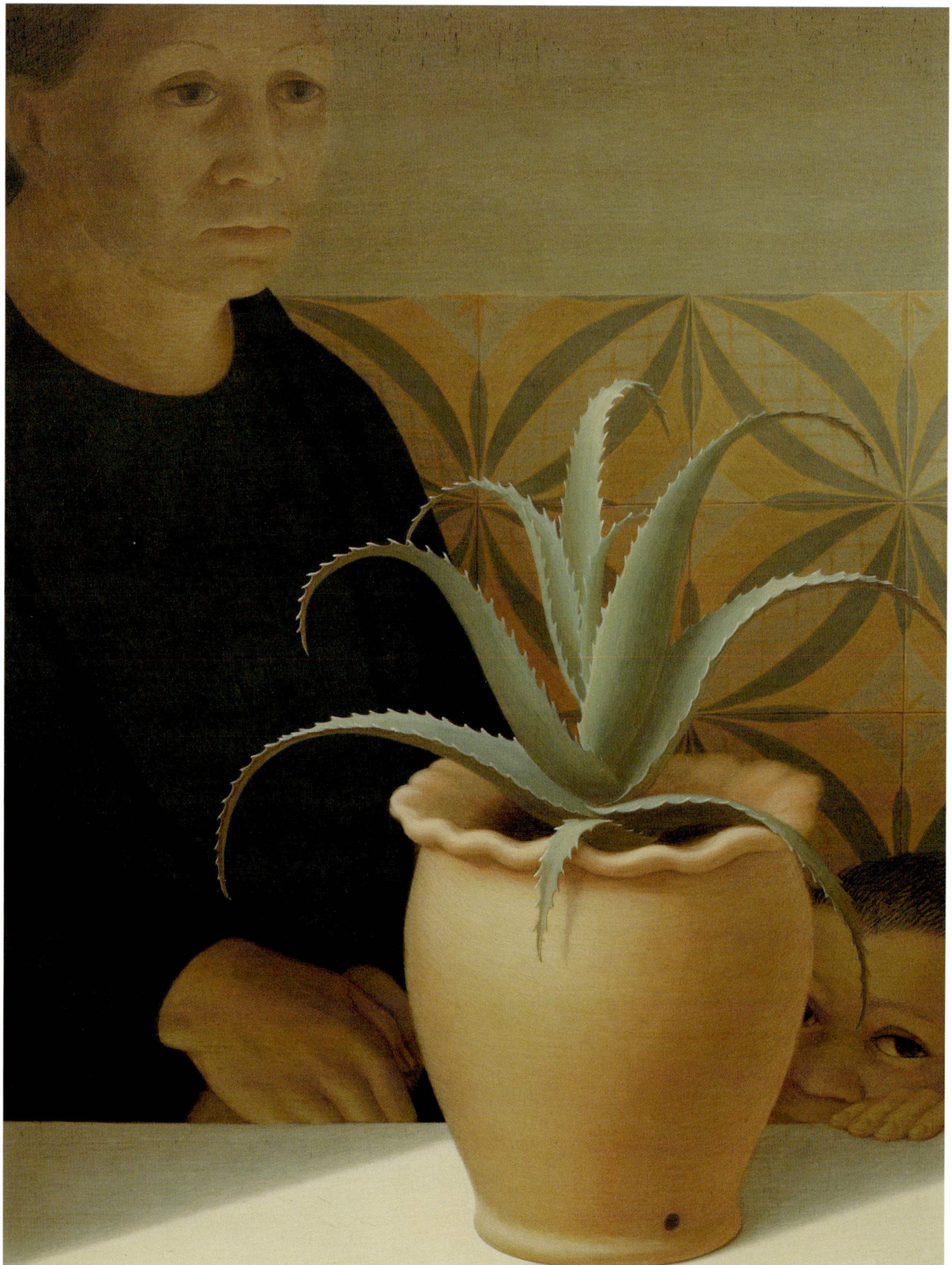

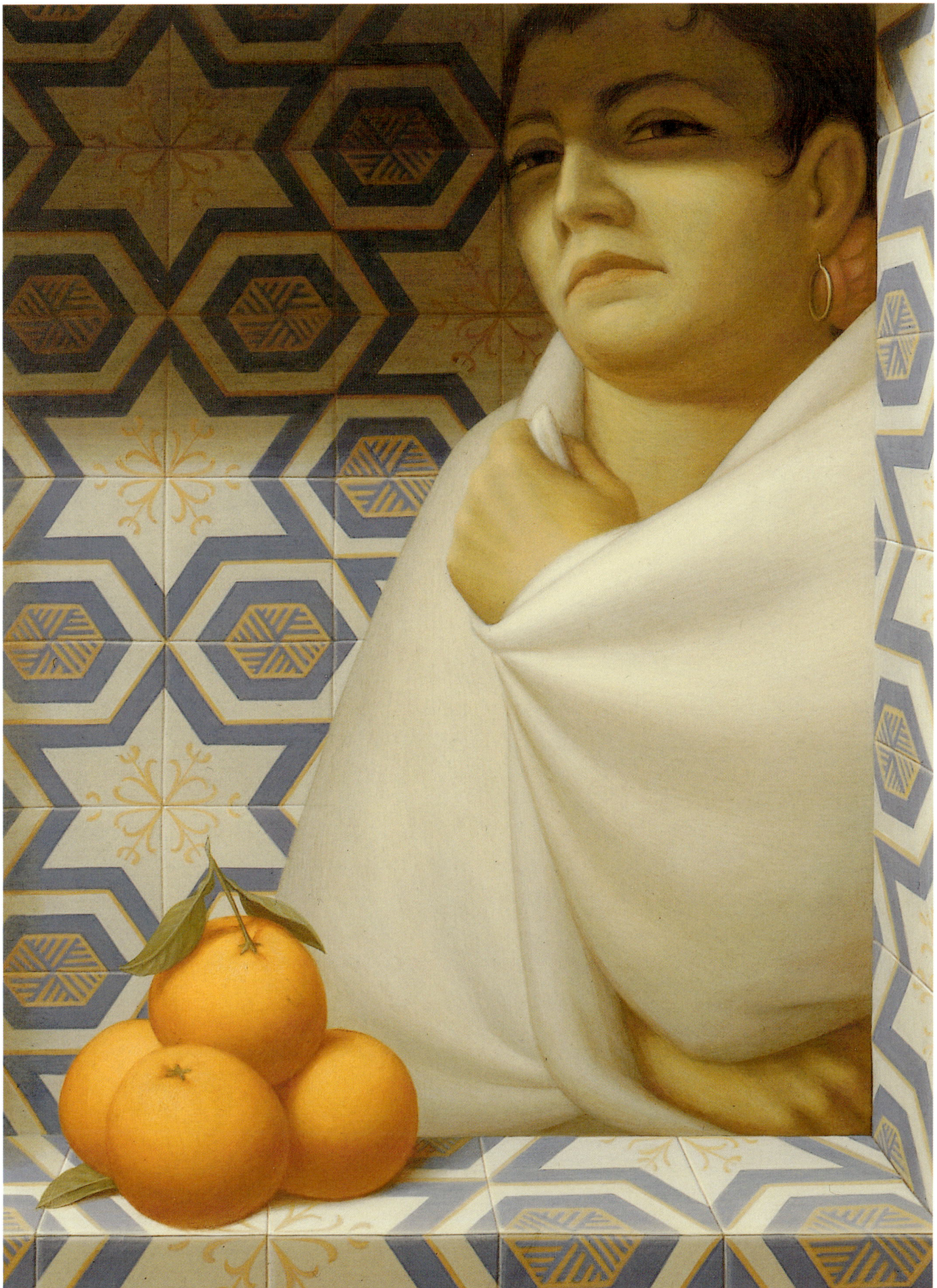

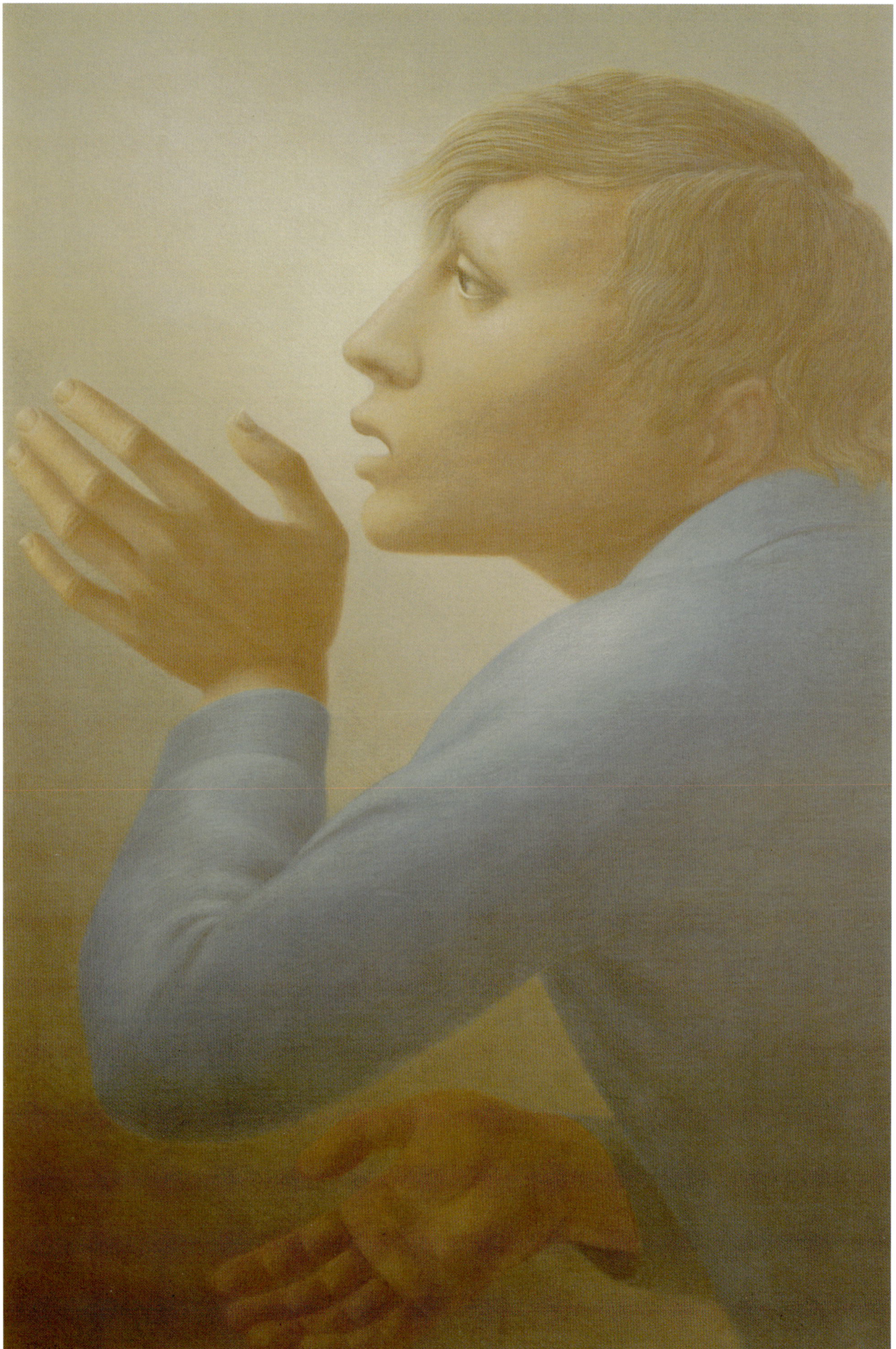

plate 52
*Orant* (1977)
Egg tempera on gesso panel
23½ × 15½ inches (59.7 × 39.4 cm)
Private Collection

plate 53
*Embrace I* (1979)
Egg tempera on gesso panel
24 × 18 inches (61 × 45.7 cm)
Collection of Anka K. Palitc

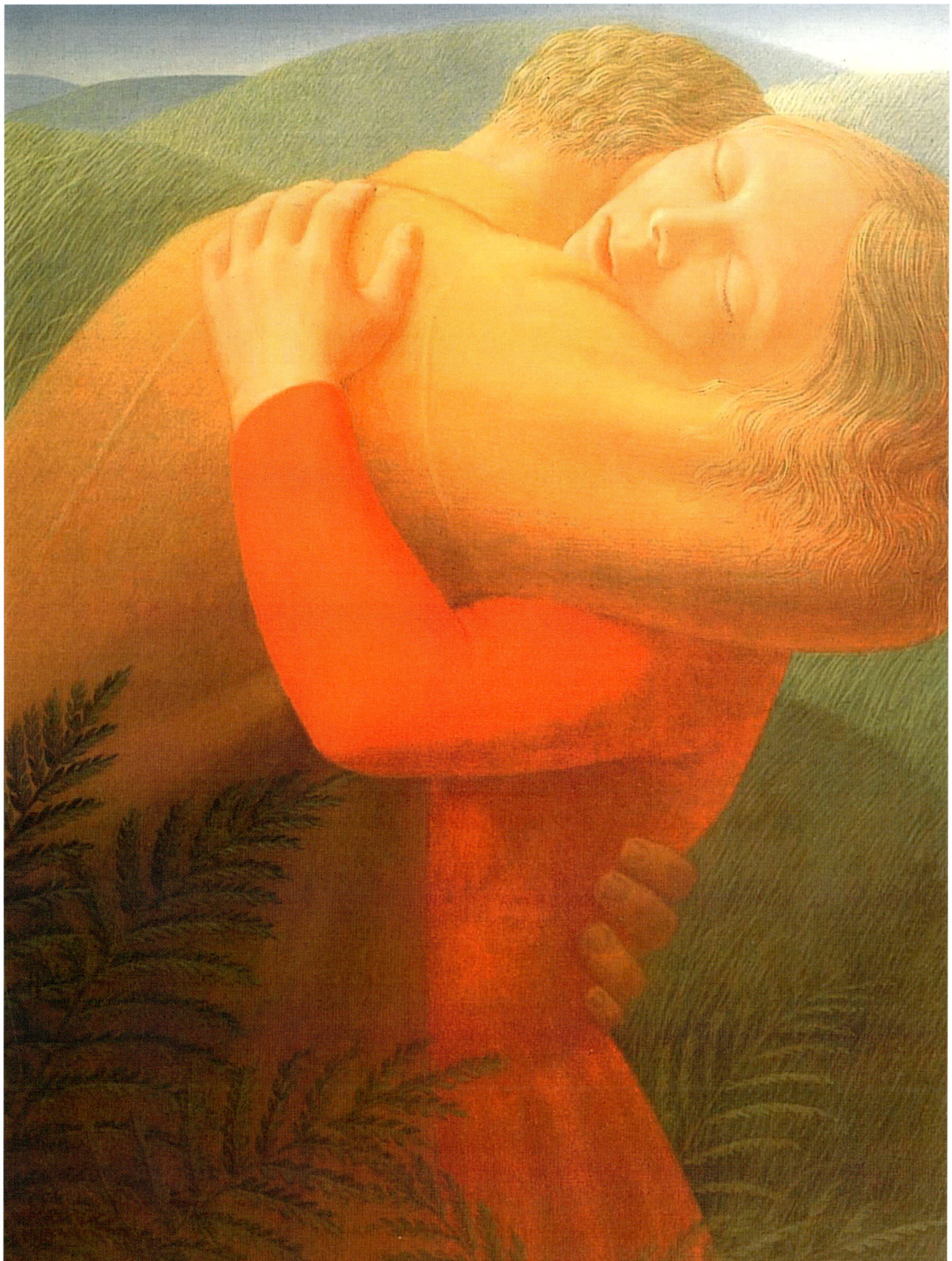

plate 54
***Un Ballo in Maschera*** (1982)
Egg tempera on gesso panel
22 × 30 inches (55.9 × 76.2 cm)
Collection of Mr. and Mrs. Mark L. Brock



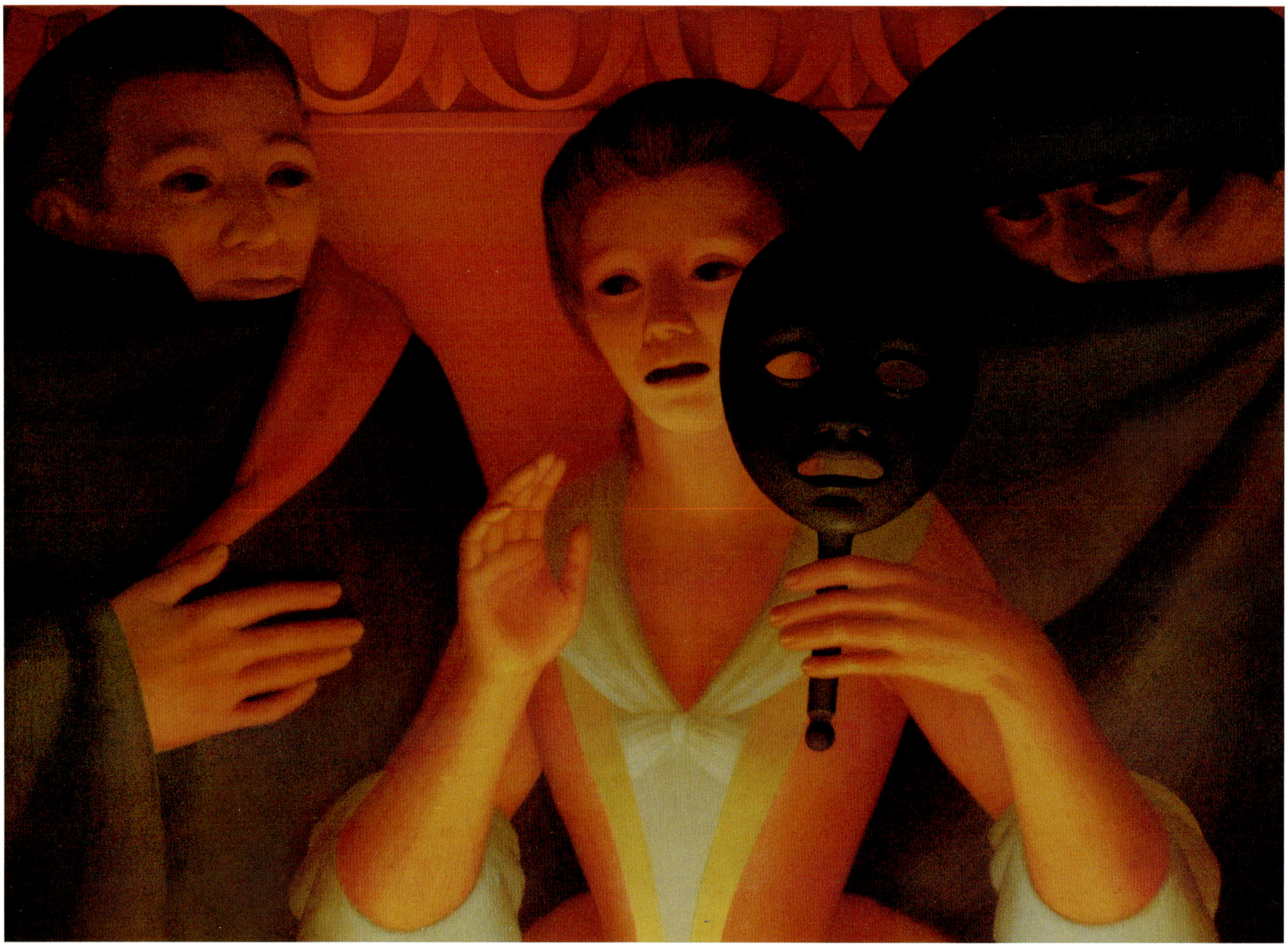

plate 55
*Waiting Room II* (1982)
Egg tempera on gesso board
19 × 37 inches (48.3 × 94 cm)
Private Collection



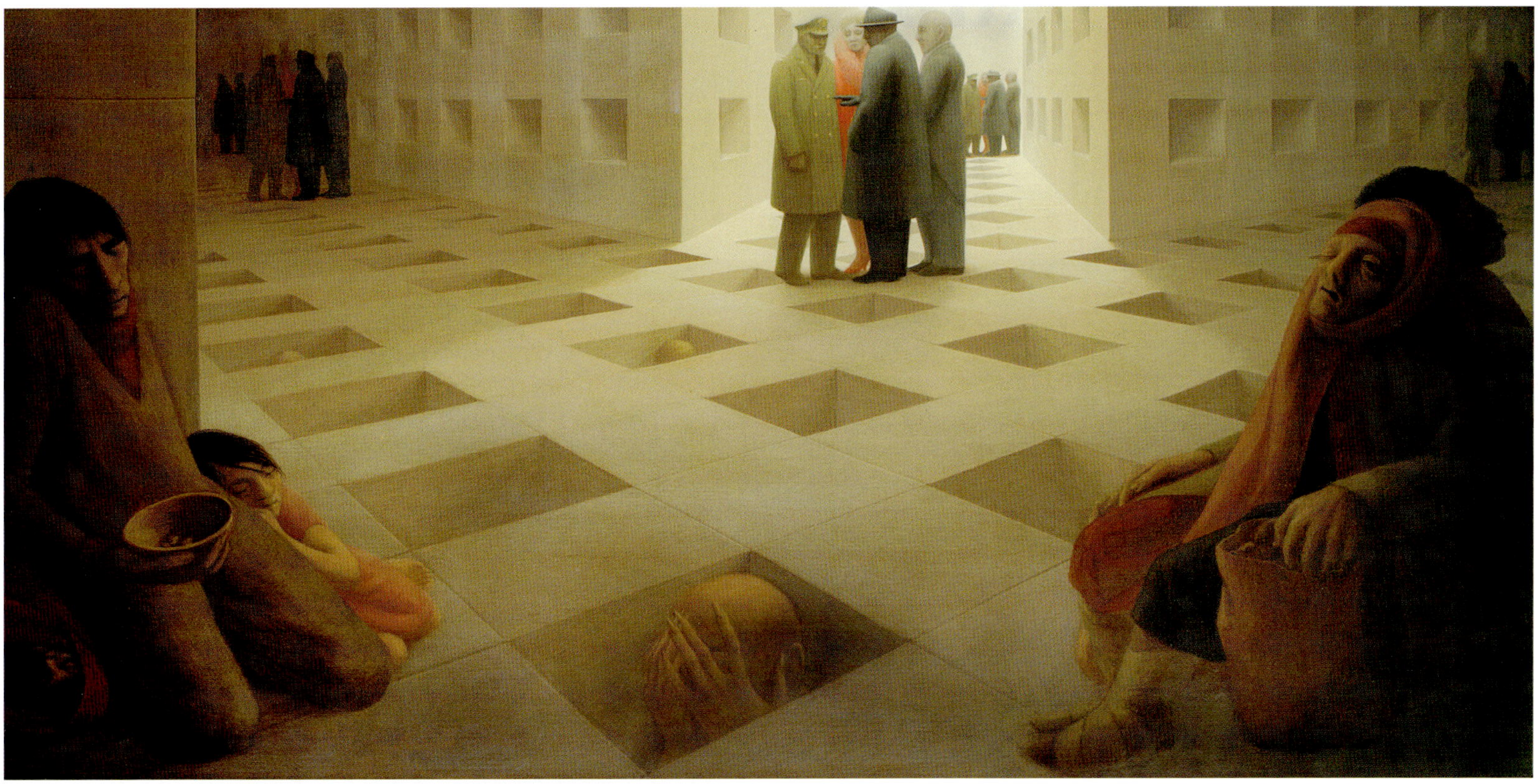

plate 56
***Girl with a Basket*** (1987–88)
Egg tempera on gesso panel
24 × 18 inches (61 × 45.7 cm)
Private Collection, courtesy James Francis
Trezza, New York



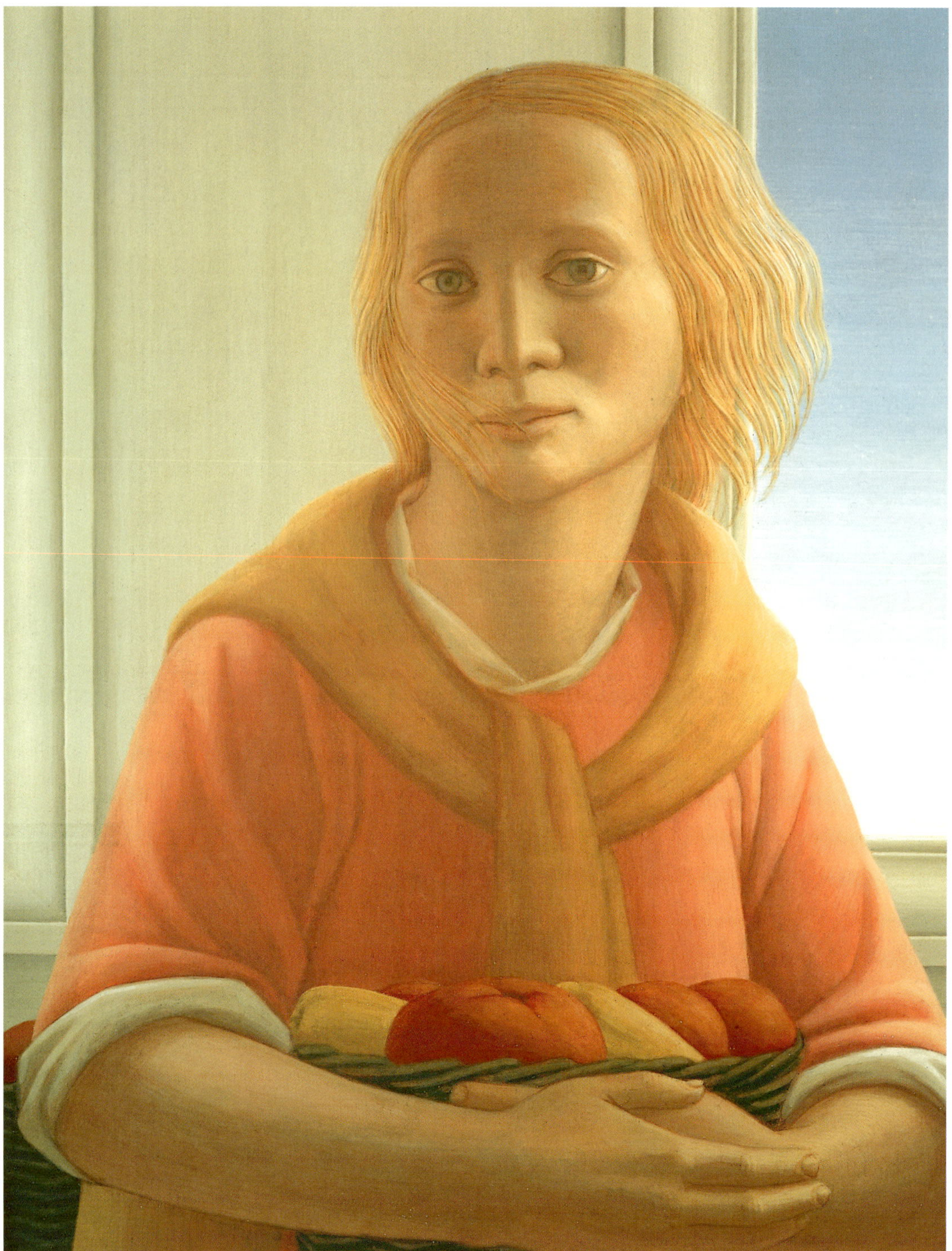

plate 57
***Woman with a Sprig of Laurel*** (1992)
Egg tempera on gesso panel
18 × 24 inches (45.7 × 61 cm)
Susan and Peter Tuteur



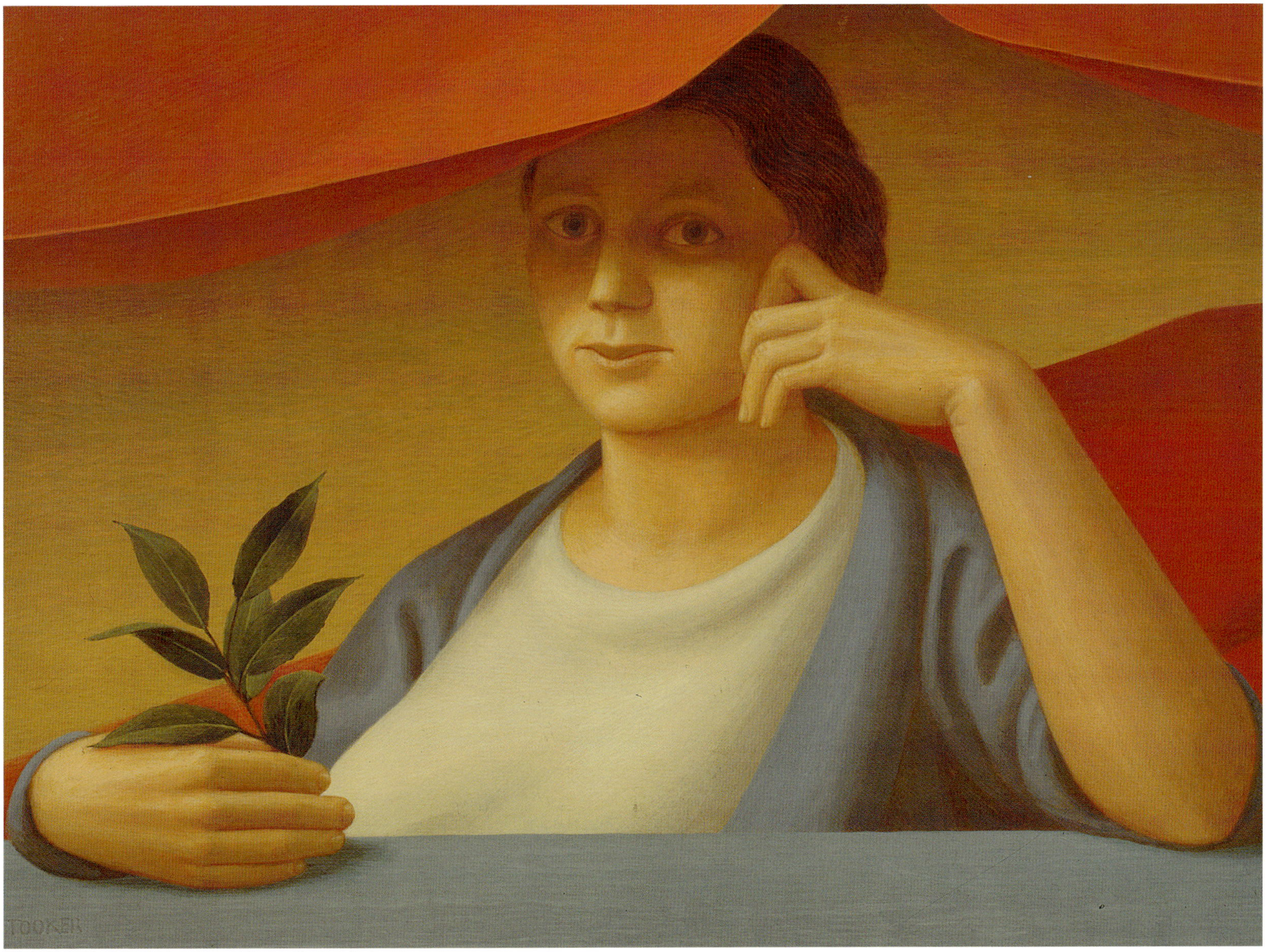

plate 58
***Self-Portrait*** (1992)
Graphite and white conté crayon on toned tracing paper
15 × 12¾ inches (38.1 × 32.4 cm)
Philadelphia Museum of Art: Purchased with the Alice Newton Osborn Fund, 2003

plate 59
***Self-Portrait*** (1994)
Egg tempera on gesso panel
14 × 12 inches (35.6 × 30.5 cm)
Private Collection, Boston, Massachusetts



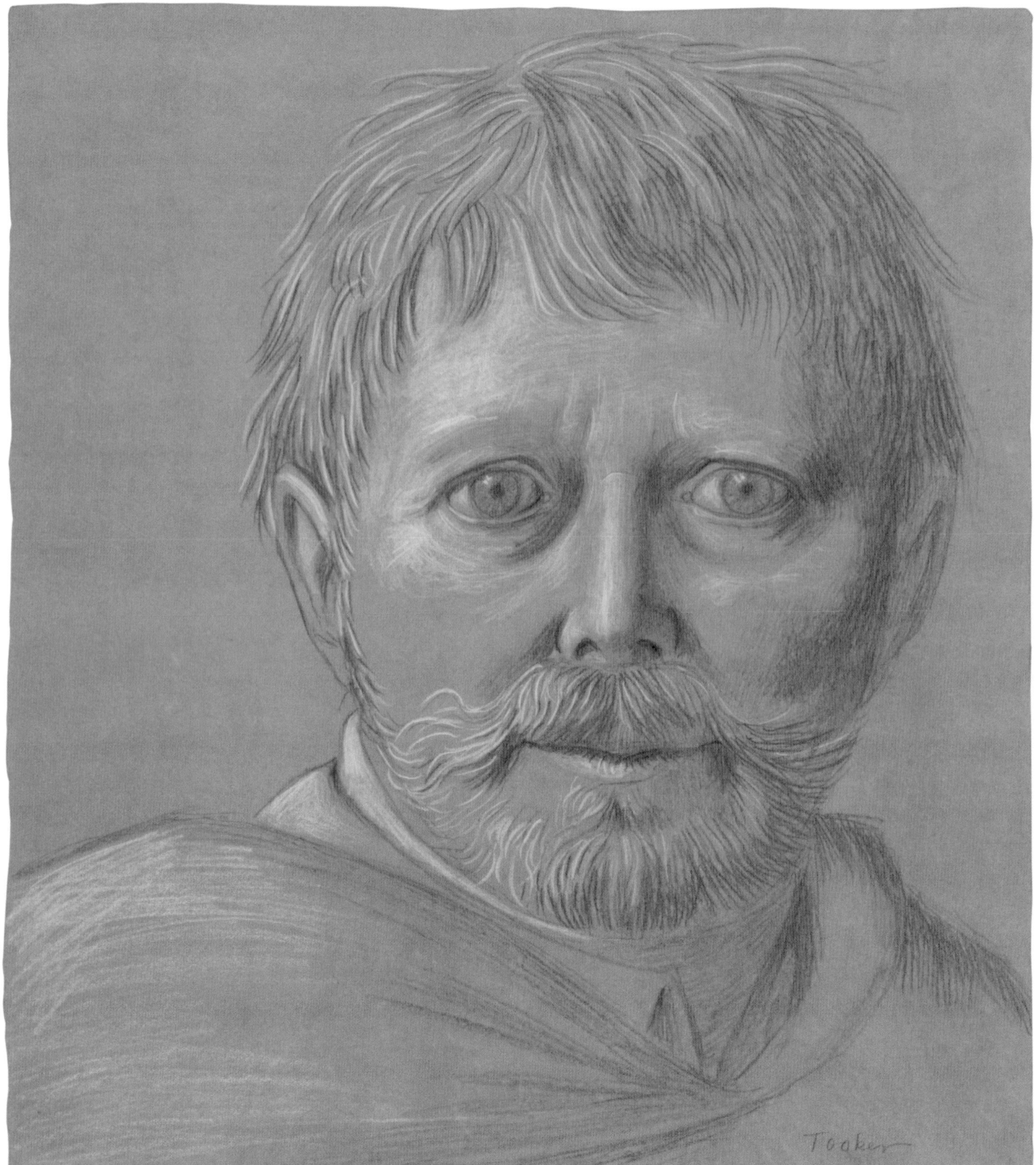

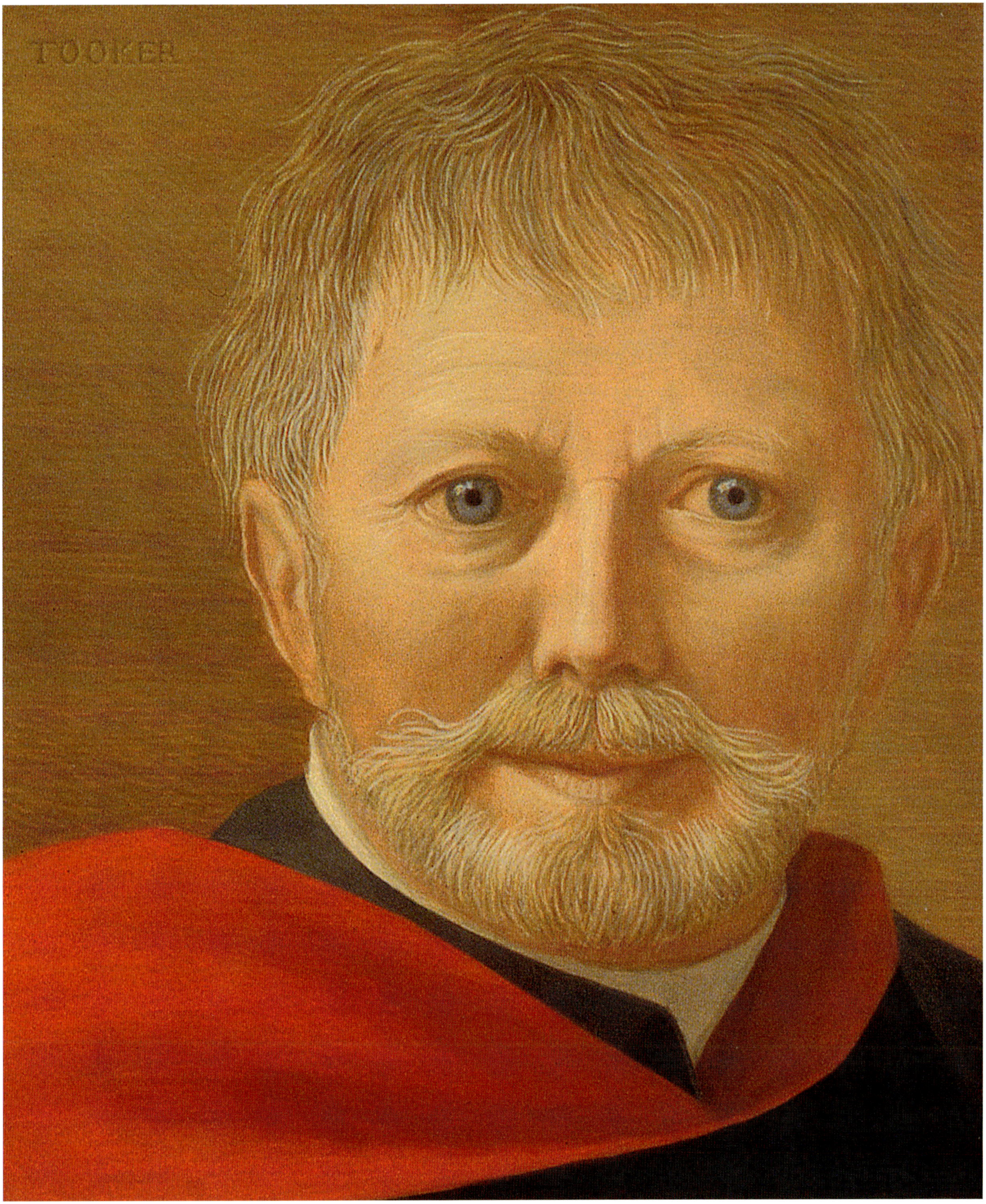
TOOKER

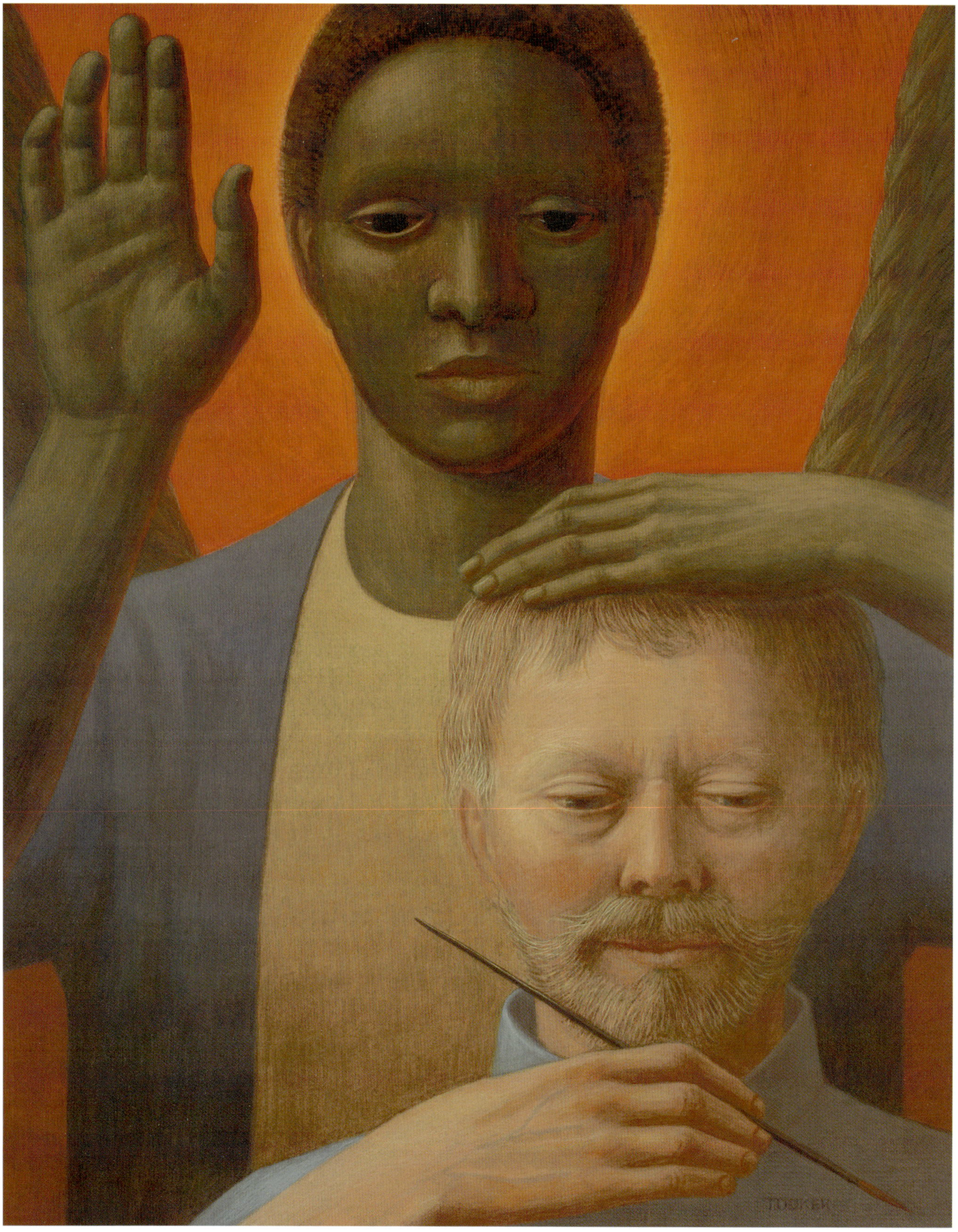
TOOKER

plate 60
***Dark Angel*** (1996)
Egg tempera on gesso panel
24 × 19 inches (61 × 48.3 cm)
Pennsylvania Academy of the Fine Arts, Philadelphia, Henry C. Gibson Fund, 2007.7

plate 61
***Man in a Tree*** (1998)
Egg tempera on gesso panel
14 × 17 inches (35.6 × 43.1 cm)
Collection of James and Barbara Palmer



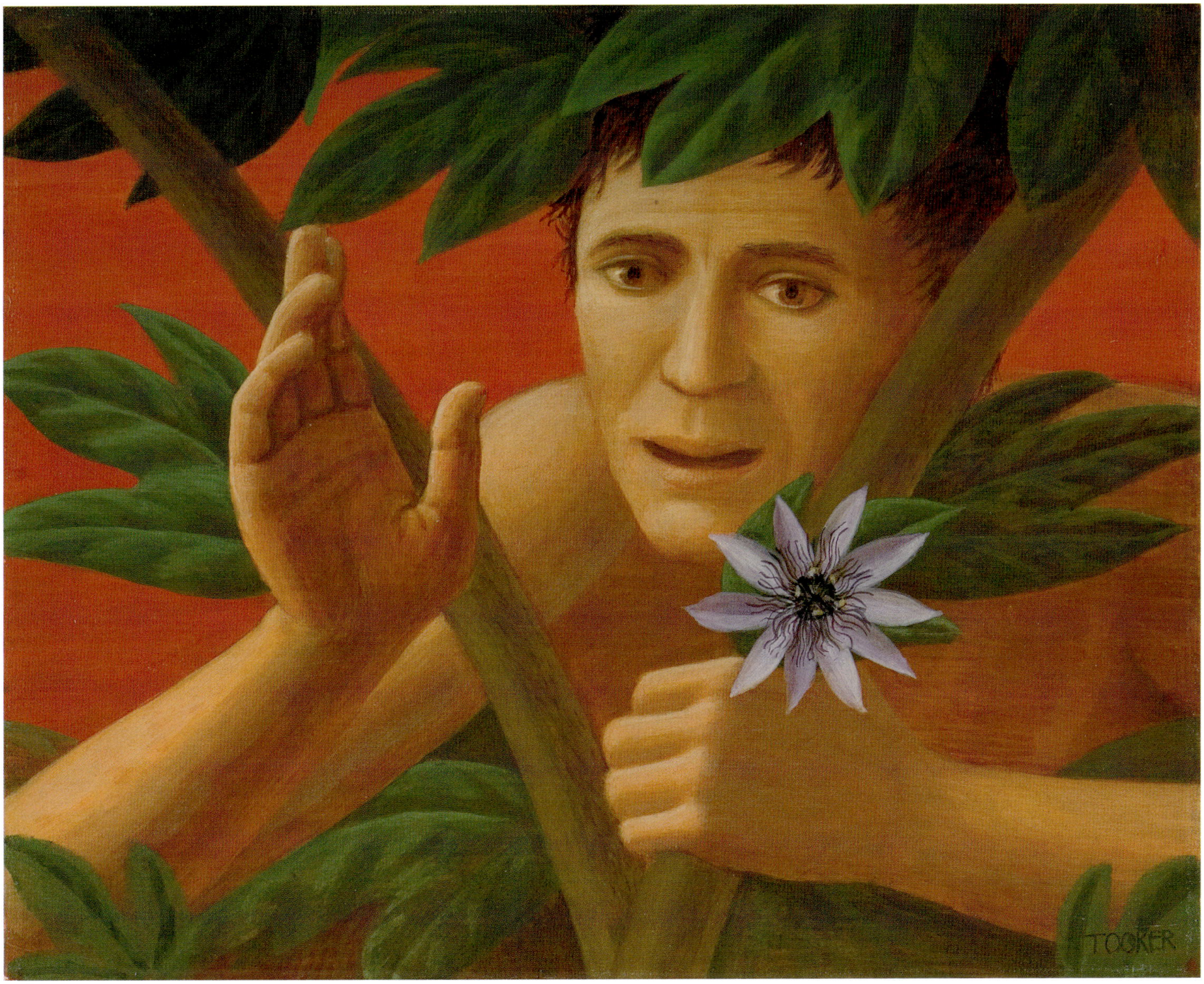

plate 62
***Embrace of Peace II*** (1988)
Egg tempera on gesso panel
18 × 30 inches (45.7 × 76.2 cm)
Reis Private Collection



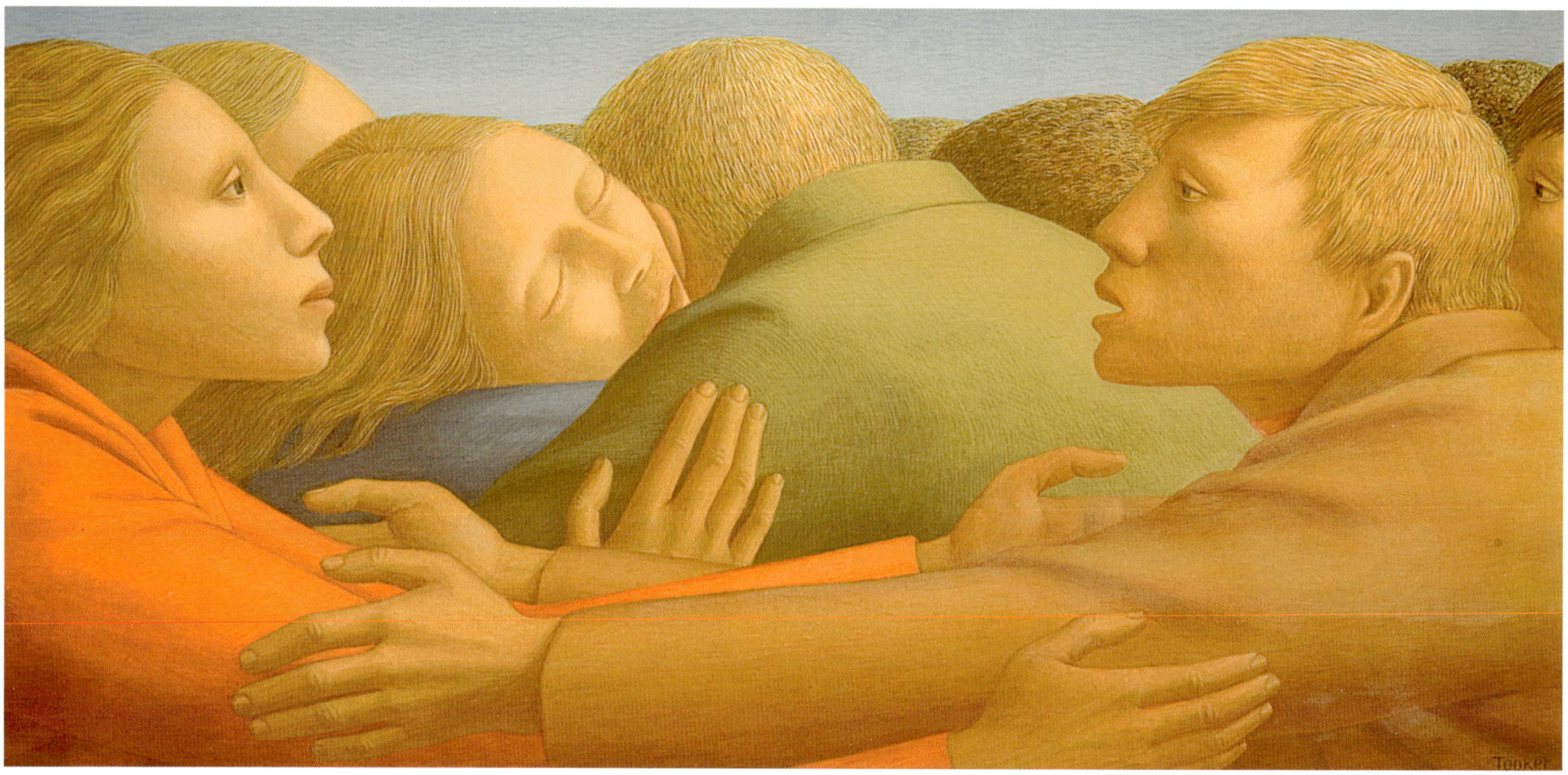

plate 63
***Landscape with Figures IV*** (1999)
Egg tempera on gesso panel
19½ × 29¼ inches (49.5 × 74.3 cm)
Pilar and Vicente Pita, New Jersey



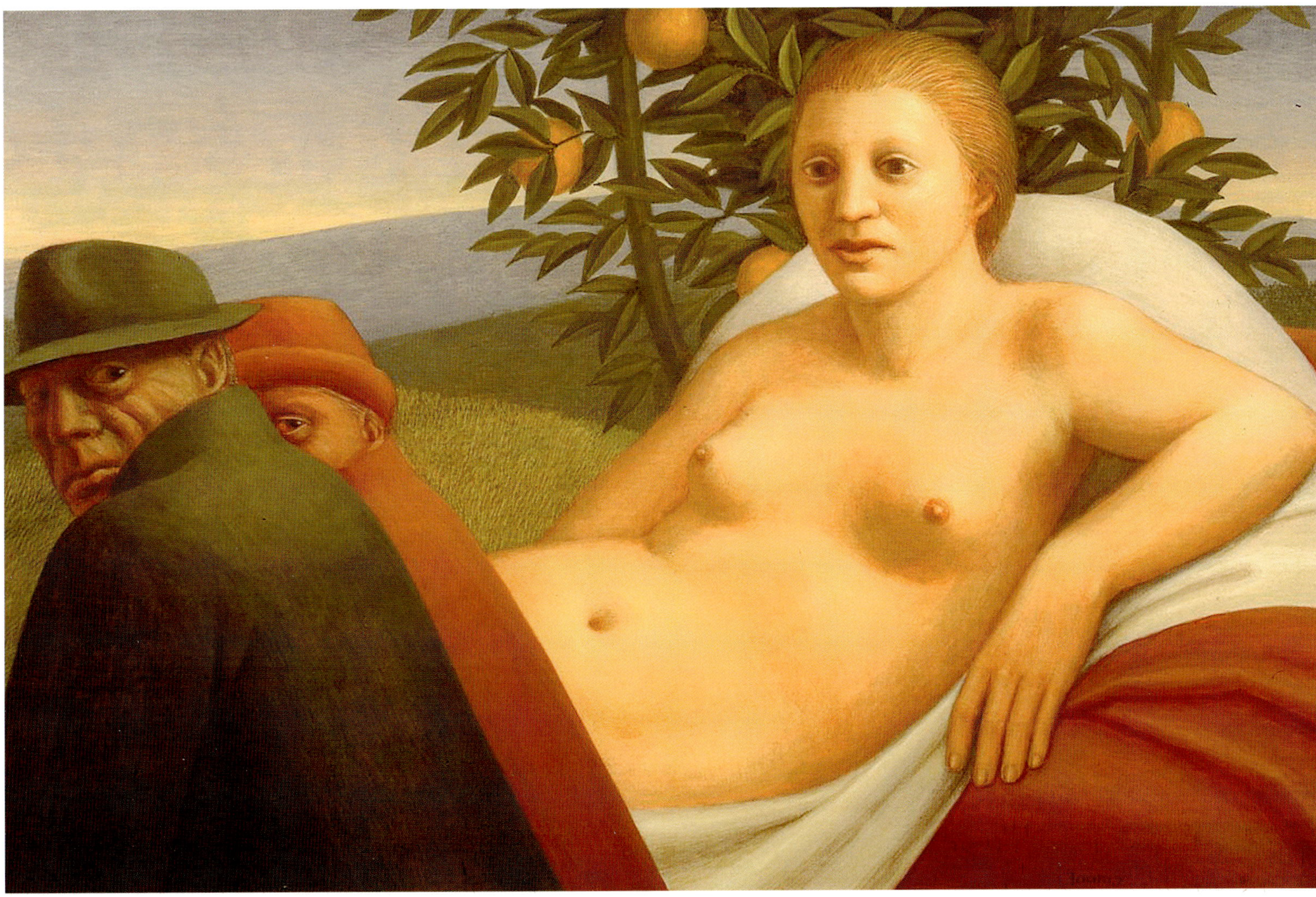

plate 64
*Father and Child* (2000)
Egg tempera on gesso panel
24 × 20 inches (61 × 50.8 cm)
Private Collection



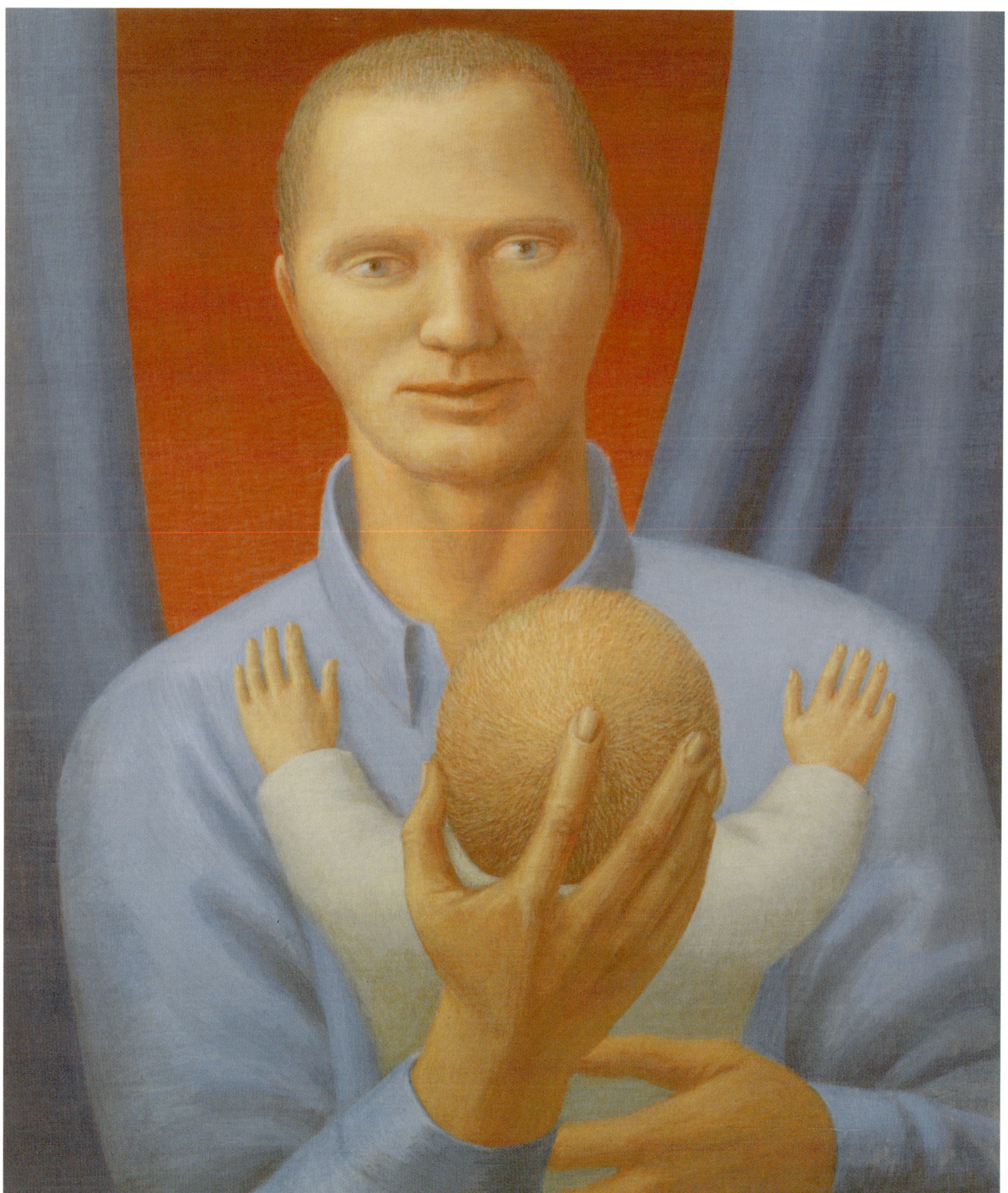

plate 65
*Girl Reading* (2003)
Egg tempera on gesso panel
15⅛ × 19½ inches (38.4 × 49.5 cm)
Courtesy of the artist and DC Moore
Gallery, New York



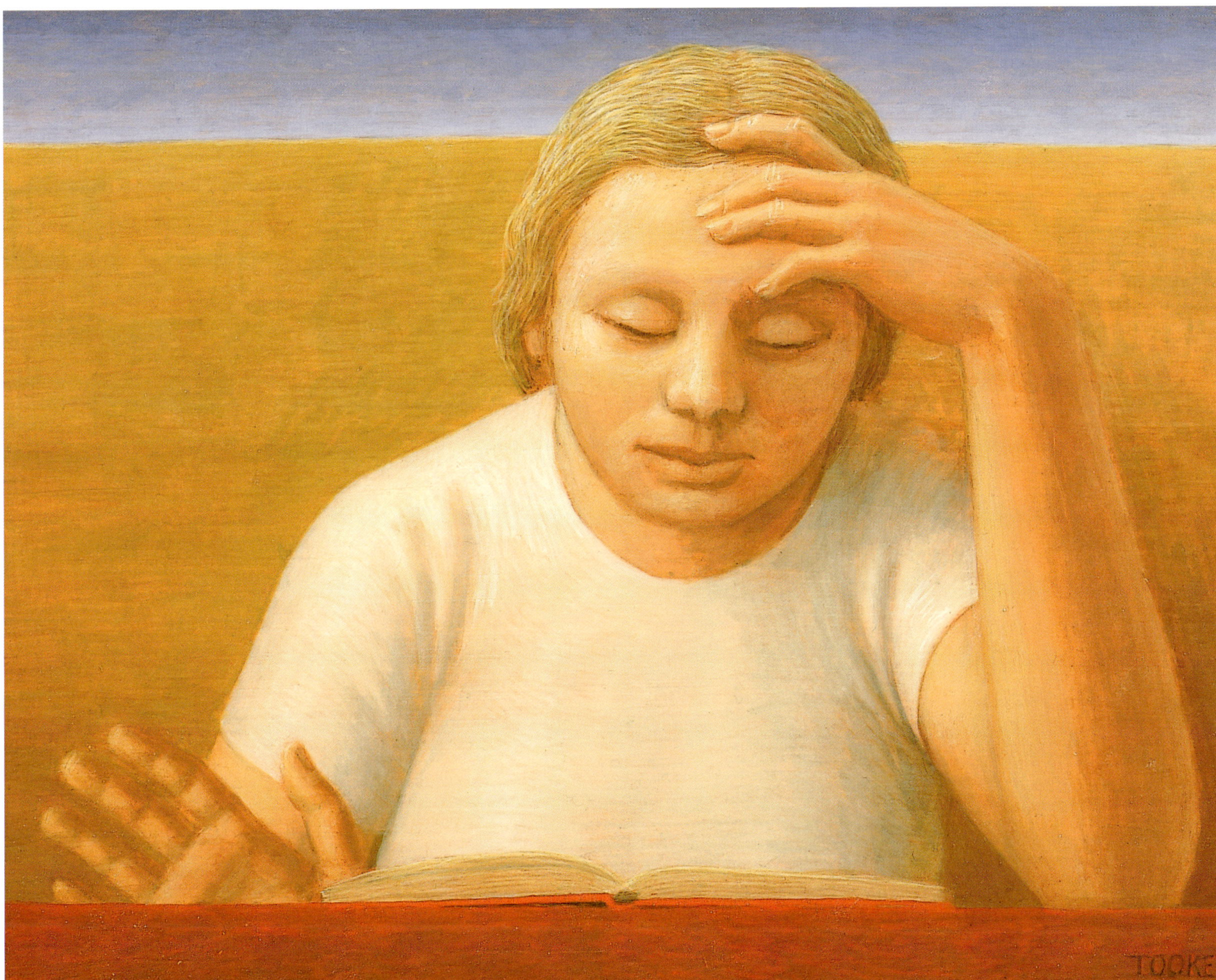

# Chronology and selected exhibition history

Marshall N. Price and Robert Cozzolino

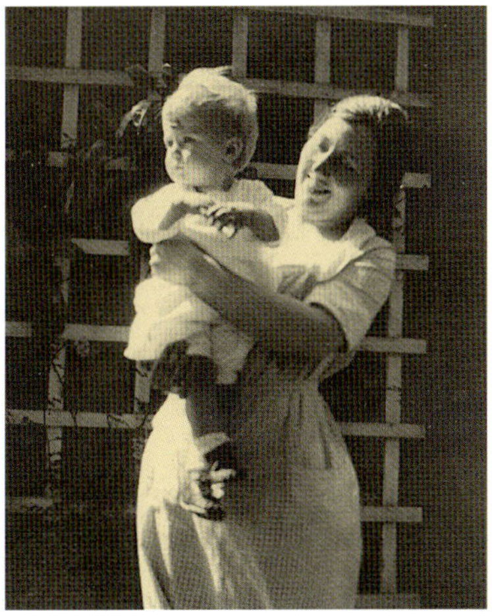

fig. 1
George Tooker and his mother, Angela Montejo Roura Tooker (*circa* 1922)
Courtesy of the William Christopher Papers, 1946–1972, Archives of American Art, Smithsonian Institution, Washington, D.C.



1920
George Clair Tooker, Jr., born, Brooklyn, New York, to George Clair Tooker and Angela Montejo Roura Tooker. During his childhood, the family moves to Bellport, Long Island (fig. 1).

1927
Tooker begins lessons in painting with Malcolm Fraser (1868–1949), a family friend and professional artist who trained at the Académie Julian, Paris; the École des Beaux-Arts, Paris; and the Art Students League, New York. An active member of artists' clubs and known in expatriate circles abroad, Fraser had known major figures of his generation, including George Inness (1825–1894), John Singer Sargent (1856–1925), and James Abbott McNeill Whistler (1834–1903). Fraser's work ranges from straightforward realist portraits to mystical Symbolist allegories on Christian themes. Tooker later recalls him as a Barbizon-inspired painter in the French tradition who taught his students under-painting and a quickly executed approach to landscape. Around this time, Fraser paints portraits of the Tooker family, including his young student.

1936
After studying at the local high school in Patchogue, New York, Tooker is transferred by his parents to Phillips Academy, Andover, Massachusetts, to improve his college prospects.

1938
Tooker graduates from Phillips Academy. Despite his desire to attend art school, he enters Harvard University to appease his parents. There he is exposed to late medieval and Renaissance painting for the first time, at the Fogg Art Museum and the Museum of Fine Arts, Boston. At Harvard, Tooker does not study fine art but paints in his own time. For a brief spell, he becomes involved with socialist and Communist political groups. He attends rallies and goes door to door to help recruit Socialist Party voters, hands out literature, and is involved in a fight as a result of his activities. After a while, he finds the group meetings dull and loses interest.

1942
After graduating from Harvard with a degree in English literature, Tooker enlists in the Marine Corps. He spends a few months in Officer Candidate School at Quantico, Virginia, before being discharged with ulcerative colitis.

1943
Tooker enrolls for two years at the Art Students League to study painting under Reginald Marsh (1898–1954), for whom he is the class monitor. While studying with Marsh, he begins painting in egg tempera. He also studies with League instructors Kenneth Hayes Miller (1876–1952) and Harry Sternberg (1904–2001). At the urging of Marsh, Tooker supplements his studies with evening class in the winter at Parsons School of Design with Jacques Maroger (1884–1962).

1944
While monitoring Saturday drawing classes at the League, Tooker meets Paul Cadmus (1904–1999), who becomes a lifelong friend. Although Marsh had taught Tooker to work in tempera, Cadmus encourages him to work in a slower, more measured way. On Cadmus's recommendation, Tooker reads Daniel V. Thompson's book *The Practice of Tempera Painting* (1936) but finds his own practice and experimentation to be most rewarding and instructive. Through Cadmus, Tooker meets artists, dancers, photographers, and writers in New York cultural circles, including Jared French (1905–1988), George Platt Lynes (1907–1955), and Lincoln Kirstein (1907–1996).

*Brooklyn Society of Artists:* [28th] *Annual Exhibition*, Brooklyn Museum, Brooklyn, New York.

1945
Provided with a modest stipend from his family, Tooker moves from his family's home in Brooklyn to a cold-water flat on Bleecker Street in Greenwich Village. He spends the summer on Fire Island, New York, with Cadmus and Jared and Margaret French (fig. 2). Tooker

fig. 2
PaJaMa
*Jared French, Monroe Wheeler, George Tooker, and Paul Cadmus on Fire Island* (1945)
Courtesy of the William Christopher Papers, 1946–1972, Archives of American Art, Smithsonian Institution, Washington, D.C.

fig. 3
PaJaMa
*George Tooker and Paul Cadmus on Nantucket Island* (1946)
Courtesy of the George Tooker Papers, 1932–1973, Archives of American Art, Smithsonian Institution, Washington, D.C.

fig. 4
PaJaMa
*George Tooker and Paul Cadmus in Provincetown* (1947)
Courtesy of the George Tooker Papers, 1932–1973, Archives of American Art, Smithsonian Institution, Washington, D.C.

fig. 5
PaJaMa
*E.M. Forster, George Tooker, and Paul Cadmus in Provincetown* (1947)
Courtesy of the George Tooker Papers, 1932–1973, Archives of American Art, Smithsonian Institution, Washington, D.C.

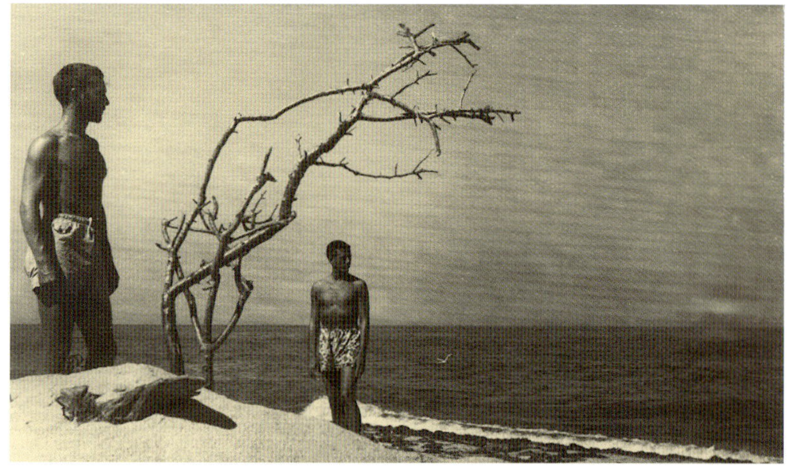



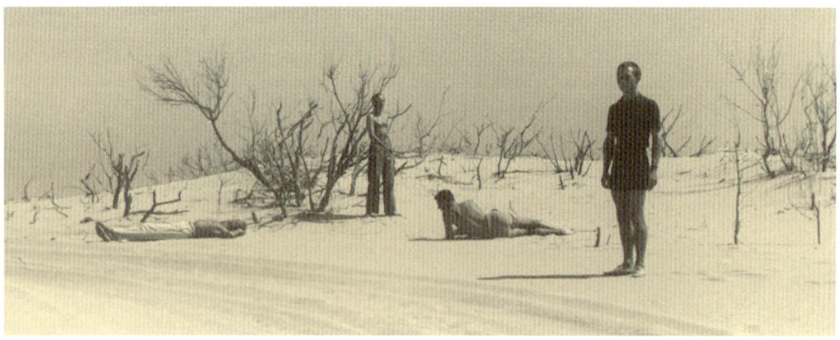

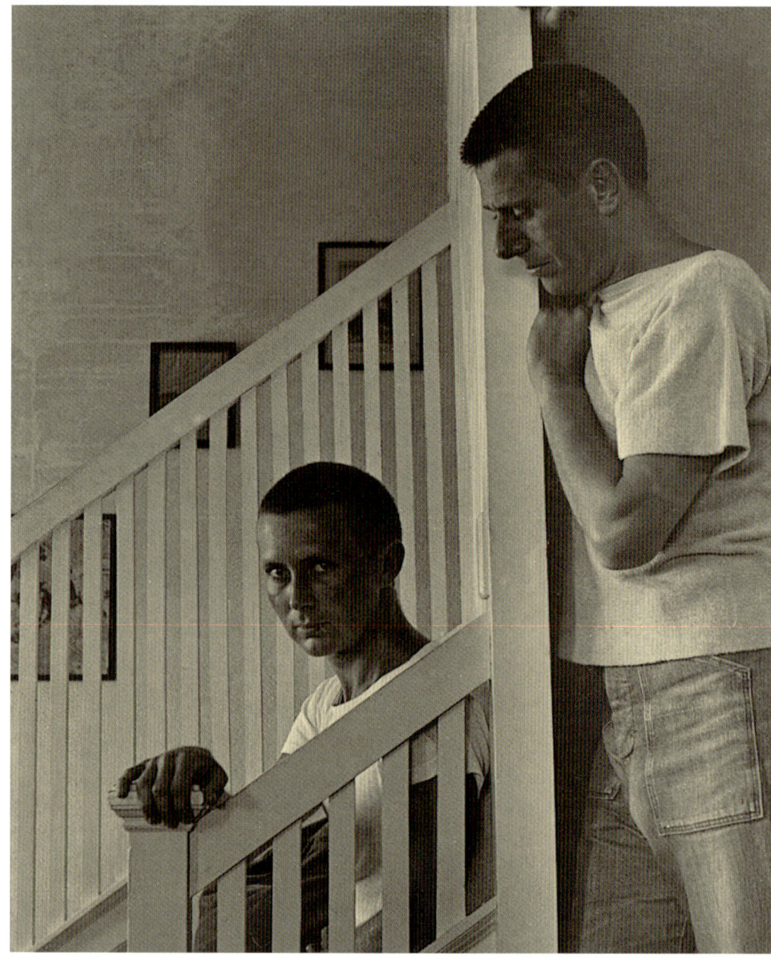

paints *Audience*, which he considers his first professional painting. It is bought by Jared French, marking his first sale.

1946

Tooker spends the summer on Nantucket Island, Massachusetts, with Cadmus and the Frenches (fig. 3).

Through Lincoln Kirstein, curator Dorothy C. Miller is introduced to Tooker's work while organizing the *Fourteen Americans* exhibition at the Museum of Modern Art, New York. Too late to be added to the catalogue, his work is nonetheless added to the exhibition. Kirstein appealed, in a handwritten note, "Is it too late for 1 more painter for your show? I have a runner up for Honoré Sharrer. He has only 4 ptgs. His name is *George Tooker*. He is very expert; he worked with *Marsh* but is nothing like him. He was a Marine and his ptg. is like Florentine 16th century but about NY."[1] *Children and Spastics* (plate 1) and *Dance* (plate 3) are included and singled out in reviews of the exhibition. It becomes a major turning point in Tooker's career.

1946 *Fourteen Americans*, Museum of Modern Art, New York.

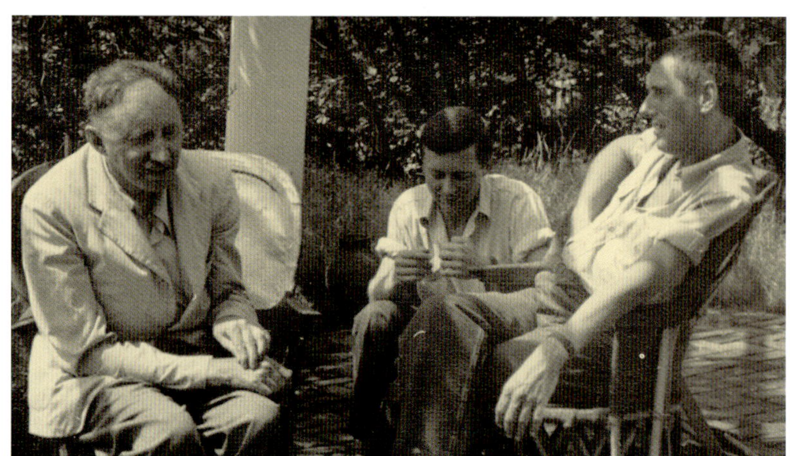

1947

Tooker spends the summer in Provincetown, Massachusetts, with Cadmus and the Frenches (fig. 4). They are joined by the writer E.M. Forster while there (fig. 5). Tooker completes his first formal self-portrait during this summer (fig. 6).

1947 *Annual Exhibition of Contemporary American Painting*, Whitney Museum of American Art, New York.

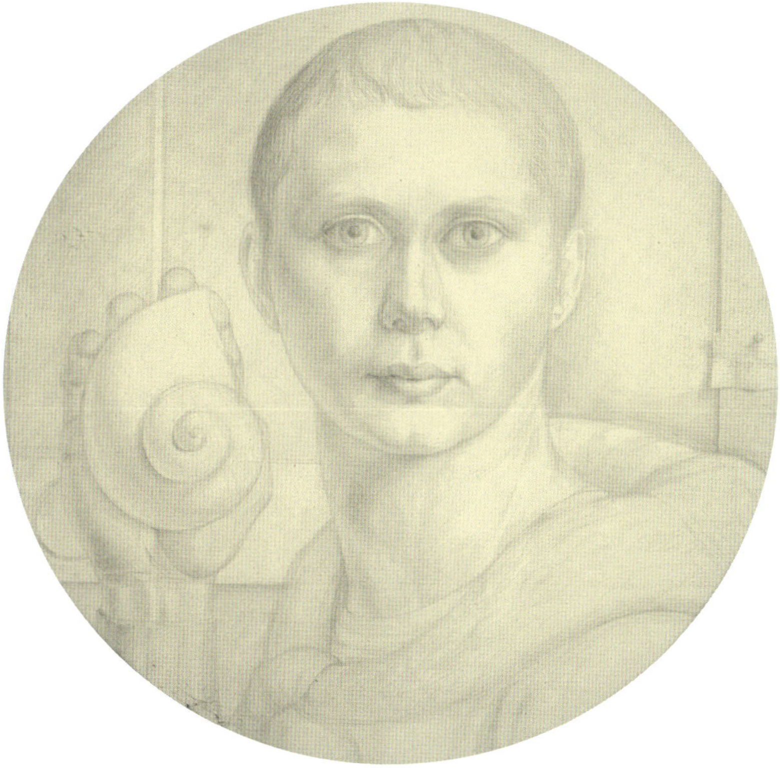

fig. 6
George Tooker
*Self-Portrait* (1947)
Graphite on paper; 17⅜ inches (44.1 cm) (diameter)
Private Collection



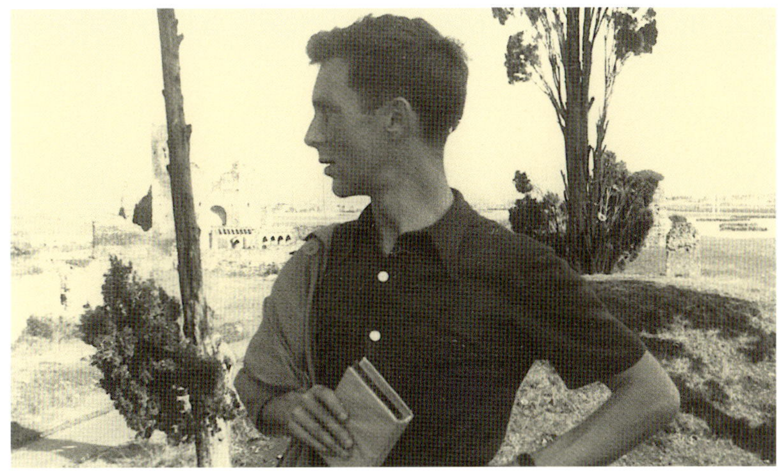

fig. 7
George Tooker in Rome along the Via Appia (1949)
Courtesy of the George Tooker Papers, 1932–1973, Archives of American Art, Smithsonian Institution, Washington, D.C.

*Painting in the United States, 1947*, Museum of Art, Carnegie Institute, Pittsburgh.

1948

Tooker spends the summer in Provincetown with Cadmus and the Frenches.

*1948 Annual Exhibition of Contemporary American Painting*, Whitney Museum of American Art, New York.

*American Painting of Today*, Worcester Art Museum, Massachusetts.

*Painting in the United States, 1948*, Museum of Art, Carnegie Institute, Pittsburgh.

1949

Tooker and Cadmus sail for Europe with the Frenches on the *Queen Elizabeth*. They travel for six months in France, Italy, and England (fig. 7), visiting numerous museums, monuments, and works *in situ*. The experience has a lasting effect on Tooker. After he returns to the United States, Tooker meets the painter and cabinetmaker William Christopher (1923–1973), who later becomes his lifelong companion (fig. 8).

*Annual Exhibition of Contemporary American Painting*, Whitney Museum of American Art, New York.

*Painting in the United States, 1949*, Museum of Art, Carnegie Institute, Pittsburgh.

1950

Tooker is included in *Symbolic Realism*, organized by Lincoln Kirstein at the Edwin Hewitt Gallery, New York, presenting Kirstein's version of mid-century Modernism. An expanded version of the exhibition, *Symbolic Realism in American Painting, 1940–1950*, travels to the Institute of Contemporary Arts, in London, England. It has the residual effect of misleadingly labeling Tooker and a group of peers—including Peter Blume, Cadmus, Kenneth Davies, French, Henry Koerner, Bernard Perlin, Alton Pickens, Charles Rain, Ben Shahn, Honoré Sharrer, Pavel Tchelitchew, Robert Vickery, John Wilde, and Andrew Wyeth—as "Magic Realists."

*1950 Annual Exhibition of Contemporary American Painting*, Whitney Museum of American Art, New York. Tooker shows *Subway* for the first time. The painting is subsequently purchased for the collection and is the first by Tooker to enter a public collection.

*1950 Annual Exhibition of Contemporary American Sculpture, Watercolors, and Drawings*, Whitney Museum of American Art, New York.

*Nineteen Young Americans*, The Metropolitan Museum of Art, New York.

*Painting in the United States, 1950*, Museum of Art, Carnegie Institute, Pittsburgh.

*Sixty Years of American Art*, Whitney Museum of American Art, New York.

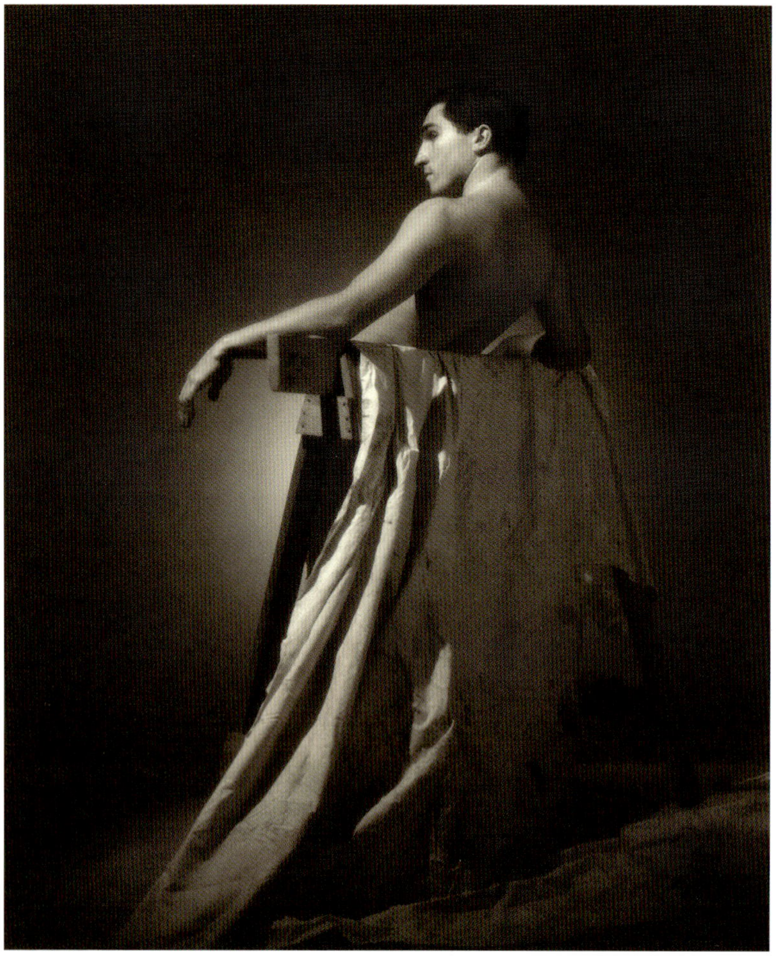

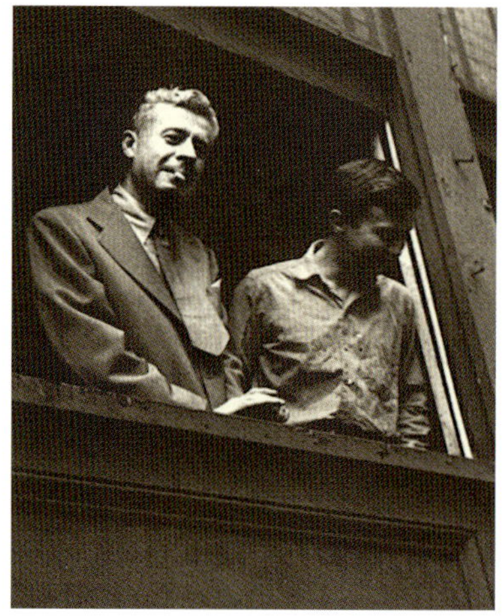

fig. 8
William Christopher, photographed by George Platt Lynes (1949)
© Estate of George Platt Lynes
Courtesy of the William Christopher Papers, 1946–1972, Archives of American Art, Smithsonian Institution, Washington, D.C.

fig. 9
Edward Lanning and George Tooker on the rear porch of the house at 77 State Street in Brooklyn (*circa* 1953)
Courtesy of the William Christopher Papers, Archives of American Art, Smithsonian Institution, Washington, D.C.



1951

Tooker and Christopher move into an illegal loft at 436 West 18th St. They make ends meet by making furniture for clients by commission. The neighborhood's ethnic diversity inspires Tooker to paint interior scenes that take their cue from storefronts, architectural details, colored lighting, and the people he encounters from day to day.

Tooker's father dies. In memoriam, Tooker paints *Sleep* (private collection), which is equally inspired by Etruscan tomb sculpture.

Tooker has his first solo exhibition, at the Edwin Hewitt Gallery, including some of his best-known works.

*22nd Biennial Exhibition of Contemporary American Oil Paintings*, Corcoran Gallery of Art, Washington, D.C.

*American Painting and Sculpture 60th Annual*, The Art Institute of Chicago.

*The New Reality*, Edwin Hewitt Gallery, New York.

1952

At the urging of Edwin Hewitt, Tooker makes a series of exquisitely crafted, surprisingly witty *trompe l'œil* still-life paintings in the early 1950s. Hewitt considers them more saleable than Tooker's urban scenes; Tooker rarely signs them.

*1952 Annual Exhibition of Contemporary American Painting*, Whitney Museum of American Art, New York.

*5th Annual Exhibition of Contemporary American Painting*, California Palace of the Legion of Honor, Fine Arts Museum of San Francisco.

*39th Annual Exhibition of Contemporary American Paintings*, Toledo Museum of Art, Ohio.

*147th Annual Exhibition of Painting and Sculpture*, Pennsylvania Academy of the Fine Arts, Philadelphia.

*The Artist's Viewpoint: The City*, The Museum of Modern Art, New York; Museum of Art, University of Michigan at Ann Arbor.

*Contemporary Drawings from 12 Countries, 1945–1952*, The Art Institute of Chicago.

1953

Following a fire that partially damages their loft, Tooker and Christopher buy and renovate an old brownstone at 77 State Street (fig. 9) in Brooklyn Heights, across the street from a Puerto Rican rooming house, which inspires *Red Carpet* (1953/54; plate 22) and several works in the *Window* series (plates 28, 38, and 39). The renovation of the house and repeated trips to Brooklyn's Borough Hall to navigate red tape and the permit department help inspire *Government Bureau* (1956; plate 27).

*Annual Exhibition of Contemporary American Painting, 1953*, Whitney Museum of American Art, New York.

*NAA Sixty-Third Annual Exhibition*, Nebraska Art Association, University of Nebraska Art Galleries, Lincoln, Nebraska.

*International Contemporary Drawings*, Toledo Museum of Art, Ohio.

1954

Through the influence of Lincoln Kirstein, Tooker is commissioned to create the stage designs for Gian Carlo Menotti's musical drama *The Saint of Bleecker Street*. Menotti had seen works by Tooker, such as *Festa* (1948; private collection), at Kirstein's home and thought that Tooker's affinity for the mood of place corresponded well to the subject. In preparation, and owing to union rules, Tooker is obliged to take the Scenic Designers Union exam, which he fails.

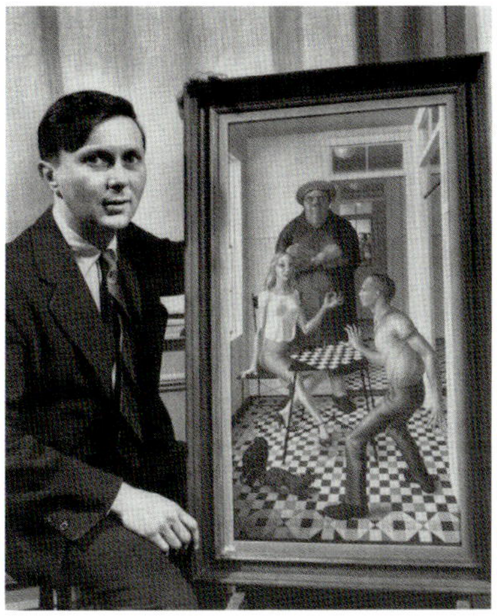

fig. 11
George Tooker with *A Game of Chess* (1946–47; plate 5), 1955
Sam Falk/*New York Times*

Tooker makes four designs for key sets in the script, however, showing a subway station, an apartment interior, a bar, and a festival scene on Bleecker Street. The designs are executed for the stage by the union artist Robert Randolph (fig. 10).

*American Exhibition of Paintings and Sculpture 61st Annual*, The Art Institute of Chicago.

*American Painting, 1954*, Virginia Museum of Fine Arts, Richmond.

*Forty-First Annual Exhibition of Contemporary American Paintings*, Toledo Museum of Art, Ohio.

*Reality and Fantasy, 1900–1954*, Walker Art Center, Minneapolis.

*Young America: Artists under Forty: Painters, Sculptors, Printmakers: Third Annual Exhibition*, Brandeis University, Waltham, Massachusetts.

1955

Tooker has his second solo exhibition, at the Edwin Hewitt Gallery (fig. 11).

*1955 Annual Exhibition of Contemporary American Painting*, Whitney Museum of American Art, New York.

*The New Decade: 35 American Painters and Sculptors*, Whitney Museum of American Art, New York.

1956

Tooker makes and paints a set of folding doors to allow privacy for his ailing mother, who has moved to the first floor of the family home. They are designed to look like a set of recessed shelves bearing a series of vignettes of personal effects, such as toys belonging to his nephew and niece (fig. 12).

*American Artists Paint the City*, 28th Venice Biennale, Italy.

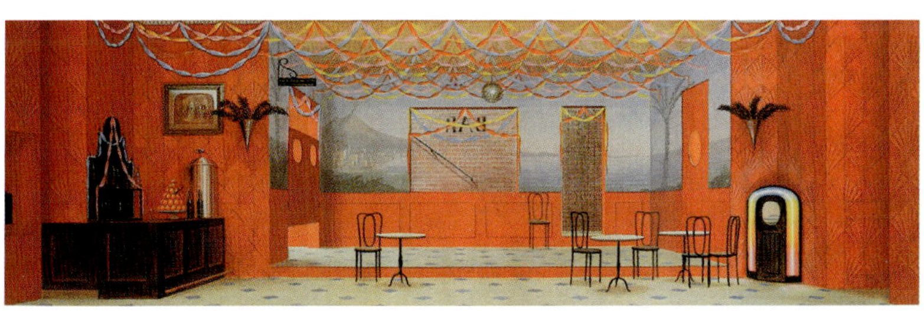

fig. 10
Scene from *The Saint of Bleecker Street* (1954)

*An Exhibition of Works by Candidates for Grants in Art, 1956*, The National Institute of Arts and Letters, American Academy Art Gallery, New York.

*Annual Exhibition of Contemporary American Sculpture, Painting, Watercolors, Drawings*, Whitney Museum of American Art, New York.

*Contemporary American Painters, 1950–1955*, The First Annual Purchase Awards Exhibition Sponsored by the Committee for Art at Stanford, Thomas Welton Stanford Art Gallery, Stanford University, California.

*Nebraska Art Association Sixty-Sixth Annual Exhibition*, Nebraska

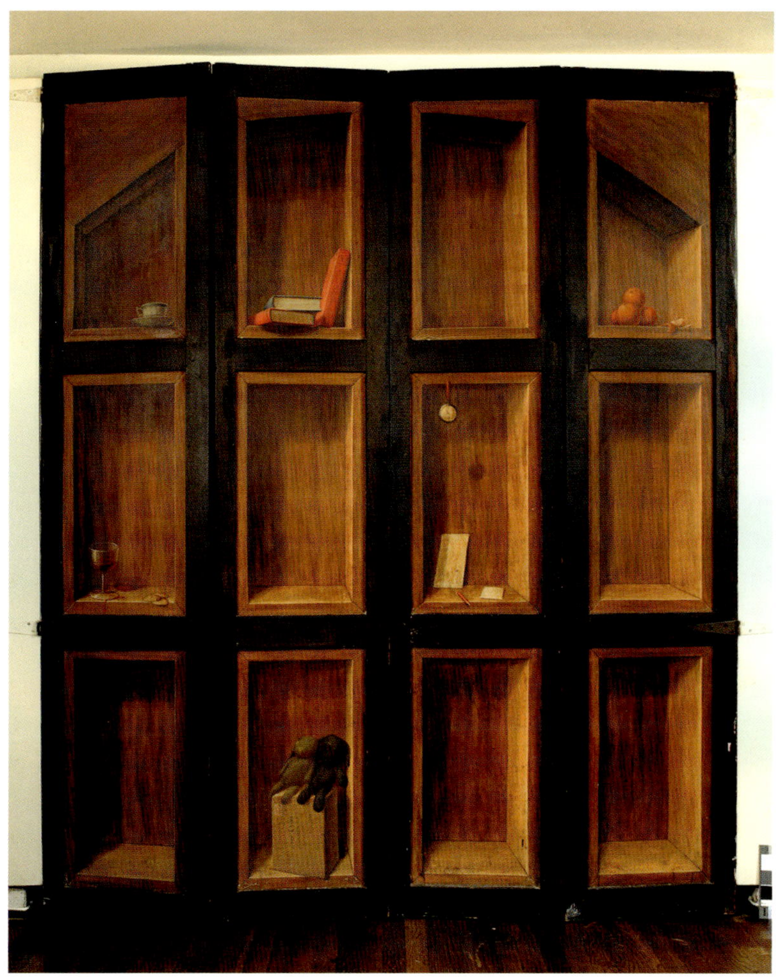

fig. 12
George Tooker
Painted folding doors (1956)
Egg tempera on wood with hinges;
96 × 92 inches (244 × 233.6 cm) (overall)
Private Collection

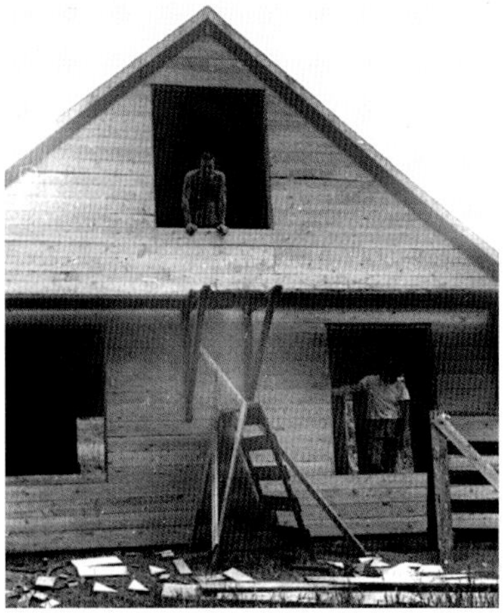

fig. 13
George Tooker and William Christopher working on their house in Hartland, Vermont (summer 1958)
Courtesy of the William Christopher Papers, 1946–1972, Archives of American Art, Smithsonian Institution, Washington, D.C.

fig. 14
George Tooker
*Farewell* (1966)
Egg tempera on gessoed masonite
24 × 23⅝ inches (61 × 60 cm)
Hood Museum of Art, Dartmouth College, New Hampshire, Gift of Pennigton Haile, Class of 1924

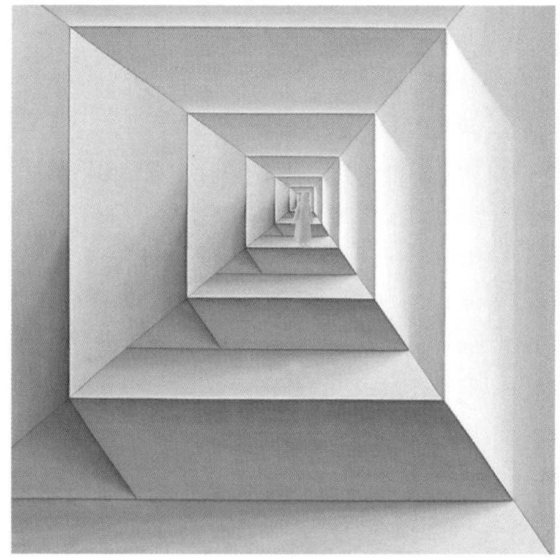



Art Association, University of Nebraska Art Galleries, Lincoln, Nebraska.

1957

*Annual Exhibition: Sculpture, Paintings, Watercolors*, Whitney Museum of American Art, New York.

*Contemporary Directions: The Realist Painters*, Silvermine Guild of Artists, New Canaan, Connecticut.

1958

Following the lead of Jared and Margaret French, who had purchased a farm in Hartland, Vermont, for Cadmus to share with them, Tooker and Christopher buy a barn in White River Junction, Vermont, for $50. They move the old barn to nearby Hartland and use it as the basis for a house, which they design and construct. The Frenches allow Tooker and Christopher to live in a small "milk house" on their property while construction is under way (fig. 13).

Tooker occasionally takes commercial work to supplement his income; he paints an illustration to accompany an article titled "The Hidden Alcoholic," for the medical journal *What's New*, 10 (winter 1959), 10–11.

*The Brussels Fair*, US Department of State. Brussels World's Fair (Expo 58), Belgium.

*Annual Exhibition: Sculpture, Paintings, Watercolors, Drawings*, Whitney Museum of American Art, New York.

*Festival of Two Worlds*, Spoleto, Italy.

1959

Tooker's mother dies. Tooker paints *Meadow I* (1960–61; plate 36) as a memorial picture. His mother's death later inspires the artist to paint *Farewell* (1966; fig. 14), a Modernist updating of the theme of the ascent of souls popular in fifteenth- through seventeenth-century Christian art.

*The American Muse: Parallel Trends in Literature and Art*, Corcoran Gallery of Art, Washington, D.C.

*American Painting and Sculpture 63rd Annual*, The Art Institute of Chicago.

*The Collection of the Sara Roby Foundation*, Whitney Museum of American Art, New York.

1960

Their house completed, Tooker and Christopher move permanently to Vermont.

Tooker receives a grant from the National Institute of Arts and Letters.

Solo exhibition at the Robert Isaacson Gallery, New York.

*An Exhibition of Works by Newly Elected Members and Recipients of Honors and Awards*, National Institute of Arts and Letters, American Academy Art Gallery, New York.

*Painting and Sculpture Acquisitions*, The Museum of Modern Art, New York.

1961

*Annual Exhibition, 1961: Contemporary American Painting*, Whitney Museum of American Art, New York.

*The Face of the Fifties*, Museum of Art, University of Michigan at Ann Arbor.

*George Tooker Exhibition*, The Katonah Gallery, Katonah, New York.

1962

Solo exhibition at the Robert Isaacson Gallery, New York.

*American Painting, 1962*, Virginia Museum of Fine Arts, Richmond.

*Art: USA: Now*, Johnson Collection of Contemporary American Painting, Racine, Wisconsin.

*Fantasy and Surrealism in American Art from the Whitney Museum of American Art*, American Federation of Arts.

1963

In an effort to supplement documentation of the space age, NASA commissions artists to create paintings on various aeronautical

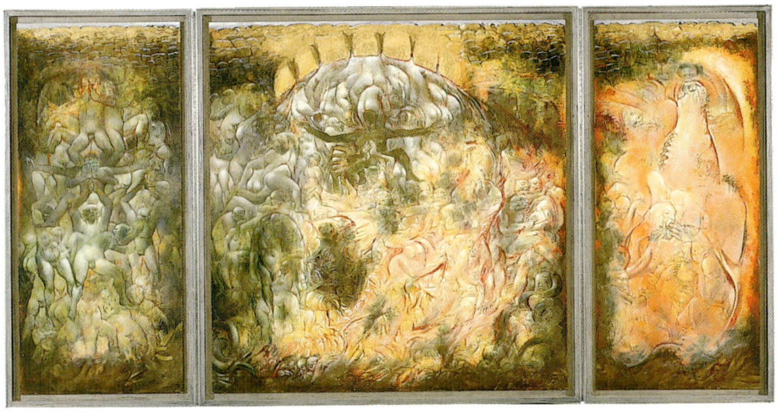

fig. 15
William Christopher (1923–1973)
*The Mammon Altarpiece* (1963)
Triptych, oil on board
45 × 84½ inches (114.2 × 213.6 cm)
(framed dimensions)
Hood Museum of Art, Dartmouth College, Hanover, New Hampshire, Gift of Tatiana de Fidler in memory of her mother, Marie Morosoff de Fidler

subjects. Tooker is asked to paint the scene inside the block house prior to the launch of a rocket. He expresses interest in painting such a work, but it does not materialize.

Although they have been committed to social justice and members of the National Association for the Advancement of Colored People (NAACP) for years, Tooker and Christopher find themselves increasingly active in the civil rights movement. They each begin a series of paintings in homage to various leaders, including Dr. Martin Luther King, Jr. (plate 37), and Malcolm X (plate 39). In this year, Christopher focuses on a series of pictures honoring Dr. King, as well as a horrific hell triptych titled *The Mammon Altarpiece* (fig. 15), which is a passionate response to the forces in human nature that oppose equality. It is ambitiously conceived as a warning to humanity and a mirror held up to reveal what may result from giving in to "the seven deadly sins."

*Annual Exhibition 1963, Contemporary American Painting*, Whitney Museum of American Art, New York.

*Painting and Drawing the Nude: Part I, The Male; Part II, The Female*, Banfer Gallery, New York.

*Paintings from the Museum of Modern Art, New York*, National Gallery of Art, Washington, D.C.

1964

Tooker receives a request from the director of the Birmingham Museum of Art, Richard F. Howard, to borrow a work for an exhibition of American painters titled *The Precise Image*. He responds by asking that Howard first provide his "word of honor" that "the museum is not segregated in any way and that Negro people are treated as equals of white people in your museum. When I receive such assurance then we can go into the matter of a suitable picture." Howard responds with surprise and resentment at Tooker's sentiments and assures him that there has never been discrimination in the museum. Tooker nevertheless declines the invitation on the basis that all of his available work is committed to a solo exhibition, but asserts to Mr. Howard that he feels "so strongly that all men are brothers whatever their color that I don't always realize that others feel as deeply committed to this as I do."[2]

Tooker and Christopher meet Dr. King at Boston University, at the dedication ceremony for the civil rights leader's donation of his papers to the library. Dr. King requested to meet Christopher after hearing of the series of paintings he had made in King's honor.

Solo exhibition at Durlacher Brothers, New York.

*Between the Fairs: 25 Years of American Art, 1939–1964*, Whitney Museum of American Art, New York.

*Magic Realism—What Is It?*, American Federation of Arts.

*Realist Paintings: Yesterday, Today and Tomorrow*, Silvermine Guild of Artists, New Canaan, Connecticut.

*Trends in Painting, 11th Annual Exhibition of Contemporary American Painting*, Bayonne Jewish Community Center, New Jersey.

1965

Tooker teaches a course titled "Life Drawing, Painting, and Composition" at the Art Students League in New York until 1968.

George Tooker and William Christopher travel to Montgomery, Alabama, in March to attend the memorial service of the Reverend James Reeb, a white Unitarian minister who was killed while marching for civil rights. They attend an additional service for the Reverend Reeb in Selma, Alabama, where Dr. Martin Luther King,

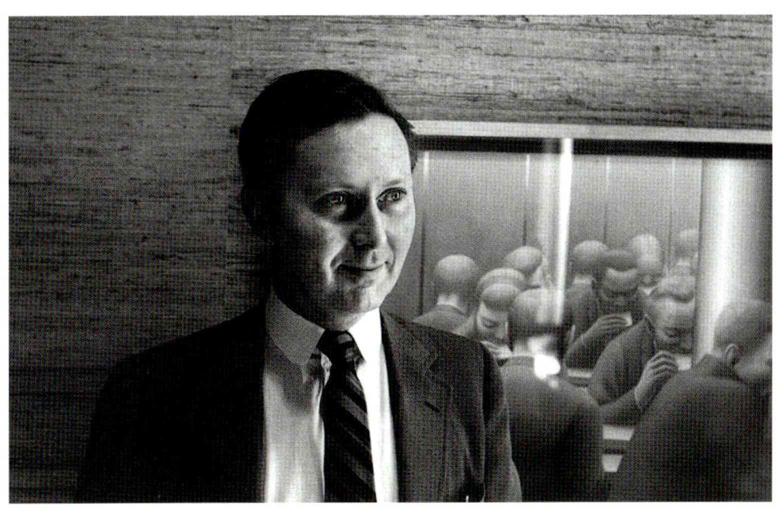

fig. 16
Tooker with *Lunch* at Durlacher Brothers exhibition (1967)
Courtesy of the George Tooker Papers, 1932–1973, Archives of American Art, Smithsonian Institution, Washington, D.C.

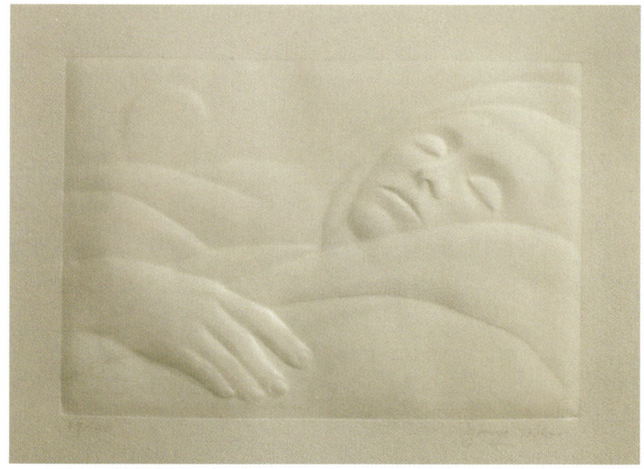

fig. 17
George Tooker
*Repose* (1975)
Intaglio print
7 × 11 inches (17.8 × 27.9 cm)
Columbus Museum of Art, Ohio: Museum Purchase, Derby Fund, from the Philip J. and Suzanne Schiller Collection of American Social Commentary Art, 1930–1970



Jr., delivers the eulogy. Following this the attendants hold a peaceful march to the Selma County Courthouse.

*1965 Annual Exhibition: Contemporary American Painting*, Whitney Museum of American Art, New York.

1966

*Annual Exhibition of Painting and Sculpture*, Pennsylvania Academy of the Fine Arts, Philadelphia.

*The First Flint Invitational: An Exhibition of Contemporary Painting and Sculpture*, Flint Institute of Arts, De Waters Art Center, Michigan.

1967

Solo exhibition at Durlacher Brothers, New York (fig. 16).

*1967 Annual Exhibition of Contemporary American Painting*, Whitney Museum of American Art, New York.

*George Tooker*, Jaffe-Friede Gallery, Hopkins Center, Dartmouth College, Hanover, New Hampshire.

1968

Owing to William Christopher's deteriorating health, he and Tooker begin to spend their winters in Malaga, Spain. Tooker maintains the apartment there until 1990.

Tooker is contacted by an advertising agency for permission to use *Landscape with Figures* (1966; plate 42) as the basis of a poster aimed at recruiting steelworkers. The irony is not lost on the artist, who nevertheless responds, "I cannot give my permission for the use of *Landscape with Figures* for any steel company since the subject of the picture is the victimization of our youth by the military–industrial complex and its servant, advertising."[3]

Tooker is elected Associate National Academician.

*American Paintings and Sculpture Lent by the Whitney Museum of Art, NY*, Palm Beach, Florida.

1969

*1969 Annual Exhibition: Contemporary American Painting*, Whitney Museum of American Art, New York.

*Human Concern, Personal Torment: The Grotesque in American Art*, Whitney Museum of American Art, New York.

1970

Tooker is elected National Academician.

1971

*The Hydeman Collection*, Fuller Memorial, Brockton Art Center, Massachusetts.

*New York, N.Y.*, ACA Galleries, New York.

*What is American in American Art*, M. Knoedler & Co., Inc., New York.

1973

William Christopher dies in Spain. Tooker remains there for most of 1973 and 1974.

*American Painting and Sculpture of the 20th Century*, Dover Art Collection, Colorado.

*National Academy of Design 148th Annual Exhibition*, National Academy of Design, New York.

Tooker collaborates with Thomas H. Garver in preparation for his first major retrospective. Though in mourning over Christopher, he gives interviews and helps clarify dates and life events.

1974

*George Tooker: Paintings 1947–1973*, California Palace of the Legion of Honor, San Francisco.

1975

Tooker makes prints for the first time, starting with the intaglio relief prints *Night* and *Repose*. In 1977, he begins a series of black-and-white lithographs, many of which are based on earlier paintings (fig. 17).

*New York, by Artists of the Students League of New York in Celebration of the Centennial Year of the Art Students League of*

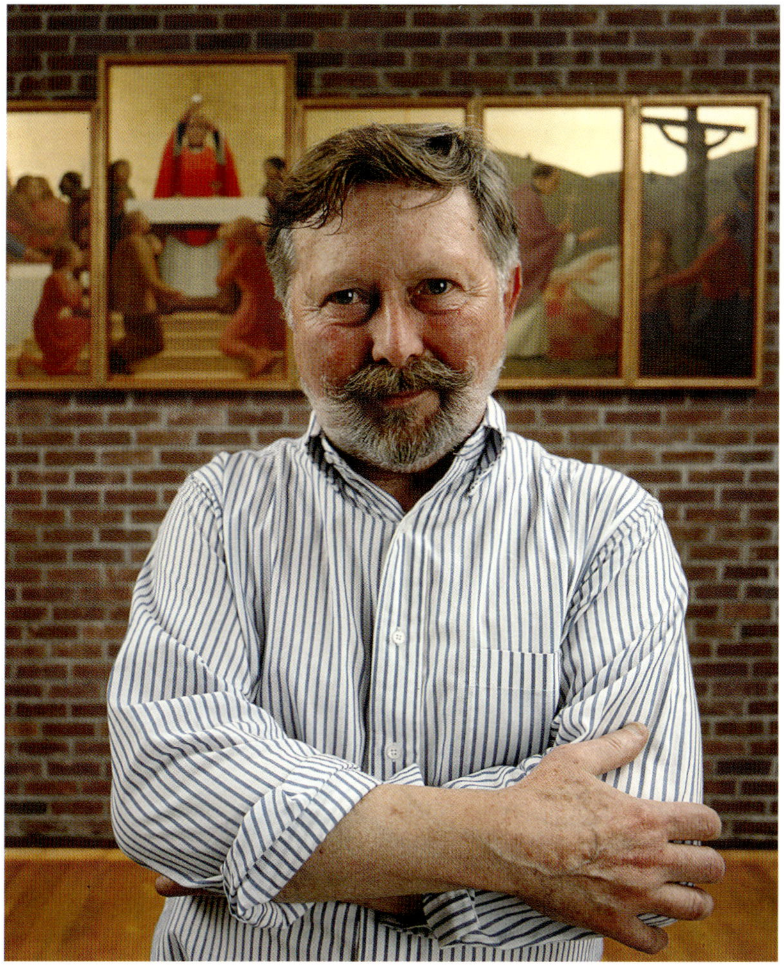

fig. 18
George Tooker with
*The Seven Sacraments*, Church of Saint
Francis of Assisi, Windsor, Vermont
(1981)
Photograph by Susan Brown
Courtesy of Chameleon Books

*New York*, Museum of the City of New York, Art Students League of New York.

1976
When Tooker's Episcopal church begins renovations, he starts attending Mass at the nearby Catholic church of St. Francis of Assisi in Windsor, Vermont. The parish priest, Father Forrest Rouelle, asks whether Tooker has considered converting to Catholicism. Tooker decides to convert and becomes a member of the St. Francis parish.

1977
St. Francis of Assisi Church burns in a fire in December. In 1979, during the course of reconstruction, Father Rouelle asks Tooker to contribute a painting for a fundraiser; instead, Tooker offers to paint something for the church building. Together they agree on the theme of *The Seven Sacraments*, which Tooker paints in 1980. The seven-panel polyptych is dedicated in January 1981 (fig. 18).
*Images of Horror and Fantasy*, Bronx Museum of the Arts, New York.

1978
*American Art, 1934–1956: Selections from the Whitney Museum of American Art*: Montgomery Museum of Fine Arts, Alabama; Brooks Memorial Art Gallery, Memphis; Mississippi Museum of Art, Jackson, Mississippi.



1979
*Artists and Architects*, New York Historical Society.

1980
*Tooker Paintings: 1950–1977*, David Tunkl Gallery, Los Angeles.

1981
After *The Seven Sacraments* is dedicated, Father Rouelle asks Tooker if he would paint the fourteen *Stations of the Cross* for St. Francis of Assisi Church. Feeling uneasy about depicting Christ, Tooker initially tells Father Rouelle that he will have to think about it. Eventually, Tooker agrees to the project and works on the panels from 1983 to 1984.

1982
Tooker is one of several artists to make a color lithograph to benefit the Metropolitan Opera. He creates *Un Ballo in Maschera* (plate 54), illustrating a scene from Verdi's opera of the same name.
*Homo Sapiens: The Many Images*, Aldrich Museum of Contemporary Art, Ridgefield, Connecticut.
*Realism and Realities: The Other Side of American Painting, 1940–1960*, Rutgers University Art Gallery, New Brunswick, New Jersey; Montgomery Museum of Fine Arts, Montgomery, Alabama; Art Gallery, University of Maryland, College Park, Maryland.
*Selected Works on Paper*, Marisa del Re Gallery, New York.
*Solitude: Inner Visions in American Art*, Terra Museum of American Art, Evanston, Illinois.

1983
Tooker receives the Governor's Award for Excellence in the Arts, Vermont Arts Council.
Tooker is elected member of the American Academy and Institute of Arts and Letters, New York.

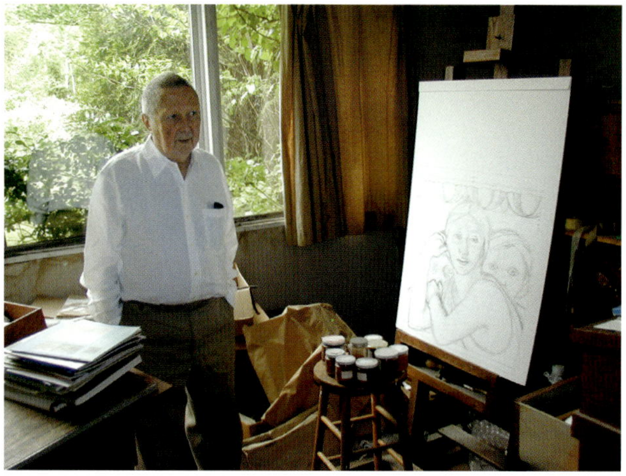

fig. 19
George Tooker in his studio with the sketch for *Sibyl* (2005), October 2006
Photograph by Thomas H. Garver



*1984 Preview*, Ronald Feldman Gallery, New York.
*Born in Brooklyn*, Rotunda Gallery, Brooklyn, New York.
*Dreams and Nightmares: Utopian Visions in Modern Art*, Hirshhorn Museum and Sculpture Garden, Washington, D.C.
*Exhibition of Work by Newly Elected Members and Recipients of Honors and Awards*, American Academy and Institute of Arts and Letters.

1984
*Contemporary Artists in Vermont*, Robert Hull Fleming Museum, University of Vermont, Burlington, Vermont.

1985
Thomas H. Garver's *George Tooker* is published, the first monograph on Tooker's life and work.
*Decades of Growth: American Painting 1920–1970*, Butler Institute of American Art, Youngstown, Ohio.
*George Tooker: Paintings, 1948–1985*, Marisa del Re Gallery, New York.
*The Surreal City, 1930s–1950s*, Whitney Museum of American Art at Philip Morris, New York.

1987
*George Tooker: Working Drawings*, Robert Hull Fleming Museum, University of Vermont, Burlington, Vermont.
*Modern American Realism: The Sara Roby Foundation Collection*, National Museum of American Art, Washington, D.C.
*The Paintings of George Tooker: Spoleto at the Gibbes Art Gallery*, Gibbes Art Gallery, Charleston, South Carolina.

1988
*George Tooker: Paintings*, Marisa del Re Gallery, New York.

1989
*George Tooker: Paintings and Working Drawings 1947–1988*, Marsh Gallery, University of Richmond.

1990
*Art What Thou Eat: Images of Food in American Art*, Edith C. Blum Art Institute, Bard College, Annandale-on-Hudson, New York.
*Cadmus, French and Tooker: The Early Years*, Whitney Museum of American Art at Philip Morris, New York.
*Close Encounters: The Art of Paul Cadmus, Jared French and George Tooker*, Midtown Galleries, New York.

1991
*The Technological Muse*, Katonah Museum of Art, New York.
*Contemporary Surrealism*, New Jersey Center for the Visual Arts, Summit, New Jersey.

1992
*Tooker's Women*, Marisa del Re Gallery, New York.

1994
*50 Years of Painting and Study Drawings*, Addison Gallery of American Art, Andover, Massachusetts.

1995
*In the Eye of the Storm: An Art of Conscience, 1930–1970, Selections from the Collection of Philip J. and Suzanne Schiller*, Terra Museum of American Art, Chicago; Greenville County Museum of Art, South Carolina; Sheldon Memorial Art Gallery & Sculpture Garden, Lincoln, Nebraska; Knoxville Museum of Art, Tennessee; Parrish Art Museum, Southampton, New York; Norton Museum of Art, West Palm Beach, Florida; Frederick R. Weisman Art Museum, Minneapolis.

1996
*Reality and Dream: The Art of George Tooker*, Ogunquit Museum of American Art, Ogunquit, Maine.

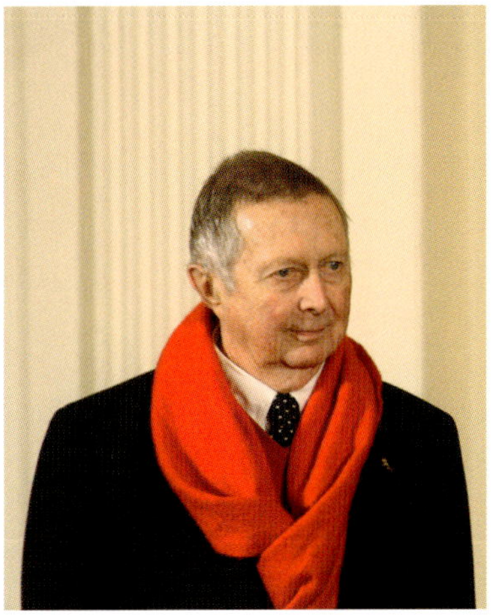

fig. 20
George Tooker received the National Medal of Arts on November 15, 2007
Courtesy of the National Endowment for the Arts



1997

*Civil Progress: Images of Black America*, Mary Ryan Gallery, New York.

*Views from Abroad: European Perspectives on American Art 3—American Realities*, Tate Gallery, London, and Whitney Museum of American Art, New York.

1998

*George Tooker: Recent Paintings*, DC Moore Gallery, New York.

1999

*The American Century: Art and Culture, 1950–2000*, Whitney Museum of American Art, New York.

*Magic Realism: A Selection of Paintings, 1925–1998*, Beth Urdang Gallery, Boston.

*Men without Women: Paul Cadmus as Curator*, National Academy of Design, New York.

*Modern American Realism: The Sara Roby Foundation Collection from the National Museum of American Art*, Everson Museum of Art, Syracuse, New York.

2000

*Figures and Forms: Selections from the Terra Foundation for the Arts*, Terra Museum of American Art, Chicago.

*George Tooker: Recent Paintings*, DC Moore Gallery, New York.

*League Masters Then: A Selection of Works by Artists Associated with the Art Students League of New York*, Art Students League, New York.

*Making Choices*, The Museum of Modern Art, New York.

Solo exhibition at the Hart Gallery, Guild Art Center, Northampton, Massachusetts.

*Twentieth-Century American Art: The Ebsworth Collection*, National Gallery of Art, Washington, D.C.

2001

*American Tableaux: Many Voices, Many Stories*, Walker Art Center, Minneapolis.

*Interwoven Lives: George Platt Lynes and His Friends*, DC Moore Gallery, New York.

*Magic Vision*, Arkansas Arts Center, Little Rock, Arizona.

*Re-presenting, Representation*, Arnot Art Museum, Corning Gallery, New York.

*Self Made Men: Male Self-Portraits*, DC Moore Gallery, New York.

2002

*Milk and Eggs: The American Revival of Tempera Painting, 1930–1950*, Brandywine River Museum, Chadds Ford, Delaware; Akron Museum of Art, Ohio; Spencer Museum of Art, University of Kansas, Lawrence.

2005

*Disegno: The One Hundred and Eightieth Annual Exhibition*, National Academy Museum, New York.

*Villa America: American Moderns, 1900–1950*, Orange County Museum of Art, California.

2007

Tooker is awarded the National Medal of Arts (fig. 20).

Solo exhibition at DC Moore Gallery, New York, including recent works, such as *Girl Reading* (2003; plate 65) and *Sibyl* (2005; fig. 19).

## Notes

1 Lincoln Kirstein to Dorothy C. Miller, Registrar Exhibition Files, exh. 329. The Museum of Modern Art Archives, New York.

2 George Tooker to Richard F. Howard, George Tooker Papers, Archives of American Art, Smithsonian Institution, Washington, D.C.

3 Quoted in Thomas H. Garver, *George Tooker*, rev. edn (San Francisco: Pomegranate, 2002), 35.

# Bibliography



### Interviews with the artist and archival sources

Grace G. Alexander, interview with George Tooker, 1967. Transcript, Archives of American Art, Smithsonian Institution, Washington, D.C.

Richard Boyle and Hilton Brown, interview with George Tooker, January 14, 1993. Research files for the exhibition *Milk and Eggs: The American Revival of Tempera Painting, 1930–1950*, Archives of the Brandywine River Museum, Chadds Ford, Pennsylvania.

William Christopher Papers, 1946–72, Archives of American Art, Smithsonian Institution, Washington, D.C.

Thomas H. Garver Research Material on Bruce Conner and George Tooker, 1973–74, Archives of American Art, Smithsonian Institution, Washington, D.C.

George Tooker Papers, 1932–73, Archives of American Art, Smithsonian Institution, Washington, D.C.

Jonathan Weinberg, interview with George Tooker, June 7, 2007.

M. Melissa Wolfe, interview with George Tooker, July 28, 2007.

### Publications and dissertations

Ackerman, Gerald. *Contemporary Humanism: Reconfirmation of the Figure*. Fullerton, California: California State University, Fullerton, 1987.

Ardoin, John. *The Stages of Menotti*. New York: Doubleday & Co., Inc., 1985.

Auden, W.H. *The Age of Anxiety: A Baroque Eclogue*. New York: Random House, 1946.

__________. *Collected Shorter Poems, 1927–1957*. New York: Random House, 1966.

Baker, Susan Jane. "George Tooker and the Modern Tradition," PhD diss., University of Kansas, Lawrence, 1994.

Benedikt, Michael. "George Tooker," in *Art: USA: Now*, ed. Lee Nordness, vol. 2. New York: Viking Press, 1963.

Benét, William Rose. *The Reader's Encyclopedia*, 2nd edn. New York: Thomas Y. Crowell, 1965.

Bénézit, E. *Dictionnaire critique et documentaire des peintres, sculpteurs, dessinateurs et graveurs*. New edn. Paris: Librairie Grund, 1976.

Bergman, David, ed., *Camp Grounds: Style and Homosexuality*. Amherst, Massachusetts: University of Massachusetts Press, 1994.

Berman, Greta, and Jeffrey Wechsler. *Realism and Realities: The Other Side of American Painting, 1940–1960*. Exhib. cat. Rutgers University Art Gallery, New Brunswick, New Jersey, 1982.

Bloom, Lisa, "Ghosts of Ethnicity: Rethinking Art Discourses of the 1940s and 1980s," in *With Other Eyes: Looking at Race and Gender in Visual Culture*, ed. Lisa Bloom. Minneapolis: University of Minnesota Press, 1999.

Cadmus, Paul. *George Tooker*. New York: DC Moore Gallery, 1998.

Camus, Albert. *Neither Victims Nor Executioners*, trans. Dwight Macdonald. Berkeley, California: World Without War Council, 1965.

Candee, Marjorie Dent, ed., "George Tooker," *Current Biography*, 19 (March 1958), 38–39.

Chauncey, George. *Gay New York: Gender, Urban Culture, and the Makings of the Gay Male World, 1890–1940*. New York: Basic Books, 1994.

Culver, Michael. *Reality and Dream: The Art of George Tooker*, Ogunquit, Maine: Ogunquit Museum of American Art, 1996.

Descartes, René. *Discourse on Method*, trans. and ed. Lawrence J. Lafleur. New York and London: Macmillan, 1956.

Duberman, Martin. *The Worlds of Lincoln Kirstein*. New York: Alfred A. Knopf, 2007.

Etlin, Richard A. *In Defense of Humanism: Value in the Arts and Letters*. Cambridge: Cambridge University Press, 1996.

Faas, Ekbert. *Young Robert Duncan: Portrait of the Poet as Homosexual in Society*. Santa Barbara, California: Black Sparrow Press, 1983.

Finkelstein, Sidney. *Existentialism and Alienation in American Literature*. New York: International Publishers, 1965.

__________. *Realism in Art: The Relation between Artistic Beauty and Real Life in Painting from Primitive Origins to Today*. New York: International Publishers, 1954.

Fletcher, Valerie J. *Dreams and Nightmares: Utopian Visions in Modern Art*. Exhib. cat. Hirshhorn Museum and Sculpture Garden, Washington, D.C., 1983.

Foucault, Michel. *Discipline and Punish: The Birth of the Prison*, trans. Alan Sheridan. New York: Pantheon, 1977.

Freud, Sigmund, "Thoughts for the Times on War and Death," in *The Standard Edition of the Complete Psychological Works of Sigmund Freud*, trans. and ed. James Strachey, Vol. XIV. London: The Hogarth Press and the Institute of Psycho-analysis, 1957.

Garver, Thomas. *A Silent Theater: The Paintings of George Tooker*. Charleston, South Carolina: Gibbs Art Gallery, 1987. (Reprinted in the souvenir program of the Spoleto Festival USA, 1987.)

__________. *George Tooker*. Exhib. cat. San Francisco: The Fine Arts Museums of San Francisco, 1974.

__________. *George Tooker*. New York: C. N. Potter, 1985.

__________. *George Tooker*. Rev. edn. San Francisco: Pomegranate, 2002.

__________. *George Tooker: Paintings*. New York: Marisa del Re Gallery, 1988.

Gear, Josephine. *Cadmus, French, & Tooker: The Early Years*. New York: Whitney Museum of American Art at Philip Morris, 1990.

*George Tooker*. Exhib. cat. Hanover, New Hampshire: Jaffe-Friede Gallery, Hopkins Center, Dartmouth College, 1967.

Graham, Dan. *Rock My Religion: Writings and Art Projects, 1965–1990*, ed. Brian Wallis. Cambridge, Massachusetts: The MIT Press, 1993.

Grimes, Nancy. *George Tooker*. New York: DC Moore Gallery, 1998.

Halley, Peter. *Collected Essays, 1981–87*. Zurich: Bruno Bischofberger Gallery, 1988.

Harper, Ralph. *Existentialism: A Theory of Man*. Cambridge, Massachusetts: Harvard University Press, 1965.

Heffernan, Ildiko. *George Tooker: Working Drawings*. Exhib. cat. Burlington, Vermont: Robert Hull Fleming Museum, 1987.

Hollister-Knepp, Gregory M. "The Sacred and the Profane: Christian and Mythological Imagery within the Œuvre of George Tooker." MA diss., Bloomsburg University College of Arts and Sciences, Pennsylvania, 1997. (Includes an interview with the artist conducted April 21, 1997.)

Hughes, Langston. *The Collected Poems of Langston Hughes*, ed. Arnold Rampersad. New York: Vintage Books/Random House, 1995.

Kirstein, Lincoln. *Symbolic Realism in American Painting, 1940–1950*. Exhib. cat. London: The Institute of Contemporary Arts, 1950.

__________. *Nijinsky Dancing*. New York: Alfred A. Knopf, 1975.

Kirstein, Lincoln, and Jerry L. Thompson. *Quarry: A Collection in Lieu of Memoirs*. Pasadena, California: Twelvetrees Press, 1986.

Lacan, Jacques. "The Mirror-Phase as Formative of the Function of the I," in *Art in Theory, 1900–1990*, ed. Charles Harrison and Paul Wood. Oxford and Cambridge, Massachusetts: Blackwell, 1992.

Leddick, David. *Intimate Companions: A Triography of George Platt Lynes, Paul Cadmus, Lincoln Kirstein, and Their Circle*. New York: St. Martin's Press, 2000.

Main Art Gallery—Visual Arts Center, *Contemporary Humanism: Reconfirmation of the Figure*. Fullerton, California: California State University, Fullerton, 1987.

Mariño, Melanie. "Disposable Matter: Photoconceptual Magazine Work of the 1960s," in Douglas Fogle, *The Last Picture Show: Artists Using Photography 1960–1982*. Exhib. cat. Minneapolis: Walker Art Center, 2003.

Martin, Reinhold. *The Organizational Complex: Architecture, Media, and Corporate Space*. Cambridge, Massachusetts: The MIT Press, 2003.

Mellor, David, "Existentialism and Post-war British Art," in *Paris Post War: Art and Existentialism, 1945–1955*, ed. Frances Morris. Exhib. cat. London: Tate Gallery Publications, 1993.

Merleau-Ponty, Maurice. *Phenomenon of Perception*, trans. Colin Smith. London: Routledge and Kegan Paul, 1962.

Meyer, Richard. *Outlaw Representation: Censorship and Homosexuality in Twentieth-Century American Art*. Oxford and New York: Oxford University Press, 2002.

Moscanyi, Paul. *The Humanist Tradition in Contemporary Painting*. Exhib. cat. New York: New School Art Center, 1968.

Pinder, Kymberly N. "Biraciality and Nationhood in Contemporary American Art," in *Race-ing Art History: Critical Readings in Race and Art History*, ed. Kymberly N. Pinder. New York and London: Routledge, 2002.

Pohl, Frances K. *In the Eye of the Storm: Art of Conscience, 1930–1970*. Exhib. cat. New York: Chameleon Books, 1995.

Post, Chandler Rathfon. *A History of European and American Sculpture from the Early Christian Period to the Present Day*. Cambridge, Massachusetts: Harvard University Press, 1921.

Read, Herbert. "Rational Society and Irrational Art," in *The Critical Spirit: Essays in Honor of Herbert Marcuse*, ed. Kurt H. Wolff and Barrington Moore, Jr. Boston: Beacon Press, 1967.

Read, Herbert, *et al.*, *The Collected Writings of C. G. Jung*. Vol. 17, trans. R.F.C. Hull. Bollingen Series XX. New York: Bollingen Foundation, and Princeton, New Jersey: Princeton University Press, 1964.

Robinson, Victoria. "Interview with George Tooker," in Elizabeth Langhorne-Reeve, *George Tooker: Paintings and Working Drawings, 1947–1988*. Richmond, Virginia: University of Richmond, 1989.

Rodman, Selden. *Conversations with Artists*. New York: The Devin-Adair Co., 1957.

Russell, James S. "Form Follows Fad: The Troubled Love Affair of Architectural Style and Management Ideal," in *On the Job: Design and the American Office*, ed. Donald Albrecht and Chrysanthe B. Broikos. Exhib. cat. Washington, D.C.: National Building Museum, 2000.

Salvan, Jacques L. *The Scandalous Ghost: Sartre's Existentialism as Related to Vitalism, Humanism, Mysticism, Marxism*. Detroit: Wayne State University Press, 1967.

Sartre, Jean-Paul. "Existentialism and Humanism," in *Art in Theory, 1900–1990*, ed. Charles Harrison and Paul Wood. Oxford and Cambridge, Massachusetts: Blackwell, 1992.

Schwartz, Barry. *The New Humanism: Art in a Time of Change*. New York: Praeger Publishers, 1974.

Sedgwick, Eve Kosofsky. *Epistemology of the Closet*. Berkeley, California: University of California Press, 1990.

Selz, Peter. *New Images of Man*. Exhib. cat. New York: The Museum of Modern Art, in collaboration with the Baltimore Museum of Art, 1959.

Shafranek, Heidi D. "The World of George Tooker: Surreal or Real." MA diss. University of Delaware, 1982. (Includes an interview with the artist conducted on June 5, 1981.)

Sheldon, William Herbert, and Stanley Smith Stevens. *The Varieties of Temperament: A Psychology of Constitutional Differences*. New York: Harper, 1942.

Sher, Gail. *Marginalia*. Chicago: Rodent Press, 1997.

Sokol, David M. *Solitude: Inner Visions in American Art*. Evanston, Illinois: Terra Museum of American Art, 1982.

Sontag, Susan. "Notes on 'Camp'," in *Against Interpretation and Other Essays*. New York: Farrar, Strauss, and Giroux, 1964.

Tafuri, Manfredo. *Architecture and Utopia: Design and Capitalist Development*, trans. Barbara Luigia La Penta. Cambridge, Massachusetts: The MIT Press, 1976.

Tunkl, David, and Merry A. Foresta, *George Tooker*. Exhib. cat. Los Angeles: David Tunkl Gallery, 1980.

Varnedoe, Kirk. *Duane Hanson*. New York: Harry N. Abrams, 1985.

Von Blum, Paul. *The Art of Social Conscience*. New York: Universe Books, 1976.

Weinberg, Jonathan. *Male Desire: The Homoerotic in American Art*. Harry N. Abrams, 2005.

Whitfield, Stephen J. *The Culture of the Cold War*. Baltimore and London: The Johns Hopkins University Press, 1991.

Whitney Museum of American Art. *The New Decade: 35 American Painters and Sculptors*. New York: Whitney Museum of American Art, 1955.

Wigmore, Jodi Ann. "George Tooker: A Reassessment of the Artist." Canadian diss., Ottawa: National Library of Canada, 1988.

Wolff, Miles. *Lunch at the Five and Ten: The Greensboro Sit-ins, A Contemporary History*. New York: Stein and Day, 1970.


**Articles and reviews published in periodicals and newspapers**


Baker, J. "Report from New Brunswick: Representation Painting in the U.S., 1940–1960," *Art in America*, 70:10 (November 1982), 19–23.

Beichman, Arnold. "Is Higher Education in the Dark Ages?" *New York Times Magazine* (November 6, 1983), 46.

Butler, Joseph T. "The Surrealism of George Tooker," *Connoisseur*, 187 (October 1974), 135.

Chave, Anna C. "Minimalism and the Rhetoric of Power," *Arts*, 64: 5 (January 1990), 44–63.

"Contemporary Florentine," *Time*, 89 (April 21, 1967), 72.

Derfner, Phyllis. *Art International*, 19 (March 1975), 38–40.

Duncan, Robert. "The Homosexual in Society," *Politics*, 1:7 (1944), 209–11.

Edgar, Natalie. "George Tooker," *ArtNews*, 61 (April 1962), 60–61.

Frankel, Stephen Robert. "The Modern Iconography of George Tooker," *Art Today* (summer 1986), 18–25.

Gablik, Suzi. "George Tooker," *ArtNews*, 63 (May 1964), 16.

"George Tooker," *ArtNews*, 50 (March 1951), 50.

"George Tooker," *The Art Digest*, 25 (March 1, 1951), 24.

"George Tooker," *The Art Digest*, 29 (January 1, 1955), 28.

"George Tooker," *Arts Magazine*, 34 (April 1960), 61.

"George Tooker," *Arts Magazine*, 41 (April 1967), 60.

Glueck, Grace. "Art: A Nostalgic Visit to 'The Surreal City'," *New York Times* (May 31, 1985).

__________. "Art in Review," *New York Times* (December 22, 2000), E46.

Grimes, Nancy. "George Tooker at DC Moore," *Art in America*, 98: 86 (July 1998), 94.

Hauser, Katherine. "George Tooker, Surveillance, and Cold War Sexual Politics," *GLQ*, 11:3 (June 2005), 391–425.

"Here: Now," *Time*, 80:10 (September 7, 1962), 36.

Kane, Marie Louise. "George Tooker's Magic Numbers," *ArtNews* 92:1 (January 1993), 29.

Kernan, N. "Interwoven Lives: George Platt Lynes and His Friends. DC Moore Gallery, New York," *Art on Paper*, 6:3 (January/February 2002), 86.

Kirstein, Lincoln. "Menotti: The Giants in Bleecker Street," *Center: A Magazine of Performing Arts*, 1 (December 1954), 3–4, 6, 8.

___________. "The State of Modern Painting," *Harper's Magazine*, 197: 1181 (October 1948), 47–53.

Kirwin, L. "Visual Thinking: Sketchbooks from the Archives of American Art," *Archives of American Art Journal*, 27: 1 (1987), 21–29.

Levin, G. "The Office Image in the Visual Arts," *Arts Magazine*, 59 (September 1984), 98–103.

McKown, R. "Spotlight Reviews 30," *Art New England*, 24 (October/November 2003), 6.

Moorman, M. *ArtNews*, 84 (May 1985), 117.

Mulski, S. "Addison Gallery of American Art, Phillips Academy/Andover: George Tooker, 50 Years of Paintings and Study Drawings," *Art New England*, 15 (April/May 1994), 63.

Munro, Thomas. "A Note on the Aesthetics of Naturalistic Humanism," *The Journal of Aesthetics and Art Criticism*, 28 (autumn 1969), 45–47.

"Negroes' Sitdown Hits 2 More Cities," *New York Times* (February 19, 1960), 16.

Pacheco, Patrick. "Point Counterpoint," *Art & Antiques*, 8: 8 (October 1991), 70–75.

Pomeroy, Ralph. "A Master of Modern Dismay," *New Lugano Review*, 8–9 (1976), 38–41.

___________. "George Tooker, Really," *Art and Artists* (1967), 24–27.

Preston, Stuart. "Current and Forthcoming Exhibitions: New York," *Burlington Magazine*, 102 (May 1960), 226–29.

"Prints & Photographs Published," *The Print Collector's Newsletter*, 25 (September/October 1994), 144–48.

Raynor, Vivien. *ArtNews*, 59 (April 1960), 55.

___________. "George Tooker," *Arts Magazine*, 36 (May 1962), 101.

___________. *New York Times* (February 22, 1985), C25.

Risatti, H.A. "Marsh Gallery, University of Richmond, Virginia; Exhibit," *New Art Examiner*, 17 (December 1989), 42.

Sawin, Martica. "Realism and Realities," *Art Journal*, 42: 2 (summer 1982), 157–59.

Sitton, Claude. "Sit-in Campaigns Spread in a Year," *New York Times* (January 29, 1961), 64.

Southgate, M. Therese. "The Cover," *JAMA: Journal of the American Medical Association*, 262: 17 (11/3/89), 2348.

Spring, Justin. "An Interview with George Tooker," *American Art*, 16:1 (spring 2002), 61–81.

"The Strange World of George Tooker," *Avant-Garde* (September 1965), 36–45.

Stroup, Jon. "Time Out," *Town and Country* (1946), 108.

Tomor, Michael A. "Magic Realism: An American Response to Surrealism," *American Art Review*, 11: 4 (July–August 1999), 142–47.

Tyler, Parker. "George Tooker," *ArtNews*, 53 (January 1955), 56.

Wechsler, J. "Magic Realism: Defining the Indefinite," *Art Journal*, 45 (winter 1985), 293–98.

Weinberg, Jonathan. "Cruising with Cadmus," *Art in America*, 80: 11 (1992), 102–109.

Wheat, Edward M. "Images of Bureaucracy in Fine Art: Salvador Dali's 'Average Bureaucrat' and George Tooker's 'Government Bureau'," *Politics & Policy*, 26: 1 (1998), 25–45.

Zucker, Barbara. "George Tooker," *ArtNews*, 74 (March 1975), 109–10.

# Exhibition checklist



*Children and Spastics*, 1946
Egg tempera on gesso panel,
24½ × 18½ in. (62.2 × 47 cm)
Collection Museum of Contemporary Art, Chicago, Gift of Mary and Earle Ludgin Collection

Study for *Dance*, *circa* 1946
Graphite, chalk, wash, and ink on paper,
13 × 20 7/16 in. (33 × 51.9 cm)
Gift of the artist (PA 1936) in memory of his parents, George Clair and Angela Montejo Roura Tooker, Addison Gallery of American Art, Phillips Academy, Andover, Massachusetts

*Dance*, 1946
Egg tempera on gesso panel,
13¼ × 20½ in. (33.6 × 52 cm)
Collection of Andrew Nelson

Study for *A Game of Chess*, 1946
Graphite on paper,
29 15/16 × 15 in. (76 × 38.1 cm)
Gift of the artist (PA 1936) in memory of his parents, George Clair and Angela Montejo Roura Tooker, Addison Gallery of American Art, Phillips Academy, Andover, Massachusetts

*A Game of Chess*, 1946–47
Egg tempera on gesso panel,
30 × 15 in. (76.2 × 38.1 cm)
Collection of Barney A. Ebsworth

Study for *How Do You Do?*, *circa* 1947
Colored pencil, graphite, and wash on paper,
26 1/16 × 19 in. (66.2 × 48.3 cm)
Gift of the artist (PA 1936) in memory of his parents, George Clair and Angela Montejo Roura Tooker, Addison Gallery of American Art, Phillips Academy, Andover, Massachusetts

*The Groping Hand*, *circa* 1947
Egg tempera on watercolor paper,
3½ × 2¾ in. (8.9 × 7 cm)
Nicholas Miles Pentecost, Courtesy DC Moore Gallery, New York

*Self-Portrait*, 1947
Egg tempera on gesso panel,
18¾ in. (47.6 cm) diameter
Curtis Galleries, Minneapolis, Minnesota

Study for *Coney Island*, 1947
Graphite on paper,
22½ × 30⅞ in. (57.1 × 78.4 cm)
Gift of the artist (PA 1936) in memory of his parents, George Clair and Angela Montejo Roura Tooker, Addison Gallery of American Art, Phillips Academy, Andover, Massachusetts

*Coney Island*, 1947–48
Egg tempera on gesso panel,
19 × 26 in. (48.3 × 66 cm)
Curtis Galleries, Minneapolis, Minnesota

*Bird Watchers*, 1948
Egg tempera on gessoed board,
26¾ × 32¾ in. (67.9 × 83.2 cm)
New Britain Museum of American Art, Gift of Olga H. Knoepke

*Cornice*, *circa* 1949
Egg tempera on gesso panel,
24 × 15½ in. (61 × 39.4 cm)
Columbus Museum of Art, Ohio: Museum Purchase, Howald Fund II

Study for *Cornice*, 1949
Graphite and wash on paper,
27 11/16 × 18⅛ in. (70.4 × 46 cm)
Gift of the artist (PA 1936) in memory of his parents, George Clair and Angela Montejo Roura Tooker, Addison Gallery of American Art, Phillips Academy, Andover, Massachusetts

Study for *Subway*, 1949
Graphite on paper, 24 × 39⅜ in.
(61 × 100 cm)
Gift of the artist (PA 1936) in memory of his parents, George Clair and Angela Montejo Roura Tooker, Addison Gallery of American Art, Phillips Academy, Andover, Massachusetts

*Bathhouses*, 1950
Egg tempera on gesso panel, 20¼ × 15¼ in.
(51.4 × 38.7 cm)
Private Collection

*Subway*, 1950
Egg tempera on composition board,
18⅛ × 36⅛ in. (46 × 91.8 cm)
Whitney Museum of American Art, New York
Purchase, with funds from the Juliana Force Purchase Award

Study for *Laundress*, 1952
Graphite and chalk on paper,
26 1/16 × 26 in. (67.6 × 66 cm)
Gift of the artist (PA 1936) in memory of his parents, George Clair and Angela Montejo Roura Tooker, Addison Gallery of American Art, Phillips Academy, Andover, Massachusetts

*Builders*, 1952
Egg tempera on gesso panel,
16 × 16 in. (40.6 × 40.6 cm)
Wayne County Public Library, Inc.

*Garden Party*, 1952
Egg tempera on gesso panel,
18 × 11¾ in. (45.7 × 29.8 cm)
Private Collection, courtesy Debra Force Fine Art, New York

*Letterbox*, 1953
Egg tempera on fiberboard,
18⅛ × 24 in. (46 × 61 cm)
Hirshhorn Museum and Sculpture Garden, Smithsonian Institution, Washington, D.C., Museum Purchase, 1993

*Jukebox*, 1953
Egg tempera on gesso panel,
21 × 14 in. (53.3 × 35.6 cm)
Mr. and Mrs. James C. Biddle

*Highway*, 1953
Tempera on panel,
22⅞ × 17⅞ in. (58.1 × 45.4 cm)
Terra Foundation for American Art, Daniel J. Terra Collection, 1992.134

*Red Carpet*, 1953 or 1954
Egg tempera on gesso panel,
16 × 20¼ in. (40.6 × 51.4 cm)
Reis Private Collection

*The Artist's Daughter*, 1955
Egg tempera on gesso panel,
24 × 12½ in. (61 × 31.7 cm)
Private Collection

*Fig Tree*, 1955
Egg tempera on gesso panel,
18 × 24 in. (45.7 × 61 cm)
Private Collection

*Window II*, 1956
Egg tempera on gesso panel,
24 × 18 in. (61 × 45.7 cm)
Collection of James and Barbara Palmer

Study for *Government Bureau*, 1956
Graphite, chalk, and wash on paper,
25¾ × 32 13/16 in. (65.4 × 83.4 cm)
Gift of the artist (PA 1936) in memory of his parents, George Clair and Angela Montejo Roura Tooker, Addison Gallery of American Art, Phillips Academy, Andover, Massachusetts

*Government Bureau*, 1956
Egg tempera on gesso panel,
19⅝ × 29⅝ in. (49.8 × 75.3 cm)
The Metropolitan Museum of Art, New York, George A. Hearn Fund, 1956 (56.78)

*Guitar*, 1957
Egg tempera on gesso panel,
18 × 24 in. (45.7 × 61 cm)
Private Collection

Study for *Waiting Room*, 1957
Graphite on paper,
27⅜ × 35⅞ in. (69.5 × 91.1 cm)
Gift of the artist (PA 1936) in memory of his parents, George Clair and Angela Montejo Roura Tooker, Addison Gallery of American Art, Phillips Academy, Andover, Massachusetts

*Waiting Room*, 1957
Egg tempera on wood,
24 × 30 in. (61 × 78.4 cm)
Smithsonian American Art Museum, Washington, D.C., Gift of S.C. Johnson & Sons, Inc.

*In the Summer House*, 1958
Egg tempera on fiberboard,
24 × 24 in. (61 × 61 cm)
Smithsonian American Art Museum, Washington, D.C., Gift of the Sara Roby Foundation

*Sleepers II*, 1959
Tempera on wood panel,
16 1/8 × 28 in. (41.2 × 71.1 cm)
The Museum of Modern Art, New York, New York, USA, Larry Aldrich Foundation Fund

*Lovers I*, 1959
Egg tempera on gesso panel,
18 × 24 in. (45.7 × 61 cm)
Collection of William T. Hillman

*Meadow I*, 1960–61
Egg tempera on gesso panel,
20 × 28 in. (50.8 × 71.1 cm)
Toledo Museum of Art: Gift of the Woodward Foundation and purchased with funds from the Libbey Endowment, Gift of Edward Drummond Libbey, by exchange, 2007.47

*Toilette*, 1962
Egg tempera on gesso panel,
20 1/2 × 17 1/2 in. (52.1 × 44.4 cm)
Linda Lichtenberg Kaplan

*Supper*, 1963
Tempera on board,
20 × 24 in. (50.8 × 61 cm)
Memorial Art Gallery of the University of Rochester. Marion Stratton Gould Fund

*Window VII*, 1963
Egg tempera on gesso panel,
24 1/8 × 21 1/8 in. (61.3 × 53.7 cm)
Terra Foundation for American Art, Daniel J. Terra Collection, 1992.168

Study for *Lunch*, 1964
Graphite, chalk, and wash on paper,
20 7/8 × 26 13/16 in. (53 × 68.1 cm)
Gift of the artist (PA 1936) in memory of his parents, George Clair and Angela Montejo Roura Tooker, Addison Gallery of American Art, Phillips Academy, Andover, Massachusetts

*Lunch*, 1964
Egg tempera on gesso panel,
20 × 26 in. (50.8 × 66 cm)
Columbus Museum of Art, Ohio: Museum Purchase, Derby Fund, from the Philip J. and Suzanne Schiller Collection of American Social Commentary Art 1930–1970

*Landscape with Figures*, 1965–66
Egg tempera on gesso panel,
26 × 30 in. (66 × 76.2 cm)
Barbara B. Millhouse

*Window VIII*, 1966
Egg tempera on gesso panel,
24 × 20 in. (61 × 50.8 cm)
Private Collection

*Teller*, 1967
Egg tempera on gesso panel,
23 1/2 × 15 1/2 in. (59.7 × 39.4 cm)
Private Collection, courtesy of EKG Art Advisory, New York

*Self-Portrait*, 1969
Egg tempera on gesso panel,
24 × 19 1/2 in. (61 × 49.5 cm)
National Academy Museum, New York, 1706-P

*Mirror III*, *circa* 1970–71
Egg tempera on gesso panel,
22 × 19 3/4 in. (55.9 × 50.2 cm)
Indianapolis Museum of Art, Gift of Edwin F. Koch, Jr., M.D.

*Ward*, 1970–71
Egg tempera on gesso panel,
20 × 30 in. (50.8 × 76.2 cm)
Private Collection

*Voice II*, 1972
Egg tempera on gesso panel,
17 1/2 × 11 1/2 in. (44.5 × 29 cm)
National Academy Museum, New York, 1758-P

*Supermarket*, 1973
Egg tempera on gesso panel,
23 × 17 1/4 in. (58.4 × 43.8 cm)
Curtis Galleries, Minneapolis, Minnesota

*Standing Figures*, 1973
Egg tempera on gesso panel,
18 × 24 in. (45.7 × 61 cm)
Private Collection

*Pot of Aloes*, 1974
Egg tempera on gesso panel,
24 × 18 in. (61 × 45.7 cm)
Private Lender

*Woman with Oranges*, 1977
Egg tempera on gesso panel,
23 1/2 × 17 1/2 in. (59.7 × 39.3 cm)
Courtesy DC Moore Gallery, New York

*Orant*, 1977
Egg tempera on gesso panel,
23 1/2 × 15 1/2 in. (59.7 × 39.4 cm)
Private Collection

*Embrace I*, 1979
Egg tempera on gesso panel,
24 × 18 in. (61 × 45.7 cm)
Collection of Anka K. Palitc

*Un Ballo in Maschera*, 1982
Egg tempera on gesso panel,
22 × 30 in. (55.9 × 76.2 cm)
Collection of Mr. and Mrs. Mark L. Brock

*Waiting Room II*, 1982
Egg tempera on gesso board,
19 × 37 in. (48.3 × 94 cm)
Private Collection

*Girl with a Basket*, 1987–88
Egg tempera on gesso panel,
24 × 18 in. (61 × 45.7 cm)
Private Collection, courtesy James Francis Trezza, New York

*Embrace of Peace II*, 1988
Egg tempera on gesso panel,
18 × 30 in. (45.7 × 76.2 cm)
Reis Private Collection

*Woman with a Sprig of Laurel*, 1992
Egg tempera on gesso panel,
18 × 24 in. (45.7 × 61 cm)
Susan and Peter Tuteur

*Self-Portrait*, 1992
Graphite and white conté crayon on toned tracing paper,
15 × 12 3/4 in. (38.1 × 32.4 cm)
Philadelphia Museum of Art: Purchased with the Alice Newton Osborn Fund, 2003

*Self-Portrait*, 1994
Egg tempera on gesso panel,
14 × 12 in. (35.6 × 30.5 cm)
Private Collection, Boston, Massachusetts

*Dark Angel*, 1996
Egg tempera on gesso panel,
24 × 19 in. (61 × 48.3 cm)
Pennsylvania Academy of the Fine Arts, Philadelphia, Henry C. Gibson Fund, 2007.7

*Man in a Tree*, 1998
Egg tempera on gesso panel,
14 × 17 in. (35.6 × 43.1 cm)
Collection of James and Barbara Palmer

*Landscape with Figures IV*, 1999
Egg tempera on gesso panel,
19 1/2 × 29 1/2 in. (49.5 × 74.9 cm)
Pilar and Vicente Pita, New Jersey

*Father and Child*, 2000
Egg tempera on gesso panel,
24 × 20 in. (61 × 50.8 cm)
Private Collection

*Girl Reading*, 2003
Egg tempera on gesso panel,
15 1/4 × 19 1/2 in. (38.8 × 49.5 cm)
Courtesy of the artist and DC Moore Gallery, New York

# Author biographies



While serving as Curator of Exhibitions at the Fine Arts Museums of San Francisco, **Thomas H. Garver** organized the first major traveling exhibition of paintings by George Tooker, which was also seen at the Museum of Contemporary Art, Chicago, and the Whitney Museum of American Art, New York, in 1974–75. Garver, the founding Director of the Newport Harbor Art Museum (now Orange County Museum of Art, Newport Beach, California) and later Director of the Madison Art Center (now Madison Museum of Contemporary Art, Madison, Wisconsin), subsequently wrote a monograph and catalogue raisonné of Tooker's paintings and graphic works, first published in 1985 and revised in 1992. He has written widely on later twentieth-century art and lives in Madison, Wisconsin.

**M. Melissa Wolfe** is Associate Curator of American Art at the Columbus Museum of Art, Ohio, and Adjunct Assistant Professor of American Art History at Ohio State University. She served in the past as Curator of Collections at the Butler Institute of American Art, Youngstown, Ohio, where she was also assistant editor and contributor to *Master Paintings from the Butler Institute of American Art* (1994). She has organized numerous exhibitions and authored catalogues, including *American Impressionism* (2006), *Sid Chafetz: A Life in Print* (2005), *American Indian Portraits: Elbridge Ayer Burbank in the West (1892–1906)* (2000), and *An American Anthem: 300 Years of Painting from the Butler Institute of American Art* (1999). She received her PhD from Ohio State University for a dissertation on the homestead photographs of Solomon Butcher, supported by a Henry Luce/ACLS Dissertation Fellowship.

**Jonathan Weinberg**, PhD, is a painter and art historian. He is the author of *Male Desire: the Homoerotic in American Art* (2005), *Fantastic Tales: The Photography of Nan Goldin* (2005), *Ambition and Love in Modern American Art* (2001), and *Speaking for Vice: Homosexuality in the Art of Charles Demuth, Marsden Hartley and the First-American Avant-Garde* (1993). He has been a recipient of several important research grants and residencies, including a 2002 Guggenheim Fellowship. Weinberg's paintings, which are in several public collections, including the Metropolitan Museum of Art, New York, and the Montclair Art Museum, New Jersey, can be seen on his Website: www.jonathanweinberg.com.

**Marshall N. Price** received his MA from Pennsylvania State University. Between 1998 and 2002, he was Assistant Curator at the Santa Barbara Museum of Art, California, where he organized a number of exhibitions, including *Gordon Kenneth Grant: A Retrospective Revisited* (2001) and *Colin Campbell Cooper: Impressions of New York* (2002). He is currently Associate Curator of Modern and Contemporary Art at the National Academy Museum and School of Fine Arts, New York. He has written on nineteenth-, twentieth-, and twenty-first-century art; his most recent exhibition and publication was *The Abstract Impulse: Fifty Years of Abstraction at the National Academy, 1956–2006* (2007).

**Anna C. Chave**, Professor of Art History at Queens College and the Graduate Center, CUNY, has published numerous essays concerned with issues of reception, interpretation, and gender in modern art practices. Her subjects have ranged historically from early Picasso and Georgia O'Keeffe to Jackson Pollock, Eva Hesse, and the feminist art movement. She is known, too, for her revisionist readings of Minimalism, including "Minimalism and the Rhetoric of Power" *(Arts*, January 1990), "Minimalism and Biography" (*Art Bulletin*, March 2000), and "Minimalism, East and West: Patronage and Aura" (*Art Bulletin*, September 2008). She has also authored monographs on Rothko and Brancusi (1991 and 1993).

**Robert Cozzolino**, Curator of Modern Art at the Pennsylvania Academy of the Fine Arts, was awarded his PhD in 2006 by the University of Wisconsin-Madison for a dissertation on Ivan Albright. He has organized numerous exhibitions at the Pennsylvania Academy and elsewhere, including *Art in Chicago: Resisting Regionalism, Transforming Modernism* (2006), *Vik Muniz: Remastered* (2005), *Light, Line and Color: American Works on Paper 1765–2005* (2005), *With Friends: Six Magic Realists, 1940–1965* (2005), and *Dudley Huppler: Drawings* (2002). His publications include catalogues for *Art in Chicago: Resisting Regionalism, Transforming Modernism* (2006), *With Friends: Six Magic Realists, 1940–1965* (2005), and *Dudley Huppler: Drawings* (2002), as well as contributions to *American Art at Princeton*, Volume 1: *Drawings and Watercolors* (2004), *New Critical Perspectives on Dalí* (2004), and *Ivan Albright* (1997).

# Index



Figures in *italics* refer to illustrations.

cma
columbus museum of art

National Academy Museum & School of Fine Arts

Pennsylvania Academy of the Fine Arts · 1805
Museum + School

Henry Luce Foundation

National Endowment for the Arts
A great nation deserves great art.

State of the Arts
NYSCA

Department of Cultural Affairs
NYCulture
City of New York

The Columbus Foundation

GCAC
City of Columbus Grants Program
Greater Columbus Arts Council

National City

Nationwide
On Your Side

Ohio Arts Council
A state agency that supports public programs in the arts